The In-Between in Javanese Performing Arts

Sumarsam

THE IN-BETWEEN IN JAVANESE PERFORMING ARTS

History and Myth, Interculturalism and Interreligiosity

Wesleyan University Press   Middletown, Connecticut

Wesleyan University Press
Middletown CT 06459
www.wesleyan.edu/wespress

Manufactured in the United States of America
Designed by Mindy Basinger Hill
Typeset in Minion Pro

The Publisher gratefully acknowledges the General Fund of the American Musicological Society, supported in part by the National Endowment for the Humanities and the Andrew W. Mellon Foundation.

Library of Congress Cataloging-in-Publication Data

Names: Sumarsam, author.

Title: The in-between in Javanese performing arts / Sumarsam.

Description: Middletown, Connecticut : Wesleyan University Press, [2024] | Includes bibliographical references and index. | Summary: "Sumarsam examines historical case studies to show how histories, traditions, and mythologies interact in Java, demonstrating how these powerful cultural sources and forces have shaped people's lives and beliefs along with the formation and transformation of Javanese performing arts" —Provided by publisher.

Identifiers: LCCN 2024011663 (print) | LCCN 2024011664 (ebook) | ISBN 9780819501264 (paperback) | ISBN 9780819501257 (cloth) | ISBN 9780819501271 (ebook)

Subjects: LCSH: Performing arts—Social aspects—Indonesia—Java. | Performing arts—Religious aspects. | Performing arts—Indonesia—Java—History. | Religion and culture—Indonesia—Java.

Classification: LCC PN1590.S6 S86 2024 (print) | LCC PN1590.S6 (ebook) | DDC 306.4/84—dc23/eng/20240318

LC record available at https://lccn.loc.gov/2024011663

LC ebook record available at https://lccn.loc.gov/2024011664

5 4 3 2 1

TO THE MEMORY OF PARTOREDJO, DIWATI, AND REDJOSENTONO

MY FATHER, MOTHER, AND STEPFATHER

CONTENTS

PREFACE

I have often received comments from my American colleagues urging me to be more explicit in my writing, to position myself more overtly as a Javanese man, performer, teacher, and researcher. This preface is my attempt to do so. I begin by sharing some events and thoughts that situate the disclosure of my personal story. Why self-disclosure? My relationship with the issues raised in this book is intimate; I will address the complex practices of Javanese expressive culture with which I have been personally involved since my childhood. Most importantly, here I offer a sketch of the personal pathways of my intellectual and artistic life, which I hope will orient the reader to the issues discussed in the book.

MY BIRTHPLACE

Approaching the completion of writing the present study, I discovered a fascinating historical event in Dander, the village where I was born.

Dhuk durung mati Ra Kuthi arep anga . . . bathara. Linungan de nira maring bhathara maring Badhander. Sah ring wngi tan ana ring wruh. Anghing wong bhayangkara angiring.	When Ra Kuti who wanted to become a King hadn't yet died, the King [who he wanted to kill] was rushed to Badhander. Going during the evening, no one knew. Only the bhayangkara troupe knew it.

(Munandar, 2021, 2; based on Brandes 1920, 3 and Kiswanto 2009, 96)

The author of the sixteenth-century *Pararaton*, from which the quotation above is taken, talks about King Måjåpahit Jåyånegårå, who reigned in the early fourteenth century, who had to run away when his kingdom was attacked and he was in danger of being killed by his enemy, Ra Kuti. The village of Badhander mentioned in the manuscript is now called Dander (though there is no evidence about when and why the name Badhander become Dander). Agus Aris Munandar (2021), a prominent archaeologist at the University of Indonesia, is almost certain that Dander was the place where Jåyånegårå and his entourage hid. The existence of Kahyangan Api (the place where fire illuminates nonstop from the ground) in nearby Dander and the inscription of Adan-Adan from the nearby village of Kalitidu strengthen Munandar's hypothesis. The former related to the place where gods descend to the earth (i.e., an important place for ritual); the latter, Adan-Adan, is a *sima* (taxed free village), the meaning of which is related to "gift." (8–11).

I am not claiming that people in Dander have any significant connection with King Jåyånegårå, but at least once upon a time they encountered the runaway king of Måjåpahit. As the word *Dander* means "generous people" (deriving from the root word *dhana* or gift and *dhare* or the holder), perhaps they were accommodating and generous to Jåyånegårå and his *bhayangkara* honor guards (6–7). By extension this also means that most likely people in Dander received a blessing from King Jåyånegårå.

The commoner-king relation portrayed in this story is at least a tangential link enabling me to claim a far-distant court culture connection, a nice story to tell in conjunction with my encounter with the Sultan of Yogyakarta and his royal family, which I will discuss in the following pages. This is because the sultan and other rulers in Central Java believe that their ancestor can be traced to the king of the Måjåpahit dynasty, not in terms of true history, but following the concept of enhancing power through one's genealogical tree: the farther back the king can mythologize his genealogy, the more powerful the king and his kingdom become (Moertono 1965).

SOCIO-HIERARCHY

It is well-known that wayang kulit shadow puppet-play performance is rich with metaphor and symbolism. From it we learn and reflect on many aspects underlying Javanese life. One of the most important is that Javanese life is structured within the scheme of socio-hierarchy, partly the result of the localization of the Hindu caste system. Javanese socio-hierarchy does not emphasize endogamy and heredity as in the Indian system, but centers on the idea of tolerance. That is, Javanese people acknowledge social stratification but seek social harmony. Wayang teaches us this idea, not in a black-and-white fashion, but in fluid, ambiguous, even paradoxical presentation.

There are some extreme examples of wayang stories representing fluidity, ambiguity, and paradox. One of them is about a comical retainer or jester, Semar, which I discuss at length in chapters 3 and 4. He is a servant with physical ugliness (big belly and fat behind) and often passes gas, but he always accompanies a knight of good character (*satriyå*), who gives him wise advice. Moreover, he is a manifestation of one of the most powerful gods. As the philosopher Franz Magnis Suseno says, "The presence of Semar in the Javanese wayang shows a deep understanding of what really is of value for humanity: it is not one's appearance, carriage or polite manners, nor one's command of the rules of etiquette that determine the degree of one's humanity, but rather it is one's inner nature" (in and translated by Meyer 2021). This implies the complexity of human communication in Java in performing socio-hierarchy; the use of language and acting out of certain behaviors are determined by the status relationships between one interlocutor and another.

In the life of Javanese court culture, stricter hierarchical systems and their practices are more noticeable than in the life of the commoners. For example, to place oneself within his or her social status, Javanese commoners recognize only the use of two speech levels (*ngoko*, or colloquial, and *krâmâ*, respectful language). However, the court has four speech levels, as well as certain etiquette and behavior. For example, *sembah*, a gesture of clapping the palms together and placing them in front of the nose while squatting on the floor, demonstrates respect to a person of a higher status.

The arrival of Western modes of education in Javanese life further expanded the socio-hierarchical structure by producing a new class of educated elites. Educated Javanese people earn a high status in society, in competition or in tandem with the existing hierarchical structure of the court tradition. This can create some ambiguity when an educated commoner meets with members of the royal family; I turn to a recent personal experience to illustrate this complexity.

In 2018 I was involved in organizing the visit of the sultan of the court of Yogyakarta to my university. I am a professor and hold the most advanced degree from an American institution of higher education, though I grew up in a village in East Java. Thus, I identify as an educated commoner. When I was assigned to introduce the sultan, I felt it necessary to be honest: as a commoner I felt very humble, but also nervous, and did not know how to act appropriately to meet the sultan face-to-face—should I do sembah, bend my body, shake hands? I ended up bending my body a bit and clapping my palms together in front of my chest, not in front of my nose. This gesture seems to be common practice for any educated nonaristocratic person when meeting face-to-face with a sultan. Additionally, because of my intellectual background, in introducing him I was able to find a way to properly explain the idea of seeking a harmonious relationship with the sultan through a Javanese philosophy called *manunggaling kawulå lan gusti*, the union of the lowest and highest status, the commoner and the king—a manifestation of the concept of unity. While recognizing social stratification, I applied a cultural strategy in seeking a harmonious social relationship.

PAYING HOMAGE TO MBAH CÅKARMÅ

When I was a young musician, my friends and I paid homage to a legendary gamelan musician and *dhalang* (puppeteer) named Mbah (Granddad) Cåkarmå by visiting his grave in Nguter, Sukåharjå, Central Java. We were told that he was a performing artist from the minor court of Mangkunegaran in Surakarta. The ritual visit had to be done at midnight, consisting of sprinkling flowers on the gravestone and a brief meditation to receive a spiritual blessing. After the ritual, we were not allowed to sleep inside the house or any place with a roof. I don't know why this practice is the way it is—I thought perhaps the more challenging the ritual, the more blessings you receive. In any event, we did it without any hindrance.

Generically, this ritual is called *ngalap berkah*, a ritual aiming to receive blessings from important figures, alive or dead, to enhance one's competency or power. Commonly, *dhalang* (puppeteers) must go through this ritual more stringently than musicians, including self-sacrificial practices, such as submerging oneself in water for hours, eating only the roots of plants or rice, and meditating at certain mystically charged locations (Hand 2016, 223–28). Obtaining power through mystical means is not an uncommon practice among Javanese people, including performers such as myself.

A long time ago, when I was a student, I complained to myself that I was not able to express myself fluently when speaking in public. I asked my friend what to do. He took me to a ritual specialist (*dhukun*), who supposedly inserted a piece of gold in the tip of my tongue (I did not feel it). When the ritual was complete, the dhukun made a surprising statement: in order to maintain my power of being a good public speaker, I must not eat mangosteen (*manggis*). But this was and is my favorite fruit! After a year went by without eating the fruit, I could not stand it—and ate the forbidden fruit. What consequence did this have? I still do not know. I was left only with a justification to fall back on if my dialogue failed to flow seamlessly in a given performance. My point is that Javanese people—myself included—often conceive of power as "real," not abstract and based on social relationships (Anderson 1996).

Returning to Cåkarmå, some decades later when I carried out research for my dissertation, I was surprised to find from my archival readings that the name Cåkarmå is mentioned in the eighteenth-century manuscript *Babad Nitik Mangkunegaran* (The Chronicle of Mangkunegaran) and in the nineteenth-century *Serat Tjenṭini*. This was a revelation to me, indeed: I believed that he was only a legendary figure, but it turns out that he was a real person. Unfortunately, I could not find out more about him since the babad mentions him only briefly, and *Serat Tjenṭini* mentions only the name Tjåkremå (the old-style spelling) in the context of the discussion of gamelan philosophy. In any event, many gamelan musicians in the area know about his grave and pay homage to him, as I did.

DUALISTIC INTERACTIONS

I share these reflections as examples of "the in-between" betwixt the real and the imagined. Mbah Cåkarmå is only a figure in my imagination but is later revealed to be a real historical figure. Power can be understood as both an abstract concept based on human relationships or as a real entity (a piece of gold in my tongue) that can be absorbed to enhance one's power. A dualistic hierarchy between commoner and royalty reflects my encounter with the sultan of Yogyakarta and his family—the interaction becomes dynamic but also ambiguous when the commoner has received modern higher education. The story of my birthplace as historically related to the fourteenth-century Måjåpahit kingdom is another case of the dynamic dualism between history and myth.

How do I approach this world of dualism? As I will mention in the introduction, my perspective is guided by a number of scholars, including Soedjatmoko, Joseph Campbell, de Certeau, and others. In my previous work (2013) I referenced the works of Victor Turner, and I returned to him again for this study, adapting his theoretical framework about dualism. I define the in-between as life experience built upon dialectically interweaving multiple dualisms: myth and reality, sacred and secular, history and myth, and so forth. This happens in the world that Turner (1979) calls "betwixt and between," neither here or there in time and space, in the liminal state. I see these multiple dialectics as encompassing the apparent and underlining facts of life in general. They can be seen underpinning Javanese culture and cultural performances. As readers will discover in examples presented throughout this book, throughout history Javanese cultural traditions have developed within the framework of these dialectical multiplicities: Hindu-Javanese; Hindu/Javanese-Islam; Hindu/Javanese/Islam-Western; oral-writing tradition, colonialism-nationalism, and so on. Wayang performance can be seen in this way: its narrative consists of hybridized Java-Hindu stories; its cultural context encompasses a mixture of sacred and secular trajectories; its religious dimension consists of mixing and matching Javanese-Hindu-Islam projection; and its innovations can include the incorporation of Western elements.

CULTURAL ARBITER?

Village and city life, informal village and formal conservatory training, mystical and worldly experience, a background in both history and myth, and teaching/performing/studying domestically and abroad—these are some of the dialectical multiple dualisms I have experienced in my life. On teaching/performing/studying abroad, I have spent more than fifty years in the United States working at Wesleyan University in Connecticut. This has been an inspirational life experience. I always cherish and highly value teaching Indonesian gamelan, music, and theater to mostly American students in the context of a liberal arts education. In the spirit of "living to learn, learning to live," I utilize, with gratitude, what Wesleyan offers, such as resources for research and conferences.

I am always appreciative when my academic colleagues take interest in my position as an arbiter of both Javanese and American culture. I am uncomfortable, however, when some insist that I should be more explicit in my academic writing by positioning myself as an "insider" Javanese person, performer, and scholar. The issue of emic-etic voice surfaces again and again. As I have stated in previous work (2013) on this topic, I concur with Perlman (2004):

> Although the search for emic musical understanding has produced rich and well-conceived literature, its pros and cons are still being discussed. Perlman rightly asserts that early ethnotheory "seemed to assume a greater degree of homogeneity and integration of culture than actually exists," hence focusing "on concepts assumed to represent a cultural consensus, ignoring issues of intracultural variability, historical change, and individual intellectual creativity." Accordingly, ethnotheory oversimplified the discourse by assuming that "musical knowledge is a single type of thing, thereby underestimating the internal heterogeneity of cognitive processes." (Sumarsam 2013, viii)

Knowing that gamelan has been present and studied by scholars in the West since the mid-nineteenth century, through various exhibitions and then through the birth of ethnomusicology in the early twentieth century, heterogeneous perspectives of gamelan are unavoidable. This means that "individuals' and institutions' viewpoints cannot be sorted in terms of a simple inside-outside dichotomy. Because the study of any music should not be only about 'outside looking in,' but also 'inside looking in and out,' or even 'inside and outside looking in and out,' I employ any line of thought that I consider relevant and useful regardless of who has produced the knowledge in question" (Sumarsam 2013, xiii–xiv).

To return to my approach as a Javanese-Western arbiter, this is illustrated best, perhaps, through a practical example of how I sometimes introduce my American students to wayang shadow puppet play—from the perspective of the film *Star Wars*. One of my favorite stories to share in class involves Luke Skywalker facing the daunting task of lifting an X-wing fighter from the depths of a river. Yoda advises him that, in order to succeed in lifting the fighter, Luke must be able to feel the Force around him. The Force Yoda refers to is the tree, the rock, and other natural entities; they serve to create life, making the life grow and producing energy that surrounds and binds human beings together. Luke complains to Yoda that he wants the impossible. Then, Yoda turns toward the submerged X-wing fighter. With closed eyes and a bowed head, he raises his arm and points toward the ship. Surprisingly, the X-wing fighter gradually rises above the water and moves forward, toward the shore.

Notice that, according to Yoda, Force or power can be obtained from elements of nature around us, everywhere. It occurs to me that I can draw a connection between Yoda and Javanese people's idea of power following Anderson's (1996) explication of the specificity of Javanese power in contrast to Western power: in the West power is abstract, based on relationships, but in Java power is concrete, emanating in nature, odd things, and art objects. Many great characters in wayang stories, such as a knight (Arjunå) and Kresnå (an incarnation of the god Wisnu), after successfully obtaining power from nature, can do what Yoda did.

I take this connection seriously. Where did George Lucas (the creator of *Star Wars*) find Yoda's cosmological idea? Apparently, he was familiar with the work of Joseph Campbell, a scholar of mythology/religion whose comparative studies include Asian religion. Lucas acknowledged learning a lot about cosmology from "Joe" (as he called him) in an interview with TV personality Bill Moyers in 1999. What is seemingly coincidental between the concepts of power in *Star Wars* and wayang turns out to relate to intercultural encounters. This example embodies the movement back and forth from Asian to Western influences that I make as a Javanese-Western arbiter. It is also another example of my intellectual life "in-between."

CODA

It is not too far-fetched to say that my life exemplifies the notion of dualisms I defined earlier: village-city life; mystical-worldly experience; historical-myth background; informal village-formal conservatory gamelan training; domestic-abroad teaching and performing. Essentially, this book is based on my lifetime of being both inside and outside wayang and gamelan. I have sought emic paths to master the arts—spending nights meditating at forerunners' graves, slipping gold into my tongue to help my words flow—and been outside wayang, exercising etic practices combing palace manuscripts and searching colonial archives for historically datable traces of verifiable people, places, and events. Wayang with its gamelan accompaniment is a multimedia performance that commands colorful and deep historical, aesthetic, religious, and emotional affiliations. In this book I continue my lifelong journey to master this complicated, profound, and changing art/ritual/entertainment—always different but somehow the same—through understanding its multiple variations from court village entertainment-cum-ritual to palace aesthetic/proof of cultural competency, from coastal mercantile entrepots to central Javanese wet rice terraces, from colonial plantation and textile factory culture to contemporary industrial estates and creative economy efforts. I view these complexities as running parallel to my own experiences in between the dialectical encounters that have shaped my pursuit of the performing arts, some of which I have shared to situate both my position and the wider issues I unpack throughout this book. If my words have failed me, I apologize for my shortcomings; I blame it on my love of mangosteen.

ACKNOWLEDGMENTS

I started my research for the present study in 2016 under the auspices of the National Endowment for the Humanities (NEH) and American Council of Learned Societies (ACLS). I was very excited that I would be able to work full time as a researcher, free from the obligations of teaching. In my application, I promised the grantors that the fruits of my research would be the publication of a book in English and Indonesian. Well, it has been more than seven years now since receiving my grants, and I have produced a book only in English, though I am still committed to translating the book into Indonesian in the near future. I would like to convey my deep appreciation and gratitude to NEH and ACLS for these endowments.

Based on this research, from 2018 onward I have written essays for publication, delivered papers at conferences, and thought about writing this book. But the privilege of being a full-time researcher free from teaching had passed. I started to worry that I would not have enough time to write a book. At this juncture, the Yale Institute for Sacred Music (ISM) came to mind, since before receiving grants from NEH and ACLS I was interested in applying for a fellowship with them. In 2019, I applied and received the ISM grant. I promised myself that I would use it only for archival research and for writing the book. I did just that, but then Covid-19 struck. The time I spent at Yale, with its rich sources of Southeast Asian and religious study and my interaction with other fellows, ended. Despite the chaos caused by Covid-19, I was able to gather scores of study materials and write about half of a very rough draft of my new book. I am forever grateful to Yale ISM for giving me the fellowship and the valuable time to be in residence at the ISM campus.

A year after the completion of my residency at Yale, I was able to complete three chapters (out of four) of a draft of this book. In October 2021, I submitted the draft to Wesleyan University Press, fully understanding that although I am on the Wesleyan faculty, I would be treated like any other scholar submitting a book proposal. The press accepted my draft for publication. Two months later, I received reports from outside readers, positive but also with some criticism and suggestions. I would like to deeply thank the staff of Wesleyan University Press for their diligent work publishing the book. To the anonymous reviewers, I am very grateful for the time you took to read and evaluate my manuscript, giving me valuable suggestions.

I feel so fortunate to have been a gamelan instructor and scholar at Wesleyan for more than fifty years. The reason I have stayed so long is that the institutional system has allowed me to make progress in my intellectual development and employment. In my initial residency in the early 1970s, I was an annually renewed visiting artist, and I also enrolled as an MA graduate student. Then my status changed from visiting artist to artist in residence with a sabbatical. I used my sabbatical time to study at Cornell University.

It has taken a long time at Wesleyan for me to earn my current status and title as a tenured Winslow-Kaplan Professor of Music. I went through many changes before achieving my current role. I have had five titles: visiting artist, artist in residence, adjunct associate professor, adjunct professor, university professor, and finally my current status, given to me in 2011. I always boast to myself that no one else in the university has had five different titles in their career there except me. I must say that the degree I received from Cornell in 1992 strengthened my chance to upgrade my status and my intellectual development. Thanks to Cornell and my advisors Professor Martin Hatch, the late Professor Benedict Anderson, and the late Professor William Austin. In any event, I am truly grateful forever to Wesleyan for its generosity in accommodating my desire to advance my scholarship, providing me with various funding to attend conferences and carry out many research projects.

I am very lucky to be a faculty member in the Wesleyan Music Department, which has been patiently supportive throughout my career. One of the most senior colleagues in the department and also in ethnomusicological circles, Mark Slobin, has been very helpful to me, giving the right direction in my writing when I need it. He was the first recipient of the Winslow-Kaplan Professorship, the title Wesleyan bestowed upon me after his retirement. I am so lucky to be friends with many colleagues from different musical backgrounds. I have attended many of their concerts, in a few cases joining in to play their music. I'll never forget playing Alvin Lucier's experimental music, and twice bringing Alvin and his group to Indonesia to play his music in Surabaya, Yogyakarta, and Jakarta. Twice I performed his infamous piece, "Sitting in the Room."

Whatever progress I have made intellectually and administratively, my love of teaching gamelan for beginning and advanced students never stops. I thank my dear colleague Professor Harjito for working with me to teach gamelan for decades. For Wesleyan, having two teachers is a luxury, but it makes the teaching of gamelan in the context of liberal arts education more effective, helping our students learn to play gamelan a bit faster. It makes it possible to spend time with students discussing gamelan in the context of Indonesian culture, showing documentary films, and providing students with a few reading and listening assignments.

There are many colleagues in the United States I have had the privilege to work with in various capacities. Ann Rasmussen, Philip Yampolsky, Sarah Weiss, Henry Spiller, David Harnish, Ben Brinner, Andy Sutton, Andy McGraw, Dustin Wiebe, and many more. Kathy Foley and Tony Day are two colleagues I consulted when I encountered difficulty working on a particular topic or approach in writing this book. I owe a debt of gratitude to all of them.

However long I have been learning English, I have never felt 100 percent confident in expressing myself, particularly in academic writing. Lauren Sweetman has been helping me edit my works for the past seven years. Her ethnomusicological and anthropological background has made her editing more than grammatical correction and improving clarity of expression; she has also made many suggestions to strengthen my arguments. My deep appreciation to her forever.

In Indonesia, I asked three colleagues graduating from the Indonesian Institute of the Arts in Surakarta to be my research assistants: Aris Setiawan, Larso Sularso, and Ciptono Hadi. They were very helpful in several ways: logistics, and hours of serious discussion and/or informal chatting while spending hours and hours in the car, in the hotel, or in my house in Solo. Terimakasih Mas. When I carried out research on wayang golèk in the central-north coastal area of Java, Gunawan Suwati (who passed away in 2021) in Tegal helped me to organize the reconstruction of an older type of wayang golèk Tegal with the late Ki Marwoto (who passed away in 2019) as dhalang. My deep appreciation to them and the musicians who performed in this project.

I would not have been able to complete this book without the support of my wife, my daughter, my son-in-law, my grandchildren, and my son and daughter-in-law. Thank you for your understanding, especially my wife, who often watched me in front of the computer and reading books for hours and hours.

I dedicate this book in memory of my biological father Partoredjo, who I never got to know and whose face I never got to remember, a cow-cart driver turned village chief who vanished around 1948 when I was only three and a half years old, a victim of colonialism/communist affairs; of my late mother Diwati (who passed away in 1983 while I was studying at Cornell), who encouraged me do whatever I wanted to in life; and of my late stepfather Redjosentono, who helped me to grow up.

NOTE ON ORTHOGRAPHY

With the exception of personal names, the spelling of Javanese and Indonesian words cited in this study follows the orthographic convention officially adopted by the Indonesian government since 1972, but citations from material written in the Indonesian and Old Javanese languages remain in their original spelling. The difference between the old and modern transliteration lies mainly in the following spellings: *dj* represents the modern *j*, *tj* represents *c*, and *oe* represents *u*.

In Javanese, *e* can take certain diacritical marks. The following is a list of vowels and consonants in Javanese that require particular notice.

TABLE 0.1

LETTER	ENGLISH EQUIVALENT	JAVANESE EXAMPLE
a	in a closed syllable (ending with a consonant), as in father	lekas
å	in an open syllable (ending with vowel, like aw in law)	bukå
c	church	celempung
d	pronounced with tongue tip touching inside upper teeth	demung
dh	pronounced with tongue tip touching palate (i.e., palatal), e.g., day	dhalang
e	about	embat
è	let	gendèr

LETTER	ENGLISH EQUIVALENT	JAVANESE EXAMPLE
é	ate	pélog
i	1. a closed syllable ends in vowel-plus-consonant., e.g., bit 2. an open syllable ends in vowel, e.g., police	alit kinanthi
ny	canyon	nyelå
o	1. a closed syllable ends in vowel-plus-consonant., e.g., bore 2. an open syllable ends in vowel, e.g., zero	pélog bonang
r	rolled r	salisir
t	pronounced with tongue tip touching inside upper teeth (i.e., dental), e.g., try	ketipung
th or ṭ	pronounced with tongue tip touching palate (i.e., palatal), e.g., later	pathet
u	1. a closed syllable ends in vowel-plus-consonant., e.g., put 2. an open syllable ends in vowel, e.g., true	wus mlaku

The In-Between in Javanese Performing Arts

INTRODUCTION

When the sun is going down, changing the day to night-time, it illuminates *imå-imå*, *gamburå*, and *ancålå*. *Imå-imå* means cloud, *gamburå* ocean, *ancålå* the tip of a mountain. God picks the young leaves of *gebang siwalan*, cutting them in equal lengths, sprinkled by *asta gangga wirantanu*. *Asta* means hands, *gangga* water, *wira* pen, *tanu* ink.[1]

Ki Warnoto 2017

The quoted text in the epigraph is the beginning of the *dhalang* (puppeteer) Ki Warnoto's opening recitation[2] to a 2017 performance of *wayang golèk* (a wayang puppet performance using three-dimensional wooden puppets). The recitation begins with a description of time and nature, followed by the physical elements of writing: the dried palm leaf (*gebang siwalan*) as paper to be written on by hands (*asta*), and water, pen, and ink (*gangga, wira, tanu*)—the elements for producing a written document. However, due to the inclusion of several old Javanese words and the text's semantic order, some of its meaning for spectators at the performance was likely unintelligible or ambiguous. Tracing the origin of this text, I found it originated from the seventeenth-century manuscript *Bhīma Svarga*, a story about the second Pandhåwå brother entering heaven to release his father from being punished by the gods.

To understand this performance, I searched for a suitable paradigm to unpack the interrelationships and meanings present in the text. Two fields of inquiry came to mind: history and mythology. They are close kin in registering the past, but for different reasons and with different processes. It is not uncommon for scholars to problematize the relationship between historical and mythological approaches, with views ranging from considering them as antithetical modes of explanation to seeing no real distinction between them (Heehs 1994, 1). *Britannica* defines them in a reconciliatory tone:

> Myth and history represent alternative ways of looking at the past. Defining history is hardly easier than defining myth, but a historical approach necessarily involves both establishing a chronological framework for events and comparing and contrasting rival traditions in order to produce a coherent account. The latter process, in particular, requires the presence of writing in order that conflicting versions of the past may be recorded and evaluated. Where writing is absent, or where literacy is restricted, traditions embedded in myths through oral transmission may constitute the principal sources of authority for the past. Hence, myths may be cited when a situation in the present is materially affected by what version of the past is accepted.[3]

In another example, in his *An Introduction to Indonesian Historiography*, Soedjatmoko (1965) is very much aware of the question of the validity of using mythology (in both literary and oral forms) as historical references. The claim is that myths are not conventional historical sources, and therefore "do not seem to yield to the conventional methods of historical examination" (xviii). Yet, Soedjatmoko goes on to argue that, in fact, Javanese mythology "does yield to conventional critical examination and does, with necessary check against non-Javanese sources, constitute a treasure house of historical information" (xix).

Soedjatmoko is useful in explaining what a historian must do to produce knowledge; that a myth-history reconciliatory approach is needed. This is crucial to my methodology, since in this book I examine how historical changes have led to the readjustment or refabrication of the meaning and context of certain events. However, people today do not necessarily know that history shapes that meaning and context. As Geertz (1973) suggests, the cultural views of contemporary people are not necessarily shaped by history or by direct social interaction, but by "a generalized set of symbolically formulated (that is, cultural) assumptions about each other's typical modes of behavior" in their contemporary society (365–66). This, in turn, prompts members of society to interpret the meaning of certain myths or dogma in a new light, different from the "original" meaning from the previous historical period. Thus, understanding the interaction or collision between myth and history rests on the shoulders of the historian.

According to Joseph Campbell (2004), who believes in mythology as spiritual reference:

> [This myth-history collision often rules] our lives, giving us everything that we live by from day to day. The collision has destroyed people's belief in these symbolic forms: they are rejected as untrue. Now, since the primary truth is not the historical but the spiritual reference of these symbols, the fact that historical evidence refutes these myths on the level of objective reality should not relieve us of the symbols. (23)

In the context of the production of knowledge, de Certeau (1988 [1974]) reminds us that the myth-history collision ought to be considered as both religious fact and religious doctrine.

> From the outset, historians take theology to be a religious ideology which functions within a broader totality that we assume can explain ideology. Can theology be reduced to the terms resulting from the operation? No, probably not. But as an object of their discipline, theology is shown to historians under the two equally uncertain forms in the field of historiography; it is a religious fact, and it is a fact of doctrine. (19)

Not unlike Soedjatmoko's myth-history reconciliation, theology is both religious fact and fact of doctrine. What the discussion in these extracts shows us is the dynamics of how we maneuver between historical evidence and mythological information: belief and fact. In examining different discursive modes to understand the aesthetic and religious meaning of Javanese performing arts throughout history (i.e., the main theme of the present study), I have come to the conclusion that it is impossible to arrive at the absolute truth of events from the historical past. As my professor of history told me decades ago, perhaps half-jokingly, what is exciting is not finding the truth, but how we go about finding the truth. Or, rather, there is no single truth, but multiple truths, hence multiple readings of the truth. In any event, de Certeau (1988 [1974]) warns us that history can become no more than a myth if it is approached "without the connection between the act that it promotes and the society that it reflects; the rupture that is constantly debated between a past and a present; the double status of the object that is a 'realistic effect' in the text and the unspoken element implied by the closure of the discourse" (44).

In this book, I present four historically situated case studies that illustrate how various histories and mythologies interact with one another in one Indonesian territory—Java. As a territory with the longest recorded history, Java presents a wide geographic zone of linguistic, social, cultural, and religious interaction that offers a very fruitful terrain for shedding light on how these two powerful cultural sources and forces have shaped people's lives and beliefs, and the formation and transformation of the form and meaning of Javanese performing arts.

HINDUIZATION

Why do we learn history? The question seems unnecessary, and the answer can be heterogenous, depending on an individual's perception. People's perception of history is the product of certain periods of particular social and political conditions, certain geographical cultural spaces, and certain levels of literacy (or lack thereof) within society (Gungwu 1982 [1979], 2). For the Javanese, the earliest perception of the past begins with a tradition that was created based on intercultural and interreligious encounters, namely the encounter with and subsequent adaptation of Indian culture. This is a process commonly called *Indianization*, a term historian Olivier Wolters (1999, 21) thought of as misleading. To him, the term *Hinduization* fits better, since it was not that Indian influences introduced an entirely new chapter in the region's history, but rather that the operation was more specifically "Hindu," a religious rather than political conception that brought about Hindu-Southeast Asian hybrid culture. Wolters goes on to say:

> Indian materials tended to be fractured and restated and therefore drained of their original significance by a process which I shall refer to as "localization." The materials, be they words, sounds of words, books, or artifacts, had to be localized in different ways before they could fit into various local complexes or religious, social, and political systems and belong to [a] new cultural "whole." Only when this had happened would the fragments make sense in their new ambiences. (55)

The Indian materials with which Java was Hinduized included the genre of sung poetry *kawya* (*kakawin*, in Javanese), which contains, among others, the *Ramayana* story and the *Mahabharata* epic. Aside from their religious significance, these Hindu tales gave impetus to the development of theatrical performances such as wayang wong dance drama and wayang kulit puppet play—the tales became primary sources for the basis of stories that have been performed by wayang performers up to the present day.

Indian music and musical instruments were also materials through which the Javanese were exposed to Indian culture (see Kunst 1968). Written evidence establishing whether Indian music was ever performed in Java during the Hindu-Javanese period from the ninth to the fifteenth century is hard to find. Nonetheless, drawings of Indian musical instruments can be found carved on the walls of a number of temples in Java, and passages about musical performance, theory, and instruments, including their association with theatrical performance, can be found in a number of literary poetic works, *kakawin*. This fact has garnered discussion among scholars regarding the influences of Indian music on Javanese performing arts.

The most important Hindu concept embraced by Javanese people was *bhakti* (devotion). In this regard, honoring the gods Siva and Wisnu became one of the most important rituals in which the performing arts were an integral part. For rulers, through this ritual "the overlord's reputation for ascetic achievement, no matter how it was gained, could be seen as exemplifying the closest relationship with Siva of anyone in his generation." Because Siva was considered the "sovereign deity who created the universe," the overlord's relationship with Siva meant that he participated in Siva's divine authority (Wolters 1999 [1982], 22).

The performing arts had an important role in this ritual of paying homage to the ruler as an emanation of Siva or Wisnu. A depiction of a ruler's glory, when sung by a bard, would reach the ends of the world, indicating that the ruler's royal authority was limitless (38). Bhakti was also demonstrated through a theatrical performance accompanied by music and singing. In the case of Måjåpahit, the king himself performed in *raket* dance drama, which made the performance lively; people would laugh constantly or weep as they were inspired by sorrow, ending in tears (Robson 1995, 92). This performance signified bhakti, as seen at the end of the play, as Prapanca, the author of *Desawarna*, describes: "When the sun was sinking low in the sky, then the King concluded [the performance], and the nobles took leave of him, wiping their lord's feet. *They said they were freed from evil, given a joy as if not of this world.*" (92; my emphasis).

The most conspicuous example of how the performing arts were used to pay homage to rulers or court officials is performance associated with royal progresses. In her work on the early history of Java, Christie (as cited by Wolters 1999) explains:

> The policy of royal progresses and the Court's dispatch of various forms of drama into the countryside. The theater helped to communicate the ruler's role. The steady increase in the numbers and categories of officials visiting the village meant that, in addition to more frequent communication between Court and countryside, more and more persons could enjoy self-esteem for participating in public life. (136–37)

In the beginning, Shaivism was a Hindu sect introduced to Java in the early centuries. Subsequently, in the ninth century, the Tantric sect came onto the scene. Its ritual, pancamakara or the "Five Ms," has been widely discussed and debated in scholarship in both Java and India. This ritual practice consisted of consuming five essential elements: madya (wine), matsya (fish), mamsa (meat), mudra (parched grain or drug), and maihuna (sexual intercourse). In Java, questions have been raised as to whether this practice was carried out by the Javanese and, if so, in what way, and whether remnants of pancamakara were still practiced centuries later after Java was Islamized.

In sum, the Hinduization of Java brought about a new Javanese tradition, which was the product of certain sociopolitical conditions, cultural spaces, and levels of literacy. This means that Indian culture underpinned the perceptions of Javanese people during the Hindu-Javanese period. Essentially, history can be seen as layers of perceptions. Subsequently, Javanese perceptions toward the Hindu-Javanese tradition further developed after the Islamization of Java, which started around the fifteenth century, leading to the Islamized Hindu-Javanese cultural tradition. Adding to this dynamic is the fact that members of Javanese society perceived the past in many ways. The question is, how do people apply their perceptions? For example, Javanese Islamic saints' application of their perceptions via proselytization in the sixteenth and seventeenth centuries would have been different from those of today's *ulama* or *kyai* (Islamic scholars). Readers will find this theme of perception throughout this book. Next, to illustrate perceptions of the Islamization of Java, and their relationship to the myth-history collision and interaction discussed earlier, I offer a personal story.

THE MAGICALLY CHARGED RELIC OF INHERITANCE

In November 2018, Wesleyan University sponsored an event to honor the visiting ruler of the Kasultanan court of Yogyakarta, Sri Sultan Hamengku Buwånå X, who came with his family and a group of performing artists—musicians, dancers, a puppeteer, and singers. The aim of the visit was to initiate cultural exchange between the Kasultanan and Wesleyan, and to produce collaborative work between Sri Sultan's artists and Wesleyan gamelan teachers and students. As part of honoring the visit of Sri Sultan, with the help of my colleagues in the Music Department, staff of the Center for the Arts, and my teaching assistant, I organized a symposium with the theme "Enacting Ethnicity and Nationalism in Indonesian Performing Arts." Sri Sultan was the keynote speaker, delivering a paper on the inheritance of Islam within court tradition, and the dynamics of his life as both the sultan and the governor of Yogyakarta. The speakers of the symposium (Andy Sutton, Roger Vetter, Lono Simatupang, and myself) each discussed aspects of the performing arts in the court of Yogyakarta.

My presentation focused on the story of the wayang play *pusåkå* (the magically charged relic of inheritance) *Kalimåsådå* (also spelled *Kalimosodo*). I pointed out, following Supomo (1997), that the storyline of *Kalimåsådå* originated in the twelfth-century literary work *Bhāratayuddha Kakawin*, written by Mpu Sedah and Mpu Panuluh during the Hindu-Javanese period (see Wirjosuparto 1968). The story tells us about the weapon Kalimahoṣadha, a book belonging to the king of Amarta (Ngamartå in modern Jv.), Yuḍiṣṭira (Yudhistirå in modern Jv.), which he used to kill his uncle Salya (Salyå in modern Jv.) in a battle between the two sides of the family, the Korawas (also spelled Kurawas or Kuråwås in modern Jv.), and Pāṇḍawas (also spelled Pandhåwå in modern Javanese).

> Then he [Salya] was struck down by the excellent weapon in the form of a book, which was gleaming and luminous, for it was a staff of jewels and gold. It pierced through his chest, and like a rainbow it drank his blood that gushed forth. Such was its power. Salya's soul then returned to the abode of the gods. (Supomo 1997, 230; his translation)[4]

Today's puppeteers still perform this story, but widely call the weapon Kalimåsådå instead. Notice how similar the words *Kalimåsådå* and *Kalimahoṣadha* are. People believe Kalimåsådå as we know it in today's wayang story derives from the Arabic phrase *Kalima Shahada* (Jv., *Kalimah Sahadat*), the Islamic sacred confession that there is no God but Allah and the Prophet Muhammad is His messenger. The transformation from Hindu-Javanese Kalimahoṣadha to Muslim-Javanese Kalimåsådå exemplifies the dynamic process of cultural transformation from Hindu-Javanese to an Islamized Java.

In my research, I looked for evidence to link Kalimåsådå to Yogyakarta court culture. I found some dhalangs performing the story in Yogyakarta province. One of them, Ki Sigit Manggolo Seputro, caught my attention because of his clear and lengthy proposition in telling the story of the connection between Kalimåsådå and Kalimah Sahadat. He concluded that Kalimåsådå became the pusåkå of the king of Mataram and his subsequent dynasty, including the sultan of Yogyakarta.[5]

In his performance, the dhalang presented a scene of the meeting between the king of Ngamartå and Sunan Kalijågå, one of the *wali* (Islamic saints) who is known to have played an important role in spreading Islam across Java. The king of Ngamartå asked Sunan Kalijågå to show him the meaning of what was written in Kalimåsådå, which was in the form of a letter. Sunan Kalijågå told the king it was the Islamic sacred confession, Kalimah Sahadat. The king then proclaimed the sunan as his teacher, and gave him Kalimåsådå. The dhalang explained that Sunan Kalijågå announced Kalimåsådå would become the pusåkå of the Javanese king and his dynasty, starting from the first king of Mataram up to Hamengku Buwånå X, the sultan who sat in the front row of the hall where I delivered my presentation. The dhalang also said that besides Kalimåsådå, the sultan owned two more sacred pusåkå: a lance (*tumbak*) named *Plèrèd*, and a golden umbrella (*songsong gilap*) called *Tunggul Någå*.

In preparing my presentation, I debated in my mind whether it would be appropriate for me to mention the names of the three most sacred pusåkå in front of their illustrious, respected owner, the sultan. Would he be offended? Eventually, in the name of academic freedom, I decided to mention them, and simultaneously declared that I have great respect for the Yogyakarta court tradition. I also apologized to the sultan for putting him on the spot by asking him to listen to me say the names of his sacred pusåkå, although I was only repeating what the dhalang had narrated. After my presentation, I approached the sultan, apologizing for the second time, to which he replied "Ora åpå-åpå" (It is okay).

This story encapsulates one of the main themes of this book: the sociocultural and religious transformation from Hindu-Javanese to Muslim-Javanese culture. The change from Kalimahoṣadha to Kalimåsådå and its enactment in wayang performance elucidates the formative, transformational, and performative contexts of cultural performance in Java, at once historical and contemporary, synchronic and diachronic. Unpacking this cultural transformation requires an understanding of the dialectical relationship between cultural representation and socioreligious action. Viewing the series of events relating to the Kalimåsådå as "texts," it is crucial to discuss the dialectical nature of cultural texts from one historical period to another.

As such, here we can see the story of the Kalimåsådå as a collision and interaction between history and mythology. Mythology should be understood as belonging to a symbolic system, while history represents a factual event. As exemplified by the story of the Kalimåsådå, a mythological symbol may become a spiritual reference. However, it may be refuted by historical evidence: the belief that Kalimåsådå derives from Kalimah Sahadat is refuted by the existence of a pre-Islamic Kalimahoṣadha from which the Kalimåsådå was invented and given a different meaning.

Regardless, reading mythology and performing arts as symbolic systems is crucial, although people may think of mythological symbols as historical facts to strengthen the legitimacy and efficacy of the myth as spiritual experience. When such a collision of myth and history is presented to the public writ large (i.e., when people are made aware that their beliefs are refuted by historical evidence), people may become upset. One of the important points I make in this book is that the link between the present and past in Javanese cultural performance is intrinsic to people's current relationship with the performing arts and tied to contemporary religious ideology. This point may trigger controversy, as I discovered several years ago after I delivered a lecture in Surakarta (Solo).

In 2016, I was invited to deliver a public lecture at the Universitas Negeri Sebelas Maret (UNS) in Solo. The story of Kalimåsådå was one of the topics in my presentation. Aside from historicizing this powerful relic of Javanese cultural inheritance, I also pointed out that in researching this topic, I encountered difficulty finding enough references to attribute the development of wayang kulit performance to Sunan Kalijågå. I could not find detailed and solid evidence of how the Sunan used wayang to spread Islam in Java. This aspect of my lecture was published in the online publication *Kompasiana* by Faishol Adib (2014). In response, some readers, who considered me a foreign scholar, posted disparaging comments, saying "why should our history be dictated by an outsider?" Another reader referenced the work of Drewes's *Het Boek Van Bonang* as evidence, though after further investigation I could not find in that work any mention of Sunan Kalijågå performing wayang to spread Islam. Only a few readers defended my position, suggesting that if lacking historical evidence is a matter of fact, readers should take that into consideration. To conclude his article in *Kompasiana*, Adib pointed out that in an academic discussion, presenting evidence is important.

It is worth noting that some scholars studying Islam in Indonesia have doubts about Sunan Kalijågå's life and activities. Makin (2016, 237), professor of religion at the State Islamic University (Universitas Islam Negeri, UIN), interpreted the name Kalijågå as deriving from *Kaliyoga*, a term referring to the transition from the Hindu-Javanese to the Muslim-Javanese period. Fox (1997, 193) questioned the life span of Sunan Kalijågå, who, according to tradition, lived during three different generations and dynasties of Javanese rulers: fourteenth-century Måjåpahit, sixteenth-century Demak, and seventeenth-century Mataram. Woodward (2011, 127) stated unambiguously that Sunan Kalijågå was a "mythical Javanese Islam saint." In his study of Chinese involvement in the introduction of Islam to Indonesia, Tan (2018, 140) pointed out that the seventeenth-century *Malay Annals of Semarang and Cirebon* mentions the sunan as an apostate Chinese Muslim of the Hanafi sect. However, the authenticity of this source has been questioned, to the degree that it might be a fabricated document (Wain 2017). Nonetheless, the perspective of Sunan Kalijågå's wickedness during his youth is often mentioned in Javanese historiography, as in *Babad Tjerbon* (Rinkes 1996, 155) and in the story performed in *kethoprak* folk drama.

The lack of conventional historical evidence of the life and activities of Sunan Kalijågå has led to these myriad interpretations. In most cases, they lean toward identifying the sunan and his activities symbolically. This tendency has led me to approach the stories of Sunan Kalijågå more in terms of signifying the symbolic meaning of his proselytizing strategy. From this premise, in the following sections I explore the meaning of the narrative revealing Sunan Kalijågå's character, which earned him the reputation as the well-known wali who introduced Islam through performing arts.

In retrospect, when I said in the question-and-answer session at my lecture at the Universitas Negeri Sebelas Maret that I could not find enough evidence about the activities of Sunan Kalijågå performing wayang, I failed to mention two important references, which do briefly show his involvement in wayang and masked dance performances. The seventeenth-century *Babad Tjerbon* mentions the sunan performing a wayang play, and it tells us that he was an itinerant dhalang known by the name of Ki Seda Brangti. When he performed, he required his audience to recite the Islamic confession as the fee for his performance. If the audience was willing to recite it, they became Muslim (Rinkes 1996, 135).[6] *Suluk Wujil*, composed in the same period as *Babad Tjerbon*, mentions the sunan performing a masked dance. In one of the stories, Sunan Bonang (the author of *Suluk Wujil*) asks his servant (Wujil) to give a particular style of earring to Sèh Malåyå (another name for Sunan Kalijågå),[7] which is a good fit for masked dancers to wear. Wujil brought the earring to Pati, the town where Sèh Malåyå was performing the masked dance. Although Sunan Kalijågå performing wayang and masked dance is mentioned in these two sources, they do not contain detailed information on how his performances spread Islam, e.g., what story the sunan performed and which part of Islamic doctrine he incorporated.

It did not occur to me during the early period of my research that I should seriously treat the narratives in these sources as symbolic actions. Following the notion that culture is a system of symbols (Geertz 1973), in the following pages I will further explore Kalijågå's deep immersion in the performing arts in his proselytizing activities to transform Hindu-Javanese to Islam-Javanese culture.

Suluk Wujil has a long discussion on wayang, but it does not tell us what story Sunan Kalijågå performed and how he employed wayang for religious proselytizing. Instead, as Cohen (2012) describes:

> The text is the product of a philosophically sophisticated wayang expert with a professional vantage on shadow puppet theatre as well as Islamic mysticism. It calls for what Ben Anderson has called a "professional reader," one well-versed in the ngelmu (esoteric sciences) necessary to comprehend the text (cf. Anderson 1990, 271–98). To understand Suluk Wujil, a professional level of theoretical competence in both wayang and theology is assumed. (24)

Here are a few examples of the stanzas about Sunan Bonang's esoteric knowledge about wayang:

> The honorable Potentate of Omniscience said,
> "The symbols for Non-Being and Being, my young friend, are
> The shadow puppets of the right and left.
>
> "Those of the left stand for Non-Being;
> Those of the right stand for Being.
> The Pandhawa stand for Non-Being,
> While the Karowa stand for Being.
> Being originates in Non-Being
> Just as Non-Being originates in Being.

The nature of reality is what is contested.
Kresna acts as the looking glass.
Kresna is the mirror for both sides in the shadow puppet theatre.
Defeat and victory are in the mirror.

"That is why they fight over the country [of Astina].
Truly, it is the nature of reality that is contested.
That is the cause for their battle.
The possession of the country is struggled over.
The Korawa princes struggle for the country
With those known as the Pandhawa.
That is a hidden sign.
That is why they fight.
They struggle over Non-Being and Being, my young friend.
Such has it been since ancient times."[8] (Cohen 2012, 31; his translation)

How do we explain the belief in the important role of Sunan Bonang and Sunan Kalijågå using wayang to disseminate Islam? I suggest this belief was constructed because of highly regarded literary works in society. That is, literary works on the sophisticated philosophical nature of wayang (as exemplified by the quotation) whose stories centered on Sunan Kalijågå and Sunan Bonang provided the basis for this belief. Even if *Babad Tjerbon* or *Suluk Wujil* are only casually known or heard of by people—like other "classic" works that are never read but are still regarded as authoritative sources of knowledge or "high culture"—these works nonetheless hold power as literary classics that allude to the importance of Sunan Bonang and Sunan Kalijågå (and other Islamic saints, for that matter) as authors of wayang philosophy, thus reinforcing the belief that Islamic saints played an important role in disseminating Islam through wayang performance.

As I mentioned earlier, myth as symbolic action is a valuable source in our search for the meaning of past events. Myth can also be considered as an allegorical marker of historical events and social processes. On the symbolic meaning of Kalijågå's life story, Quinn (2019) explains:

For many Javanese Sunan Kalijågå's life story is literally true, but for others it is an allegory rather than history. Sunan Kalijågå is an embodiment of Javanese Islam and his life story parallels the evolution of Islam in Java, with each stage marked by a name change. It begins with Islam's comfortable vassalage under Hindu-Buddhist rule (Radèn Mas Said) and proceeds through violence, pillage and war (Brandhal Lokåjåyå) to peaceful proselytizing (Sheikh Malåyå) and finally to mass conversion and Islam's integration into the culture of Java (Sunan Kalijågå). The saint's life also captures stages in the development of personal spirituality: from youthful innocence and self-indulgence, to outrage and rebellion, to the awakening of self-awareness and responsibility, and ultimately to the energy and peace unlocked by spiritual maturity. (50–51)

The last sentence of Quinn's quotation is worth emphasizing: the story of the sunan should be understood as symbolic action, portraying someone who has gone through different stages in his spiritual development. In other words, what Quinn describes is the symbolic meaning of Sunan Kalijågå's inner character.

For our discussion, it is important to explore the presence of the performing arts in the context of the history of Indonesian Islam. I suggest that implicitly indicated in Kalijågå's myth is his deep immersion in Javanese performing arts. In this regard, I turn to a manuscript from the court of Surakarta entitled *Sĕrat Suluk Warna-Warni Tuwin Wirid Syattariyah* (Various Books and Poems and Syattariyah Teachings) to point out the relevance of the story of Déwå Ruci in Javanese wayang as an allegorical marker of the transformation from the world of Hindu-Javanese to Islam-Javanese.[9]

Based on a pre-Islamic *Mahabharata* epic, but Javanese in origin, the story revolves around the second of the Pandhåwå brothers, Bimå, searching for the water of life. After successfully resolving obstacles (i.e., tests from gods), Bimå meets a dwarf god named Déwå Ruci, who is also a miniature of himself. Déwå Ruci invites him to enter his stomach. There, Bimå sees boundless ocean, empty and unidirectional space, and four colors: black, red, yellow, and white. Déwå Ruci explains to Bimå the meaning of these colors and their mystical realization.

We learn from literary evidence that the story of Déwå Ruci is based on the pre-Islamic, Old Hindu-Javanese poem *Nawaruci*. Arps (2011) coined the term "resacralization" to indicate the transformation of *Nawaruci* to Yåsådipurå's literary work *Déwå Ruci*, composed in the late eighteenth century. Comparing the two, Arps concludes that Yåsådipurå employed miscellaneous Sufistic ideas and images from a variety of sources, indicating his deep knowledge of Islam. It is likely that his Islamic perspective was drawn from his own religious experience as a practitioner of *tarekat* (Sufi brotherhood).

In her recent study, Meyer (2021) similarly states that the Old Javanese story of Déwå Ruci "was reworked into a Sufi text in modern Javanese poetry" (676) and describes the transformation of the main figures from the story of Déwå Ruci to the story of Nabi Kilir, or Khiḍr in Arabic. Reputedly inspired by Yåsådipurå's *Déwå Ruci*, the story of Nabi Kilir was composed by Imam Anom of the Kasunanan court of Surakarta in 1884. Subsequently, in 1993 it was rewritten with the title *Serat Linglung Sunan Kalijågå (Seh Malåyå).*

The story of Nabi Khiḍr, which can be found in the Quran (Surah 18:65–82), is about the meeting between the Prophet Musa and "one of Our servants," the Prophet Khiḍr. Musa is asking Khiḍr to be accepted as his follower, and to be taught about "something of higher truth" that he learned from Allah.

The main similarity between the story of the Prophet Kilir and Sèh Malåyå is the teaching of mystical knowledge through the symbolic meanings of certain colors. In *Déwå Ruci*, Bimå plunges into the ocean in search of the water of life. There, he meets Déwå Ruci, who asks Bimå to enter his stomach to receive mystical doctrines. In the Nabi Kilir story, Sunan Kalijågå is trying to reach Mecca for pilgrimage by swimming in the ocean. In the ocean he meets Nabi Kilir who, like Déwå Ruci to Bimå, teaches Kalijågå mystical knowledge.

In "The Tenth Saint and His Antecedents," Quinn (2018) explains how the authors of the story *Sèh Malåyå* were reworking Déwå Ruci into their story. Here, I present Quinn's (14) example of the convergences and differences between the two stories: the dialogues between Bimå and Déwå Ruci and between Sèh Malåyå (i.e., Sunan Kalijågå) and Prophet Kilir.

BIMÅ MEETS DÉWÅ RUCI

Bimå is instructed by his teacher and mentor Durnå to seek the water of life in the ocean.

In the middle of the ocean, Bimå meets with Déwå Ruci, a mini replica of himself.

Déwå Ruci instructs Bimå to enter into him through his ear.

Inside, Bimå finds a vast ocean and meets again with Déwå Ruci.

Bimå receives mystical instruction from Déwå Ruci.

SUNAN KALIJÅGÅ MEETS NABI KHIḌR

Sunan Kalijågå is instructed by his mentor Sunan Bonang to make a pilgrimage across the ocean to Mecca.

On the seashore, or in the ocean, Sunan Kalijågå meets with Nabi Khiḍr, who has the appearance of a small child.

Nabi Khiḍr instructs Sunan Kalijågå to enter into him through his ear.

Inside, Sunan Kalijågå finds himself floating in a vast emptiness, or in an ocean without horizons. He meets again with Khiḍr.

Sunan Kalijågå receives mystical instruction from Khiḍr.

Regarding the transformation of the story of Déwå Ruci to the story of Nabi Kilir, which is marked by Bimå replacing Sunan Kalijågå and Déwå Ruci substituting for Nabi Kilir, Meyer (2021) explains:

> The narrativization of Sunan Kalijaga's story in the *Seh Mlaya* makes particularly evident certain narrative and aesthetic continuities between pre-Islamic and Islamic Java, as it narrates Sunan Kalijaga's path to becoming a *wali* by grafting it onto the pre-Islamic *Dewa Ruci* narrative, with the narrative structure and symbolism of the originally Hindu-Buddhist text staying mostly intact. As it crosses religions, the *Seh Mlaya* narrative has proved to be a productive point of inquiry into the ways in which Javanese Muslims appropriated pre-Islamic aesthetic forms and integrated them into a new religious framework (Arps 2011; Quinn 2018, 676).

In addition to learning of the important role of Sunan Kalijågå in Islamizing Java through the performing arts, we also learn from other manuscript evidence of the depth of the Islamic environment at the court of Surakarta in the early to mid-nineteenth century. The Islamic environment at the Javanese courts has not been given much attention. This is because our understanding of the court literary works, which we believe to be the works *par excellence*, has for the most part been based on Hindu tales in their modern Javanese language versions. For example, several prominent court poets were known for translating the Old Hindu-Javanese *Mahabharata* epic and the *Ramayana* story into modern Javanese literary works, including Yåsådipurå I (see Florida 2019) and Ronggåwarsitå's well-known *Puståkå Råjå*. Evidence shows, however, that aside from being well-known Javanese literati, these court poets were also Sufi devotees, avid readers and composers of *Suluk* (Islamic mystic song), and authors. For example, Ronggåwarsitå compiled treatises of Islamic mystical doctrines in the work *Wirid Hidayat Jati*, which Florida (174) characterized as bearing resemblance to Syattariyah Sufi teachings. In this way, Ronggåwarsitå and other court poets' works are similar to that of ethnographers, as they are manifestations of—following Gilbert Ryle, as adapted by Geertz (1973, 6)—"thinking of reflecting" and "the thinking of Thoughts." As such, their mythological narratives of the Islamization of Java contain valuable historical evidence supporting our understanding of Kalijågå's narrative as symbolic action.

Reading Kalijågå's narrative as told by the court poets illustrates the significance of Kalijågå's way of Islamizing pre-Islamic aesthetic forms. Meyer identifies this by looking at the way in which Sunan Kalijågå desires to achieve a true understanding of God's guidance (*hidayat*). Here is a conversation between Kalijågå and his teacher, Sunan Bonang:

Seh Mlaya said softly:
"I, your servant, am very grateful."
Kalijaga offered his reverence.
"But your servant says to you, lord:
I ask for all of it:
The truth of the Most High
that is called faith and guidance [hidayat]."[10] (Meyer 2021, 680)

The narrative implies that Sunan Kalijågå was studying Islam in depth. The hidayat likely came from two sources: a Ghazālīan concept widely circulating in Islamic Southeast Asia at that time, and the instruction of Sunan Kalijågå, which came from the brotherhood Syattariyah's thought and practice (9). Meyer also found another source adapted in the Kalijågå narrative, al-Gahazali's *Bidayat al Hi-dayat* (The Beginning of Guidance) on a form of Sufi doctrine. Viewed in this way, by paralleling Bimå with Sunan Kalijågå and Déwå Ruci with Kilir (the Javanese name of the Prophet Khiḍr) in the wayang story of Déwå Ruci, we can see the depth of Kalijågå's immersion in the world of wayang, along with its relationship to Islamic Sufism.

MYTH AS CONDUIT FOR SPIRITUAL EXPERIENCE AND PROSELYTIZATION

Discussing the mythological narrative of Sunan Kalijågå reminds us of the interaction and collision between myth and history that underpins this book. In the following discussion I propose that through mythology, one's status can be socially enhanced. Mythology can also be a conduit for referencing and experiencing magico-religiosity. In other words, for Javanese people, mythology is more than storytelling. For example, one of the ways that Javanese kings have enhanced their power is by creating a genealogical tree. In the words of Moertono (1968, 62–63), "The more august persons, real or *legendary*, it incorporated and the further back it went, the greater the king's prestige" (my emphasis). It is fitting, therefore, that Javanese rulers created their genealogical trees including such figures as Adam and Eve, the Hindu gods and goddesses of the *Mahabharata* and *Ramayana* tales, Hindu-Javanese rulers, important figures from indigenous Javanese stories, Islamic rulers and saints, and ancestral founders of the present Mataram dynastic kingdoms.

Mythology can also become a religious reference to strengthen people's spirituality while they carry out important tasks. For example, gamelan makers, in carrying out their work, must disguise themselves with the names of mythological figures, for example prince Panji and his entourage (the main characters of the twelfth-century indigenous Javanese story). In so doing, they can endow themselves with the spiritual power and physical stamina they need to safely produce a good gamelan set.

In another example, we know historically that the Indian writing tradition was introduced to the Javanese in the early centuries CE. After a process of localization, passages from ancient manuscripts often became hymns or mantras, as is the case with the mantra that opens certain wayang performances (I will address this topic fully in chapter 3). The Kalimåsådå and *Kalimahoṣadha* are two further cases in point, involving the sanctity of scripts—both are written documents: *Kalimahoṣadha* a book, Kalimåsådå a letter. Perhaps we can think of the English word *scripture*, from the root "script," indicating a sacred book of writing descended from God. The Veda of Hinduism and the Quran of Islam are also scriptures, the sacred writings descended, respectively, from many gods (deities in Hindu) or one God (Allah in Islam). By extension, the scripts themselves are also sacred. It does make sense, therefore, that magical power is attributed to *Kalimahoṣadha* and Kalimåsådå. Commonly, the term *Jimat*, from the Arabic *azimat* (power), precedes *Kalimåsådå*, hence *Jimat Kalimåsådå*, the sacred letter.

This discussion reveals the richness of the content and context of Islam in Java as the religion has been localized, becoming the Islam-Javanese religio-cultural tradition. After other Islamic schools of thought (*mazhab*) were introduced to the archipelago, Indonesian Islam became a plural Islam with many different interpretations of the religion, which have given rise to different traditions. The dynamic of Indonesian Islam has been further complicated by the recent emergence of the radical Islamic movement and the localized incorporation of Western-influenced, global cultural trends (Sumarsam 2018, x). As I have explained elsewhere, such developments have often triggered heated debate on the place of performing arts in socio-religious life. In this regard, the prominent historian Ricklefs (2012, 392) argues that because of the recent deepening Islamization of Javanese society, the older art forms such as wayang and gamelan have been culturally denatured. To the extent that these art forms have revived at all, it is only because local authorities support them for the purpose of tourism, or for marking unique local identities. Moreover, he goes on to say that even if Islamic reformers do not aim to discredit older art forms, eventually modernization and the globalization of entertainment will lead to their abandonment.

Ricklefs's pessimistic opinion about the future of traditional performing arts deserves pondering, but it is too early to declare such a drastic prediction. What is clear is that, as a multimedia performance genre that commands colorful and deep historical, aesthetic, religious, and emotional affiliations (Anderson 1996;

Arps 2016; Kayam 2001; Mrazek 2005; van Groennendael 1985), wayang has inspired wide-ranging discourses. The multifaceted meanings of wayang are sustained and thickened by the fact that in our contemporary world, wayang also illuminates (a) the effects of Indonesia's sociopolitical and religious conflicts, (b) Java's cultural encounters with global Western influences, and (c) Java's deepening Islamic conservatism. Thus, we are witnessing the change, continuity, and expansion of the meaning, content, and context of wayang.

Regarding change and continuity, I have observed a trend starting in the 1980s where wayang mythology is used for religious propagation and *pengajian*, a religious activity to strengthen people's piety. As noted earlier, according to Javanese tradition, Sunan Kalijågå did precisely that: he used wayang performance to spread Islam. Although detailed evidence of the sunan's performance of wayang is lacking, this belief has inspired contemporary preachers to follow suit, incorporating wayang scenes in their oratory as well as a score of levities and light musical interludes in their preaching. While it is true that in the past, Islamic values and doctrines have been incorporated into wayang stories implicitly (Sumarsam 2013), today's preachers do so explicitly. For example, they may Arabize the name of wayang figures and Islamize their behavior. The incorporation of scenes full of humor and light musical interludes raises new questions about the appropriateness of levity and popular culture in religious propagation whose aim is to facilitate congregation with Allah.

In another wayang trajectory, in the period leading up to the independence of Indonesia in the early twentieth century, Indonesian nationalists used wayang as a metaphor in their political discourse. One example is Tjipto Mangoenkoesoemo's stand on constructing Indonesian national ideology, in which he emphasized the importance of the rights of association and assembly. Shiraishi summarizes Tjipto's characterization of the situation, using wayang characters as reference: "He then compared the Indies government to Pandhita Durna [a cunning priest of the kingdom of Ngastinå] and the sunan to the king of Ngastina in the wayang of the Mahabharata cycle and said that the purpose of the SH [Sarekat Hindia, an organization he founded] was to fight, like Pandhawa, against the Indies government and the nobility for the freedom of the Indies." (Shiraishi 1990, 189)

Tjipto was also very concerned about the moral decay of the Indies government, referencing the knight (*ksatriya*) character of the son of Arjunå (the middle brother of Pandhåwå), Abimanyu. When his grandfather refuses to give him permission to search for his father, he steadfastly stands by his request: "No, grandfather! You cannot refuse to grant my request, for I have made up my mind to seek my father" (Tjipto Mangoenkoesoemo 1928, in Shiraishi 1990, 124). Responding to his grandson's insistence, the grandfather says: "Good, my son! I see that I have not taught you the qualities of ksatriya in vain. In your decision I recognize your ksatriya-nature, which cannot be thwarted by any kind of hardship—nay, more, which in every hardship finds a mighty spur to still greater efforts. Once again, you do honor to your caste by your determination" (124).

The use of wayang as political metaphor continues today, especially among Indonesian national figures, politicians, and cultural commentators with Javanese backgrounds (see Pausacker 2004). This includes the late President Abdulrahman Wahid (Gus Dur), who contextualized wayang with respect to nationalism and Islam; and the head of Parliament Fadli Zon, whose satire of President Joko Widodo referenced the story of the clown Pétruk becoming king (Pétruk Dadi Ratu), a story that originated within the context of colonialism, which I will discuss in chapter 4.

OVERVIEW OF CHAPTERS

Cultural formation and transformation, the collision of history and mythology, text and context in cultural performance, aural and written tradition, levity and religiosity: these topics will be unpacked in the four chapters of this book. The book is not a strict history of the performing arts, although its chapters are arranged loosely in chronological order. Rather, in each chapter I discuss aspects of these issues.

In chapter 1, "Indian Origin and Inspirations: Old Javanese Literary Works and Cultural Performances," I examine the aesthetic and religious meaning of certain contemporary musical practices, tracing their Indian roots in literary works and iconographic evidence from the ninth to the fifteenth centuries. In so doing, I selectively follow, review, and comment on musical practices and contexts that have been studied by a number of scholars, including A. Becker, J. Becker 1993, Hadiwidjojo 1953, Poerbatjaraka 1987, 1868, 1940, Widdess 1993, Acri 2014, 2015, 2010, and Gomperts 2002. Each author discusses the connection between Javanese and Indian musical practices and the performing arts. They trace the meaning of certain musical practices, for example the names of gamelan tones, which Becker links to the significance of Hindu-Buddhist philosophy in the period of medieval Java. Widdess, Gomperts, and Acri deeply and meticulously do the same. Stutterheim's study of the genesis of court jesters in the old Javanese period was based on a long speech by the learned prince of the court of Surakarta, Hadiwidjojo.

In chapter 2, "Center-Periphery, Court-Rural Dynamics: Performing Arts on the Move," I consider how Javanese mythologies have moved and transformed from one cultural site to another—center to periphery—examining literary and/or theatrical forms in different contexts within their historical periods. For example, East Java, where some myths originate, was once a center, until its political and cultural decline led the center to move to Demak and its vicinity. The north coast area became the periphery at the time Mataram's power arose. The stories of Panji, Damarwulan, and *Mahabharata* and *Ramayana* have moved from one center to another, changing their web of significance. One element of myth is that it has sustained its prominence as a way of enhancing spiritual power. For example, it has become a tradition for gamelan makers to name themselves after Prince Panji or members of Panji's entourage to seek a blessing from their ancestors to produce the best gamelan safely. Similarly, some dhalang wayang golèk in the north coast area of Java use a mantra to open their wayang performance by quoting texts from the seventeenth-century manuscript *Bhīma Svarga* to obtain blessings from God.

In chapter 3, "Linking the Present to the Past through Preaching, Ritual, and Levity," I discuss the dynamics of modern Islamic preachers, each of whom has a distinct style, particularly in pengajian, the gathering meant to strengthening people's religious piety. In contrast to a formal religious gathering, such as Friday's mass prayer in the mosque, pengajian is commonly held in the community to celebrate holy days as well as rite-of-passage events. Commonly defined as "live religion," the preacher delivers his sermon through oratory containing Islamic values and examples of ideal behavior for Muslims. Most preachers deliver their oratory in a mixture of Indonesian and Javanese language that is easy to understand and entertaining. Even if the sermon uses elaborate language structures, assonance, and rhyme, such as the preacher Kyai Abdurochim's oratory, the content is full of humor. Adding to the entertainment value are musical interludes interspersed with the oratory. The interludes are mostly in popular music styles, such as light pieces of gamelan and Indonesianized and Islamized Western popular music (e.g., *dangdut*) using a rock band, gamelan, and/or Indian musical instruments. Some preachers, such as Gus Muwafiq, also insert a number of wayang scenes, presenting them in a mixture of storytelling and humorous commentary. Discussion of music and wayang often features in the preaching. In mesmerizing ways, the preacher tells his audience about the transformation from Hindu-Javanese to Muslim-Javanese culture, including the transformation of the Hindu pancamakara ritual to traditional Javanese slametan, marking a shift from a wild to a respectable ritual.

In the final chapter, "Discourses on Wayang from the Nineteenth Century to the Present," I focus on contemporary discourses of the performing arts in the context of colonialism and Indonesian nationalism. I mentioned the story of the clown Pétruk becoming king being used as a satire about President Joko Widodo.

I discuss this example further, tracing the genesis and meaning of the story from its inception in the nineteenth century to its contemporary transformation. I apply Margana's (2019) hypothesis that the creation of the story was directed by the Dutch Resident in Yogyakarta by reading closely the script of the story as it appeared in the nineteenth-century manuscript *Serat Kondha Ringgit Purwa* from the Kasultanan court of Yogyakarta. I expand the discussion to include contemporary perspectives on wayang and Islam, examining the perspectives of the fourth president, Abdulrahman Wahid (Gus Dur), and other contemporary national figures on wayang, social harmony, and Islam.

CODA: THE IN-BETWEEN

To recapitulate: what has emerged from the present study is a myriad of diverse perspectives in the discourse of the development of Javanese cultural tradition, which arises after a long history of intersociocultural and interreligious encounters, from the ninth century to the present time. But the availability of historical evidence from one period to another is not even—the farther back the history, the less evidence is available to us. The lack of conventional historical fact has made it possible for people to liberally interpret the meanings of past events, linking them to contemporary events in various ways. The study shows dynamic interaction, collaboration, and collision between history and mythology. The paucity of historical evidence has also enabled the creation of culturally contextualized myths that are presented in the form of an imagined world. Therefore, mythology can be useful for reconstructing history by reading between the lines. A myth can also become a spiritual reference point for people since its content often relates to the existence of divine beings. In this regard, the link between spirituality and religion should be explained. The practice of conventional religion consists of a formal institutionalized process (e.g., through religious gathering in the mosque or church) directed toward achieving personal or collective union with God. Spirituality can be obtained both formally and informally. Commonly, the informal way of achieving spirituality is through events associated with community activities. This is what scholars called "lived religion" (Rinallo et al. 2013), that is, those practices and rituals carried out by religious laity in their everyday lives, consisting of a range of activities that may have religious significance or contain spiritual potency. For example, music and theatrical performances can be presented in preaching activity by religious leaders and in religious festivals. It is not uncommon to see gamelan and wayang play presented side by side with religious songs, display of magically charged relics of inheritance, and prayer.

In my previous work on cultural hybridity, which denotes people from different religions and traditions or worldviews coming into contact with one another, contacts between cultures "bring about a wide register of multiple identity experiences and intensive cultural communication" (Sumarsam 2003, 1). In the case of intersociocultural and interreligious encounters as driving forces of the formation of cultural hybridity, my study finds that the newly formative tradition does not end up only in a happy fusion and synthesis; rather, as individuals or communities position themselves within diverse perspectives, ideologies, and religious pluralities, conflict, ambiguity, and ambivalence become part of the dynamic of hybridity.

In a sense, we are entering the world of "times in-between and spaces in-between" as explained by Turner (1979, 234–43) in his well-known essay "Betwixt and Between: The Liminal Period in Rites de Passage." The concept of "the in-between" is about the process of sociocultural change and continuity, the state of transition, a becoming, and a transformation affecting the performing arts. Turner calls this process "the rite of passage" from which a "liminal phase" is created; that is, the period of time and space in a "no-man's-land betwixt-and-between the structural past and the structural future as anticipated by the society's normative control of biological development." (Turner 1990, 11). Whereas the present study employs synchronic and diachronic approaches to performing arts from different localities and social hierarchies, understanding their multiple variations is the heart of the matter: as I mentioned earlier, the present study unpacks performing arts from court village entertainment-cum-ritual to palace esthetic/proof of cultural competency, from coastal mercantile entrepots to central Javanese wet rice terraces, from colonial plantation and textile factory culture to contemporary industrial estates and creative economy efforts.

In this regard, Turner's (1982) study about a transition from ritual to theater would be a useful framework to adapt. As I summarized his point in my previous works (Sumarsam 2013, 73):

> He proposes two abstract categories of cultural performances: (1) those of "tribal" societies, linked to recurrent calendrical events; and (2) those of industrial societies, as leisure activities. The former evokes "liminality," the state of ambiguity, of being "out of time" or in "social limbo," that both performers and audience (in the general sense of the words) experience during a ritual process. The latter creates a "leisure" event, a "play," that "provides the opportunity for experimentation with variable repertoires," consistent with the manifold variation made possible by developed technology . . . Turner maintains that in aesthetic drama the liminoid is removed from ritual process and also "in-

> dividualized." He goes on to say that "the solitary artist *creates* the liminoid phenomenon, the collectivity experiences collective liminal symbols. This does not mean that the maker of liminoid symbols, ideas, images, etc., does so *ex nihilo*; it only means that he is privileged to make free with his social heritage in a way impossible to members of cultures in which the liminal is to a large extent the sacrosanct."[11]

To show the best illustration of the notion of liminality or the in-between, I will briefly detour to Bali, since the interrelated opposite is the hallmark of Balinese culture and cultural performance. One of the best examples of this aspect of Balinese performing arts is the role of clowns (*penasar*) in mediating between the world of the audience and the world of gods and kings. The fact that "the clowns banter with spectators, teasing the royal characters and making ironic comments about the sacred Sanskrit songs that are sung in praise of the gods" (Jenkins 1994, 22) is an example of clowns living in the world of in-between.

Another example of interrelated opposites is the belief in Balinese cosmology that good and evil are inextricably linked to each other, that demons and gods coexist with the same dynamic tension (22). The best example of this concept in Balinese performing arts is the ritual performance of the encounter between Rangda and the lion mask called *Barong*. "Barong is an archetypal spirit of benevolence, and his clashes with Rangda are charged with extraordinary spiritual potency for the Balinese. Although their battle is enacted regularly in every village, neither Rangda nor Barong is ever allowed to kill the other. They always fight to a draw, achieving the dynamic tension between good and evil that defines the Balinese vision of life" (23).

Characterizing theatrical production as I have described makes us aware of the dualistic interaction in search of the balanced coexistence of good and evil through creative exploration in society during the time of transition. It also shows the complexity of the processes of formation and transformation of culture and cultural performances in the context of sociocultural change throughout history. To this end, what is essential in this study is making the connection between the past and the present in performing arts, which is unpacked in the context of their interhistorical, interreligious, and intercultural experiences and practices. In this regard, contemporary performing arts can be seen as a collection of juxtapositions: synchronic and diachronic trajectories on the one hand, and on the other hand a presentation of the intersections between peripheral, central, national, and global perspectives.

ONE

Indian Origin and Inspirations

Old Javanese Literary Works and Cultural Performances

> 9. His efforts [of granting freehold to a monastery] may result in the welfare of the sacred foundation, and all people may enjoy themselves and obtain pleasure in sight-seeing. The *tangkil hyang*[1] *Si* Nalu recited the Bhima kumāra, dancing like Kicaka.
>
> 10. ka *Si* Jaluk recited the *Rāmāyana*, blowing flutes and making buffoonery; *Si* Mungmuk (and) *Si* Galigi showed *vayang* in honor of gods and presented (above all) Bhimaya-Kumara.[2]
>
> *Sarkar 1959, 96*

Taken from an inscription issued in the name of King Balitung in 907 CE, this epigraph is one of the most quoted texts among scholars studying old Javanese culture for a number of reasons. The most important reason—and its point of relevance to the topic of this book—is the fact that it is the oldest evidence available to us that mentions the various genres of performing art: singing, storytelling, wayang performance, and music. From another section of the inscription, we learn about the context: the performances were staged for the celebration of the granting of freehold to the monastery of Dalinan (Supomo 1993, 2, based on Naerssen 1937 and Sarkar 1972, 85–98).

The mention of the story about Bimå (Bhima) and the dancing of Kincåkå (both are characters from the *Mahabharata* epic) and the reading of the *Ramayana* story suggests the popularity of these two epics. We know that the Sanskrit-based Old Javanese poetic work (*kakawin*) *Ramayana* is the oldest surviving literary work available to us from the Central Javanese period; it was composed during the middle of the ninth century (Supomo 1993, 2, based on Robson 1980 and Zoetmulder 1974, 217–33). Given the magnitude and high quality of *Ramayana Kakawin*, it is not too far-fetched to assume that at that time, there must have been a long and very active literary tradition. Therefore, as Supomo (1993, 2–3) asserts, "the two Sanskrit epics, the *Ramayana* and the *Mahabharata*, must have had their honored place . . . even if there are no traces of the *Mahabharata* from the Central Javanese period among the corpus of Old Javanese manuscripts." The charter from which the inscription is taken further mentions si Nalu reciting *Bhimakumara* and performing Kincåkå's dance, clowning by si Mungmuk, and wayang performance by si Galigi using a story of *Bhimaya Kumara*. These references support the possibility that the *Mahabharata* was equally as popular as the *Ramayana*.

Although the charter does not detail the story of *Bhimakumara* and Kincåkå, we know that Bimå and Kincåkå (Javanese, Kicaka or Kincåkårupå) are two characters from the *Mahabharata* epic. Bimå is the second brother of Pandhåwå. Kincåkå is the prime minister of King Matswåpati of the kingdom of Wiråthå. Scholars give different meanings to *Bhimayakumara* or *Bhimaya-Kumara*. Sarkar (1972) suggests that *Bhimaya-Kumara* is a corruption of the word *Bhīmaja-Kumāra*, referring to the son of Bimå (i.e., Ghaṭotkaca), hence the story of Ghaṭotkaca. Zoetmulder (1974, 209) interprets it as "the Young Bhima" and "Bhima as Lover." Holt (1968, 128) thinks it is simply a story of Bimå as a hero of the *Mahabharata*. We know from the Indonesian version of the fourth book of the *Mahabharata*, *Virāṭaparva*[3] (Phalgunadi 1992), and also from contemporary wayang performances, that Bimå must confront and fight Kincåkå, who lusts for Salindri (Yudhistirå's wife in disguise), but Salindri rejects the lusting Kincåkå. In Javanese wayang performance, Bimå kills Kincåkårupå and his brother Rupakincåkå. In any event, such evidence led Zoetmulder (1974) to confirm the existence of wayang performance in the Hindu-Javanese period (the tenth century), though no evidence exists specifically describing its form.

There is another aspect of performance mentioned in the charter that Supomo (1993, 3) pays attention to: the act of *macarita* (recitation), as in "si Jaluk recited a story of Ramayana." He suggests that this was a tradition of the public reading of literary works, which may have been inspired by the same tradition in India called *harikatha*. This tradition is still being practiced in Bali, called *mabasan*.

Thus, we see that by the tenth century, the Indian literary work had been adapted by the Javanese. In light of this fact, it is useful at this juncture to discuss the development of literacy in the early history of Java. This is relevant to our discussion because theatrical performances were based on and inspired by these literary works.

We know from the historical evidence available to us that the rise of international trading in Asia in the early centuries CE made possible the advancement of Javanese intellectualism and cultural development. That is, Indian merchants served as a conduit for the introduction of Indian culture in Southeast Asia. Most likely, the merchants brought with them Brahman priests, who were then responsible for introducing literacy, religion, and culture to people on the mainland and islands of Southeast Asia.

Script is a fundamental element of literacy. After investigating inscriptions on stone or copper plate from the first millennium CE, scholars have identified a number of Indian scripts that existed in Southeast Asia (see Hunter 1996; Supomo 1996).[4] The Pallava script, named after the Pallava dynasty of South India, is one of them. In Indonesia, inscriptions written with this script can be found in Kutai and West Java from the fifth century. In the mid-eighth century, the Pallava script evolved to become Kawi script, marking the beginning of the development of Javanese literacy. The term *kawi* refers to the Javanese rendering of *kavya* (Sanskrit court poetry). This script was used for writing literary works on *lontar*, a common material that served as the main form of written documents for centuries to come. By this time, the Sanskrit meter and Sanskrit-based Javanese language had become common for the literary form of the poetic genre *kakawin*.

While Indian merchants initially introduced Indian culture to Java, by the eighth century intellectuals and priests of local Indianized royal courts had become the main agents spreading literary works. Essentially, the literary world belonged to the elite. Those from elite and royal backgrounds made it possible for the Javanese to adapt the highly elegant, stylized, and strictly formalized rules of Sanskrit poetic genres. The aim of such literary adaptation was to legitimize and enhance the power of Javanese rulers, since Javanese people considered Indian traditions as having a high degree of prestige.

A verse of kakawin illustrates these highly regulated metrical rules: each stanza consists of four lines of the same length; each line must have a fixed number of syllables; and each syllable should be recited according to its fixed duration—either short (∪) or long (–). See, for example, the following text from *Jagaddhita*, Canto 1/1:

∪
– – – | ∪ ∪ – | ∪ – ∪ | ∪ ∪ – | ∪ ∪ ∪ | ∪ ∪ ∪ | – ∪ – | ∪ –
saṅ śūrâmrih ayajña riṅ samara mahyun i hilaṅa nikaṅ parāṅmukha
līlakâmbaṅ urā sĕkar taji ni keśa niṅ ari pêjah ing raṇāṅgana
ūrnā niṅ ratu māti wija nira kuṇḍa nira nagara niṅ musuh gĕsĕṅ

sāhityâhuti tĕṇḍas iṅ ripa kapökan i ratha nika suśramâṅlaga.
(Supomo 1993, 55; see translation in note)[5]

Due to these strictly regulated metrical rules, writing kakawin was a highly disciplined literary act. For the poet, the challenge was to fulfill the metrical requirements while at the same time reflecting the content of the kakawin. Essentially, writing and performing kakawin was a spiritual exercise, which had spiritual effects on the listeners. Knowing that his works were dedicated to the king, the author made his best efforts to write the poem. Underlining the concept of *dewa-raja* (god-king, a belief that the king is a divine universal), the literary yoga, as a form of homage to the king, promoted his invincibility, making the world more prosperous.

Scholars studying Javanese kakawin agree that much of their content was inspired by Indian kavya (Creese 2004; Supomo 1996; Zoetmulder 1974). Scholars also agree that many kakawin impart religious experiences and practices. Unlike Indian kavya, however, Javanese kakawin were also designed for aesthetic enjoyment and entertainment. As Creese (2004, 23) explains, "One of the major roles that kakawin poets performed was that of 'soother of cares' (Panglipur lara), a function shared with poets in other literary traditions in the Indonesian and Malay world."[6] Creese explains further:

> [By] capturing in verse the beauty of the natural world, the emotion of love, and the heat of battle, poets created a universe in which the audience could leave behind their everyday concerns and be transported to the heroic realm of war, love, and adventure, swept away by exquisite language, pleasing meter, apt metaphor, bawdy jokes, and clever allusion. In other words, kakawin were designed to entertain, to be sung and performed in public, and to appeal to a live audience drawn from all classes of society. While the "paying" audience may have been the elite members of the inner court, performances were watched by all those who could attend, whether rich or poor, villager or court official. Even for the poet's wider audience, the spiritual benefits of hearing the stories were considerable. In addition, didactic elements in kakawin, particularly those pertaining to proper conduct, or dharma, were aimed at society in general. (23)

The richness of cultural and religious experience in Javanese kakawin were represented mostly by the great Hindu tale *Ramayana* and the *Mahabharata* epic. These two great literary works sustained the Javanese fascination with Hindu mythology for centuries to come. Throughout Javanese history, they were copied, recopied, and translated into the middle and modern Javanese language by *pujangga* (*pujonggå* in modern Jv., royal court poets and chroniclers). In addition to its continual transformation in literary works, the stories were also carved on the walls of ancient temples. For example, the ninth-century gigantic monument Borobudur in Central Java presents the story of Buddha. The ninth-century Dieng Temple, also in Central Java, includes the names of Pandhåwå characters from *Mahabharata*. *Ramayana* was depicted on the wall of the ninth-century Hindu temple Prambanan and the temple of Panataran in East Java. Stories from *Mahabharata* were also carved on the walls of the temple of Pananggungan in East Java. Interestingly, scenes from the indigenous Javanese story Panji (which I discuss in chapter 2) were also depicted on the walls of the same temple.

It is worth noting that the function of *candi* (temples) was not unlike that of kakawin: they were "a sanctuary of the gods where ceremonies were performed at which gods were thought to be present, and a place of worship, where homage is paid to them and at the same time to deified royalty and to the royal ancestral spirits" (Stott et al. 2003, 11–12). It makes sense, therefore, that writing kakawin is described as an "act of worship . . . sometimes likened to building a temple," and that "the fruit of his [the poet's] devotion, the kakawin, is described as a candi bhasa or 'language temple'" (Supomo 1996, 24). As Mpu Tantular, the author of *Arjunawijaya*, states: "The purpose of my praise is to implore Him to pay heed to the homage of one who devotes himself to poetry. . . This is what I ask as I build my temple of language on my writing board" (24).

Understanding the temple as a place of worship can be seen from two different angles. First, the candi itself is a sanctuary where acts of worship take place. Second, stories depicted on the walls of temples often portray heroic characters believed to be the ancestors of Javanese people and/or the manifestation of their kings.

EVIDENCE FROM KAKAWIN

As noted earlier, priests and intellectuals in the Hinduized Javanese royal courts were responsible for the production of literary works, and they chose the most elegant, stylized, and strictly formalized rules of Sanskrit poetic genres to adapt and produce. It is relevant to ask what kinds of literary traditions existed in Java before the introduction of Indian forms during the ninth century. What kinds of performing arts existed at this time? Unfortunately, as Zoetmulder (1974, 3–8) explains, except for limited passages of Sanskrit inscriptions and Chinese sources, there is not enough evidence to build a clear understanding of pre-Hinduized Javanese literacy.

Robson (1983) suggests that wayang performance may have existed before Java was Indianized. His hypothesis is based on the existence of several indigenous Javanese terms. The *Ramayana Kakawin*, the first kakawin composed in Java in the mid-ninth century, contains a number of indigenous Javanese terms not taken from Sanskrit, which suggests the practice of indigenous Javanese arts, including singing, poetic recitation, wayang, drama, and oratory. Robson explains:

> One of the terms found there is widu. The meaning of this is, however, fairly clear, as it is related to the Malay bidu and biduan, "a singer at a shamanistic seance." The word widu is thus indigenous Javanese, that is, it is not taken from Sanskrit or some other foreign language, and so we can assume that the widu's work too was of an indigenous origin. A widu's activities are clarified by a verb following the noun; thus we find the widu mangidung, the widu who sings songs—seeing that "song" and "poetry" are the same concept in Java, here we have evidence of the performance of poetical texts. In later literary sources we also find widu amacangah; amacangah means to recite tales of the past, perhaps in the form of genealogies. And finally we have the expression widu mawayang, found in the Old Javanese Rämäyana (24.1 12), a text datable to the middle of the ninth century. From this it seems that the widu also performed a kind of drama, possibly the same as the shadow-theatre of today. The context where the words are found suggests that the widu mawayang was "homeless and unattached" and did not stand in particularly high regard. Probably alongside the sophisticated written literature of which the Rämäyana itself is an example there also existed a repertoire performed by lowly practitioners wandering the countryside. (293)

Robson strengthens his point by drawing a connection between *widu* and *kidung*, a sung poetic genre from the Middle Javanese period. Kidung is believed to have magical powers to ward off evil and prevent illness, even today. This indicates that the basic meaning of the term has survived to the present. The widu was linked to ritual, drama, and the deeds of the ancestors, likening him to the figure of the dhalang, whose performance of wayang and exorcisms persists in contemporary Java. With this in mind, Robson suggests that a form of wayang performance must have been occurring during the time of the writing of *Ramayana Kakawin*.

Robson does not specify what kind of wayang performance could have existed, due to the lack of evidence. However, it is clear to him that a widu was the main performer, a priest-like master of ceremony whose performance included singing or reciting poetry. It appears wayang performed by the widu-cum-priest was a type of religious ritual. Robson also offers an interesting proposition, linking the term *widu* from the pre-Hindu Javanese period to *kidung* from medieval Java, and likening the widu to contemporary puppeteers performing exorcisms.

If widus had a very important function in society, why did the author of *Ramayana Kakawin* assert their status as lowly performers, homeless and unattached? Here Acri (2015, 67) enters in the discussion. First, Acri takes issue with Robson's assertion that widu is related to biduan and comparable to contemporary puppeteers. Acri argues that there is no convincing explanation regarding the indigenous traits of widus as proposed by Robson. Acri (2014) reviews works by Robson (1983), Stutterheim (1956), Becker (1993), and other scholars, who link some premodern Javanese performers and performances with South Asian Shivaism-inspired medieval Javanese traditions. According to Acri, these scholars' "approach is rigorous, and their hypotheses are convincing, [but] their conclusions need to be fine-tuned in light of the newly available textual and visual evidence, and especially of our better historical grasp of Sivaism in both South Asia and Nusantara" (Acri 2014, 14).[7] Acri aims to fill this gap. To appreciate his argument in full, I refer readers to his fascinating discussion. For my purposes, I focus on an aspect of Acri's discussion connected to the identity, position, and function of widus as discussed by Robson.

Doubtful of the link between the widu and the biduan, Acri (2010) reviews the work of Robson (1983), Damais (1970), Gomperts (2002), Aichele (1969), and Drewes (1925). Aichele (1969) asserts that *widu* is a generic term for singer, mask-dancer, actor, buffoon, or shadow-player. Aichele also explains: "From the verses of Ramayana it is clear that in Medieval Java, the shadow-player is an itinerant comedian, whose profession expelled him from his home, who should remain solitary and who cannot maintain friendship nor conduct a regular family life" (as cited in Acri 2010, 64). Acri (65) also points to information from the Javano-Balinese *Tutur Śevaśāsana* that refers to those who perform like a widu, "namely '[a] person of an inferior status (having an occupation which is considered inferior),' and linking them—along with *avayaṅ* 'wayang players,' *menmen* 'musicians,' *ijo-ijo* and *abacangah* 'reciters'—to the lowest category of people in the social scale such as *śūdras*, 'members of the fourth estate,' *caṇḍālas*, 'outcasts,' and *mlecchas*, 'barbarians.'" In sum, scholars agree on the link between widus and religious ritual. However, that Old Javanese society considered them as a group of outcasts, itinerant and lowly performers, has led scholars to consider the widu as an ambiguous figure with an ambiguous position. Other passages from kakawin allegorically describe widus as mendicant ascetics. This is a peculiar pairing: performer-cum-ascetic.

In any event, scholars agree that a number of performing arts genres existed by the tenth century, including wayang, although its form cannot be definitively identified. Even during the Hindu-Javanese period, when evidence about performances emerges in Javanese kakawin, no specific detailed information can be found about forms of wayang. The most commonly invoked reference that suggests wayang performance was a shadow puppet play is a passage from the *Arjunawiwaha Kakawin* composed in the eleventh century. This is part of a conversation between Arjunå and the god Indrå about the true value of power and pleasure (see Zoetmulder 1974, 209–10).[8]

> For if you look carefully at it and see that the world drives us to distraction, put an end to it. If you seek enjoyment, heaven and so on, and find them, even so you will suffer pain. In difficulty because of how the five senses obstruct us, we are suddenly confused and dazed, not realizing that we ourselves have been blinded by the objects of desire.
>
> For example, someone watching wayang puppets weeps, is sad, foolish and easily moved, though he already knows that it is only chiseled leather that moves and talks. This is like the man who is attached to the objects of the senses, even to the point of not recognizing that their true nature is unreality, and every form of existence is an illusion. (Robson 2008, 57, 59)

It is clear that carved leather puppets were used in this wayang performance. However, the passage is not explicit as to whether the performance was a shadow puppet play. The sentence "every form of existence is an illusion" at the end of the second verse perhaps implies it was indeed a shadow puppet play.

Zoetmulder (1974) offers stronger evidence about shadow play from his reading of passages from five kakawin: *Bhomantaka*, *Harsawijaya*, *Bharatayuda*, *Wretasancaya*, and *Sumanasantaka*. Passages from these kakawin describe wayang shadow play, though it is mentioned in simile, as part of the journey of certain figures and/or nature. Passages from a section of *Bhomantaka Kakawin* describe the journey of a group of holy seers, likening them to wayang puppets while they are flying in the sky. As evening approaches, "seeking shade in the clouds they were now indistinctly visible, then reappeared like wayang puppets projecting against a white screen, the light of the sun serving as the stage-lamp" (210). In another passage, the author mentions wayang in descriptions of nature when a figure, Samba, passes through the mountains: "Swiftly his chariot carried him along the road, which slopes down from the mountain ridge to a piece of flat terrain where recently rain had fallen. The rice-fields were shrouded in a haze, as though hidden behind a *kelir*. The banana-trees moving gently were the wayang puppets" (210).

Zoetmulder (1974) further identifies passages from *Hariwangsa* and *Bharatayuda Kakawin* that mention musical accompaniment for wayang performance. Like the description of wayang in *Bhomantaka*, wayang and music are mentioned indirectly as simile. In *Hariwangsa*, we find the following description: "In the rice-field along the slopes of the mountain, the trees were wayang puppets against the screen of the all-enveloping transparent mist. For songs they had the soft calling of the kuwong, and the bamboo-rattle in the ravines provided the salunding" (211). From *Bharatayuda*: "In the river the clatterers arranged in rows were like the salunding of the wayang. The hollow bamboos through which the wind played were like flutes, following its lead. The small gongs were provided by an orchestra of kungkangs (a big frog producing a booming sound) in the ravines. The shrill sound of the grasshoppers constituted the incessant accompaniment of the cymbals (kamanak)" (211).

From these descriptions, we can conclude that wayang performance was accompanied by one or more instruments and singing: singing and *salunding* (from *Harsawijaya*), or salunding, flutes, small gongs, and *kamanak* (from *Bharatayuda*). It seems the salunding, perhaps a xylophone with bamboo or metal keys, was an important instrument in wayang performance. This is reminiscent of the importance of the instrument called *gendèr* in modern Java and Bali. Regardless, as I have mentioned elsewhere in discussing musical ensembles in early Java (Sumarsam 1995), a smaller ensemble, with or without singing, is characteristic of the Hindu-Javanese style. In other words, larger ensembles as we see them today developed in later centuries.

An important point needs to be made regarding scholars' quest to perceive the past based on written documents. The documents of this era were inscribed in stone or on metal plates, such as the charter attributed to King Balitung mentioned earlier. The majority of documents contain literary works in prose or poetic meters (kakawin). While what is written in much of the kakawin is an adaptation of Indian literary works, such as the *Ramayana* story and *Mahabharata* epic, certain indigenous Javanese aspects were incorporated into them. This fact has led scholars to study not only the Javanese adaptation of Indian literary works, but also the content of literary works as invaluable evidence of Javanese historical events. Moreover, scholars have examined these texts to glean insights from the perceptions of the writers into social structures, rituals, monuments, and stories. In other words, for scholars studying Old Javanese literary works, interpretation of the past is at the heart of the matter. In light of the sizeable number of written documents and the long timeframes scholars have to deal with, it is not surprising to find theoretical disagreements among them, as in the case of Acri's critique of Robson.

Why do we care about history? This question often surfaces in my mind. More specifically, what is the use of perceiving the past? I alluded to the answer to this question earlier. That is, remnants of our perceptions of the past, as drawn from Old Javanese literary works and inscriptions, can be discerned in all sorts of artifacts and cultural expressions that still exist and are practiced in contemporary Java today. As such, the arduous quest to link contemporary cultural and socioreligious practices with their possible genesis has occupied scholarly inquiry. To this end, in the following sections—and indeed, this book as a whole—I aim to enrich discussion about the connection between the past and the present, as seen through interhistorical, interreligious, and intercultural experiences and practices in Javanese performing arts. I begin this discussion in the remainder of this chapter with a review of discourses in the scholarly literature.

DISCOURSES ON EARLY JAVANESE MUSIC

The dialectic tension between "speaking the past," i.e., remembering, conserving and repeating, and "speaking the present," i.e., innovation and creativity, is what gives any culture its vitality. A pronounced emphasis one way or the other is deleterious. Too much remembering leads to an inertia, a treadmill of repetition and dullness. Too much forgetfulness leads to the belief that the present is one's own creation, or the creation of one's immediate past. This amnesia has sometimes led to the attribution of many Javanese cultural performances to the influence of colonialism . . . , or exclusively to Islam . . . , or pure reincarnation of a "Hindu-Buddhist" past. Constantly renewed cultural texts, stories and performances preserve the past while not becoming copies of the past; i.e., they become palimpsests. (Becker 1993, 167)

Wayang and gamelan music, two of the most celebrated cultural performances in Indonesia, are traced in ancient inscriptions, literary works, and pictorial evidence from the early centuries CE. It is commonly understood that there are links between religion and these two performing arts genres. In his study of twentieth-century wayang play, Anderson (1996) concludes that there is a pervasive presence of compelling "religious mythology which commands deep emotional and intellectual adherence" (16) in the genre. It is not surprising, therefore, that the topic, form, and historical development of wayang and its musical accompaniment have occupied scholarly attention since the early nineteenth century.

Scholars studying early Javanese performing arts encounter a number of challenges. First, the extant documents are mostly literary works written in the Sanskrit-based Old Javanese language *kawi*; hence, the knowledge of and ability to read kawi is required. Second, since Old Javanese belles lettres are adapted from Indian literary works, linking them to the Indian art of writing, comparative study with Indian culture cannot be avoided. As noted earlier, these literary works were composed during the Hindu-Javanese period and based on Indian metrical rules. To a large degree, these Indian-based literary works were also imbued by local circumstances. Scholars agree that much of the Old Javanese literature was, by and large, adaptations of or inspired by Indian kavya. For this reason, scholars cannot avoid tracing and comparing the content, context, and even aesthetic embodiment of Old Javanese kakawin with Indian kavya. Following this wide trajectory in studying old Javanese performing arts, Judith Becker (1993) traces the concept and meaning of listening to gamelan in the period of medieval Java. As I summarize in the following sections, Becker shows us that the religious meanings of early Javanese music persist among elite Javanese in contemporary Java.

Analogical Approach to Gamelan Tones

Much of the work of early scholars involved the codification of musical instruments, with some suggestive reconstruction of ensemble forms and their meanings. Becker's (1993) approach in searching for the meaning of gamelan in the present and its link to the past is systematic. She uses a palimpsest metaphor to explain the transformation of gamelan's cultural meanings. She defines *palimpsest* as "a tablet on which previous writing is erased, and then written upon again, on which the previous inscription still shows through, albeit faintly" (167). In other words, despite historical change, new meanings cannot completely erase the cultural practices of the past. Instead, traces of previous cultural practices and artifacts appear infused in the new culture. Becker asserts that the vitality of any culture is the result of the dialectic tension between speaking the past and speaking the present. In this regard, in her study of contemporary didactic expositions written by "a select and elite group of elderly men" from Surakarta and Yogyakarta, Becker uncovers a hidden musical meaning whose genesis is traced to the aesthetic and religious meaning of Javanese music in medieval Java (the period from the eighth to the fifteenth century). Among the selected didactic manuscripts, Becker focuses on the work of Sastrapustaka (1984) entitled "Knowledge of Gamelan Revealed." In this treatise, Sastrapustaka relates the names of the tones of gamelan to the human body:

> The tone Barang (thing) refers to the form of the head of a person
>
> The tone Gulu (neck), the passage way leading from the head
>
> The tone Dhadha (chest), the source of human life
>
> The tone Lima (five), the beauty of nature and art, springing from the five senses (pancèndriya)
>
> The tone Enem (six), feeling (rasa, six feeling which cause feeling to have six aspects). (as cited in Becker 1993, 62–65)

Examining Sastrapustaka's analysis of gamelan tones, Becker explains:

> The systematic way in which he piles one analogy upon another—building a dense interpretive net within which one aspect of the music, the names of the tones, relate to the human body and ultimately to the cosmos is a rhetorical strategy highly developed in Old Javanese literature and in Tantric texts. Juxtaposing Sastrapustaka's story with quotes from Old Javanese literature, from writings on kebatinan sects and from medieval Indian Tantric literature suggests the similarities between them in the ways of expression, the congruences in what it is possible to say, and the correspondences concerning what constitutes spiritual knowledge. (59)

In this regard, Becker links the five names of gamelan pitches with Buddhist *cakra* (also spelled *chakra*), the visualization of center energy, especially the main scriptural teachings of Tantric Buddhists and Saivites. Three sacred syllables of these texts from medieval Java—Om, Ah, and Hum—correlate with the three important upper cakra—the head, neck, and heart. It is these upper three cakra that Sastrapustaka associates with the first three keys of gamelan tones—Form, Way, Live. The other two tones refer to Love and Feeling. Becker (1993, 70) explains that there are a number of different systems of cakra: five, six, seven, and even ten cakra. The five cakra are mentioned in an Old Javanese Saivite Ganapati-tattwa text (79). Subsequently, Sastrapustaka corresponds the five notes-name analogy to the five senses and expands it to the six *rasa* (*pancaderiya* and *sadrasa*). The overall point is that Becker convinces us of our sympathetic understanding of Sastrapustaka's analogical proposition.

Furthermore, Becker notes that Sastrapustaka expands his analogical proposition to the exploration of the meaning of *rasa sejati* (true rasa), which comes from the pitch *lima* (referring to the feelings emanating from the five senses), which, with pitch *enem* (attraction, residing within the heart) completes the true rasa. Thus, the analogy of gamelan tones (*barang*, *gulu*, *dhadha*, *lima*, *enem*) to form, path, life, attraction, and feeling is now complete, which implies that the aim of experiencing artistic study of gamelan is not only to cultivate physical skill, but also rasa sejati. That is, that rasa and beauty are found within the spiritual and physical self (i.e., meditation). Becker sees Sastrapustaka's rasa and rasa sejati in the doctrine of a tenth-century thinker, Abhinavagupta, the most influential aesthetic philosopher of Buddhist and Saivite Tantricism. According to Abhinavagupta, the aim of experiencing aesthetics is the pursuit of enlightenment, in which:

> The limited "I" is completely absorbed into Siva or Bhairawa, the adored object: everything vanishes from the field of consciousness. Aesthetic experience, on the other hand, requires the presence of the latent traces of delight, etc. . . . Aesthetic enjoyment consists in the lasting of one's own consciousness; this lasting is endowed with extreme pleasantness (Beauty), which abstains from a contact with the various latent traces of pleasure, pain, etc. (Abinavagupta, as cited in Gnoli 1968, 82–83n4, quoted by Becker 1993, 89)

To support her argument, Becker links this mystical-aesthetic experience toward achieving enlightenment to several references, including the work of Zoetmulder, one of the most prominent scholars of Old Javanese literature. In his now classic *Kalangwan* (1974), Zoetmulder explains that all Old Javanese kakawin (except *Ramayana*) always start with *manggala*, an invocation by the poet for his effort to produce a beautiful poem in order "to attain union with an internally visualized, meditative deity" (90). It is the aim of producing "beauty" (*lango*, *lengeng*, *lengleng*) that manggala explicitly states, which according to Zoetmulder is best translated as "rapture."

In this regard, Becker reminds us of Sastrapustaka's important point that the spiritual self is the peak of the aim of studying (i.e., performing and listening to) gamelan music. Whereas Sastrapustaka identifies spirituality in gamelan music through his interpretation of the names of gamelan tones, Becker utilizes another Javanese point of view to support her argument. Soerachman (1980), a member of the Javanese elite, describes the journey to achieve his spiritual self through meditation by listening to certain gamelan pieces. While Sastrapustaka informs us at a conceptual level, Soerachman informs us directly, with the hands-on use of gamelan as a conduit to achieve a spiritual self. Soerachman asserts that certain pieces are appropriate to trigger oneself to inspire meditation. He draws from the meanings of the names of certain gamelan pieces to discern their practical use for meditation. That is, *gendhing* (gamelan compositions) are suitable for meditation because the meanings of their names are, according to Soerachman, in congruence with the step-by-step practice of meditation:

1. Begin by sitting while listening to *gendhing Kinanthi Teplek.*
2. *kinanthi* = with
3. *teplek* = sit up straight
4. Begin to focus the mind and senses while listening to *gendhing Laras Driya.*
5. *laras* = to gather, collect [to tune]
6. *driya* = senses, thoughts

7. If meditation attains divine inspiration (*sasmita/ilham*), then listen to *gendhing Asmara Dana.*
8. *Asmara* = *samar* (dim, vague, indistinct) [*asmara*, "love," "passion"]
9. *dana* = gift from the Lord
10. When meditation is to finish, then "make oneself one with" *gendhing Kinanthi Sandung.*
11. Kinanthi + with
12. Sandhung = trip over, stumble [?]

(Soerachman 1980, as cited in Becker 1993, 93–94)

Unlike Sastrapustaka, Soerachman does not use an analogical approach to understand the names of gendhing and does not use references. One might be suspicious of Soerachman's motivation. For accuracy, Becker (93) sometimes inserts into the text the "correct" meaning. For *Laras Driya*, Becker adds the translation of *laras* as "to tune." With *Kinanthi Sandhung*, Becker adds a question mark [?] about the meaning of *sandhung*. If Soerachman's interpretation is not a case of "the end justifies the means," at the least the meaning of *gendhing* as relating only to meditation denies a more diverse context and content. Within the circle of gamelan intellectuals, it is common to link the name *Asmaradana* with the name of an Old Javanese kakawin, *Smara Dahana* (Love and Fire). *Asmaradana* can stimulate various affects, from lively to subdued, depending on the *irama* (context) in which the piece is performed. *Kinanthi Sandhung* is known as a piece to express lust and is often performed to accompany romantic scenes in wayang wong or kethoprak dance drama.

An Aesthetic Understanding of Text

Judith Becker's explication of Sastrapustaka's and Soerachman's interpretations of the meanings of gamelan tones and names of gendhing serve as an attempt to develop what Alton Becker calls an "*aesthetic* understanding of a text" (original emphasis; text refers to culture). Becker asserts that in interpreting text, non-Javanese "must learn to use new conventions of coherence, invention, intentionality, and reference."

> For aesthetic response to be possible a text must appear to be more or less coherent, the mythology it draws upon and presupposes must be more or less known, the conventional intent of the creator or speaker of the text in relation to one's own role as hearer/reader/interpreter must be relatively well understood, and even the more basic assumptions about how words relate to thoughts and the things of the world have to be more or less shared. (Becker 1979, 240)

Becker's guidance is very useful, not only for non-Javanese scholars, but equally for Javanese scholars as well. Essentially, the crux of the matter is that one should realize the challenge of trying to understand the relations of text to context in the pursuit of an aesthetic understanding of that text—in his case, the aesthetic of wayang performance. As he politely states, by no means are all relations explored in his long, far-flung article, implying there are still issues that can be explored further. In other words, understanding text in context requires multiple and multilayered processes.

This is in line with Judith Becker's (1993) assertion regarding the tensions in ethnomusicology as a discipline between (a) musicians who play, those who think and feel the music; (b) scholars who write about music and musical sound; and (c) scholars who write music as cultural expression. Although Becker prefers to align herself with only the third category, the discussion is more dynamic and richer with the inclusion of perspectives from the first and second categories. From the perspective of the third category alone, Becker concludes that meanings in gamelan or dance performances are "multiple, many-layered and constantly shifting."

> When one writes or reads about the "meaning" of a dance or a gendhing or a poem or a statue, "meaning" must be understood as referring to an overlay of individual interpretations. No performance can have exactly the same meaning for every listener or every performer. Each listener brings his or her own experience to an event and understands the event within the framework of a personal history. Complete consensus on the meaning of a performance or complete overlapping of individual meanings never happens.
>
> Thus, meanings in the music of the gamelan or in dance performances are multiple, many-layered and constantly shifting. No single strand, no one interpretation can capture the various nuances, the subtle suggestions communicated by an artistic performance. Meaning inheres in a complex system of relationship—overt, covert, implied or explicit—that pertain between the listener and the performance (1–2).

This idea of the multiple ways of giving meaning to the performing arts is a well-thought-out proposition, though Becker limits her study "to understand the frame of reference of the writing of a select and elite group of elderly men (all of whom have since died) from Yogyakarta and Surakarta" (2), and does not examine the perspectives of diverse performers and listeners from different social classes. This limitation is understandable, considering the far-flung, complex, wide-ranging topics and issues of discourses and practices of Javanese performing arts from the medieval period to contemporary Java that Becker studied. By exploring aspects of Old Javanese aesthetics and religion as they intersect in the performing arts, past and present, Becker highlights the overlapping and multilayered meanings of gamelan.

REFLECTION AND DISCUSSION

Becker (1993, 167) describes "the dialectic tension of 'speaking of the past' and 'speaking of the present.'" It is often the case that description of the performing arts by Javanese people (insider's voice) tends to glorify their past and present. This has happened since the early twentieth century, when Javanese elites created the adjective *adiluhung* (great beauty, "classical," refined, respectable, beautifully embodied in them) to characterize their performing arts (Florida 1995; Pemberton 1994; Sumarsam 1995). Focusing on the concept of adiluhung, Javanese tend to ignore *anèh*, odd or out-of-the-norm elements of cultural expression. The case of *canthang balung*, the court jokesters, which I discuss later, is an example of anèh. I suggest that this odd element has historical precedence—it may be a manifestation of palimpsests, unerased cultural practices of the past, as Becker (1993) proposes in her theoretical approach to contemporary Javanese cultural performances.

Antinomian Canthang Balung

Among Javanese court dance genres in the Kasunanan Court of Surakarta, *serimpi* is one of the highly refined dances. It has graceful and highly stylized movement, with choreographed shifting of positions in an orderly, well-designed fashion. Serimpi is accompanied by gamelan playing refined music, which smoothly transitions from one section to another. Yet, in the middle of the performance a peculiar stylized vocal interjection is heard—*Éééé, yoooooook, hayu tå, yå tå*—performed by a pair of male singers. Called *senggakan* or *alok*, this stylized interjection is auditorily conspicuous, that is, louder than the sound of the rest of the ensemble.

As a student at the conservatory and academy of gamelan in Surakarta (1962–1970), I learned to play pieces for serimpi dances. I did not learn to sing senggakan, but when I first listened to it while playing my instrument, I was surprised—I had no idea of the significance of this intense vocal interjection. In retrospect, I question why neither I nor my friends ever asked our teachers—many of them were *kraton* (court) musicians, and they did not explain it to us. Perhaps due to our belief that the kraton were the center of Javanese culture, producing *alus* (refined) cultural performances, we just accepted what we learned. We became used to the sounds of the peculiar senggakan without asking why it was performed within the highly refined serimpi dance and its musical accompaniment.

Two decades later, in the late 1980s, while writing my dissertation (eventually my first book [Sumarsam 1995]), canthang balung was one of the subjects I stumbled upon, in the context of court culture in colonial Java. Relying on secondary sources, Soewandi (1938) and Stutterheim's (1956) works, I examined the roles of canthang balung in the context of the court ritual, inside and outside the court. For the former, "the task of the canthang balung included guard duty, performing senggak or alok (short vocal interjection) and keplok (clapping) with the gamelan to accompany serimpi dances, and to dance at the garebeg festival when the king departs to inner court" (Stutterheim 1956, 95). In addition, once a year, they had a special duty "to play the clown in a procession of the garebeg mulud festival to celebrate the birth of the Prophet Muhammad."

In the procession, when the canthang balung arrived at the outer hall of the court (pagelaran), they clowned in as funny a way as they could, including imitating dogs mating. This was because if the prime minister laughed at the clowning of the canthang balung, he had to pay them. This was no longer done at the time of the writing of Soewandi's report in the late nineteenth or early twentieth century (1938). According to Stutterheim (96), "This custom was abolished probably for the sake of decency because many European of the Resident's (later Governor's) retinue were present at the grebeg ceremony." (Sumarsam 1995, 121)

Outside of the court ritual context, I was surprised to learn that canthang balung were employed as the head of *talèdhèk*.

The duties of the lurah badhut [canthang balung] included issuing identification cards (serat pikekah) to be purchased by the talèdhèk, to show the dancers' legal status as dancer and prostitute. To get this identification card, the dancer had to pay to Gunalewa an annual fee of ten wang (equal to 8 ½ cents in Javanese currency at the time). If the dancer did not have this identification card, she could be reported to the government (nagari) and be arrested.

It was also the duty of the lurah badhut to always be ready whenever the court officials demanded the dancers perform in a court celebration. For this reason, the lurah badhut had their own talèdhèk living in their houses, which were also brothels. Besides Gunalewa and Sukalewa of the Kasunanan court, the Kepatihan and the Mangkunegaran also had their own lurah badhut.

The practice of prostitution presented the courtiers and the Dutch colonial government with moral problems, including the exploitation of the talèdhèk by lurah badhut, fighting between the clients of the lurah badhut in their brothels and the breakup or marriages caused by the prostitution. Therefore, sometime around the beginning of the twentieth century the courtiers and the Dutch government abolished the authority of the lurah badhut to control talèdhèk, and the court to administer the talèdhèk directly. They were given the same status as lurah badhut, as abdi dalem (persons in the service of the king). Perhaps at this time two low-ranking canthang balung, Sukaastama and Gunaastama, were added. (121–22)

It may be surprising to learn of the promiscuous cultural practices embedded in this aspect of court culture. At the same time, the court produced aesthetically deep, refined performing arts within a context "tinted" by antinomian behavior. How do we explain this paradox? In thinking about this question, I searched for further references to canthang balung. I stumbled upon a speech delivered by Gusti Pangeran Harjo Hadiwidjojo, a son of King Paku Buwånå X who was educated at Leiden University in the Netherlands. As the head of Radyapustaka Museum, in 1953 he delivered a lecture about canthang balung, explaining in detail their duties and lives.

Hadiwidjojo (1953) describes in depth the peculiarity of the performance of canthang balung at the court of Surakarta and their odd lifestyle. At first, he was not sure that talking about canthang balung and their promiscuous work was necessary, since he and his audience lived in a different era. He thought that many people, including himself, did not care about them anymore. At this juncture his position as a Dutch-educated person took over his intentionality. With the encouragement of his colleagues, he meticulously listed the definitions of canthang balung from dictionaries and oral information from both Dutch and Javanese sources. He concluded that canthang balung were extraordinary personnel. They were not clowns, not musicians, not a common thing, but a sacred phenomenon. At times, their performances were tied to a religious procession. He insisted that although they performed clownish dancing, the context in which they performed was religiously significant. For example, they performed in conjunction with the Islamic Muludan religious procession. They danced to the sound of the gamelan composition (gendhing) "Rambu," an opening piece from the performance of the sacred gamelan Sekatèn. This confirms an important fact: canthang balung dances were not clowning, but were related intimately to religious expression.

Hadiwidjojo describes the task of canthang balung at length:

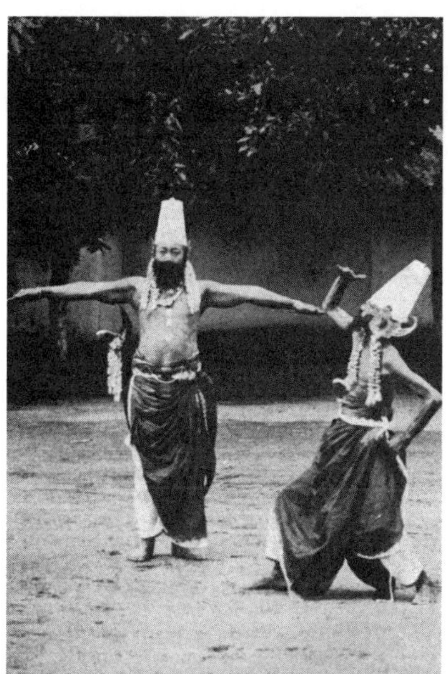
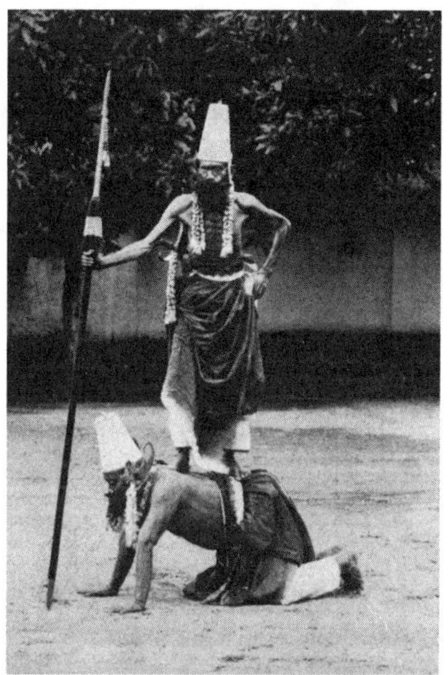
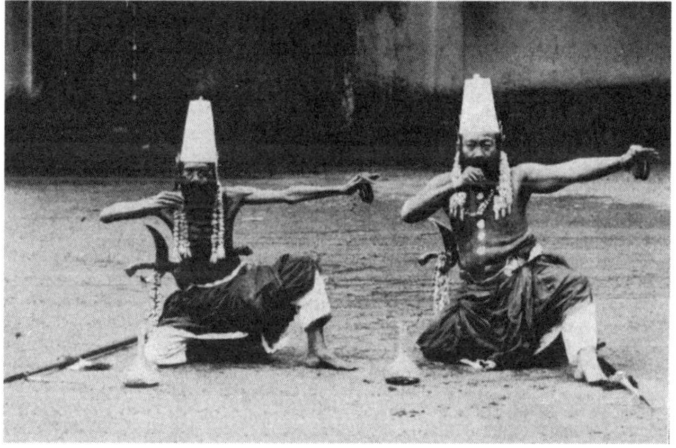

FIGURE 1.1 Canthang balung performing *vliegen* (flying), *grappenmakerij* (clowning), and *gadjah ngombé* (drinking elephant). Brandts Buys 1933, 299.

> Therefore, if I am not mistaken, originally canthang balung is the head of a procession whose task was to lead a presentation of the offering to pay homage to our ancestors, forebears, pioneers, etc. In today's context, they are religious chiefs (*kaum* or *pengulu*). In the context of the Buddhist era, they were priests, brahman. Therefore, the pengulu performs ritual in the mosque = [is the same as in] the temple [the pengulu does not perform ritual] before the king, as how nowadays *wilujengan* ritual is commonly done in the house. [Islamic] Mulud Nabi ritual = [is the same as] when the ritual was carried out by and in the temple. I assume you all know that *mulud* in Arabic means the celebration of birth (*weton*). Hence the celebration of the birth of temple = [is the same as] in the Buddhist tradition in Bali, it is called *odalan*—this [odalan] might be an old tradition. Subsequently, the ritual was Islamized by *wali* (Islamic saints). Because of the strong influence of the [Islamic] power, it continues to be practiced in the form we see it today. Subsequently, people don't know the original practice of canthang balung. Their status as priests declines to clowns. (4, my translation)

Hadiwidjojo's speech enriches our discussion of canthang balung by including in our discourse an "insider" perspective (a court intellectual), layered upon my "outsider" work (a non-court intellectual studying court culture). Hadiwidjojo positioned himself as an unbiased scholar, a learned member of the aristocracy. Had he presented his speech as a member of the royal family from an adiluhung perspective, he would have most likely skipped discussion of this particularly peculiar court cultural practice. He claimed he received information from insider informants, including his father, King Paku Buwånå X, and the leader of the court musicians, R. T. Warsadiningrat.

Apparently Hadiwidjojo had observed canthang balung for roughly two decades before he gave this speech at the Radyåpuståkå Museum in 1953. An essay on canthang balung written by Dr. W. F. Stutterheim (1956 [1935]), "A Thousand Years Old Profession in the Princely Courts on Java," demonstrates this fact. The article, which I have relied on in my discussion of canthang balung, addresses a possible connection between an image of a man or two in brahman dress facing a dancing girl, and contemporary canthang balung and their practices at the court of Surakarta. Published in *Bijdragen tot de Tall-, Land- en Vokenkunde* #9 in 1935 and republished in a book entitled *Studies in Indonesian Archaeology* (1956), Stutterheim states, "As early as 1932, through the kindness of Pangeran Aria Kusumayuda and Pangeran Aria Hadiwijaya [Hadiwidjojo], I obtained a few accurate notes concerning the nature of the activities of these canthang balung; these notes I reproduce here in extensio" (94). In the same article, Stutterheim also mentions similar but simpler canthang balung practices in the court of Yogyakarta; his information was solicited from long-time Yogyakarta residents, a Dutch physician named Groneman and an interpreter, Mas Sujana Tirtakusuma.

The only idea that Stutterheim offers in this article is the connection between the image carved on the wall of Borobudur—a dancer or dancers dancing with a man or men in brahman dress—and its possible link to contemporary canthang balung and their practice at the court of Surakarta. In this regard, he concludes that the official relationship of canthang balung "to the dancing-girls, their function at the serimpi-dance and finally the wearing of a beard, which usage is preserved in Surakarta, [is] sufficient indication that we are dealing with the present holders of the same profession, or a profession most closely related to that which the Borobudur-reliefs represent" (Stutterheim 1956, 98). To strengthen his argument, Stutterheim refers to Moen's (1924) article on the practice of Buddhism in the twelfth-century Singhasari kingdom among a particular sect whose practitioners enjoyed the Five Ms (i.e., *mada*, drinking liquor; *maithusa*, sexual intercourse; *mudra*, meditation; *matsya*, eating fish; and *mamsa*, eating meat), which was "still found in the so-called chanṭang balung, two bearded 'buffoons' with the upper part of their body naked and with yellow strips, whose duty it is to become fuddled in public with gin or arak and to dance in an intoxicated state. These court functionaries not so very long ago received their official income by keeping dancing girls and prostitutes. Their name, probably a nick-name, is probably due to the fact that originally they performed their 'dance' on the *ksetra* [cemetery], 'rattling with bones' (nyantang balung)" (as cited in Stutterheim 1956, 99). Notably, Hadiwidjojo (spelled Hadiwijaya in Stutterheim's essay) was the main contributor to Stutterheim's essay.

Priest-cum-Dancer / Singer / Performer / Buffoon

One may doubt the proposed link between the twentieth-century canthang balung and similar figures, characters depicted on the walls of the ninth-century Buddhist monument Borobudur, and in the peculiar twelfth-century ritual practice, perhaps because of the long lapses in time. However, in examining passages from Old Javanese literary works, this link cannot be ignored. Acri (2014, 2010) meticulously investigated this link by examining Javanese and Indian manuscripts and the studies of other scholars. In a recent essay, Acri and Wenta (2022) revive Moen's idea of the Buddhist Tantric practice in twelfth-century Singhasari represented by a well-known terrifying Bhairawa statue in Kediri, associated with the kings Kertanegara and Adityavarman in Sumatra. For further discussion, the following section draws from Acri's study. I'll begin by quoting passages from the ninth-century *Ramayana Kakawin*:

Once upon a time, the *kuvoṅ-bird* and starling (*jalak-bird*) had a lively conversation. They were despising each other. Kuvoṅ-bird accused starling of encamping near the weaver-bird. Starling became enraged, comparing kuvoṅ to an unworthy *vidu* (wayang-player). Ironically, kuvoṅ was also an official.

[Starling:] You are *taṇḍa* [official]! You have a very mean "palace," living in holes in the ground. You are stained, kuvoṅ! Homeless, unattached, while leading the life of a vagabond performer, a vidu (wayang-player), but you are endowed with manifold abilities, having magical powers! (Translated by Acri 2011, 62)[9]

Two adjectives come to mind in reading the episode: allegorical and theatrical. It is allegorical because birds were used to satirically represent ascetic and political characters (53). It is theatrical because the subject matter is presented in a dramatic manner. According to the starling, kuvoṅ, the bird, and the vidu, the wayang performer who the bird represents, are enigmatic figures. Why was the vidu, who was endowed with many abilities and magical power, also an official, homeless, and unattached to his community? Who was the vidu? Was he a singer, a puppeteer, a mendicant priest, an official, or an antinomian (one who rejects social norms and morality)? Scholars who have studied Old Javanese literary works (e.g., Acri 2011; Robson 1983; Zoetmulder 1974) define *vidu* as any combination or all of the above. The point is that the episode tells us that around the ninth century, we find interesting, intriguing, and lively discourses on Javanese cultural performance traditions. What is relevant to our discussion is the case of vidu as having a paradoxical character. He was a singer/dancer and buffoon, but also an official and priest who had magical power, representing an antinomian practitioner.

Apparently, the description of this paradoxical figure can be found in other passages of the *Ramayana Kakawin* and other kakawin. For example, in the thirteenth-century *Sumanasantaka Kakawin* we find an intriguing description of episodes similar to the description of vidu from *Ramayana Kakawin*. The author tells us about a wedding between Prince Aja and Princess Indumati, which includes episodes of a performance:

All the comedians made [the audience] roll around laughing. They were dancing furiously, engrossed in [observing? Joking about?] their [exposed] penises, [their faces becoming] tense with effort. A "dwarf" [as tall] as the span of a kəbəh [danced] animatedly, then became suddenly afraid at last. He was laughed at [by the audience when] he was taken by a sudden fright as a "dwarf" [as tall] as the span of a *baṭaṅ* arrived.

A *pirus* acted the part of a *menmen*; through his dirty jokes he caused laugh-

> ter. His mistress cleverly followed "in style" by enacting [the gesture of] urinating. As his man saw her, he looked fiercely at her and sniffed, full of excitement. He followed her and they mated, [acting] like goats; when he gazed in her eyes, he suddenly showed his teeth.
>
> Those who were reciting [tales] raised a laugh, and all of them were eager to be jeered. The sacred maidens disliked to have as masters the young male dancers. Those playing the human-puppets were all equally skillful, and they caused vehement laughter. The old men were laughing with open mouths; screaming loudly, they suddenly lay sprawling on the ground. (Acri 2014, 9; his translation)[10]

It is indeed fascinating to read the depiction of both male and female characters clowning, dancing, and pantomiming bestial sexual intercourse. Acri (8) is of the opinion that these characters were ascetics-cum-performers representing Saiva figures. However you perceive these passages, either symbolically or at face value, the point is that by identifying the exhibitionists with performer-cum-ascetic figures, we enter the highly evocative topic of Tantrism, whose pancamakara ritual involves sexual orgies, drinking alcohol, eating flesh, etc. Literature on Tantrism in India and its transformation in Java, in the past and present, is overwhelming. It is not the place here to discuss in detail this fascinating but controversial subject. However, a brief remark on the practice of Tantrism related to the Five Ms is useful.

In traditional Indian society, the main purpose of Tantrism is the quest for power through an ascetic lifestyle in a monastic community with worship focused on certain deities, such as Visnu, Siva, and Sakri. Siva ascetic movements rose in the thirteenth century, distinguishing themselves with regard to their practices, symbols, lifestyle, and theology, which led to two movements: (a) the conservative and orthodox or right-handed branch, which emphasized esoteric teaching and practices on the extensive use of *mantra* (repetitive sacred utterances), *mandala* (sacred diagram), and *mudra* (symbolic hand gestures); and (b) the left-handed (inauspicious) radical movements that promoted the partaking of the illicit Five Ms: *mada* (wine) *mamsa* (meat), *matsya* (fish), *mudra* (parched grain)—which was probably an intoxicant—and *maihuna* (sexual congress; Olson 2015, 42–43). This transgression of social norms can be found in Tantric practices, such as in Hindu and Buddhist Bhairawa or Kali Tantra; they are considered the left-handed, "hard core" branch of Tantrism (Padoux 2002). Padoux explains:

> The main reason for this antinomian behavior appears to be the wish, by so doing, to participate in the dark, chaotic, undisciplined, and very powerful forces

that are normally repressed and kept outside the pure, orderly, circumscribed world of the Brahmin. This wish, incidentally, implies a belief in a world pervaded by power, a power supposedly at its utmost in that outside world. Such transgressive practices include the transgressive ritual use of sex.

The use of sex is not found in all Tantric traditions. It is not prevalent, but present nonetheless, in the Saiva and Sakta groups that have a Kapalika origin or background and that have kept, if only symbolically, the Kapalika culture of the cremation ground with its cult of the Yoginis and its erotico-mystic rites and notions. (20–21)

For the most part, studies of the concept and practice of Tantrism are based on religious literature. This fact has led me to ponder whether reading religious texts can be interpreted as representing literal practices or symbolic, metaphysical statements. A well-known scholar of Tantra practice, White (2003, 7), wondered about this question, since to him "not all religious language is literal in its intentionality." However, following Shulman (1993), White asserts that the tendency toward a literalization of symbolic statements or practice is a hallmark of these "hard core" Tantra movements. According to White, during the medieval period in India, the king and his royal family became the main clientele of this particular Tantra. This Tantra was also introduced to Southeast Asia, which then became the royal culture as well as the religion of the popular masses there (White 2003, 12). As mentioned by Stutterheim earlier (quoted from Moen's work), left-handed Tantrism existed in Java in the twelfth- to thirteenth-century East Javanese Singhasari kingdom.

Returning to the question of whether the reading of religious texts should be perceived as literal or symbolic, to what degree did the literalization of the Five Ms happen in Java? It is difficult to answer this question definitively. The important point for this discussion is whether the remnant of any of this antinomian behavior can still be found in contemporary Java. As mentioned earlier, Hadiwidjojo (1953) and Stutterheim (1956) link the antinomian behavior of canthang balung to a Buddhist sect whose practices included the execution of *pancamakara* (the Five Ms). In her discussion of the link between Sastrapustaka's treatise on gamelan and Buddhism in medieval Java, Becker (1993) agrees with Stutterheim that "The reliefs at Borobudur and Prambanan [Stutterheim, 1956, 93] may indicate Pasupata monks in the 'marked' or first stage of spiritual practice" (177). Regarding Tantrism's link to canthang balung, Becker (following Stutterheim) says:

When the garebeg festival was over and the great *sekati* gamelan were returned at 2:00 a.m. to the building that housed them, the *canthang balung* followed the procession, alternatively hopping on one foot during one *gongan* (musical cycle marked by a gong stroke), then on the other foot during the succeeding *gongan*. When the gamelan procession reached the building where the gamelan are kept, the *canthang balung* performed a caper imitating dogs in heat. Strange and inappropriate behavior by palace officials would not in itself identify these men as remnants of a Pasupata monkhood, but they formerly carried as well as Saivaite seal of office. Their official seal was representation of a *lingga-yoni*, the oldest and most widespread of Saivaite symbols. (Stutterheim 1956, 96, as cited in Becker 1993, 178)

Acri (2014, 37) fine-tunes Becker's point, proposing a link between canthang balung and the practice of Pasupata in India: "On account of the markedly antinomian features displayed by these dancers," he suggests that "it is more likely that they represented the remnants of even more extreme Saiva groups," collectively called *Kapalikas*, also known under the general label of *Siddhas*. Acri goes on to say:

Those practitioners were scornfully depicted as supernaturally endowed, yet evil, sorcerers who often posed as false Brahmans or ascetics; they sang, danced and played in theatrical performances they encouraged the practice of drinking alcohol and engaging in sex with female attendants, whom they admitted into their order (cf. Bloomfield 1924); and their attire included ornaments and musical instruments made of (allegedly human) bones, as well as human skull parts thereof. The etymology of the (nick-) name *canthang balungs* would perfectly make sense in a Kāpālika milieu, for the "rattling bones" may be nothing else than a local variant of the rattle-drums (*damaru*) made of bones that constituted one of the most characteristic marks of the Śaiva Kāpālikas. Also indicative of a Kāpālika origin may be the strings of flowers adorning their naked bodies, which is reminiscent of the garland of flowers offered to the gods (*nirmālya*) worn by Atimarga ascetics, and the emphasis on laughter, which is reminiscent of the observance *aṭṭahāsa* or vehement laughter prescribed by the Pāśupata observance (pāśupatavrata). The detail, reported by Stutterheim (1956, 97), that on certain occasions the naked body of the *canthang balungs* was daubed over with horizontal stripes of yellow boreh unguent is in harmony with the image of *jənu* (= *boreh*) unguent pouring down on excited dancing peacocks (and, arguably, pigeons) in RK [*Ramayana Kakawin*] 24.105, and also resonates with the practice of smearing a yellow orpiment over the body or hairs and beard associated in certain Sanskrit texts with practitioners of the Bhairavamārga. (37–38)

Let us pay attention to two of Acri's points (following Stutterheim): the image of canthang balung is reminiscent of the excited dancing of peacocks or pigeons as described in *Ramayana Kakawin*, and also resonates with certain practices of Indian Bhairava Tantrism. In other words, Acri strengthens Stutterheim and Hadiwidjojo's assertion that Tantric practices in early Java (or India for that matter) were a palimpsest (to borrow Becker's term) of canthang balung performance. Furthermore, Acri makes a fascinating assertion: the image of canthang balung reminds him of the ambiguous identity of widu, linking widu with the observance of a certain Tantric sect called *Pasupata* and other related Saiva groups. Their practices include bathing in ashes, dancing, playacting, and antinomian behavior. Some of these groups may include more extreme practices, such as the drinking of alcohol and sexual promiscuity. Acri's argument is also strengthened by the fact that widu held extremely low status in the Saiva hierarchy.

TRACING AND RETRACING INDIC ROOTS

In tracing the Indic roots of literary works and contemporary cultural performances in Java from different angles, especially from linguistic and archaeological study, the challenge is always how to interpret textual (written) and physical (pictorial) evidence. The Java-India intercultural encounters of the past were a reality, and can be seen in pictorial evidence and written documents. In this respect, scholars are interested in finding out how Java-India interactions influenced the formation of Javanese cultural traditions. I have described the interpretation and reinterpretation of certain subjects by different generations of scholars, sometimes yielding different results and always enriching the discourse. In most cases, a definitive answer to an historical question about a certain cultural performance is hard to find. Nevertheless, the fact that almost all the Old Javanese literary works were adapted from Indian works fuels interest in understanding this transformation, what has changed, and what local aspects have remained.

It should be clear by now that this chapter and the rest of the book aim to address the manifestation of cultural remnants of the past in modern Java. As I mentioned earlier, the *Mahabharata* epic and the *Ramayana* story are the most conspicuous of these remnants; they continued to be adapted as the basis of stories for wayang performance even after Java was Islamized in the fifteenth century and have persisted in Javanese performing arts to the present day. For this reason, the Indian influence on Javanese wayang play is a topic that has continually occupied scholars.

Alton Becker (1979) explains how a puppeteer may expand his text (i.e., narrative) by singing a verse from Old Javanese sung poetry at the beginning of his performance. For example, the text of the song sung by the puppeteer in the first scene of wayang performance begins with this sentence: *Leng leng ramya-nikang, sasangka kumenyar, O. Mangrengga rumning puri* (Beautiful was the moon that shone over the palace where the women lived). Becker notes that this sung poetry—quoted from the twelfth-century *Bharatayuda Kakawin* written in the Sanskrit-based Old Javanese language—cannot, almost in its entirety, be understood by the wayang audience or even by the puppeteer. Moreover, the content of this sung poetry is unrelated to the moment of the story. How do we interpret this unintelligible song as presented in the present action? Becker (1979) explains that this is an example of Javanese art invention in which the history of a performance genre is displayed by quoting ancient poetry. As history advances, the puppeteer continues to expand his motifs and characters, "working on an expanding text which expands through space and time far beyond his imagination," but still "from the body of mythology he believes in" (229). The result of this process of invention is a performance consisting of a collage of motifs and characters exhibiting both past and present.

This multiplicity of events and perspectives within the content of wayang performance, presented in different performance contexts, has led to diverse ways for the audience to watch wayang:

> There is no assumption that everyone will be interested in the same thing at the same time; someone will always be dozing. The setting for a wayang is non-compulsive, more like a Western sports event than serious theater. It is not shameful or embarrassing to sleep through what someone else is enjoying. Jokes, philosophy, action, poetic language—each has different appeal to different people, depending on their own mental make-up, which is often described in a way parallel to the Indian theory of rasa and guna. (230)

As such, the diversity of content in wayang performance builds "thick texture" aesthetic experience. Asking himself why he (an old man) liked wayang, Becker's answer was "*Asalnya Ramai!*" which means "Above all because it is bustling/complex/busy/beautiful!" The word *ramai* derives from the Old Javanese word *ramia*, which originated from the Sanskrit word *ramya*, which means "pleasing, beautiful." Giving the etymology of this word is a way for Becker to explain the semantic change from "beautiful," as in the poetry a dhalang sings in the beginning, to beautiful because it is bustling and complex, which indicates that "Sanskrit words, like Sanskrit stories, are recontextualized in Java" (230).

Becker's point is that the recontextualization of Sanskrit stories happens as part of the way in which a dhalang builds a multiplicity of events and perspectives into his performance. Furthermore, Becker (1979, 224) examines the structure of a wayang performance in terms of its epistemological formation and transformation. He proposes that there are four major epistemologies in any story of wayang performance: (a) that of the demons—the direct sensual epistemology of raw nature; (b) that of the ancestor heroes—the stratified, feudal epistemology of traditional Java; (c) that of the ancient gods—a distant cosmological epistemology of pure power; and (d) that of the clowns—a modern, pragmatic epistemology of personal survival. All four epistemologies coexist in a single wayang. That is, nature time, ancestor time, God time, and the present are all equally relevant in an event, though for each the scope is different. The linearity of the Aristotelian notion of Western drama that produces unambiguous temporal-causal sequences cannot be applied to wayang performance, whose plot structure is based on multiple timeframes and multiple epistemologies.

Sears (1994) offers a different perspective than Becker. Through her investigation of Sanskrit aesthetic theory in an ancient Indian literary work on the performing arts, *Natyasastra*, Sears suggests that the Aristotelian nature of the wayang play can be traced from this ancient Indian treatise. That is, that the different performative elements mentioned in this ancient treatise are apparent in their articulation in wayang performance. The first element comprises the four character types discussed in *Natyasastra*, which fit with a number of characters in Javanese wayang: the self-controlled and vehement type, Bimå and Duryodhånå; the self-controlled and lighthearted type, Kresnå; the self-controlled and exalted type, Arjunå; and the self-controlled and calm type, Yudhistirå. In Javanese wayang, clowns generally support their master, which matches the clowns described in *Natyasastra*. The second element is plot. Sears identifies two kinds of plots mentioned in *Natyasastra*—principal and subsidiary plots—which are also similar to Javanese wayang. The use of different levels of language is the third element: superhuman language is for the gods, noble language is for the kings, and there is the common language of Barbarian origin, with other subtle categories. The use of different levels of language is also common practice in Java and Javanese wayang. Finally, *Natyasastra* discusses colors as an important indicator of mood and emotional state. Here, the focus is not so much on the facial colors of Javanese wayang puppets, but on the various temperaments of a puppet character, or *wondå*.

One of the difficulties in studying the early history of Javanese shadow puppet theater is the absence of evidence to determine its form and practice. Some scholars have suggested Javanese wayang must have originated from India or China (see Gomperts 2002, Mair 1988), though again without clear evidence. Sears (1994) asserts that Indian shadow play developed only in the seventeenth and eighteenth centuries, much later than the development of Javanese wayang.

Is it possible that Indian shadow puppet play originated from Java or Bali? Evidence for this is very thin. Consequently, Sears examined implied evidence from the content of the Indian-adapted Old Javanese literary works, and discovered that works prior to the eleventh century do not help in reconstructing wayang performance. Instead, Sears found evidence of Javanese poets' familiarity with the use of literary embellishment (*alamkara*), an important practice for Balinese puppeteers to ornament or digress from the narrative of their performances. This is particularly compelling since Balinese puppeteers use Old Javanese kakawin as basic texts for performance. And, according to Levi (as cited in Sears 1994), a text from the first book of the Javanese *Mahabharata* mentions a text connected with Sanskrit theater.

Sears (1994) acknowledges that none of the evidence can prove the Indian origin of Javanese wayang. In this connection, she mentions the Sanskritization of Tantric ideas and practices in India and subsequently in Java, which led to literary yoga and the historical link between Indian aesthetic theory and Javanese poetic works. Sears also mentions the wandering performer, *widu mawayang* (widu performing wayang) mentioned by Zoetmulder (1974). As noted earlier, the discussion of Tantrism and widu highlights the difficulty of defining Javanese wayang performance and the performing arts more generally. Sears observes that Zoetmulder's findings on tradition derive from *Natyasastra*, which found expression in wayang and other kinds of performances during the twelfth-century Kediri period. This was the time when Indian aesthetics became firmly rooted in both kakawin and wayang. Sears concludes this discussion as follows:

> The fact remains, however, that we know very little about the contours of performance tradition at that time. There may in fact have been two or more distinct performance traditions, and it is possible that the court kakawin were performed with pictures painted on scrolls rather than with puppets—and that the puppeteers led itinerant village troupes like the wandering performers (widu mawayang) described by Zoetmulder. Various performance practices probably were found in the Old Javanese courts, and all must have included the oral presentation of written or oral poetic and dramatic texts. (Sears, 109)

I present Sears's explication of the Indian influence in Javanese wayang at length to show not only the richness of the interpretative development of the structure and aesthetic of wayang performance, but also because we cannot ignore the depth of the Hinduization of Java. With this premise in mind, in the following sections I discuss the presence of ancient Indian music theory and practices in a numbers of Sanskrit-based Old Javanese literary works.

Studies by Widdess and Gomperts

Earlier, I discussed Becker's (1993) work on linking contemporary gamelan aesthetics and religious meanings to music of the past. Because of her focus on these two aspects, she discusses musical structure and practices only in passing. In contrast, Widdess (1993, 186–96), a prominent British ethnomusicologist with expertise in South Asian music, proposes an interesting hypothesis regarding the connection between rhythmic and scale organization in early Indian music and contemporary Javanese gamelan. Widdess argues that in the eighth century, Indian and Javanese music had similar organization and ensembles. However, in their subsequent development, each evolved away from the other. In the case of Indian music, starting in the twelfth century, the influence of musical practices from Islamic Central Asia brought about certain characteristics as we know them today, namely the predominance of solo and improvisatory performances of singers or string and wind instruments. Gamelan, on the other hand, developed into a large ensemble of percussion instruments performing fixed compositions in a limited number of scales and modal systems, but retained its older, Indian style of organization. To prove his hypothesis, Widdess offers evidence from *Natyasastra*, the ancient elaborate treatise concerning dramatic performances in which music and dance feature prominently. According to Widdess, the early theory of rhythm in India, similar to modern Javanese gamelan, "is measured by exclusively binary units, called kalā. According to the tempo and style of the piece, this kalā could comprise two, four, or eight equal beats, called matra . . . The length of the matra is considered to be constant; the length of the kalā is consequently variable" (188). Widdess asserts that this musical feature is shared with modern gamelan: kalā is likened to *gatra* (a unit of four notes) in gamelan. "Secondly, the kalās were grouped together into larger units of measurement, just like in gamelan music the gatra are grouped into gongan . . . The third point of comparison is that since the kalā could comprise two, four, or eight beats, the value of the beat remaining constant, then we have here something analogous to the Javanese concept of irama or rhythmic levels" (189).

Widdess next compares the melodic organization of Javanese gamelan and Indian music; the two appear to have little in common. On the one hand, gamelan has two scale systems, *sléndro* and *pélog*, with a limited number of modes or *pathet*. On the other hand, Indian music has a large number of scales, from ten (North India) to seventy-two (South India), and hundreds of modes or *raga*. Again, Widdess's explication is drawn from music theory mentioned in *Natyasastra*.

A comparison of the more or less equal intervals of the pentatonic sléndro and the large and narrow intervallic patterns of pélog with the ancient Indian scales of *Saḍja-gramā Nātyaśāstra*, and *Madhyama-gramā* yielded little compatibility (see figures 1.2 and 1.3). However, delving deeper into *Natyasastra*, Widdess discovers that in practice, three pentatonic systems are used, deriving from the seven-tone heptatonic Saḍja-gramā, whose two tones are either suppressed or omitted altogether. The result is like three of the five-tone set or pentatonic scale in pélog gamelan (see figure 1.4). The connection between sléndro and the Madhyama-gramā system is less convincing, perhaps because the intervals of sléndro evolved to a more equal distance, a hypothesis advanced by Curt Sach (1945) to which Widdess refers (194). Widdess suggests that "only at the deepest levels of structure [are we] likely to find any meaningful parallels with Indian music" (192). Widdess does not claim to prove that gamelan scales derive from Indian scales. Such a claim requires more evidence of the introduction and transformation of Indian musical scales to Southeast Asia, and their adoption as Southeast Asian scales. Generally, what is relevant to my discussion is that Widdess highlights that some Indian musical terminologies, instruments, and rules of poetic meter appear frequently in Old Javanese kakawin and Javanese

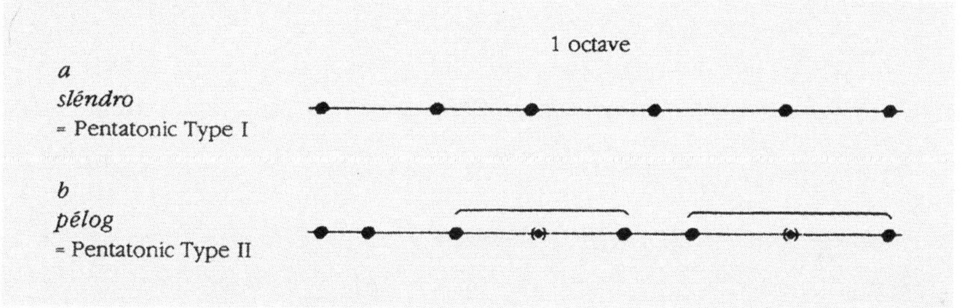

FIGURE 1.2 *Sléndro* and *pélog* pentatonic types. Relative interval sizes between note symbols are approximated. The pitch indicated by a dot enclosed in parentheses is also used for other pélog pentatonic types. Adapted from Widdess 1993, 192. Reproduced by permission of the School of Oriental and African Studies, University of London.

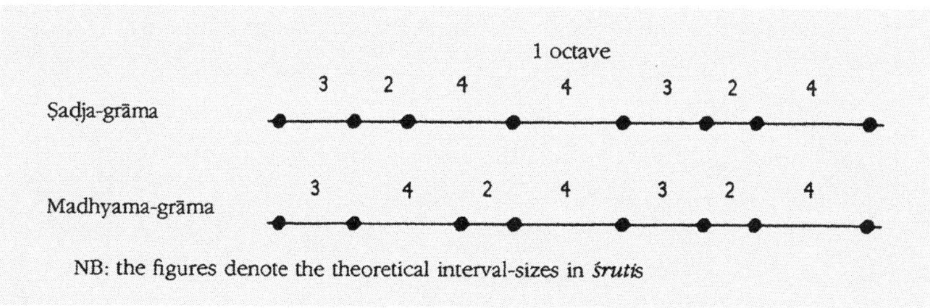

FIGURE 1.3 Ṣaḍja-grâma and Madhyama-grāma. Adapted from Widdess 1993, 192. Reproduced by permission of the School of Oriental and African Studies, University of London.

reliefs; hence, the possible connection on a theoretical level between Indian music and gamelan cannot be ruled out.

Furthering this discussion, Gomperts (2002) provides a wider scope and evidence base than Widdess. Gomperts first briefly introduces the tuning and modal systems of early Indian music. Next, he discusses references to them in Indian-inspired Old Javanese literary works, tracing back aspects of contemporary musical practices in Java and Bali to early music theory in India. In the following sections, I highlight particular points of relevance.

Our earlier discussion on Indian-inspired Old Javanese literary works showed that poetic traditions are pervasive in the work of Old Javanese authors. This also suggests the importance of singing, since kakawin were meant to be sung. In the epigraph at the beginning of this chapter, I mentioned a ninth-century inscription concerning kakawin recitation by Jaluk of the *Ramayaṇa* [*si Jaluk macarita rāmāyana*]. Most likely, this recitation was presented in the form of singing with musical accompaniment. The following quotation is from the *Ramayaṇa Kakawin*, describing the recitation and musical practice in question:

> Vālmīki addresses Kuśa and Lava: "Please, sing our venerable *Rāmāyaṇa* [epic]. In the king's outer courtyard, you should recite it in [the] presence of all *brāhmana*-s and *kṣatriya*-s including those who are entitled to listen to your singing (O.J. *kidung*) of King Rāmadeva. Take great care, men, in the [musical] usage (Sk. *prayoga*) of the tones (Sk. *svara*) which are bound together (O.J. *ikêt*) . . . Then, with never flagging high spirits, you should sing twenty chapters [which] should be recited (Sk. *uccārana*) in continuously sweet (Sk. *mardava*) speaking (O.J. *amadisata* < Sk. *vādisat*). [You should also] use (O.J. *weh*) transitions (O.J. *putus*) of tempo (Sk. *pramāṇa*). Do not render it in the vernacular language (Sk. *prākṛta*, i.e., Old Javanese) without my instructions. If the king asks you, tell [him] that you two (O.J. *kālih*) are my disciples. Here is the *vīṇā* with its enchanting (O.J. *konang-unang*) tones (Sk. *svara*) [which was a] gift of the holy Nārada. Play (O.J. *gupit*, lit. pluck) the secondary scale (Sk. *mūrchanā*) [on the *vīṇā* that accompanies] the cheerful singing (Sk. *gīta*) [of the *Rāmāyaṇa* epic]. When singing for the king, my grandchildren, do not let your thought stray because he is the father of all creatures. Do not seek gain by usury grandchildren! You should not quarrel with people about wealth (or: gold) when you are in the hermitage. Tomorrow morning, you should start singing. These were Vālmīki's orders to Kuśa and Lava." (580–81)

This text mentions multiple musical practices, including a sweet recitation with temporal transitions, classical courtly language, vīṇā as an accompaniment of the recitation, and the gupit (to pluck with plectrum?) style of playing vīṇā. According to Gomperts (2002), the names Kuśa and Lava derive from the Sanskrit term *kuśīlava*, bards who sung or recited the story of *Rāmāyaṇa* while accompanying themselves with musical instruments. As indicated toward the end of the excerpt, the teacher gives Kuśa and Lava an arched harp, vīṇā, which was a gift from Nārada, a god proficient in music.

Notably, instead of using the Indian term, the author of the *Ramayaṇa Kakawin* preferred to use Javanese kidung sung poetry. This suggests the poetry was sung in a Javanese manner, and the author perhaps knew the subtlety of musical practice. This is further the case with the use of the term *mūrchanā*. After comparing the section in which the term appears with the corresponding Indian Sanskrit version, Gomperts (577) concludes that the Old Javanese author must have known music theory well, since the term *mūrchayitvā* in the original Indian text, which means the verb "having tuned," was correctly rendered to the noun "secondary scale." That is, in early Indian music, each grāma-rāga of the seven-tone system has a secondary mūrchanā scale, the starting tone of which is one of the seven different tones. Gomperts points out that grāma-rāga and its secondary mūrchanā scale serve important functions in accompanying dramatic moods in theatrical productions:

Regarding musical instruments, we learn from the quotation that vīṇā seems

TABLE 1.1 Grāma-rāga in the development of Indian dramatic moods

Grāma-rāga	*Dramatical situation*	*Modal characteristics*
Bhinna-ṣaḍja	In certain songs related to the entry of the hero in a situation in which he is inclined toward the use of all implements or tools	*Sa-grāma*, scale: *Sa Ga# Ma Dha Ni#*, *murchanā* starts with *Dha*, initial: *Dha*, dominant: *Dha*, final: *Ma*
Mālava-kaiśika-madhyama	For love in separation in the entry to the female apartments	*Ma-grāma*, scale: *Sa Ri Ga Ma Pa Dha Ni#*, *mūrchanā* starts with *Pa*, initial: *Sa*, dominant: *Pa*, final: *Ma*
Bhammāṇa-pañcama	In travel along a path in summer by those overcome with weariness and in forests	*Ma-grāma*, scale: *Sa Ri Ga Ma Pa Dha Ni#*, *mūrchanā* starts with *Sa*, initial: *Sa*, dominant: *Sa*, final: *Ma*

Created by the author. Adapted from Gomperts 2002, 577.

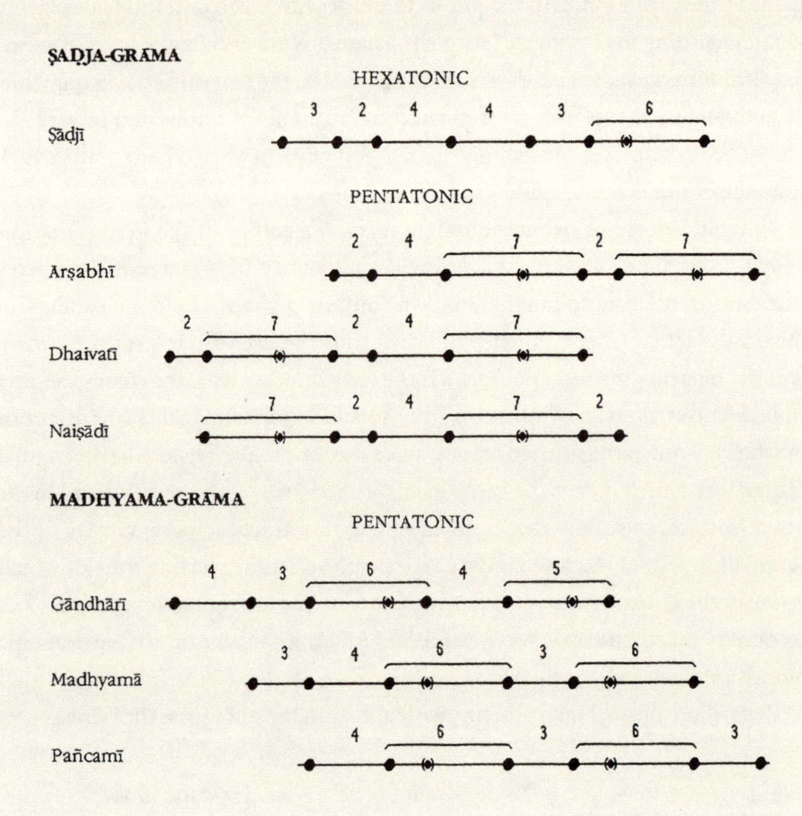

FIGURE 1.4 Three pentatonic systems deriving from the seven-tone heptatonic Ṣaḍja-gramā. Reproduced by permission of the School of Oriental and African Studies, University of London.

to be one of the most important instruments for accompanying recitation. This instrument does not exist in contemporary Java, though it is depicted on the walls of temples, such as in the ninth-century Buddhist monument Borobudur, in a relief of the Jolotunda sacred bathing place in East Java (fifteenth century), and in the form of bronze statues found in Nganjuk in East Java and Bantul in the province of Yogyakarta (tenth century; Gomperts, 584).

What might have relevance to linking modal classification in Indian music with gamelan is the frequent mention of vīṇā in the twelfth-century *Bharatayudha*. In the following passages of *Bharatayudha*, the singing of woodcocks is likened to a song accompanied by vīṇā. In a scene in the royal garden, ladies in attendance were having a good time, exchanging poems and playing delightful music until they fell asleep.

> As the morning dawned, the sun was as red as the tired eyes of a love-sick woman. The sounds (Sk. *śabda*) of the *kokila* birds in the *kanigara* trees were like quivering songs (O.J. *kidung*) of passion. Like [sung] words (O.J. *wuwus*) to the accompaniment of a wipanca [harp J (Sk. *wipanci*)] was the crowing of the wood-cocks in the cages. Peacocks shrieked and bees ravished the flowers in the beautiful private quarters. (585)[11]

It is worth noting that the puppeteer of traditional wayang performance uses this sung text to mark the transition from the second major part (pathet Sångå) to the third part (pathet Manyurå) of his performance. In an all-night performance, this happens at around 3:00 a.m. It is a well-known and standard practice in traditional Javanese wayang performance to refer to the three major divisions of the play. Each is named after the modal system (pathet) of the music: pathet Nem, pathet Sångå, and pathet Manyurå. Thus, there is an intimate relationship between time of the day or night, the mode progression in the music, and dramatic moods and emotion.

It is unknown whether the choice in this verse was inspired by an Indian way for structuring time in the performing arts, though this cannot be ruled out. The relationship between modal systems and dramatic moods was important and well established in ancient Indian theatrical production, as seen in Gomperts's three examples of grāma-rāga that accompany dramatic situations (see previous figures). From the perspective of the theory of modal classification, in both Indian music and gamelan each modal system is governed by the importance of certain tones as the parameter that defines them (see table 1.2 for an example of a gamelan modal system).

Vīṇā is also mentioned in the Old Javanese version of *Mahabharata*. In a story of the five Pandhåwå brothers living in exile, the fourth book of *Mahabharata*, Wiråthåparwå, mentions Dropadī (the wife of Pandhåwå), who had lost all desire to live after an attempt by the prime minister of Wirata, Kincåkå, to rape her. In her anguish, she embraces Bimå (the second brother of Pandhåwå), who was sleeping. Reflecting on the story, the text says: "It seemed as if a *vīṇā* in the shape of a bottled-gourd (O.J. *lawu-wina*, Sk. *Alābu-viṇā*) manifested a narrative that used (Sk. *prayoga*) the musical tone (Sk. *svara*) *Gāndhāra*" (Gomperts 2002, 582). The author of Wiråthåparwå also used vīṇā as a metaphor in military archery: "in warfare, for you, your bow (O.J. *laras*) is like playing on (sk. *lakṣana*) the viṇā" (582).

TABLE 1.2 The hierarchical functions of tones in the pathet modal system

Pathet ("Mode")	*Tone: Lower kempyung ("fifth")*	*Tone: Upper kempyung ("fifth")*	*Tone: Dhing*	*Tone: Dhong ("tonic")*	*Tone: Pelengkap ("supporting tone")*
Pathet nem	5 (må)	6 (nem)	1 (ji)	2 (ro)	3 (lu)
Pathet sångå	1 (ji)	2 (ro)	3 (lu)	5 (må)	6 (nem)
Pathet manyurå	2 (ro)	3 (lu)	5 (må)	6 (nem)	1 (ji)

Gāndhāra

The mention of Gāndhāra in this text reminds me of Poerbatjaraka's (1987) hypothesis of the genesis of the gamelan instrument gendèr, from Gendhara, a Buddhist center in medieval India. As I discuss in prior work (Sumarsam 2014, 329), Poerbatjaraka was interested in analyzing the genesis of gendèr after reading Kunst's opinion that the *sléndro* or *saléndro* scale came to Java together with the name of the Shailendra dynasty (note the similarity between the words) by way of the kingdom of Sriwijaya in South Sumatra. Poerbatjaraka presumes that Mahayana Buddhists from Gandhara were responsible for bringing the sléndro instrument gandhara to Sriwijaya, then to Java. Subsequently, the instrument gandhara became *gendèr* in Javanese gamelan.

How did *gandhara* transform to *gendèr*? As a linguistics professor, Poerbatjaraka (1987) explains the transformation in terms of etymological interpretation and wordplay. First, it is not uncommon for words ending with syllables *èk*, *èl*, *èt*, and *èr* to have originally ended with *ak*, *al*, *at*, and *ar*, such as *suwèk* to *suwak*; *dhèdhèl* to *dhadhal*; *sèrèt* to *sarat*; and *cèrèt* to *carat*. Second, when Indian words ending in "a" are turned into Javanese, the "a" ending disappears, such as *Singapura* to *Singapur*, and *daca* to *das*. Therefore, it is not impossible that the word *gendèr* derived from *gendara* by way of *gendar* (which happens to be the name of a Javanese cracker, *karak gendar*, shaped like gendèr keys). Poerbatjaraka strengthens his argument by pointing out that in wayang performance, Gândhara is the land of the birthplace of Dewi Gendari (the mother of Kurawa brothers), and in Old Javanese literature the word *gandhara* refers to a musical instrument.

I see some problems with Poerbatjaraka's hypothesis. First, in claiming that *gandhara* is the name of a musical instrument, he relied on Juynboll's dictionary, but Juynboll uses a question mark. Second, after examining the meaning of *gandhara* in the work of Zoetmulder (1974), Phalgunadi (1992), and Gomperts (2002), I have come to view Poerbatjaraka's identification of *gandhara* as a musical instrument as incorrect. Poerbatjaraka translated a passage from Wiråthåparwå, "*hanan kadi lawu-winâ myaktâ-[katha]-ken ikang swara-gandhâra-prayoga*" as follows: "Or, like a gourd-lute, she clarified the voice of the *gandhara*, which was played together" (Poerbatjaraka 1987, 275). Relying on Gomperts (2002, 582), the translation should be: "It seemed as if a *vīnā* in the shape of a bottled-gourd (O.J. *lawu-winā*, Sk. *Alabu-vīnā*) manifested a narrative that used (Sk. *prayoga*) the musical tone (Sk. *svara*) *Gāndhāra*." Hence, *gandhara* refers to a musical tone, not a musical instrument.

Actually, Poerbatjaraka knows that gandhara is one of the musical tones, since two pages later he states that gandhara is one of the tones of the seven-note Indian scale saptaswara, from which the Javanese pélog scale originated. Poerbatjaraka (1987, 280) identifies the names of the saptaswara tones as follows: *sadhya*, *risabha*, *gandhara*, *madhyama*, *pancama*, *dhaivata*, and *nisada*. As we see, the name of the third degree is *gandhara*. Perhaps due to his focus on the instrument gendèr and its similarity to the sound gendara/gandhara, Poerbatjaraka did not realize that in the same essay he himself identified gandhara as the name of a tone. In any event, Poerbatjaraka is correct to suggest that Mahayana Buddhism in South Sumatra and Java originated from Gandhara. Comparative study of the representation of Buddha by Revire (2017) shows that the Gandhara style of portraying Buddha is depicted in the Mendut temple in Central Java, implying that the spread of Mahayana Buddhism in Java from India via South Sumatra happened between the seventh and ninth centuries.

Widdess (1995, 23) notes the tendency to name scale degrees and raga "after marginal regions (in relation to the cultural heartland of the Ganges basin) and ethnic groups of low social standing or foreign origin." He gives two examples: *niṣāda/Naiṣhādī* is named after an impure community living in the Rajasthan region; and the tone *gāndhāra* and its corresponding jati-name *Gandhari* is named after the region of Gandhāra in the southern entrance to the Hindu Kush. Widdess goes on to say that "this region was an important channel of musical influences to and from Central Asia, and its musical importance is reflected in the use of the term *Gandharva* (inhabitant of Gandhāra: cognate with Greek *kentouros*) to mean a celestial (or mortal) musician, and *Gāndharva* (that which pertains to the Gandharva to mean musical art, especially the non-Vedic ritual music described in BHNS [Bharata: *Natya-sastra*] and DD [Datilla: *Dattilam*])" (7). Gomperts (2002) indicates that *gandhara* is the third primary scale (grama) in ancient Indian music. After all, Poerbatjaraka is correct to identify Gandhara as a possible region where certain Indonesian gamelan scales originated. His error was that what has been transferred to Indonesia is not a musical instrument called *gandhara*, but a tone or perhaps a tone system. His assertion that *gendèr* derives from *gandhara* may result from his intuitive interpretation as a linguist.

Earlier, I discussed Becker's (1993) study of the association of the meaning of gamelan tones with Buddhism as proposed by Sastrapustaka: the tone *barang* (thing) refers to the head of a person; the tone *gulu* (neck), to the passageway leading from the head; the tone *dhadha* (chest), to the source of human life; the tone *lima* (five), to the beauty of nature and art; and the tone *enem* (six), to feeling, or rasa. Notably, as Gomperts (2002) points out, some of these names have overlapping meanings with those of Indian tones, suggesting the terminological influence of the Indian concept of saptaswara on contemporary Javanese gamelan:

> The meaning of the Sanskrit *Sadja* (lit. born of six), *Madhyama* (lit. center, middle), and *Pañcama* (lit. fifth) are related to the Modern Javanese tones *Nĕm* (lit. six), *Tĕngah* (lit. center, middle) and *Lima* or *Gangsal* (both lit. five) respectively. In Indian music, the seven tone names are also associated with body parts. *Madhyama* and *Pañcama* also are associated with the throat and chest respectively. The Javanese tone names *Ḍaḍa* or *Tĕngah* both denote chest, and *Gulu* or *Jangga* both stand for throat. (587)

Gomperts acknowledges that the other three names of Javanese tones deviate from the Sanskrit tones or their associations: bem or panunggul, pélog, and barang.

To make the comparison between Indian and gamelan notes clearer, table 1.3 illustrates the tone names of Indian saptaswara with their traditional syllabic abbreviations and etymological meaning.

To recapitulate, Gomperts and Widdess offer invaluable insights in tracing the links between Java's musical present and its musical past of Indian origin. As is the case of historical research writ large, such an endeavor is fraught with difficulty. In a review of Widdess's (1982) book on the ragas of early Indian music (now a classic in the field of Indian music study and historical ethnomusicology), Clayton (1998) warns readers:

> [Although there is a] substantial amount of technical writing on early Indian music, the interpretation of such material is hampered by a number of factors. Texts are likely to be corrupt and unreliable; the tendency of authors to claim, both explicitly and implicitly, the authority of earlier texts in support of their

TABLE 1.3 The Indian seven *svaras*

Degree	*Name*	*Abbreviation*	*Derivation*	*Meaning*
1	*ṣaḍja*	*sa*	*ṣaḍ* (six) + *ja* (born)	Born of the six organs of utterance
2	*ṛṣabha*	*ri*	*ṛṣabha* (bull)	Bellowing like a bull
3	*gāndhāra*	*ga*	*gandha* (fragrance)	The fragrance note
4	*madhyama*	*ma*	*madhya* (middle) + the superlative suffix *ma*	"Middlemost"
5	*pañcama*	*pa*	*pañca* (five)	The fifth note
6	*dhaivata*	*dha*	perhaps from *dhī* (perceive, think)	Unclear
7	*niṣāda*	*ni*	*ni* (down) + *sad* (sit)	The final note

Adapted from Rowell 1992, 55. Reproduced by permission of University of Chicago Press.

assertions means that a degree of skepticism must be employed in assessing descriptions of musical practice; and the technical vocabulary, of which many of the terms have shifted in meaning over the centuries, is itself a minefield. (164)

Clayton quickly clarifies, however, that Widdess is aware of these pitfalls, and that Widdess uses methodological thoroughness and imagination to overcome them to an impressive degree. Nonetheless, this caveat should be kept in mind in any study involving the historical reconstruction of musical practice and culture.

If these challenges are pervasive in the study of early Indian music, which has relatively well documented ancient music theory and notation, examining early Javanese music is even more difficult due to the lack of evidence—no substantial Javanese music theory and notation has been found dating before the twentieth century. To carry out research on early Javanese music, one must glean insights from scattered material in passages on old inscriptions of Old Javanese literary works. Since these documents are largely adaptations of Indian written poetry and prose, tracing their Indian genesis to understand what kinds of musical practices may have existed in early Java has been the go-to methodology of contemporary scholars. I commend Acri, Becker, Gomperts, Sears, and Widdess for their studies of the religious, literary, and musical practices of Java's present and their link to the same in the past. They all apply, in the words of Clayton, "a combination of historical textual interpretation, musical analysis and what might be termed an ethnomusicological instinct—that is, a concern with the people involved—with the result that historical sources are revealed as evidence of once-living musical tradition as performed by real musicians." (164)

As I stated in the introduction, intercultural and interreligious encounters are the main themes of the present study. In this chapter, I have discussed the earliest encounters between Hinduism and Javanese culture. What's at stake is the dynamic process of these encounters and the results of that process. With evidence available to us from the early period of Javanese history (from the ninth to fifteenth century) and taking into account studies by several scholars, I have traced the formational and transformative processes resulting from this encounter, which brought about the new hybrid Hindu-Javanese cultural tradition.

Our understanding of this dynamic, formational, and transformative process is based on multiple perceptions, drawn from both historical evidence (i.e., old manuscripts and iconographic evidence) and contemporary evidence. In this regard, the connections between past and present events are laid out, thereby epitomizing the main theme of the book.

I continue this theme in the next chapter, but the analysis revolves around the ways in which cultural objects, especially myth and performing arts, have moved from one cultural landscape to another. Focusing on myths originating from East Java, the Panji and Damarwulan stories and the story of Bimå Svarga, I show how these stories have travelled through land and sea to other parts of Java and other islands, even as far as the mainland of Southeast Asia. In their new cultural landscapes and contexts, these cultural objects have become localized to suit local cultural ambience.

TWO

Center-Periphery, Court-Rural Dynamics

Performing Arts on the Move

Carved on the wall of the fourteenth-century temple on the slopes of Mount Penanggungan in East Java, the image in figure 2.1 shows Prince Panji amorously teaching his betrothed princess Condråkirånå (also spelled Candrakirana) to play an Indian plucked-string instrument. This is one example of evidence of the presence of Indian musical instruments depicted on the walls of ancient temples. There are many such examples in other temples in Central and East Java. Moreover, hundreds of names of Indian musical instruments and Indian musical terms appear in the passages of Sanskrit-based Old Javanese literary works, such as the *Ramayana*, *Bharatayudha*, *Bhomakawya*, *Ajunawiwaha Kakawin*, and others (see Kunst 1968). Despite the prominent presence of Indian musical instruments, terminology, and theory in the early centuries of Java, we do not have any solid evidence to show that Indian music and/or dance, or theatrical performance for that matter, were ever performed in Java at that time. Nonetheless, the iconography of this image, containing a juxtaposition of indigenous and foreign elements—a Javanese prince playing and teaching an Indian musical instrument—provides insight into the social and historical context of the Panji story.

THE PANJI AND DAMARWULAN STORIES

There are several versions of the Panji story. What they have in common is a love story between a prince and a princess as the main theme. The love story revolves around various episodes involving separations, difficulties, adventures, and the use of disguises, before their ultimate reunion. *Journeys of Desire*, the

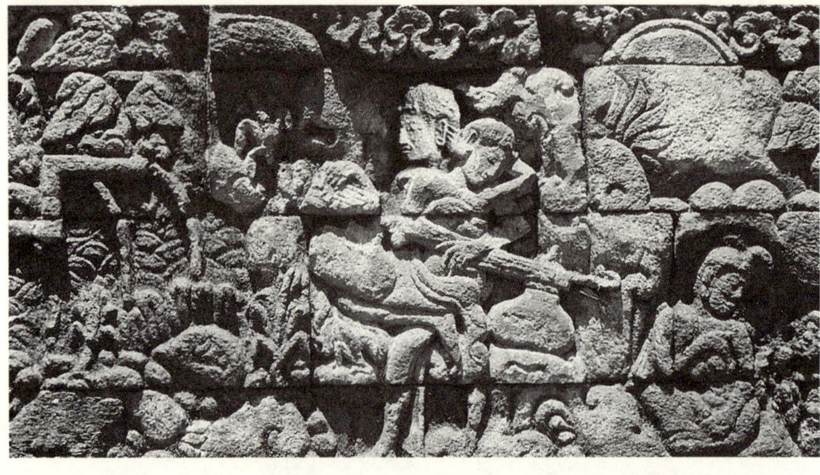

FIGURE 2.1 A panel at the Temple of Kendhalisådå depicts Prince Panji giving a music lesson on an Indian instrument (*vina*) to his betrothed wife. Adapted from Kunst 1968, fig. 64. Reproduced by permission of Springer Publishing.

title of Vickers's (2005) book on the Balinese Panji Malat story, encapsulates well the central theme of the story. Here is a synopsis of the Panji story, which I quote from Zoetmulder (1974):

> There are four kingdoms whose kings are brothers: Koripan or Kahuripan (= Janggala = Keling), Daha (= Kadiri = Mamenang), Gegelang (= Urawan) and Singhasari. The marriage between the crown prince of Koripan and the princess of Daha is the main theme of all the Panji stories. The prince is generally called *raden* Panji or *raden* Ino, but bears one or more other proper names besides . . . ; the princess is commonly designated by the name *raden* Galuh [or Candrakirana, L. K.] . . . At the beginning of the story they are already betrothed, but the princess vanishes and Panji leaves the *kraton* to go in search of her. Both assume different names. Those of Panji generally indicate his irresistible charm in love: Malat Rasmi, Waseng Sari, Wideya . . . , and these are used as titles for the various poems. Often he lives unrecognized in the vicinity of his love. It may also be the princess whose identity remains long unknown. The stories invariably end with recognition of the partners, general rejoicing and a wedding. Panji's great love for the princess of Daha does not prevent him from getting involved in other amorous escapades. On the other hand he proves his valor in battle when on his search he roves about with his band as a *ksatriya* from a foreign country, destroying one enemy *kraton* after the other, or when he comes to the assistance of the king whose hospitality he enjoys, if the latter

is attacked by the ruler of another country whose request for the hand of the princess has been rejected. (428)

Some scholars (Berg 1954, Poerbatjaraka 1940, 1968, Ras 1973, Robson 1971) are of the opinion that the names of some of the characters of the main kingdoms and some of the events that appear in the stories suggest that it is associated with the history of East Java during the time when the political and cultural center resided there, around the twelfth to fifteenth centuries. In other words, the Panji story is assumed to represent certain historical events. Whether this is true or not, it has been discussed and debated by these scholars and others.

It has been suggested that two historical events and kingdoms might be connected to the Panji story, namely events in the kingdoms of Kediri and Måjåpahit and their complex network of kingship. For the Kediri connection, the Panji story is in reference to King Erlangga (also spelled Airlangga), whose kingdom was divided into two, Jenggala and Kediri. The love story of Panji and Sekartaji or Condråkirånå involving separation, difficulty, and adventure references the split of the kingdom. Eventually, the divided kingdoms were united, hence the formation of the kingdom of Måjåpahit under the reign of Hayam Wuruk. The eventual union of Panji and Condråkirånå is supposed to reflect the united kingdom.

From another perspective, in his study of *Wangbang Wideya*, a Panji story written in Bali in the second half of the sixteenth century, Robson (1971) takes issue with the idea of a single basic Panji story. Instead, he suggests that the many Panji stories were variations on the theme of Panji and Condråkirånå's journey and separation, which can be "expanded to include a great variety of episodes, elaborate descriptions and repetitions" (12–13). Hunter (2007, 27) sees the Panji story from a *kakawin* perspective, as a symbol of the struggle of any young prince to become a noble warrior prince (*kshatriya*). These perspectives show that the Panji story can reflect both historical fact or fiction, or lie somewhere in-between.

Evidence of the Life of the Performing Arts through the Panji Story

Scholars have studied the connection between the two forms of Panji narrative representations—as narrative art in written literature (prose or poetic form) and in visual arts (pictorial representation on the reliefs of temples). However, another important form of narrative art has not been fully explored: narrative form that is reenacted in the performing arts, such as in various kinds of wayang performances. Sedyawati (1993, 175) is right to say that there must have been an intimate relationship between narrative art in stone, oral and written literature, and the performing arts. This is highly probable since almost all literary works of the Panji story contain episodes of wayang performance (Poerbatjaraka 1968, 387). Although this is a play within a play, it can be considered as evidence of the life of the performing arts in society at that time.

How often was the Panji story performed as wayang or in any other theatrical genres when the story began to appear in the fifteenth century? The lack of evidence makes it impossible to answer this question with certainty. Knowing that contemporary masked dances and masked dance dramas (*wayang topèng*) are the genres in which the Panji story has been commonly performed, it is logical to examine the earliest existence of masked theatrical genres.

Examining a number of ancient inscriptions, archaeologist Haryono (2006) identifies the ninth-century Kuti inscription as containing evidence of masked dance performance, for example in the sentence "*hanapuka warahan kecaka tarimba hatapukan haringgit abanyol salahan.*" The sentence is difficult to translate, but it seems clear that from the root word *tapuk* (mask), *hanapuka* and *hatapukan* refer to dancing with and/or wearing a mask; *haringgit* refers to puppet theater, and *ambanyol* to jester (3). Haryono (6) also discusses the Lantakan inscription, dating from the same century, which mentions *atapukan*: *pinda atapukan prana 30 hop rarai winehan pirak dha I kinabaihannya* (thirty pairs of masked dancers, all young boys, each was given *perak*), and the Mantyasih III inscription, containing the description *atapukan si giranghyasen* (the performance of masked dance was delightful).

According to Cahyono (2014), who has researched masked dances in today's city of Malang and its vicinity, the earliest existence of masked dances was between the eighth and sixteenth centuries. At that time, several large kingship centers (*kadatwan* or *kraton*) and their vassals were important patrons of various kinds of masked theatrical genres. However, as a consequence of the Islamization of Java, since the sixteenth century masked dance performances at the kraton gradually declined, though villages around those centers in the areas at the foot of Mount Kawi and Mount Bromo (Tengger Caldera) preserved masked dance drama performance until the mid-twentieth century (314).

In spite of the mention of the masked dances in these inscriptions, there is no evidence to show that they performed the Panji story. Cahyono (2014) states that the earliest mention of masked dances performing Panji stories is in the fourteenth-century inscription *Pabanyolan*. According to historians, the fourteenth and fifteenth centuries were the heyday of the Måjåpahit kingdom. We learn from the *Negarakertagama*, a literary work containing political and sociocultural descriptions of Måjåpahit, that to celebrate the prosperity of the kingdom, each year a Caitra festival was held with food and drink in abundance.

The festival was "the demonstration of social and cosmic community by fraternization, rejoicing at the beginning of a new period and feasting at abundance of good things" (Pigeaud 1962, 214). Food of all kinds, intended for commoners from different regions, was freely provided. The kidung singing and the female dance *juru i angin* and the male dance *buyut* (perhaps more like today's *tayuban*, a dance party for male guests), provided lively entertainment.

Along with other performances, *Negarakertagama* also mentions *raket* (a play with singing and dancing) being performed at the festival. Interestingly, the king himself performed raket.

4. Årya Raṇḍhikāra had neglected to address the King.
So Årya Mahādhikāra joined him to say together
That the nobles desired to watch him perform rakĕt—
"Ah!" was all he said, and went back to make an improvisation.

5. Prince Kṛtawardhana acted as *pañjak* for him in the meantime;
There in the hall in the centre it was hastily arranged.
His Sori was a singer, and his Tĕkĕs was Rahajĕng—
Seeing that it was for the sake of amusement, it simply aroused mirth.[1]

6. He withdrew when the King arrived to take up his role:
His song was of a different kind, causing the onlookers to be delighted.
His sori was brisk, fittingly handsome and accomplished.
And the latter's song made veiled allusions, giving the onlookers deep pleasure.

7. The king was exceedingly handsome, in his full costume,
And he had eight Tĕkĕses who, being his minor wives, were truly beautiful.
They were of noble descent, clever and thoroughly versed in what to do.
So when he did the jesting-scene they let comments drop that were to the point. (Robson 1995, 92)[2]

There is no contemporaneous evidence to show that raket as mentioned in *Negarakertagama* performed the Panji story. According to tradition, *wayang bèbèr*, a form of storytelling in which a puppeteer scrolls and unscrolls a series of paintings, was created during the reign of the last king of Måjåpahit at around the fourteenth century (Anderson 1974, Sayid 1980). The transition from Hindu-Javanese to Islam-Javanese, which involved the movement of political and cultural centers from one place to another, may be the reason for the absence of written documents; alternatively, older documents may have gotten lost. Hence, little evidence can be found about cultural performances in Java in the sixteenth and seventeenth centuries.

Evidence of the Panji Story from Bali

Lacking evidence of Javanese cultural performances using the Panji story, scholars have searched for evidence from other places in Indonesia, especially the neighboring island of Bali. The island is one of the best places to find such evidence for several reasons. During the Islamization of Java, Javanese people who wished to continue embracing Hinduism migrated to Bali. In their new home, the Javanese migrants rebuilt and reconceived their Javanese life, including the writing of sung poetry (*kidung*) whose content and perspectives projected their Hindu-Javanese worldview. From their literary works and cultural performances, we can learn much about cultural performances that reenacted the *Mahabharata*, *Ramayana*, and Panji stories.

While the fourteenth-century *Negarakertagama* mentions a performance called *raket*, possibly a masked dance genre, evidently raket is also mentioned in the seventeenth-century kidung *Wangbang Wideya*. Robson (1971) has studied this kidung intensively and translated it into English. The story begins with the crown prince agreeing to let Wangbang Wideya present his raket performance. Rangga Wicitra played Kulante, Ajaran-Wirapaksa played the reverend teacher, and Banyak Sudira played the music.

> 59b. "Caraŋ Leŋkara, sir, will crack the jokes." Raden Siŋhamatra laughed, and then those who were to perform the *rakĕt* made ready. The Crown Prince gave instruction to inform Raden Wiratsari of it; His eunuch went to invite her, and arriving bowed and made an obeisance to the lady.
>
> 60a. He said, "Madam, your Highness should also come and watch the *rakĕt lelaŋkaran*," the Crown Prince says.
>
> 60b. Indeed it is a new kind of *gambuh*, and Apañji Wirastraswara's performers are the very best." Raden Warastraswari said nothing. (87)[3]

In his study of the Balinese text of the Panji story, *Malat*, which is performed in a play with singing and dancing called *gambuh*, Vickers (2005, 109) points out that the earliest reference to gambuh play can be found in *Wangbang Wideya*. As can be seen in the excerpt, the author of *Malat* equated gambuh to raket. We know that gambuh dance drama in Bali performs the Panji story. Hence, it is possible that raket as mentioned in *Wangbang Wideya* also performed stories connected to the fourteenth-century Panji narrative.

Furthermore, in his study of *Malat*, Vickers offers rarely mentioned evidence of a shadow puppet play called *wayang gambuh*, which exists as a collection in only a few places (Blahbutuh, Sukawati, and Pamecutan). The gambuh puppets have iconographic similarity to Javanese wayang gedhog puppets. Vickers's informant in Blahbutuh told him that the two sets of puppets were brought to Bali from Blambangan in the eastern corner of East Java, when the kingdom of Blambangan was under the suzerainty of the king of Mengwi in the seventeenth century.

Hinzler has a different explanation of this episode. She suggests that wayang gambuh was brought from Java to Bali in 1698 by Panji Sakti, the ruler of Buleleng, whose vassals included Blambangan and Pasuruan in the extreme eastern parts of Java, across a bay from Bali. She is of the opinion that Balinese wayang puppets represent the older type of Javanese puppets because they resemble human depictions that were found in East Javanese reliefs from the period of Måjåpahit and Singhasari. She hypothesizes that the creation of new style of wayang puppets, including wayang gambuh, happened between the mid-fifteenth century and 1706, the main reason being the Islamization of Java, which forbade the representation of human beings (Hinzler 1981, 53). This opinion is commonly held by scholars (Hobart 1987, Holt 1968, Wagner 1988). As I have described in previous work (Sumarsam 2011):

> [The law of the Islamic orthodoxy] considers music and figural imagery as seductive arts that compete with the Qu'ran, i.e., as a source of imaginative and visionary powers. This is ground for idolatry, as the weak-minded may be tempted by this figural imagery. This religious position on human depiction explains the lack of statues in mosques (though two-dimensional figures are still allowed) and the preference for calligraphy and symmetrical abstract patterns (Hodgson 1977, 504). The assumption here is that the prohibition of seductive imagery brought about an extreme stylization of Javanese puppets, a stylization that was meant to extremely distort human anatomy in order to avoid problems and to keep wayang approvable. Made as a complete two-dimensional figure, a wayang puppet has long arms and stylized eyes (only one eye is usually depicted), stylized nose, mouth, hair, and ornately stylized attire. Thus, we can say that Islamic ideology inspired a revision of Javanese puppets. (51)

One aspect of the Panji story is particularly worth noting. Sometimes the story depicts cultural performances such as *wayang kulit* (a shadow puppet play) and *wayang topèng*—i.e., a play within a play—in which Panji and his entourage are portrayed as performing artists. Here is a summary drawn from Poerbatjaraka's

(1968) synopsis of *Hikayat Panji Kuda Semirang*, which was composed in 1837, though according Poerbatjaraka it contains old elements of the Panji story:

> Once upon a time, Panji and his brothers, Brajanata and Wirapati, served the king of Gegelang. In the meantime, after winning a battle, Prince Semirang (Candrakirana in disguise) arrived in Gegelang, also to be a servant of the king. Anytime Semirang appeared before the king, Panji felt as if he was his beloved one. While in Gegelang Panji and Semirang often met each other, playing gamelan. Meanwhile, another of Panji's brothers, Perbatasari, was searching for his brothers in Gegelang. Before he arrived in the city, he disguised himself as a puppeteer named Surengrana. His entourage disguised themselves as his musicians (*panjak*). The group met a woman, nyai Rangga, in the market. She asked the group to stay in her house. There she asked the puppeteer about his background. The puppeteer said that he came from Palembang. His mother, who came from Benggala, had long been living in Java, in the mountain of Danuraja. The wayang group was well taken care of by nyai Rangga. Once in the evening Surengrana successfully performed wayang, which earned him popularity in the town. Subsequently he performed wayang from one night to another, in the house of important figures in Gegelang. Eventually Panji also wanted to watch Surengrana's wayang performance. When Panji and the puppeteer saw each other, they were aware that they knew each other, but they did not tell everyone. The puppeteer started his performance, enacting the story of Boma. The spectators were fascinated with his performance skill. So much so that the king of Gegelang wanted to watch the wayang performance; he invited the wayang group to perform in his palace. When the king saw the puppeteer, he was reminded of the face of his brother when the king was still young. The performance began, performing the story of Rama. Semirang wanted to meet the puppeteer, but he worried that his disguise from being the princess of Daha would be known. Therefore, Semirang and the puppeteer felt they should know each other only from a distance. (33)

Notice that wayang with stories from *Mahabharata* and *Ramayana* were performed in and outside the court, suggesting that at the time wayang was a popular performance. This makes sense, considering that by the time the story of Panji appears, wayang performance featuring Hindu stories had already existed for more than three centuries. The question is, what about performances reenacting the Panji story at that time? Cahyono (2014) suggests that the Islamization of Java brought about a decline in performances of the Panji story in East Java. Interestingly, in eighteenth- and nineteenth-century Central Java, wayang shadow puppet plays and theatrical genres performing the Panji story flourished. Before discussing this further, I will examine another story, Damarwulan, which also originated in East Java and had significant development as a celebrated performance in nineteenth century Central Java.

The Damarwulan Story

Like the Panji story, the story of Damarwulan is also associated with the kingdom of Måjåpahit. The theme of the story is a power struggle between the Queen Suhita of Måjåpahit and Bhre Wirabumi of Blambangan. There are two important versions of the story. According to *Serat Pararaton* (composed in the early sixteenth century), during the time when Måjåpahit was ruled by King Hayam Wuruk, the eastern part of Java was granted to his son Bhre Wirabumi. After the death of the king, his successor, Wikramawardana, placed his daughter on the throne. This action was disputed by Bhre Wirabumi, hence the Måjåpahit-Blambangan conflict. In the Damarwulan story, Ménakjinggå (Bhre Wirabumi) is very eager to marry the Queen Kencånå Wungu (Suhita), but the queen rejected his love. Instead, she sent a village boy named Damarwulan to attack Ménakjinggå, and Damarwulan decapitated him and presented his head to the queen. Damarwulan was then installed as the king of Måjåpahit. A tangential but important line of the story is that during Damarwulan's residency in Måjåpahit, the daughter of Prime Minister Logendèr, Anjasmårå, fell in love with him.

Babad Blambangan tells us a different version of the Damarwulan story, starting with King Brawijaya of Måjåpahit installing Ajar Gunturgeni to the throne of Blambangan because of his power to defeat the enemies of Måjåpahit. Ajar Gunturgeni (or Pamengger) had no children, but he had a dog. He transmogrified the dog into a human so that it could become his successor as king of Blambangan. However, the transmogrification was imperfect, such that his head did not change to a human head but remained a dog head. The rest of the narrative is the same as the first version of the story. Margana (2007) describes the historical significance of this story:

> Bhre Wirabumi, Pamengger, and Menak Jingga probably all refer to one and the same figure. If the first is accepted as the more historical figure, the latter two must actually be personifications of the first. . . . Whoever the writer of the epic of Damar Wulan was, he must have been someone who was passionate about the glory of Majapahit. Menak Jingga's attitude was considered inhuman and promptly associated with doglike behavior. Probably, the writer of the *Babad Blambangan* was averse to accrediting such a questionable person as Bhre Wirabumi or Pamengger, to the Blambangan family tree. (24)

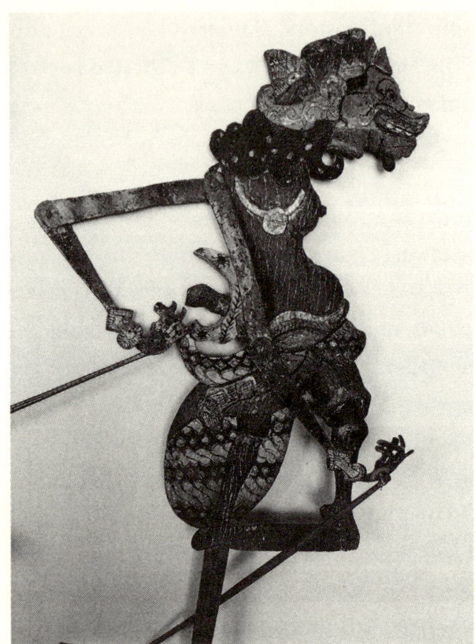
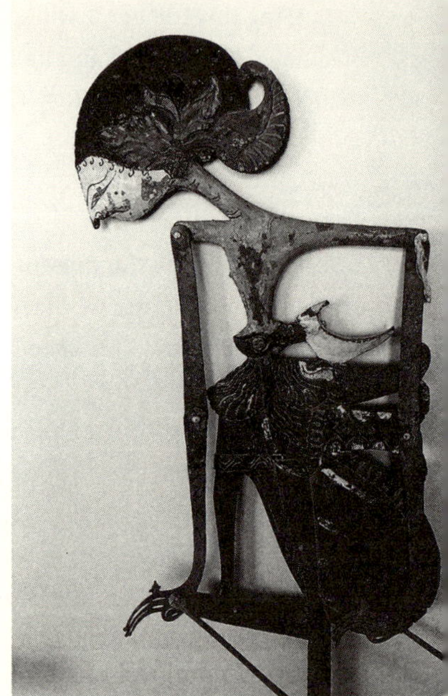

FIGURE 2.2 Ménak Jinggå and Damar Wulan of Wayang Krucil. From the collection of Wesleyan University. Photographed by the author.

Therefore, he created a villain, Ménakjinggå, who could assume all the more detestable attributes of Pamengger. In other words, the writer recognizes Ménakjinggå as one of the Blambangan kings, but describes him as genealogically unrelated to the main line of the family. This was probably an attempt to expunge any political stain on the Blambangan ruling dynasty. The different versions of the history and traditional historiography of Blambangan have led to several versions of the story of Damarwulan. The portrayal of Ménakjinggå as having a doglike head is commonly known and depicted in theatrical performances, except in the nineteenth-century Central Javanese court performances, as I discuss later.

EAST JAVANESE STORIES ON THE MOVE

As Cahyono (2014) points, the Islamization of Java was a factor in the decline in patronage of masked dance performances by Javanese royalty in East Java, as well as the disappearance of kingship centers themselves. Interestingly, Islamization was also responsible for the preservation and wide dissemination of the Panji story, both orally and in manuscript form. The rising centers of maritime trade along the north coast, led by elite communities of Muslims, were the main reason for the downfall of the previous inland centers of power and kingship in East Java. These developments led to the intensification of trade, both domestically and abroad. Ras (1985) explains the result of these developments:

> The elite consisting of traders in these towns had bourgeois-progressive perspectives and aspirations with international orientation. This caused the development of culture. During the North-coast period, Javanese culture experienced a renewal: many old traditions were dropped, changed with new traditions and new ideas received from the outside world that were then assimilated. Since the 15th century, the Muslim population in many North-coast towns was gradually increasing; by the 16th century Islam was clearly dominant. In spite of this development, people's favorite entertainment remained indigenous Javanese performances: dances and gamelan music, *wayang* theatre, singing, and so forth. We know this fact from rather old Javanese texts, such as *Suluk Wujil*, and also from sources outside of Java. We learn from *Hikayat Lembu Mangkurat* from South Kalimantan that, "After the king of Kauripan in Candi Agung sits down sadly for some time, the Prime minister Lau says: 'I beg your pardon your majesty, I heard news from many trading sailors that in the kingdom of Giri people are very noisily entertaining themselves day and night with all kinds of wayang and mask-dance performance, *gambus* [dance drama], and dancing, because the king is very clever, according to people. If your majesty is interested, let us send a messenger to Giri, so that your sadness will be brought to happiness.'" Then it is said that Patih Lau was summoned to go to Giri, near the town of Gresik, "to borrow people who are skillful in performing *wayang*, mask-play, dance, *gambus*, *joged* dance, and *gendot* dance." This kind of evidence was strengthened by Javanese texts from *Serat Sastramiruda* (Kusumadilaga 1930). From this book we know that the renewal of wayang—the appearance of the puppet and the structure of the story and its gamelan accompaniment—started from the Coastal period, and was sponsored by walis, especially Sunan Giri, Sunan Bonang, Sunan Kudus, and Sunan Kalijaga. (vii)

We learn from Ras about the Pasisir as a hotbed of political and cultural activities, where traditional performing arts developed and spread throughout Java and beyond. As Vickers (1993) points out, Southeast Asian maritime trade made it possible for a cosmopolitan interweaving of cultures to occur. In the case of Java's north coast, maritime trade led to the formation of Pasisir community complexes, which facilitated intellectual exchanges and movements of people, literature, and performing arts in the area. Vickers also (2005) eloquently demonstrates the dynamics of such intraregional interactions found in the Balinese kidung poetic text *Malat* and other literary works. More generally, Pigeaud (1967, 6–7) maps the expansion of literature during this period, beginning in East Java and moving both eastward and westward through literary centers such as Gresik, Demak, Cirebon, and Banten. In other words, the Panji story has travelled widely throughout Java, to other Indonesian islands, and beyond. Despite the dissemination of the Panji story through literature, Vickers (2020, 269) suggests that it more likely spread through oral means and performance than through narrative forms.[4]

Recall the image at the opening of this chapter: Panji teaching an Indian musical instrument. The hybrid nature of the image—a Javanese prince teaching his princess to play an Indian musical instrument next to an image of the ocean—can be thought of as a metaphor for cultural exchange through transoceanic journey. Although the story never reached India, it spread throughout the Indonesian Archipelago and can be found in present-day Malaysia, Myanmar, Thailand, Laos, Vietnam, and Cambodia. The spread of the story was facilitated by the rise of maritime trade across Southeast Asia. For example, the prosperous trading center at Patani, on the east coast of the Malay Peninsula, had exchanges with many parts of Asia, resulting in the Panji story also taking root there and in neighboring Kelantan in both written and oral literature (Rattiya 1988, Robson 1996). From Patani, the Panji story travelled to Ayudhya, and then to Cambodia and Myanmar (Burma).

As Puaksom (2007) explains, a Thai manuscript of an *Inao* story, *Aindarwuntha*, was written for the Burmese court dance performance *Eenaung* (from *Inao*), which reenacts a version of the Panji story. Following Aung's (1956) classic study, Puaksom examines how an extant Thai Panji manuscript once belonging to a court dance troupe from Ayudhya was brought to Burma by its army after it sacked Ayudhya in 1767. It is also possible that the Panji story was carried to Ayudhya by a Javanese Muslim prisoner of war from the Patani court, and that this version of the story was subsequently translated into Thai, where it became the basis for dance drama productions (Puaksom 2007, Rattiya 1988, Robson 1996). Though evidence of this transmission is not very solid, it supports the possibility of the dissemination of the Panji story through both oral and written forms.

EAST JAVANESE STORIES AS CELEBRATED PERFORMANCES IN JAVANESE COURTS

As I noted earlier, Panji and Damarwulan became prominent stories in eighteenth- and nineteenth-century Central Java. In what context were these stories introduced to Central Java? According to Carey (1997, 77), the political relationship between Surabaya and Mataram had something to do with this transmission. In the seventeenth century, Surabaya was at the peak of its power. When Sultan Agung of Mataram subjugated Surabaya, the relationship changed from antagonistic to allied. It was in this context that the Damarwulan story, in both oral and literary form, was introduced to Central Java. This is a plausible hypothesis, although contemporaneous evidence of such transmission is lacking. However, the nineteenth-century perspective from the court of Central Java supports this hypothesis. According to the learned courtier and wayang expert Kusumadilaga (1930, 163), Pangeran Pekik of Surabaya, who was married to Sultan Agung's sister, introduced a wooden puppet performance (*wayang krucil*) to Mataram. The wayang krucil puppets introduced to Mataram were made of leather. Kusumadilaga (Kusumådilågå) goes on to tell the story of subsequent rulers recreating the shape and temperament (*wondå*) of wayang purwå and wayang gedhog. In the year 1659, Paku Buwånå II of Kartåsurå summoned a prominent carver to create a Pangeran Pekik style of wayang krucil, in the form of a wooden puppet modelled after Pangeran Pekik's leather puppet of wayang krucil. The performance was accompanied by a gamelan Lokananta that was tuned to a special tuning system called *miring*. The ensemble consisted of gong-type instruments (*kethuk*, *kenong*, and *kempul*), *kendhang* (drum), and a metallophone (*saron*) (166).

It is quite interesting how much the Central Javanese courtiers admired East Javanese cultural tradition, as seen in their creation of new mythology that often contained East Javanese stories as the genesis of their cultural traditions and icons. For example, Kusumådilågå mythologized the origin of *tayuban*, a social dance in which female dancers are hired to dance with the guests, from the time of Buddhism:

> It was the dancing of celestial nymphs to the accompaniment of the sound of *katawang* [heavenly musical sound?]. At the time of Janggala [a twelfth-century kingdom in East Java], it is said that Prabu Suryawisesa entered the inner palace, he was met by the queen in the middle of the *paringgitan* quarter [the space between the inner and outer hall]. There the queens danced to the accompaniment of gamelan slendro. Thus, tayuban dancing originated in the reign of Prabu Suryawisesa. (178)

Kusumådilågå seems to say that the queen dancing when she met the king inspired the creation of tayuban. The point is that the Javanese royal family attributed to East Javanese the power of the past as the origin of their cultural practices.

In another example, a famous dancer/choreographer of the mid nineteenth-century Mangkunegaran palace, Tondhåkusumå, mythologized the genesis of the court cultural icons from ancestral mythology of the past. In *Serat Kyai Gulang Raryå* (1870), he wrote that *bedhåyå sångå* dance was created at the courts of Segaluh, the story encompassing a series of ancient kingdoms, beginning from Pajajaran, then Måjåpahit, Demak, and Mataram. It is not clear whether the bedhåyå sångå to which Tondhåkusumå referred was the most sacred bedhåyå dance in the court of Surakarta performed annually for the coronation of the king as we know it at present. The dance with nine (sångå) dancers is the only one we know as the most sacred bedhåyå in the court of Surakarta it is called *bedhåyå Ketawang*, and in the court of Yogyakarta, *bedhåyå Semang.*

As I noted briefly in the introduction, Tondhåkusumå also created a story of Panji Inokertapati as being responsible for making the first gamelan on earth. The story goes as follows. Because the earth had not had gamelan as good as the Heavenly gamelan Lokananta, Panji wanted to make the first gamelan, asking his brothers and servant to be his assistants:

8. [The prince Panji] took special pleasure in warriorship
and in leadership.
However, in his heart,
he felt most pleasantly
to hold audience with his family and his court officials.
The prince Panji knew in depth the art of singing,
and was expert in performing gamelan.

9. Therefore, he was unhappy in his heart
that he hadn't yet found in the earth
gamelan similar to Heavenly gamelan Lokananta.
As the incarnation of the god Wisnu,
Immediately it came to his mind
to make gamelan.

10. The prince Panji summoned
his four brothers and his deformed
servants, also four of them,

to assist him.
In making the gamelan, Asmarabangun was
ready to work, sitting down
at once, in the usual manner of working.

11. He holds the *uthuk* device.
Its left and right side are used to flip over [the gamelan material].
The young brother Jungut,
stands by in front of his elder,
holding tongs to take the material out,
bringing them to the base.
The base is made of black stone.

12. Those who pound the would-be gamelan are
Raden Wirun, who holds a small hammer;
Andaga holds a medium-sized hammer;
a large hammer is held by Raden Kalang;
Dhoyok, Bancak, Sebul, Palèt are bellowing.
There are four bellows,
large, medium, half-medium, and small size. (24–25)[5]

This is an example of the use of mythology as spiritual reference. Calling themselves by the name of Panji and his entourage, the gamelan makers attained spiritual experience so they could safely and successfully produce the best gamelan. The name disguises employed by gamelan makers have been known from the early twentieth century onward. Mangkunegårå VII, the king of the minor court of Mangkunegaran (reign 1916–1944), gave Kunst (1973, 138) the following information: The chief smith assumes the name of Panji Hinokertapati or Panji Sepuh. The first assistant is his half-brother, Panji Charangwaspå or Panji Nem. The next assistants are Handågå, Wirun, Kartålå (they are Panji Sepuh's half-brothers, out of his secondary wives), then his inseparable servants (*punåkawan*) Bancak and Doyok; Panji Nem's punakawan Sebul and Palet; Panji Sepuh's youngest sister, Ragilkuning; and Panji Sepuh's learned jester, Jangkung. In today's practice, usually only the leader of the gamelan makers assumes the name Panji (Suwardi 2020, personal communication with author).

Becker (1988) thinks the necessity of the name disguise among gamelan smiths occurs because gamelan making is the act of carrying out dangerously powerful forces.

> [Smiths in Java and Bali] place themselves in the spiritually dangerous position of imitating an evolutionary process, or hurrying along the natural changes of the earth. By the use of fire, they not only accelerate the slow transformations of ores in the earth, but from dull ores they produce objects of wonder such as gongs and the iron dagger known as *kris*. The transformations brought about by the smithy both imitate and excel those of the earthly forces—the smithy's job is precariously close to blasphemy, yet without the support of the blasphemed One, he has no hope of success. (386–87)

Becker's proposition is sensible. Another similar idea is the belief that a *keris* (kris), and by extension gamelan instruments, may endow power because the fabricated metal is the result of the union between ore from the earth and a meteor falling from the sky (Haryono 2014). The symbolic Javanese expression of addressing the earth as Ibu (mother; i.e., Ibu Pertiwi or Mother of the earth) and Bapa (father; i.e., Bapa Angkasa, Father of the sky) has deeper symbolic meaning in terms of paying homage to nature (150).

In addition to mythologizing East Javanese stories for spiritual reference, the courts of Central Java experienced efflorescence in the arts, including the production of literary works containing East Javanese and Hindu stories. This happened in the context of what scholars call the "renaissance" in literature (Pigeaud 1960, 235). A long conflict within the royal family, which resulted in the permanent division of a single Mataram kingdom into two major courts, was followed by a time of increasing order and tranquility that brought about renewed interest in poets producing works. The flourishing of literary works containing all sorts of stories inspired performing artists to reenact them in theatrical performances. One in particular, *Serat Kandhaning Ringgit Purwa*, which was written during the seventeenth or eighteenth century, inspired the development of the court style of wayang and other theatrical performances reenacting stories from East Java.

We know that the wayang play performing the Panji story is called *wayang gedhog*. Wayang gedhog, together with masked dance drama (*wayang topèng*), were known as highly elaborate performances in the late nineteenth and early twentieth centuries, especially in Central Javanese courts. A literary work known for its encyclopedic content, *Serat Tjenṭini*, composed between the late eighteenth and early nineteenth century, often mentions various performances, including wayang shadow play, wayang play with wooden puppets, dance, dance drama, masked dance, and magic shows. Masked dance performance in the Panji story was one of them; the term *gambuh* referred to this masked dance, which was used interchangeably with the terms *bagor* and *wayang topèng*. A few stanzas of *Serat Tjenṭini* (late eighteenth century) suggest the popularity of the masked dance using the Panji story at this time. In a gathering, Kulåwiryå asks others about:

5. The best performance to be invited for tonight's performance.
"Should it be wayang play, *gambyong* dance
Or *bagor* masked dance? From the three
Which is the best?
Choose one of them."
Wiråbåjrå says,

6. "It is up to you, master,
Which one you like."
Kulåwiryå's brother says, "For me
Bagor is the best,
With the story of Nåråwongså, or Jåyåkusumå."

7. All things considered, people here
Prefer only a performance of
Masked dance. Many people will come to watch,
Rather than watching ringgit
Or tlèdhèk dance, wayang krucil or purwå performance.
The masked dance will be watched by a lot of people. (199)[6]

Another example of a refined and elaborate performance of wayang gedhog (including its gamelan accompaniment) comes from *Panji Asmåråbangun*, a Panji manuscript composed in the mid-nineteenth century:

9. The princess was entertained,
making her happy.
For this evening,
the prince Inowanengpati
would like to see a wayang show.
Raden Kuda agrees.

10. The handsome one is asked to perform the wayang.
The gedhog puppets have been set up.
The screen and blending lamp have been installed.
The wayang puppets are new,
looking illuminating are the puppets' golden paint.
The puppets are very well shaped.

11. Ki Sogèng and Ki Cêkruk
are assisting the puppeteer.
Gamêlan has been arranged.
Those who play the music
are his family.
The district officials are in attendance.

12. The rebab player is Dyan Wukirsantun,
the drummer Raden Permadi,
Dyan Jâyâmarutâ plays bonang
panerus. Dyan Andâgâ
plays bonang barung.
Gong was played by Jayèngpati.

13. Saron, gambang, celempung,
salukat, kethuk, and kenong [were also played].
Attending wedânâ is complete.
Raden Wasi Jayengresmi
was always sitting behind the puppeteer.
Raden Panji was assisting him.

14. Raden Panji Asmârâbagun
sees the play behind the screen,
together with his wife laying down.
Kusumâ Jinali and ladies-in-attendance
see the play close to the screen. . . .

17. The audience is jam packed,
their hearts very engrossed.
The puppeteer is well versed with his pronouncement
in unfolding his story.
The musicians are handsome,
sounding the Walgitâ piece to tell the story.

18. When Panji Anom
serves in Pânârâgâ, Panji Kasatriyan attacks Bali, crossing the narrow sea.
He wins the battle. (*Panji Dadap* 1980 [mid-nineteenth century], 170–71)[7]

Indeed, wayang gedhog is known for its refined and elaborate performance. In 1963, my gamelan school reconstructed a performance of wayang gedhog by Ki Madyåpradonggå, the only dhalang who knew how to perform this wayang. I watched the all-night performance. I noticed that the scenes and subscenes of the story contained more variety than the usual wayang kulit purwå. The narrations are often longer, with detailed descriptions and elaborate language about the scene. The pélog-only pieces for accompanying the play are known as sophisticated and in a variety of forms. Many *sulukan* mood songs are much longer and elaborate than sulukan for wayang kulit. The interactions between the puppeteer and the musicians are meticulous, since certain sections of a song should match perfectly with the character and the manner of their actions, such as the songs sung by the clowns. This highly refined performance of the Panji story is remarkable if we compare it with the East Javanese performance of folksy wayang krucil or klithik.

Wayang Topèng and Langendriyan *in Javanese courts*

Earlier I mentioned the period of renaissance in literature after the permanent division of the court of Mataram into two major (Kasunanan in Surakarta and Kasultanan in Yogyakarta) and two minor courts (Mangkunegaran in Surakarta and Paku Alam in Yogyakarta). These literary works contain Panji, *Mahabharata*, *Ramayana*, and Damarwulan stories, such as *Serat Kandhaning Ringgit Purwa* (The Book of the Narration of Wayang Purwa), *Serat Panji* (The Book of Panji), *Serat Langen Driya* (The Book of Langen Driya), *Serat Damarwulan* (The Book of Damarwulan), *Serat Kandha Ringgit Tiyang* (The Book of the Narration of Wayang Dance Drama), as well as literature about performances such as *Buku Kawruh Topèng* (The Book of the Knowledge of Masked Dance), *Buku Pakem Topèng* (The Guide Book of the Masked Dance), and *Serat Pakem Ringgit Gedhog* (The Guide Book of the Wayang Gedhog). This literature continued to inspire the development of wayang, dance, and dance drama performances until the nineteenth century, especially in Javanese courts.

It is worth noting that the sociohistorical context in which a poet writes his works influences the content of those works. According to Kumar (2020):

> [Paku Buwånå IV (reign 1788–1820)] was a serious devotee of the Panji story, writing numerous Panji works and also dressing as Panji in court dance drama. His Panji works are set in a wider world than that of *Wangbang Wideya*. In particular, he seems to have been considerably preoccupied with the aggressive Makassarese, who play a major role in three of his compositions that

were probably *wayang gedog lakons*, namely *Panji Dadap*, *Panji Raras*, and *Panji Sekar*. (138)

Like other Panji stories, the story of Paku Buwånå IV's Panji also revolves around Panji's quest to find or journey with his beloved and his entourage, involving disguises and battles with their contenders. In a scene in *Panji Dhadhap*, Panji disguises himself as the king of Keling, Dhadhapwasesâ. He goes to the kingdom of Jambi with his chief minister Dhadhapnarantåkå. The minister enters a competition to marry the daughter of the king of Jambi, Prabu Kiswårå. The competition requires that he kill an elephant named Balitung, the favorite domestic animal of King Jambi's daughter Retnå Turidhåwilis. One of his contenders is the prime minister of the kingdom of Makasar, Gunåsarontå. Eventually, Dhadhapnarantåkå wins the competition, but before his official meeting with the king's daughter, the king of Makasar and his army attack the kingdom of Jambi. It is told in the story that the Makassarese (Buginese) are known as a very aggressive enemy. The following stanzas describe the brutality of the army from Makasar's attack on the army of the kingdom of Jambi:

17. The assigned kings were attacked
and stricken from behind.
The leader,
i.e., the commander who makes the last decision,
was Aryå Bagaspati.
He brought with him
eight brave and powerful fighters.

18. The exceptionally powerful army unit of four thousand,
and four thousand cavalrymen,
were assigned
to enter the battle.
The gong, drums, and trumpets were sounded.
The cheering was ear shattering,
as if the sky was full of sound. . . .

20. The forty thousand Buginese soldiers holding swords,
riding horses,
were attacking, striking.
pushing viciously, slashing [with swords]
the marching army [of Jambi].

They [the forces of Jambi] were very surprised,
because they were attacked from the rear.

21. Crying in fear and in disgust were those soldiers who were wounded with swords.
Many arms were cut off.
They were run over by horses.
They tried to strike back, but not fast enough.
Pushing and upside down were they,
one was stacked on the top of the others,
asking each other what's going on.

22. The commander Jurumalang [of the kingdom of Jambi] angrily asked,
"Where is this attacking army are coming from?
They carry out deceitful acts,
attacking us from the rear,
without orderly manner,
as if they are forest wolfs,
stupid army."[8] (Paku Buwånå IV 1980 [1780–1820], 170–71)

A brief history of Makasarese is useful here. The Makasarese live in South Sulawesi. They are one of the largest ethnic groups in the area, aside from the Bugis and the Toraja. People often think that the Makasarese and the Bugis, who live next to the Makasar area, are the same ethnic group. Regardless, they both are known for being seafarers. This working distinction was intensified for the Makasarese when in 1669 Makasar, the principal center of sea trading outside Java, was taken by the VOC (the Dutch East Indies Company). "A number of Makassar noblemen left for Java, where they joined the struggle against the Dutch and their Boné allies, fighting either with Trunåjåyå of Madura in east and central Java (1674–1678) or with Banten's Sultan Agung Tirtåyåså (1682–1684) in west Java. Other Makassar emigrated to Sumatra and even to Siam" (Pelras 1996, 145).

In the same period and the same context, the Buginese sided with the Dutch in taking over Makasar. According to Pelras:

> Makasar became the major point of embarkation not only for its [Bugis community's] own fleet but also for the Bugis fleets and the Bugis adventurers who set off in search of wealth and fame for the western parts of the archipelago, now their main area of maritime activity since the Dutch had restricted their access to the eastern islands. From the Riau archipelago, where many of them

had settled in the vicinity of the Johor court, at a strategic meeting point of the local and international trade routes, they extended their activity in various directions, including that of the Malay peninsula. (145)

In addition, the Bugis assisted the Dutch in their conquest of the Mataram kingdom in Java (Hall 1981, 373).

It seems that the author of *Panji Dadap* knew the history of the presence of the Makasarese in Java, but he may have treated the Makasarese and the Buginese as indistinguishable; they both were known for their bravery in war and piracy, although Pelras (1996, 309–10) has debunked the notion that the Buginese were fierce pirates. In *Babad Giyanti*, Yåsådipurå often mentions the Buginese as being fierce combatants: "The commander of Mataram forces was very disappointed, since his forces lost the battle with the Buginese. . . . They acknowledge that fighting with the Buginese cannot be taken lightly." In the *Serat Soerja Radja* of the Kasultanan court of Yogyakarta, the enemy from Europe, assisted by troops from Makasar, Ternate, and the Buginese, were portrayed as infidels from overseas (Ricklefs 1974, 192–93). The *Serat* mentions the arrow dance (*beksan djemparing*) and the lance dance (*beksan djebeng*), perhaps to commemorate the war noted previously. In the court of Kasunanan Surakarta, *Wirèng Andågå-Bugis* (in which Panji's entourage duels a Bugis combatant) was created. The dance ends with the Buginese combatant losing the battle. In recent times, the ending of the dance was changed to the two dancers shaking hands, capturing the spirit of camaraderie between different ethnic groups.

In spite of the fighting between the army from South Sulawesi—for the most part siding with the Dutch—and the Javanese court army, after the decline of the colonialism, Javanese courts assigned Bugis and Dhaèng Makasar as honor guards. In the Kasultanan of Yogyakarta, their duty is to participate in court processions, especially during the religious festival to commemorate the birth and the life of the Prophet Muhammad. A group performs processional music in an ensemble consisting of European snare drums, the Sulawesi wind instrument *puwi-puwi*, a Javanese drum, and a handheld gong.

All in all, in the nineteenth century, wayang topèng and wayang gedhog were highly developed at the courts of Surakarta and Yogyakarta (for Yogyakarta, see Wiratama 2021). As I mentioned earlier, Javanese courtiers and poets produced literature (poetry or prose) that inspired the development of the performing arts. Such literature also included books about the history and practice of the performing arts. The book of *Kawruh Topeng* (1985 [1832]) is one example. Published first in the *Sasadara* journal, the book contains background to and performance practices of masked dance drama. The anonymous author attributes the creation of this wayang topèng, which has been popularly performed in the north coastal area, to Sunan Kalijågå. The author explains that it was introduced to and adapted by the court of Surakarta through the village of Palar, near the court city of Surakarta. When it became a court performance, the connection between the masked dance drama in the court and in the village was sustained, because a few court dhalangs moved to the village.

What is worth noting here is that, according to this book, when the masked dance drama was adapted by the court of Surakarta, it became a highly sophisticated performance. Next, I translate a description of a scene of the antagonistic King Klånå, including its gamelan accompaniment. The scene begins with the dancing of the king's giant soldiers:

> For the dance of the giant soldiers, the gamelan accompaniment was gendhing "Jangkrik Gènggong." Then, human soldiers or ministers entered, followed by [the clown] Sembunglangu. After the conclusion of the dance, they all sat in front of the would-be king's throne. Then, with the gendhing softly played, the dhalang narrated to the court audience. . . . After performing a transitional part of the piece, ladrang "Gandrungmanis" was sounded. In the wayang tradition, this gendhing is called "Talakbodin" or "Bendrong." The first dancer entering [the dance arena] was the young Klånå Trijåyå, who after dancing sat in front of the soldiers. Then, the gendhing was played softly, accompanying King Klånå who was dancing in the mood of falling in love, while the dhalang narrated the scene, with the clown clowning. After a transitional part of the piece, the gendhing was played at a faster tempo, accompanying King Klånå *kiprah* dancing. After the completion of the kiprah dancing, the gendhing changed to "Gencong." Then, the gendhing was played softly, while King Klånå sang a falling-in-love-mood song. When the gendhing reached the *inggah* section of gendhing "Eling-Eling," King Klånå changed his dancing movements and his singing. When the gendhing changed to gendhing "Logondhang," King Klånå changed his dance movements again. When he concluded his dancing by waving to his soldiers (who all moved up front), then the gendhing changed to gendhing "Bedrug" in a fast tempo. The young Klånå moved forward, saluting to and standing in front of the king. All the soldiers, one after another, saluted the king. Then, the young Klånå moved forward, facing the king, and together they danced kiprah. Both Klånå were dancing in the same variations. After the completion of the kiprah dance, gamelan stopped playing. The two Klånå sat down facing one another. Then, the dhalang sang a mood song; all the masked dancers sang together with the dhalang, singing the song "Sastradhatan." After the conclusion of the singing, the dhalang narrated about what was needed,

> followed by the departure scene, which was accompanied by gendhing "Plajengan Srempegan" at a moderate tempo.

I present this lengthy quotation to show the complexity and sophisticated nature of the scene. Its dancing and music, and the interaction between the dancers and the music, were far more complex than what we know them to be in today's masked dance drama.

Earlier I described the East Javanese story of Damarwulan as a semihistory of the kingdom of Måjåpahit. Like the Panji story, when the Damarwulan story was introduced in the courts of Yogyakarta and Surakarta, it transformed into a sophisticated performance, especially in the dance opera *Langendriyan* in the minor court of Mangkunegaran.

Langendriyan was created in the mid-nineteenth century by Tondhåkusuma, the well-known dancer/choreographer in the Mangkunegaran palace during the reign of Mangkunegårå IV. Aside from its refined and sophisticated performance, what is distinctive about *Langendriyan* is that both male and female character roles—strong, refined, demonic, and clown—are performed exclusively by women. This came about because of the history of *Langendriyan*. The central figure of the opera was the European Kiliaan Godlieb (perhaps Indo, a mix of Javanese and Dutch parentage). He owned a batik factory in a suburb of Surakarta, which is known as a suburb of Godlieban. Observing a dozen or so ladies drawing batik patterns while also singing, Godlieb came up with the idea of a performance whose actors were singing. He discussed his idea with Tondhåkusumå, who then created *Langendriyan*. There is no written evidence about the choice of Damarwulan for the story of the opera, whether the batik woman singing really inspired the genre, or if the idea came from Tondhåkusumå or Godlieb.

In a prior work (Sumarsam 2003) I described the form of *Langendriyan*.

> The musical feature of *Langendriyan* is the interactive singing of poetic forms by the singer/dancers accompanied by the gamelan. The gamelan also accompanies a fight scene with the piece called *Srepegan*. When the singer/dancer is about to sing the poem, the player of the *keprak* (a wooden box, sounded to guide the dancers in their movements) cues the drummer, who then cues the ensemble for *sirep* (a quiet moment); in this moment, most of the instruments drop out, except a few instruments that are needed to accompany the song. Besides *Srepegan*, there are also other gamelan compositions accompanying various scenes, such as a romantic scene and the exchange of tense words before a battle scene. The music of *Langendriyan* is quite complex, involving

a highly interactive activity of the dancers/singer, keprak player, drummer, and other musicians; it is a combination of singing, dancing, choreography, and drama. (61)

Decline and Reconstruction

In the introduction, I touched on why the courts in Central Java paid attention to and created refined theatrical performances of East Javanese Panji and Damarwulan stories—both were associated with the last Hindu Javanese kingdom of Måjåpahit. That is, this cultural transformation is part of the concept of the legitimation of kingship through succession usurpation and the cult of glory (Moertono 1968, 52–82). "Another means of enhancing royal glory was the king's genealogical tree. The more august persons, *real or legendary*, it incorporated and the further back it went, the greater the king's prestige" (62–63). The attribution of the courts of Central Java to East Javanese myth is one of the means for enhancing the power of a ruler through the genealogical cult of glory. As Moertono (63) explains, "The Javanese mind strove to syncretize the two different cultures of Hindu religion and Islam in order to establish the desired continuity; the kings of Mataram were therefore provided with a double genealogy," Hindu and Muslim.

This genealogical transformation reflects Kusumådilågå's story about the origin of tayuban dancing from the time of Buddhism. Furthermore, Kusumådilågå (1930 [1870], 178) says, "At the time of Demak [the period of Islamized Java], tayuban was performed by santri [of an Islamic sect called] Dulguyering Birahi. The introduction [of the piece for tayuban] was dhikir prayer. The song was accompanied by [musical instruments] angklung, kendhang, and terbang. There were also male or female santri who were summoned to dance. The melody was similar to gendhing sléndro or pélog." Kusumådilågå ends his story by saying, "Later, tayuban became the entertainment of Javanese people both in the village and in the city. The commoners or the elite, if the held wedding celebration, circumcisions, and the like, held tayuban entertainment" (178).

As I have pointed out, wayang gedhog and wayang topèng (both of which reenact East Javanese Panji and *Langendriyan* stories) became celebrated performances in the Central Javanese courts of Surakarta and Yogyakarta. Wayang topèng was also known outside of these courts, for example in the Klaten and Gunung Kidul regency in Yogyakarta province. However, throughout the twentieth century these theatrical performances sharply declined, and in some cases disappeared. Competition with theatrical performances based on the stories of the *Ramayana* and the *Mahabharata*, especially wayang kulit and wayang wong, caused this decline. The rise of modern, Indonesianized Western-style entertainment, such as popular music, film, and television, also contributed to this decline.

There have been recent attempts to revive wayang gedhog and wayang madyå by faculty members of the Institut Seni Indonesia (Indonesian Institute of the Arts) in Surakarta. The communities in which wayang topèng still exists, such as one in Klaten, have also tried to revitalize the masked dance drama (Adi 2018, Sawega 2014). Major efforts to repopularize the Panji story have also been carried out at several festivals under the sponsorship of the Ministry of Education and Culture in collaboration with local provincial governments. In 2018, festivals took place in several cities—Denpasar, Pandaan, Malang, Blitar, Kediri, Yogyakarta, and Jakarta—each of which presented the Panji story in both traditional and newly composed dance or dance drama forms.[9] Organizers also invited groups from Thailand and Cambodia to perform. In addition, a collection of more than 250 ancient tales from all over the world was curated by Leiden University library (2017) and included in UNESCO's Memory of the World program. This recognition has given impetus to Indonesian artists and authorities to revive and revitalize cultural performances and scholarly discussions of the Panji story, though it is still too early to know whether these encouraging developments will bear positive results.

One of the points that has emerged from the discussion of the indigenous Javanese Panji and Damarwulan stories concerns the intimate relationship between myth and spiritual experience. The context from which this point emerged is the process of transformation from East Javanese to Central Javanese cultural traditions. All in all, to understand fully Javanese performing arts throughout the history of socioreligious change, we must explore the interweaving of their content and contexts as they evolve from one period of time to another. The following sections follow the same trajectory of discussion, focusing on Hindu stories as they have intermingled with Islamic and local stories, especially in the north coastal area of Java.

THE CASE OF BIMÅ SVARGA: WAYANG GOLÈK IN TEGAL[10]

In 2017, toward the end of my fieldwork in Java, I met Gunawan Suwati, a musician, a dhalang (puppeteer) of wayang golèk and wayang kulit, and one of the leading artists in the north coast city of Tegal, who actively promotes local traditional performing arts. I told him that I was interested in studying the history and contemporary practice of wayang golèk. Gunawan suggested I document an older Tegal style of this wayang performance. He felt that the older style of

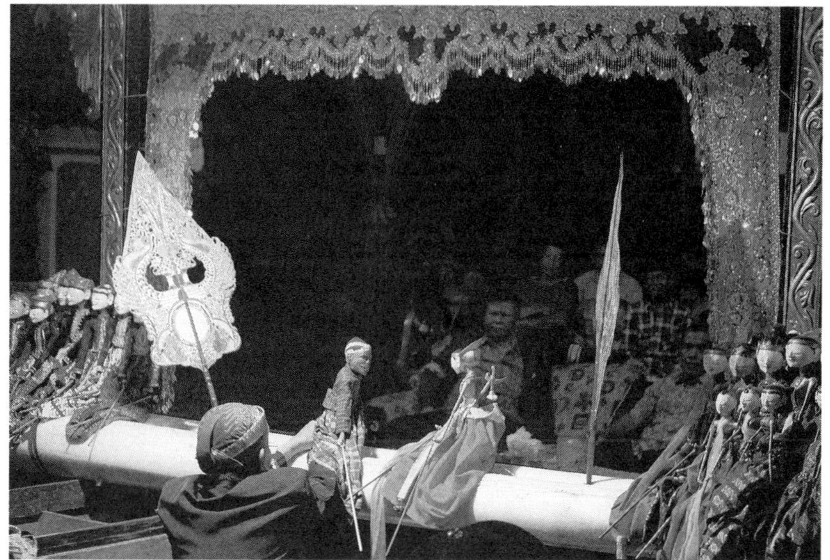

FIGURE 2.3 Wayang Golèk Cepak in Tegal. Photography and videography by Ciptono Hadi, Much Cholid, and Jepri Ristiono.

wayang golèk had become diluted by the adaptation of elements from contemporary wayang kulit.[11] Since I have long been interested in the history of Javanese performing arts, I accepted Gunawan's suggestion with open arms (see Sumarsam 1995, 2013). I agreed to work with him to organize a performance and to help find musicians and dhalangs who would be interested in this documentation project. This turned out to entail an extensive analytical trajectory in terms of the history, content, and context of wayang golèk and wayang performance in general.

A continuing conversation with Gunawan culminated in a performance and documentation of wayang golèk, which was performed by the dhalang Ki Warnoto and accompanied by musicians organized by Gunawan. On the morning of November 28, 2017, the wayang stage and gamelan ensemble were assembled under a tent in front of Gunawan's house. Gunawan's friend lent his set of wayang golèk puppets and wayang stage paraphernalia for the occasion. The late Ki Enthus Susmono, a well-known dhalang of wayang kulit and wayang golèk (and also the governor of the Tegal regency) provided his gamelan set, also without charge. As with most wayang golèk performance today, the stage equipment included a sound amplification system.

That morning, Ki Warnoto and the musicians rehearsed, guided by Gunawan. They focused their rehearsal on a few pieces that the musicians seemed to have a hard time remembering. I was told that the drummer, who formerly accompanied Ki Warnoto's performance, had passed away; therefore, Gunawan invited a drummer from another town who had never accompanied a Ki Warnoto performance. I noticed that during the rehearsal, Ki Warnoto and the drummer spent some time working on matching the drum patterns with the puppet movements. The rehearsal ended at around noon. A lunch was provided for the performers. After lunch they dispersed.

At around 7:00 p.m. the musicians and dhalang, fully attired in traditional costume, gathered to prepare for the performance to be documented, and then had dinner. At 8:00 p.m. the performance began with a musical overture. Unlike the musical overture of a wayang kulit performance, which consists of pieces in the pathet manyurå mode, a musical overture for wayang golèk consists of pieces in pathet sångå.[12] After the overture ended, the dhalang signaled to the musicians that he was about to open the show. The musicians played a piece named "Kawitan Tegal" to accompany the first scene of the play. After removing the *kayon* (a puppet representing the tree of life), which had until then occupied the middle of the screen, thus signifying the beginning of the play, Ki Warnoto introduced two *parekan* (ladies-in-waiting) puppets, having them dance to the lively drum rhythms played by the ensemble. A puppet representing the king then entered and took his seat on a throne. A signal followed from Ki Warnoto for the music to accelerate. At a certain point, most of the instruments became silent in a section known as *sirep*, in which the music plays softly to accompany the dhalang's narration of the scene. In wayang golèk Tegal, this is called *ngabor*.[13] The following is the dhalang's opening narration.

> When the sun is going down, changing the day to nighttime, it illuminates *ima-ima*, *gambura*, and *ancala*. Ima-ima means cloud, gambura ocean, ancala the tip of the mountain. God picks the tip of the single leaf of *gebang siwalan*, cutting it in the same length, sprinkled by *asta gangga wirantanu*. Asta means hands, gangga water, wira pen, tanu ink. People debate about tablets [and writing], no one can confirm the difference. There are those who consider tablets as older than writing, and vice versa. Because of the arrival of new life, we find a new creation in the form of books of revelation [?] until the end of the world. The issue is that, before the tablet exists, writing has existed. Before the writing exists, the tablet has been available. After the disappearance of the tablet and writing, poets get together for reckoning the letters. As the ink falls on the tablet, it has led to the creation of sixty-two letters. Of the sixty-two letters, thirty of them are thrown to the direction of the north, falling on the land of Bandi (India?), Israel, and Arab or Mesir. The letters are still written in bold [?], and haven't yet been given vowel symbols. In the future, when the

vowel symbols are added, the form of books of revelation [?] until the end of the world, will lead to the creation of the holy books of Jabur, Bible, Torah, and Quran. (Video documentation, Sumarsam 2017)[14]

The town of Tegal is in the western part of the north coast of Java. History informs us that in or around the fifteenth century, Islam was introduced to Java, first in the north-central coastal area, then to the rest of the coast and interior of the island. Although historical evidence of the genesis of wayang golèk is hard to find, the fact that it reenacts Islamic stories suggests that its earlier existence and development took place in Java's north coastal area. According to tradition, one of the *walisångå* (the nine Islamic apostles believed to be responsible for introducing the religion in Java and beyond), Sunan Kudus, created wayang golèk. From the political/cultural center in the north-central coast of Java, wayang golèk spread to other parts of the north coastal area.

Today, wayang golèk exists in the cities of Batang, Pemalang, Pekalongan, Tegal, Cirebon, Indramayu in the central and western coastal area, and in the Pasundan area in the interior of West Java. To the south of Tegal, wayang golèk can be found in the Kebumen and Banyumas areas in the south-central interior of Central Java. The opening narration quoted previously is also performed by puppeteers of wayang kulit in Cirebon and Banyumas. It is interesting to note that some puppeteers of Balinese wayang kulit also use the same sentence "asta gangga wirantanu" in their narration, making us think about the history and geographical distribution of this text. I will return to this topic in the next chapter.

Although the stories performed in wayang golèk relate intimately to Islam, the text of the opening of the narration, revolving around the sentence "asta gangga wirantanu," is taken from the story of the Hindu-Javanese kidung sung poetry called *Bimå Svarga*, which was written in the seventeenth century on *lontar* (dried palm leaves). The part of the narration that mentions "asta gangga wirantanu" is from an episode of dialogue between Bimå (the second of five Pandhåwå brothers) and Bathårå Guru (the godhead Siva). It is part of the story of Bimå rescuing his father Pandu from hell. Pandu was placed there as a punishment from the gods for his wrongdoing.

As the narration comes from a written manuscript, it is useful to discuss the origin of written tradition in Java. In the first chapter, I discussed the origin of writing technology—the Indian scripts for writing and rewriting kakawin poetic forms containing Indian literary works. I now turn to the relationship between written tradition and oral tradition, and the process of the adaptation of written text for the opening narration of wayang golèk and wayang kulit in Java and Bali. Ki Warnoto began his narration with the beauty of nature and a description of ancient writing. It then goes on to describe a metaphorical world generated by letters, with the letters as the source of holy books of different religions. Although the opening narration is essentially a mantra, a hymn to power and potency (Foley 2002, 88) where the puppeteer asks for blessings from deities and *dhanyang* (local ancestors), the narration also reminds wayang audiences that they live in a multifaith world.

As a whole, Ki Warnoto's narration informs us about the contemporary local cultural space where wayang golèk was cultivated and performed. This locality is linked to the history of the early Islamization of Java. As the text moved from one region to another, intercultural and intellectual exchanges occurred between the areas where the text was recited by puppeteers. Considering the evolution of the text since the manuscript was written in the pre-Islamic era has led me to think about cultural and socioreligious transformation throughout Java's history. Indeed, the text in its various forms has been performed since its inception and is still used by some puppeteers today. The transformation from written text to oral expression has further prompted me to think about the relationship between literacy and orality. Finally, this narration invites us to investigate ritual in action, since the text is a mantra to ensure a safe performance.

As with any wayang performance, the opening narration of the first scene Ki Warnoto recites is an invocation, a mantra, a literary yoga, the aim of which is to seek "the power of potency" (Foley 2002, 88), offer an apology to the gods (Zurbuchen 1987), and/or request the gods' blessing so the performance will proceed without hindrance. For the audience, the mantra conveys more than a supernatural connection; it is also enjoyed as an aesthetic presentation. I define aesthetic enjoyment in wayang as an interplay between dramatic action and its ornamentation. The dramatic action includes those aspects of performance that directly relate to the storyline, while ornamentation refers to other art forms—music, dance, literature, and visual arts such as painting and carving—that are integral to, and closely collaborate with, the storyline. These arts not only produce effects that are peripheral to the plot of the story, but at times they become the focus of enjoyment, drawing the spectators' attention away from the storyline (Sumarsam 1984, 107). When a juxtaposition of two or more ornamentations occurs—for example between soft-sounding music and literary/stylized language of narration—a deep aesthetic enjoyment can be experienced by the audience. This is what the audience might experience when listening to Ki Warnoto's invocation. That is, while the storyline is backgrounded, the beauty of the language and musical accompaniment is foregrounded.

However, the difference between Ki Warnoto's invocation and the invocations of wayang kulit is very striking. In large part this is because the beginning of his invocation makes no mention of anything related to the story presented in the scene. He begins by reciting poetic phrases about the sunset and its effect upon the environment, describing the practice of ancient writing and the origin of alphabets that inspired the creation of a few holy books. The narration that explicitly mentions the story only appears after a long discourse that has no relation to the story. This is strikingly different from the invocation in a wayang kulit performance. As illustrated in the following extract, the opening narration of a Ki Anom Soeroto's wayang kulit performance mentions the name of the palace (in other words, it directly relates to the storyline) after only a couple of sections of poetic phrases at the beginning of the invocation:

> Vanish, be still be brought to a close. Which city then is prime among the eminent decad of antiquity: prime stands for first, eminent for excellent decad for ten, antiquity for the beginning. Though many are the gods' creatures overlain by the skies supported by the earth, enclosed by the oceans, and many are enthralling in the extreme, still the state now extolled has no match. Where to find a single land that bears ten names; such could only be the land of Astina, or Gajah Oya, or Liman Benawi; it is named the land of Astina, for it was founded by the late king Hasthimurti. It is called Gajah Oya or Liman Benawi: before it came to be a city, on the site it occupies stood the remains of an elephant's palace. It is made the opening of the story. For though one search a hundred lands one could not find two in a thousand, not even ten. As the land is long and lofty, littoral alpine, fecund, abundant, bustling, opulent, secure, ordered, AND prosperous. (Translated by Arps 2016, 117–18)

The rest of the narration is a long description of the glory of the kingdom. Only a few sentences at the end of the narration mention the essential content of the story's plot. As the text shows, in a traditional wayang kulit invocation, after only a few opening sections Ki Anom Soeroto has already mentioned the name of the kingdom and its location. In the wayang golèk invocation, there is no mention of the name of the kingdom and its location until a long description of various topics that have no relation to the plot of the story are recited. This fact makes me eager to explain the significance of Ki Warnoto's invocation.

My immediate response to Ki Warnoto's performance was curiosity. When he recited the words *asta gangga wirantanu*, I asked myself what he was referring to. When I heard the word *mangsi* (ink; in the text, *tanu* is the word for ink), I could only think of the practice of contemporary writing, as this word is still used in present-day Javanese. However, according to the *Old Javanese-English Dictionary* (Zoetmulder 1982), *mangsi* is an Old Javanese word for ink. When Ki Warnoto explained the meaning of these four words, indicating the practice of writing, using the hand, water, pen, and ink, I still did not understand the reference. Only after he spoke the words *gebang siwalan* (a palm leaf or tree) did I begin to understand that Ki Warnoto was talking about the process of writing with the hand, water, a pen, and ink on a dried palm leaf. I had two questions: Why did he adapt the description of ancient writing for his invocation? And what is the origin of the text with the theme "asta gangga wirantanu"?

The Origin of the Text, Coastal Concentration

I was fortunate that in my literary research on this topic I stumbled upon an article written by a philologist at the National Museum of Indonesia, Gunawan (2017), "Manuscript Production and Akṣara Mysticism in the *Bhīma Svarga*." Gunawan directs us to the village of Kabuyutan Ciburuy in West Java as the place where the text originated. He mentions a number of manuscripts containing the story of *Bhīma Svarga* written in Old Javanese. He refers to a contemporary wayang performance in the coastal area of Central Java in which the variants of the texts that mention asta gangga wirantanu have been immortalized (10). This is a variation of the same text of Ki Warnoto's invocation.

The story of *Bhīma Svarga* goes like this: Bimå, the second oldest of the five Pandhåwå brothers, wants to rescue his father Pandu from hell after the gods punished him for his grave sin of shooting a deer with an arrow. After going through a series of trials—especially fighting with the guardians of hell—Bimå rescues his father. Subsequently, he meets with the god Siva (Guru) to have a discussion, part of which deals with the origin of *puståkå* (book or manuscript):

> Bhīma: There is more, Guru. I would like to ask you, how did the earliest manuscript turn black, until it was said to be the best, how was this done?
>
> Guru: I would like to talk to you, Bhīma. The earliest manuscript turned black. The gebang leaf, cut in the same manner lengthwise and widthwise, [is then] transformed into life by the gaṅgā, vīra, and tanu. Gaṅgā is water, vīra the pen, tanu the ink. The smoke of the oil lamp is rubbed in copper shells, dissolved in the *laṇḍa* of the *kepuh* tree, mixed with lac, [and then all] mixed in the right doses into the inkwell. This is what is called ink. Its role in the making of books is well-known. (10)

There is no colophon to indicate when *Bhīma Svarga* was written, but in the context of other manuscripts that mention this story, this manuscript must have been written in the early part of the sixteenth century, before Java was fully Islamized. This conjecture is corroborated by other evidence, including the existence of a Bimå cult during the Måjåpahit period (Duijker 2010), and

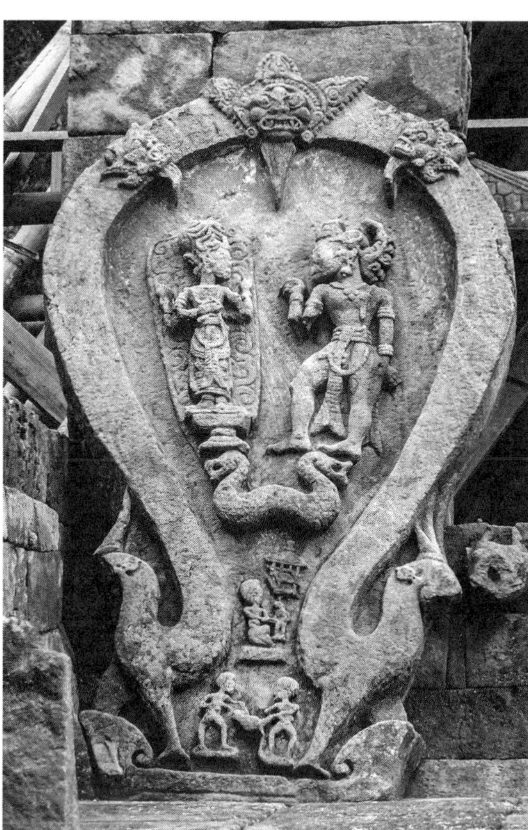

FIGURE 2.4 Bima in conversation with Siva. Candi Sukuh, Central Java. Photographed by the author.

the presence of Bimå in iconographic forms, such as carved figures on the wall of Candi Sukuh, built in the fourteenth and fifteenth centuries, which contain the scene of Bimå in conversation with Siva (see figure 2.4).

The text of *Bhīma Svarga* also includes a description of the process of producing ink by mixing the residue of oil lamp smoke with the liquid of the kepuh fruit. This description also appears in invocations by Balinese dhalangs. This fact suggests that the two manuscripts might have come from the same period of intercultural exchange during the heyday of maritime trade around the sixteenth century. Like the Panji story, the story of *Bhīma Svarga* originated from East Java in the period from the twelfth to sixteenth centuries, when the area was a political and cultural center. How was the story introduced to other parts of Java? As with the journey of the Panji story, the answer lies in the world of Southeast Asian maritime trade, which made possible a cosmopolitan interweaving of cultures and led to dynamic exchanges of intellectuals and movements of people, their literary works and performing arts.

As noted earlier, Ki Warnoto's invocation differs strikingly from a similar invocation in wayang kulit. As my research focuses on tracing older cultural artifacts along the north coast of Java, I ask whether dhalangs of wayang golèk in the Tegal area adapt the same texts in their invocations. From the limited number of performances of wayang golèk that I have seen I cannot say that this is the case. Unsatisfied, I examined videos of wayang golèk performances and found that some dhalang wayang golèk in the Tegal region also use them, as do wayang golèk in Indramayu and the Pasundan regions of West Java. However, unlike wayang golèk in Tegal and Indramayu, whose plots are based on Islamic and local babad stories, wayang golèk in the Pasundan area reenact stories based on the *Mahabharata* and the *Ramayana*. As I continued my research, I also found that some dhalang of wayang kulit in Cirebon, Banyumas, and Cilacap adapt the same texts. My interest in the use of the texts deepened when, after reading Hooykaas (1973) and rereading Zurbuchen (1987), I found that Balinese dhalangs also use the same texts. With just a few exceptions, the distribution of the texts is concentrated along the north coast area. Asian maritime trade from the fifteenth century made possible the dissemination of Javanese stories—including the Panji story, *Bhīma Svarga*, and others—throughout the Pasisir and beyond.

From Pustaka to Pusaka

The fact that Ki Warnoto and other contemporary dhalangs use portions of sixteenth-century texts containing the theme of asta gangga wirantanu as an integral part of their invocation suggests that the Hinduization of Java is the root cause of this transformational process. The implication is that within the Hinduization process the Javanese were introduced not only to Hindu religion but also to written tradition. In this regard, the Javanese considered written tradition as having special significance. However rudimentary, writing was considered a very valuable tool to document and disseminate knowledge, especially literary works (*pustaka*, *puståkå*). Hence, the Javanese venerated written documents and considered them powerful objects; so much so that the physical material on which the document was written (*lontar*, palm leaf) was also believed to be imbued with sacred power (*sakti*). A written document is not only *pustaka* but also *pusaka* (*pusåkå*), an heirloom or magically charged object, from which power can be acquired.

It is worth noting that the two words are semantically very close. In fact, one of the meanings of *pusaka*, as defined by Poerwadarminta in his dictionary *Baoesastra Djawa* (1939, 504), is a letter of advice, *layang piwekas awujud pitutur*, indicating that the two words *pusaka* and *pustaka* are related to each other. In this regard, Florida (1995) offers a useful explanation for the importance of *pustaka* (manuscript) being held in high esteem as *pusaka* (heirloom).

> First, the manuscripts are usually old and hence wear the patina of age that is among the marks of spiritually charged objects in Java. As material objects, the manuscripts are physical sites upon which the extraordinary powers of former writers and readers may have rubbed off. And so they offer the possibility of powers by contagion. Second, the manuscripts are esteemed for their rarity. Access to manuscripts in Java is reserved, if not quite as reserved as many believe. Third, the manuscripts are esteemed for having been inscribed in Javanese scripts. The exaltation of these scripts has its own history. There are, for example, a number of nineteenth-century writings that specifically treat the hidden meaning, and power, of Javanese scripts in relation to Javanese bodies. (35–36)

Florida focuses her discussion on the manuscripts housed in the courts of Java in the nineteenth century. This belief in the power of pustaka can be traced from one of the main aims of the poets in writing literary works: as an act of worship. In his study of kakawin, Zoetmulder (1974, 172) identifies the words *lango, lengeng, lengleng* as reflecting the way poets expressed their emotions to worship the god of beauty. "What they convey is a feeling that is perhaps best rendered by 'rapture.' It is a kind of swooning sensation, in which the subject is completely absorbed by and becomes lost in its object, the appeal of which is so overwhelming that everything else sinks into nothingness and oblivion" (172). This magico-religious behavior of the poets was observed by and resonated in the minds of the Javanese, so much so that they treated puståkå (manuscript) as pusåkå. Perhaps the idea of manuscripts containing power was deeply felt by the author of *Bhīma Svarga*, so that he felt it necessary to describe in detail the technical means of writing to reinforce the notion of venerating written tradition.

The adaptation of certain texts used for invocation also relates to this veneration of expressing knowledge through written documents and the physical objects on which knowledge is written. One might also think of this phenomenon as analogous to a symbolic expression of *curigå manjing warongkå* (the union of the dagger and its sheath) when Javanese people talk about the mystical union between the content (*isi*; i.e., the blade of the dagger) and the receptacle (*wadhah*; i.e., the sheath of the dagger).

My examples show that in Java, the intimate court-rural relationship has engendered a dynamic interplay among repertoires and idioms, as well as between written and oral traditions. The Javanese place a high value on ancient print production, so much so that they consider ancient manuscripts as magically charged objects. This tradition is still sustained in twenty-first-century Java, as seen in the invocations by dhalang Ki Warnoto and his contemporaries in the north coastal area of Java, inland Central Java, the Sunda area of inland West Java, and Bali. These regions, with their long history of maritime trade and intercultural and religious encounters, have played a significant role in the spread of manuscripts and stories throughout Southeast Asia.

To recapitulate, tracing the connection between present and past events, in chapter 1 I investigated certain contemporary cultural practices as palimpsests of the old cultural traditions, from the Hindu-Javanese period in the early history of Java. In this chapter I have examined cultural practices that resulted from Java's openness to and localization of Indian culture. In this regard, written tradition, which produced inscriptions and manuscripts, and the rise of maritime communication, had important roles in documenting cultural practices and spreading them from one cultural space to another. In a similar vein, I discussed three Hindu or indigenous Javanese myths—Panji, Damarwulan, and Bimå Svarga—which developed in East Java, the political and cultural center at the time, that subsequently spread throughout Java, Bali, and other islands. Special attention was given to the transformation of Panji and Damarwulan stories when they were adapted and developed into Javanese cultural icons at the major and minor courts of Surakarta and Yogyakarta. The story of Bimå Svarga was discussed in terms of its travel throughout the north coastal area of Java and Bali and its subsequent localization.

Whereas the discussion thus far has focused on the palimpsest of Hindu-Javanese cultural practices up to the nineteenth century, in the next chapter I examine their transformational manifestation as part of Islamic proselytizing activities. I consider how certain prominent Islamic figures from the sixteenth century to the present have influenced the Islamization of Hindu-Javanese cultural traditions, and the role of the performing arts in carrying out religious proselytization.

THREE

Linking the Present to the Past through Preaching, Ritual, and Levity

A popular and charismatic Islamic preacher, Ahmad Muwafiq—known intimately as Gus Muwafiq—began preaching at the 2019 graduation ceremony at Sekolah Tinggi Ilmu Tarbiyah (Higher Learning of the Science of Religion) in Tuban by explaining the problem of the initial Islamization of Java. He said that Java was the most difficult place to be Islamized, because the land was very haunted (*paling wingit*). Java's central power, the kingdom of Singåsari and Måjåpahit, controlled over one-third of the world. When the multinational forces of Mongolia attacked Måjåpahit, they were defeated by Ronggalawé's forces of Tuban. After defeating Mongolia's forces, the process of the Islamization of Java was attempted but to no avail. Why? According to Gus Muwafiq:

> [It was] because apparently a very extreme Hindu sect had existed in Tuban and its vicinity, including the inland of Central Java. This very extreme sect was known as Bhairawa Tantra. The Bhairawa Tantra sect did not solely represent Hinduism, but not solely Buddhism either. It came about in the period of the mixture of Hindu and Buddhist traditions. The Hindu tradition teaches people about *dharma* [good deeds] and about restraining passion and lust. Hence, according to Hinduism, when a noble human being dies, he undergoes *moksa* [body and soul vanish]. One can moksa after experiencing *upanisad*. Upanisad means the ability to dismiss one's identity to the extent that no one can know him. In addition, he should behave in the manner of the earth [*kebumian*]. Kebumian is a way of life, similar to the life of the earth. The more people urinating on the earth, the more fertile is the earth. The more people hoeing the

earth, the more fertile is the earth. Thus, the more people insulting the earth, the more they benefit from it.

Furthermore, he should experience *upawasa*. In upawasa, one should sit in silence, not eating, not drinking, not touching his wife. In so doing, his body becomes smaller and smaller, then in a blink of the eyes, he disappears, moksa. In some places in Java, this upawasa ritual was not effective—many people were unsuccessful in carrying out upawasa, that is, the body became smaller and smaller. But if you are not strong enough spiritually, because your mind is remembering your wife, remembering your sheep, it [the process of *moksa*] stops. . . . This is the context that brought people to embrace a new opposite sect, a sect that allowed them to indulge their lust and passion [*ngumbar hawa nafsu*], known as *pancamakara* or the Five Ms [*malima*].[1] This ritual consists of the gathering of men and women, all are naked, placing *arak* liquor and human *tumpeng ingkung*[2] [sacrificial food] in front of them. For what reason? To release their lust and passion. Their lust of arousal beneath the stomach was fulfilled by practicing freely sexual cohabitation. To prevent them from thinking too much, liquor was drunk. To prevent their stomachs from making cracking sounds [a sign of being hungry], they were given tumpeng to eat. Essentially, what they needed was *ngrågå sukmå*. In carrying out ngrågå sukmå, which means the exit of the soul [from the bodies], in order for the bodies to stay in place, they were given human flesh to eat. . . . Consequently, this act resulted in the creation of a new, very extreme kind of sacred knowledge.[3]

Gus Muwafiq then explained the creation of three black magics: black magic to steal, to kill, and to make women fall in love. Referencing evidence from Turkey, Gus Muwafiq pointed out that 1,500 *ulama* (Islamic scholars) led by Sayid Aliyudin disappeared, thought to have been devoured by Javanese people who had acquired the black magic. Subsequently, a powerful ulama from Turkey, Sayid Samsudin Al Bakir Al Parsi, whose body was very strong, was sent to Java. There he was known as Sèh Subakir from Tidar mountain in Magelang, Central Java. Subakir chased the Javanese people who had embraced black magic in all directions, leading them to settle in new places, establishing new communities of black magic. When Sèh Subakir reached his old age, a son of ulama Jumadi Kubra from Tuban named Iskak continued this task. Iskak married Subakir's daughter, Dewi Sekar Kedu. The marriage resulted in the birth of Sunan Giri of Gresik. Those Javanese who practiced black magic ran to Bali. There, they taught Hindu Tantrayana, including a form of black magic called *léyak*. Others settled in Kediri, teaching the pancamakara ritual. To confront these people, members of the ulama community assigned a powerful ulama by the name of

Sunan Bonang; he was the son of Sunan Ngampel. Eventually, people who carried out the pancamakara ritual surrendered to Sunan Bonang, begging him to save their lives. Sunan Bonang responded:

> Alright, I will not kill you, but you have to change your behavior. The ritual of circumambulation can continue; it is okay, but don't be naked. Men and women shouldn't be naked, should not do sexual cohabitation. Drinking liquor is not allowed . . . change it to boiling water, coffee, or tea. Regarding tumpeng, it is *halal* [not forbidden], no problem. Regarding chicken ingkung, [I mean] human ingkung [food for sacrifice], it should be replaced by chicken ingkung." These requirements were imposed by Sunan Bonang. Regarding the mantra of *ngrågå sukmå*, [Sunan Bonang says that] it should be replaced by the *tauhid* sentence, *lhailahhailolah*. [If we don't know all of this,] it indicates that we don't have up-to-date information. Even if we know that now tumpeng can be found in many places, including Malaysia, we still don't know that actually Sunan Bonang was the one who continued to facilitate rituals with tumpeng sacrificial food. (Muwafiq's sermon)[4]

Gus Muwafiq then warned his congregation that as the followers of walisångå, members of a Nahdlatul Ulama organization, they must not be influenced by the idea that the tumpeng food ritual derives from Hindu-Javanese culture. Tumpengan is not the practice of *musryik* (idolatry), like pancamakara is. Gus Muwafiq further explained other aspects of Islamization, such as covering speakers with cloth, as is used in preaching. Animal sacrifice, which had been carried out by the Javanese during the Hindu period, was readjusted to the form of today's Islamic *Idul Korban* animal sacrifice. Gus Muwafiq concluded, "Therefore, I always say, if there are people who say that tumpengan is musryik, tell them [that it is not]. But if they steadfastly insist, cannot be corrected, approach them, slap their lips [laughter of the audience]."

In keeping with the themes of this book, Gus Muwafiq's speech raises questions around how people perceive the past, and how people use those perceptions to connect events through time. In his sermon, Gus Muwafiq revealed his view of Java's past and its links to the present: the glory of the fourteenth-century Måjåpahit kingdom and the difficulty of Islamizing the haunted land of Java; the Bhairawa tantra sect that produces the bizarre pancamakara ritual and its Islamic transformation; and the historical link of his subject matter to the local ambience in Tuban, where Gus Muwafiq was preaching.

In chapter 1, I discussed the link between Hindu-Buddhist traditions in medieval Java and certain contemporary Javanese cultural performances, including how the meanings of gamelan tones relate to certain Hindu-Buddhist practices in early Java (Becker 1993). Becker only briefly touches on Tantric practice and does not mention pancamakara, one of the most important rituals of Buddhist Tantrism. Although Becker discusses contemporary Javanese gamelan and court ceremonial dances, she does not mention *canthang balung*, the court jokesters whose work included singing vocal interjection with gamelan to accompany serimpi dance, clowning in Islamic religious festivals, and leading the talèdhèk dancer-singers. A number of scholars believe that canthang balung are inextricably linked to the practice of Hindu-Buddhist Tantrism (Acri 2014, Stutterheim 1956, Sumarsam 1995). In contrast, Gus Muwafiq pays special attention to the pancamakara ritual and how it was appropriated to become an acceptable ritual practice in today's Javanese-Islamic hybrid culture.

It is to be expected that preaching differs from an academic presentation. In producing academic knowledge, the subject matter should be discussed with a more objective argument, supported by theory and evidence, and delivered in formal language. Academic writing is aimed at a circle of learned readers. Preaching may or may not involve academic practicalities, depending on the preacher and in what context it is delivered. Regardless, the most salient aspect of preaching is that the preacher engages in real-time interactions with a heterogenous congregation, both learned and lay people. In addition, a preacher may implicitly or explicitly align himself to a particular social or political organization. In Gus Muwafiq's case, he was very explicit in declaring himself a member and the voice of Nahdlatul Ulama (NU), one of the largest Islamic sociopolitical organizations in Indonesia.

Muslims consider the Prophet Muhammad as the first and model preacher (Arb., *khatib*, Jav., *ketib*), providing moral and sociopolitical content to supplement and confirm the guidance provided in the Quran, including impelling men to propagate its message (Antoun 1989, 67). Antoun qualifies, however, that in Arabia, the tradition of public speaking also existed in the pre-Islam period in the roles of "the poet (*sha'ir*), the chief (*sayyid*)—who was often said to be the possessor of spiritual gifts—and the soothsayer (*kahin*), who delivered oracles in rhymed prose, blessed followers, cursed enemies, and acted as faith healer" (67). These pre-Islamic orators had different ethical and sociopolitical significance in their positions as brave warriors and public spokesmen for the tribe:

> His insignia were the lance, staff, or bow, indicators of the military honor of the tribe. In the public arena or verbal competition along with the poet he heaped glory on his own tribe and opprobrium on its opponents, comparing deeds, origins, and noble (ignoble) qualities. In the early Islamic period the *khatib*

retained many of his earlier attributes, but now the role took on a primarily religious significance inasmuch as Muhammad's preaching was to Muslims, and boasting about tribal valor was devalued in the new Islamic ethos. (67–68)

It is also worth noting that since the beginning of Islam in Arabia in the seventh century, the mosque was not only a place for worship, but also for asylum, for discussing important public matters, and for travelers to rest. A *mimbar* (elevated seat of honor) is placed in the middle-center of the mosque as a symbol of religiopolitical authority, from where important public pronouncements are made and khatib (preachers) deliver sermons every Friday. Antoun (67–68) reminds us, however, that the khatib was not the only Islamic preacher. There were a number of spokesmen who could be called pre-preachers, who worked to propagate Islam, but not from the mimbar of the mosque at the Friday sermon. Three types of these spokesmen were very active in propagating the religion: *wa'is* (admonisher), *mudhakkir* (reminder), and *qass* (teller or edifier of religion). It was not uncommon for these pre-preachers to be criticized for their somewhat wild behavior when preaching, which included singing (rather than reciting) the Quran, draping mimbar with multicolored garments, feigned weeping to show they had entered a mystical experience, and applying oil and cumin to their faces. Ibn al-Jawzi, a famous Islamic scholar in twelfth-century Baghdad who wrote about these pre-preachers, admonished them for their unconventional behavior, including violent body movements, crying out for help, and crowding unrelated men and women together (70).

The kinds of preaching during the beginning of Islam in Arabia that Antoun describes are still being practiced in contemporary Indonesia. Indonesians use the term *dakwah* (from Arabic *da'wah*) to denote activities to strengthen and deepen Muslims' faith, although it might also mean religious propagation (i.e., converting people to Islam). In Java, the term *pengajian* (the study of Quran, liberally applied), in reference to the main meaning of *dakwah* (*dhakwah*), is more commonly used. Pengajian can be held for all sorts of purposes, such as rite-of-passage events, Islamic holy days, celebrating events in educational institutions, and political events.

Following the trend of its spread throughout the Muslim world, dakwah entered Indonesia in the first half of the twentieth century, particularly after Indonesian independence in 1945, and rapidly developed during President Suharto's New Order regime from the late 1960s onward. Meuleman (2011) explains how social, economic, and political developments had a large impact on the development of dakwah activities:

> The gradual and interrelated processes inherent in the rise of living standards, the extension of education to increasingly large sections of the population, urbanization, the development of non-agricultural economic activities, and the rising influence of foreign cultural, social, intellectual, and spiritual models all contributed to the growth of new spiritual needs and questions which were addressed in diverse ways by these dakwah movements. (239–40)

The various circumstances from which dakwah movements developed have contributed to their rich content and context.

Gus Muwafiq appeared during the high point of these circumstances, particularly in relation to education, urbanization, the influence of foreign (especially Western) cultural and social models, and the expansion of new technology and modern media to disseminate information. Gus Muwafiq's preaching also has been shaped by an era of deepening Islamization in Indonesia (see Ricklefs 2012), which has led to ongoing conflicts among Islamic factions and increasing intolerance among heterogenous Indonesian Muslims. But before I discuss these conflicts, in the following sections I will further examine Gus Muwafiq and his preaching.

INTERTEXTUALITY

From the quotation at the beginning of this chapter, we may sense that Gus Muwafiq has a keen interest in the history of Islam. He acquired his knowledge of history through study at the Indonesian State Islamic University Sunan Kalijågå (Universitas Islam Negeri Sunan Kalijågå) in Yogyakarta from 1990 to 2010 (Ainur 2019). Born in Lamongan in East Java, in 1974 he studied Islam at a number of *pesantrèn* (Islamic boarding schools), mainly Pesantrèn Lirboyo in Kediri, also in East Java. Gus Muwafiq was an Islamic activist, once appointed the secretary general of the Southeast Asian Islamic Student organization. He was also a very active member of Pergerakan Mahasiswa Islam Indonesia (PMII, the Student Movement of Islam in Indonesia). Perhaps because of his multifaceted background, the fourth president of Indonesia, Kyai Haji Abdulrahman Wahid, trusted Gus Muwafiq to be his personal assistant. Thus, Gus Muwafiq's knowledge of Islam led him to become a well-known preacher, orator, activist, and expert in Islamic history.

To understand Gus Muwafiq's discussion of the Buddhist-Javanese pancamakara ritual, we must trace the sources or "texts"—written and spoken—that informed the "texts" of his oratory, in what can be viewed as a process of intertextuality. Searching for sources that would inform my understanding of Gus

Muwafiq's analysis of pancamakara, I found Sunyoto (2004). Sunyoto references a study by Moen (1924) on pancamakara ritual performed in honor of King Adityawarman, and assumes that during the period of Hindu-Java the same ritual was carried out in a cemetery called Ksetra. Today we know that a suburb called Setra located near the Ampel mosque in Surabaya. Sunyoto assumes that the name *Setra* derives from *Ksetra*, the place where the pancamakara ritual was performed. According to Sunyoto, Sunan Ampel was the leader who Islamized pancamakara to become the ritual meal called *kendurèn*, which derived from the Persian tradition of *kenduri*, a ritual meal in honor of the wife of Prophet Muhammad.

My aim here is to trace the sources Gus Muwafiq used to construct his presentation. I am also interested in understanding how Gus Muwafiq processed and manipulated these sources to meet the needs of his main audience. His statements, as well as comments from important Islamic figures and intellectuals, make clear that his oratory is directed toward a younger, millennial audience. Gus Muwafiq presents sermons in a lighthearted style, utilizing storytelling and humor. Tofik Pram, the editor of a recent book by Gus Muwafiq, praises him for his proselytizing at a time when Indonesia was threatened by the radicalization and politicization of Islam (Muwafiq 2019, 17). One blurb written by Dr. Oman Fathurrahman of Universitas Islam Negeri (Islam State University) Syarif Hidayatulah Jakarta particularly caught my attention for its characterization of Gus Muwafiq's preaching:

> Reading this book, I feel I was sent to another world. Usually, I learn about the history of Islamic acculturation in Nusantara local culture through written documents, which is rigidly presented academically, and sometimes makes me bored. This book is different. It contains Gus Muwafiq's oratory (*tuturan*) in the form of light-hearted stories about how Islam descends to the earth; it arrives and dialogs with the diverse cultures of Nusantara. Some of his oratory can be characterized as imaginative or in the language of santri, *khayal*. But his style does not minimize the important message of its content, that is, that Indonesia has unbroken sociocultural roots and capital. That capital is the manner in which people practice religion, which is flexible, adaptive, and willing to accept diversity, without losing the principals and foundations. In order to be accepted, preaching for millennials should be in this style, indeed. Through this book, Gus Muwafiq appears as a unique preacher (Fathurrahman, as cited in Muwafiq 2019, book blurb).

It is striking that Faturrahman uses the word *imagination* (*khayal*) to characterize parts of Gus Muwafiq's propagation. On the one hand, from a Sufi perspective, imagination functions as a powerful intermediary that enables human beings to remain in constant contact with the infinite and absolute (Akkach 1997). On the other hand, in secular terms, *khayal* means "fantasy," or "empty imagination." As such, we may ask in which category Gus Muwafiq's story of the Islamization of pancamakara falls. This is difficult to answer. Depending on their backgrounds, audiences may receive and respond to the preacher's story differently.[5]

The question also persists as to whether this transformation of pancamakara actually happened as Gus Muwafiq and others attest. What evidence, beyond the views of the individuals expressed previously, supports this claim? As I highlighted in chapter 1, scholars agree that pancamakara (the Five Ms) of Bhairawa existed during the Hindu-Javanese period. Does evidence exist indicating how pancamakara was Islamized?

Following other scholars, in chapter 1 I proposed that the antinomian behavior and profession of the canthang balung court servants were linked to Buddhist Tantrism and colored with eroticism, albeit confined to the context of court culture. This reminds me of my prior description (Sumarsam 1995) of peculiar behaviors in Sufi *dhikir* (chanting in praise and remembrance of Allah) mentioned in *Serat Tjenṭini*, a literary work composed in the early nineteenth century. The author describes the opening of a mass of whirling dhikir, in which participants, with eyes covered by batik cloth or paper, formed a circle, held their breath intermittently, and cried unconscious with shaking heads, the male and female devotees acting out various behaviors:

50. They were everywhere, one on the top of the other,
    Like banana trees that had been cut down.

51. Men and women mixed together,
    Those who were on the top of the other did not mind.
    The ones who were naked were not concerned,
    There was no punishment.
    That was the way of the people of Dul Birahi,
    Whoever achieved superiority, no questions were asked
    About their behavior.
    Those santri whose èlmu was inferior
    Surrendered their wives' bodies and souls,
    Presenting them [to the superior ones] for whatever purposes.
    (*Serat Tjenṭini* 1912–1915, 5–6:92)[6]

Participants in dhikir employed all sorts of techniques "to open up [their] consciousness to the attractions of the supra-sensible world: sacred numbers and symbols; colors and smells, perfumes and incense; ritual actions and purifications; words of power, charm-like prayers and incantations, with music and chants; invocations of angels and other spirit beings; even the use of alcohol and drugs" (Trimingham 1971, 199).

If we compare these techniques with pancamakara in Tantric practice, assuming that consuming meat and fish was part of the ritual, one action is missing: erotic or sexual behavior. However, in his work on the Sufi tradition of Dul Birahi,[7] Zoetmulder (1994) describes sexual promiscuity and nakedness as integral to the dhikir ritual. He suggests that sexual promiscuity and nakedness are similar to Pasupatas, Kapalikas, and other Buddhist tantric practices in India. Furthermore, Zoetmulder (237–38) asserts that the term *birai* is "a bastardisation of bhirawa, birawa, or birawi." Though the meaning of *birahi* in Malay is "in anguish" or "to be mad about" something, it appears that the word is closer in meaning to getting oneself into a state of ecstasy; hence pointing to the primary meaning of *bhairawa*. To strengthen his point, Zoetmulder quotes passages from *Suluk Lonthang*, which explicitly describes *ambirawa*, the act of bhirawa:

> If you wish to know the true science, ask for one who is already *bhairawa*, who has all doctrines ready to hand (?) (or, who takes what comes to hand?), who knows how to speak the language of heresy, who knows the evil that is within him, who does wrong intentionally and praises all of this, who does not concern himself about permitted or forbidden or consider what is obligatory or recommended, who already possesses an immaterial body. (228)

Suluk Seh Malaya confirms the ultimate aim of achieving the state of identity with God:

> He who is perfect, he who has been chosen, is not afraid when death comes. That perfect one, his form is not visible, because the realm has already become prosperous indeed. The meaning of the perfect one [is that] He has destroyed that place. The seven worlds have already been destroyed, for his destruction of this world is already complete, [having become] one in kind with Ambirawa.
>
> The king of the world that has just been created, his name is Ambirawa. The six worlds, they are all destroyed; vanished is the eastern direction, as well as the west, south, north, what is above as well as what is below, and also wood and stone, together with the earth and sky, the space reverberating in the wind and water, the ocean and fire. (Acri 2019, 293)[8]

Discursive Modes of Interpretation

Next, in tracing the intertextuality of Gus Muwafiq's discourse, I discuss how he gives an Islamic meaning to Javanese performing arts. In this regard, I focus on his use of *tembang*, a form of Javanese sung poetry, in his preaching.

Gus Muwafiq freely acknowledges the important role of Javanese performing arts in the promotion of Islam. Oftentimes, his discussion begins with a caricature of or anecdote about music. For example, in a show of pride in Javanese gamelan music, he says:

> Arabia has a musical instrument called *terbang* [frame drum], made of wood and leather. Europe has the musical instrument guitar, made of wood and *tali* [rope]. For these instruments, they only have to cut wood and rope. Easy. But Indonesia has musical instruments called gamelan, made of metal. It is only Indonesia who has mastered the advanced knowledge of mining and metallurgy who can make musical instruments from metal. Thus, do not be ashamed to be a member of the Indonesian nation. (YouTube video, uploaded by Prasetyo, 2019)[9]

Obviously, Muwafiq's comment about the material of musical instruments is problematic since there are many musical cultures whose instruments are made of metal. He also skips the fact that some guitars use string made of metal, not tali.

Gus Muwafiq also states that by nature, Javanese people like to sing. As an example, he sings the beginning of a song (a lighthearted or children's song), and makes a funny comment about its reference to a duck, *menthog-menthog tak kandhani* (ducks, let me tell you). He says, "It is odd that you people talk to ducks." Then, in a serious manner, he explains that because Javanese people like to sing, they composed the song "Sangkan Paraning Dumadi" (Origin and Destination of Life). He goes on to say that this song is a vehicle to remind people to remember the creator of life, Allah. The songs he references are from a genre of Javanese sung poetry called *mâcâpat.*

Mâcâpat are forms of Javanese sung poetry consisting of eleven songs. Each song is composed according to certain metrical rules: (a) a fixed number of lines per stanza, (b) a fixed number of syllables per line, and (c) a fixed vowel that the last syllable in each line must contain. For example, a stanza of the song *Pucung* consists of four lines. The first line has twelve syllables with the final vowel sound "u." The second line has six syllables with the final vowel sound "å." The third line has eight syllables with the final vowel sound "i." The last line consists of twelve syllables with the final vowel sound "a."

MÅCÅPAT PUCUNG

Ora urus karemané nguwus-uwus	12 syllables, end on u
Uwosé tan ånå	6 syllables, end on å
Mung batiné muring-muring	8 syllables end on i
Kåyå butå buteng betah nganiåyå	12 syllables, end on å

Måcåpat are meant to be sung and involve melodies in which a text is intoned. Each måcåpat song creates a certain emotion, mood, or character. Table 3.1 lists all måcåpat with their syllabic count, end-vowel indication, and character or mood, based on Hardjowirogo (1980 [1952]). The måcåpat are grouped according to their use, as detailed in bold.

Aside from describing this general character of the songs, Hardjowirogo (195) specifies their use as appropriate for the following:

Dhandhanggula	The most fluid or generic;
Sinom	the opening, middle, or end
Kinanthi	of a story
Mijil	Speech
Pangkur	Love and instruction
Durma	Love and apprehension
Asmaradana	Love and tension
Maskumambang	Passion or serious instruction
Megatruh	A concerned mood
Pucung	Apprehension
Gambuh	Sadness and great apprehension
	Apprehension and regret
	A pleasant feeling
	Instruction about a rather tense subject

Comparing måcåpat with Old Javanese *kakawin* (see chapter 1), one notices their differences: måcåpat stanzas consist of a varying number of lines and syllables per line, while in kakawin, each stanza has an equal number of lines and syllables per line. Despite these differences, that both kakawin and måcåpat are meant to be sung and the rule of syllabic and line quantity are observed suggests that, to a certain extent, there is a continuous transformation from the kakawin to the måcåpat genre. Additionally, the timeframe of the creation of måcåpat cannot be established with certainty. Poerbatjaraka (1952) suggests that the oldest måcåpat is the Islamic moralistic tale of Koja Jajahan, which was

TABLE 3.1 Måcåpat songs with their syllabic count, end-vowel indication, and character or mood

NAME	I	II	III	IV	V	VI	VII	VIII	IX	X	COMPOSER
The following five måcåpat are suitable for the opening of the story, though they should be matched to the content of the song. Dhandhanggula is the best fit for this.											
Dhangdhangula	10-i	10-a	8-é/o	7-u	I	7-a	6-u	8-a	12-i	7-a	Sunan Kalijågå
Sinom	8-a	8-i	8-a	8-i	7-i	8-u	7-a	8-i	12-a		Sunan Giri Kedhaton
Kinanthi	8-u	8-i	8-a	8-i	8-a	8-i					Sultan Adi Erucakra
Mijil	10-i	6-o	10-é	10-i	6-i	6-u					Sunan Geseng
Pangkur	8-a	11-i	7-a	12-u	8-a	I					Kangjeng Sunan Murjapada
The next two are suitable for expressing a dramatic mood.											
Durma	12-a	7-i	6-a	7-a	8-i	5-a	i				Kangjeng Sunan Bonang
Asmaradana	8-I	8-a	8-e/o	8-a	7-a	8-u	8-a				
The next two are suitable for expressing a concerned mood.											
Maskumam-bang	12-i	6-a	8-i	8-a							Kangjeng Sunan Majagung
Megatruh	12-u	8-i	8-u	8-i	8-o						Kangjeng Sunan Giri Parapen
The next song is suitable for when the mood is slacking down.											
Pucung	12-u	8-i	8-i	12-a							Kangjeng Sunan Gunungjati
The next song is suitable for unfolding rather intense moral instruction.											
Gambuh	7-u		12-i	8-u	8-o						Natapraja

Created by the author. Adapted from Hardjowirogo (1980 [1952]).

probably composed in the seventeenth century. In spite of Hardjowirogo's mention of composers of måcåpat (most were known by tradition as Islamic saints or important figures), no contemporaneous evidence can be found to confirm that the songs were composed by those individuals. What is certain is that by the eighteenth and nineteenth centuries, this form of sung poetry had become a common literary language for all kinds of literary works, including history, religion, myth, and romance.

An interesting facet of this discussion is how people interpret the meaning of the word *måcåpat* and each of the names of the måcåpat songs. The oldest Javanese-Dutch dictionary (Gerick and Roorda 1901) has an entry for *monca-pat*, described as: "Abbreviated to *måcåpat* or *macepat*; in Krama (High Javanese) also sometimes *monca-sekawan* = the four closest villages lying to the east, west, south, and north of a village, its neighboring village." Måcåpat are often interpreted as deriving from this kind of classificatory thinking, though it remains unclear how singing måcåpat is connected to this clustering of villages or cosmological arrangements, let alone its connection with Islam.

Gus Muwafiq's preaching on the connection between måcåpat and Islam follows this kind of classificatory thinking. In many of his sermons he suggests that måcåpat means reading the four elements (*barang papat*), which are the companions of our soul residing inside our body. Two of them reside in the left soul, called *jin qorin*, the other two in the right soul, a negative force called *kun afaldol*. These Islamic elements were Javanized, called *kadang papat lima pancer*. According to Javanese tradition, the kadang papat are four elements that accompany a baby in his/her birth: water, placenta, blood, and a gut attached to navel, the center (pancer). Gus Muwafiq concludes by interpreting the meaning of each name of the måcåpat songs, sequencing them as a portrayal of human life from birth to death:

> Thus, we are taught to sing the songs of life. The first song is called *Maskumambang*. What is *Maskumambang*? It means the floating (*kumambangé*) of the soul as it descends to the world. . . . Because Maskumambang means the descending of the soul, after [the soul] is residing inside the body for nine months, then people should experience the song *Mijil*. . . . After [the baby] comes out [is born, *mijil*], it becomes a child, the song for this is *Kinanthi*. The child should be given guidance through religion and ethics (*kanthi*). . . . After *Kinanthi*, then *Sinom* follows. It means becoming a young man (*enom*) who is very stubborn, who cannot be advised. The next one is even worse than Sinom, that is *Asmårådånå*. When you fall in love (*ketaman asmara*), even a cat's excrement tastes like chocolate. Thus, I should leave the young man to

> *Kyai*. . . . Whatever they become [in their lives], the important thing is that they are required to study religion. . . . After Asmaradana passes, the song *Gambuh* follows. It means boys and girls are in accord *(jumbuh)*, marrying and beginning family life. After Gambuh, the next song is *Dhangdhang Gulå*, meaning the meeting of cooking ware (*dandang*) and sweet taste (*gulå*, sugar), which imply experiencing the sweet and bitter in life. After Dhangdhang Gulå, the next song is *Durmå*. People should perform good deeds (*darma*) [for society] . . . Then the song *Pangkur* follows—the time comes to leave behind the world (*ngungkuraken*), . . . to find a clear path to unite with Allah . . . by praying in the mosque. If you do not leave behind the world by entering the mosque to pray, you will be followed by the song *Megatruh*. Your body and soul will be taken out. The final song is *Pucung*. Here you are wrapped with white cloth (*dipocong*), . . . to be brought to enter a narrow door. That's why an old man is called *buyut*, to be ready to enter the narrow door.[10]

In this example, Gus Muwafiq's oratory highlights the use of wordplay or etymological interpretation as a strategy to understand and teach about life and the importance of religion through the interpretation of the names of mâcâpat songs.

Alton Becker (1979) similarly describes the use of etymological interpretation as a strategy among puppeteers in Javanese shadow play to find the meaning of the word in question. Called *jarwå dhåsok* (also spelled *jarwo dhosok*, forced or imposed interpretation), etymologizing is not intended to discover the original meaning of the words, but is rather an attempt to discover the "intrinsic 'properties' of the letters, syllables, and, finally, the whole words" (Emerson 1948, 18, as cited in Becker 1979, 236). Becker explains this by giving an example of the English word *history*, which on the one hand (a) can be traced to the French *histoire*, Latin *historia* (a narrative of past events), Greek *istoria* (learning by inquiry), and then to *istor* (arbiter, judge), hence back in time to a possible Indo-European origin. On the other hand (b), *history* can be interpreted as deriving from "his" and "story," also referring to an account of the past, but from contemporary men's perspective, seeing women as having a secondary role in life. The question is not which one is correct or wrong, but what is the purpose of the etymologizing strategy. In reference to jarwå dhåsok in Javanese discourse, Becker suggests that the Javanese consider the second etymology, as in men's story, seriously as an important part of the text in order to understand the world. To do so he illustrates jarwå dhåsok in a narration by the puppeteer when stating the name of the giant king Niwatakawaca from the story of *Arjunawiwaha* (Celebrated Arjunå):

> The king who ruled this land is called Maha Prabu Niwata Kawaca. And his name means "one who wears armor that may never be pierced" which, in our time, means "one who could not be defeated," for he and all his people believed that and acted as if that were true. His name is made of three words, Ni, Wata, and Kawaca. Ni or nir is from the word *nirwana*. Nirwana means freedom from desires, freedom from the past, freedom from the future, something which cannot be likened to anything. In other words, the Great God. *Wata* means blind, without vision. Kawata comes from *Kaca*, which means mirror. Hence, his name, Niwatakawaca, means a mirror that is broken, a mirror which has lost its ability to reflect the truth, the Great God. When he was young he was called Nirbito, which comes from Nir and Bito. Nir is, as was said, from *nirwana*. Bito means afraid. For although all feared him, he was himself a coward and turned away from the Great God. (238)

We learn how the puppeteer was pervasively describing the character of the giant king as "one who could not be defeated" but also as "a mirror blind to nirvana." Although the former meaning is not the same as the latter, "both are true and both, along with the childhood name of the king, tell us about him" as a ruthless character (238).

Ultimately, this discussion helps us understand how meaning is constructed. It should be common knowledge by now that meaning is constructed based on context. As such, there is no absolute truth—truth is relative (Taylor 1978). This does not mean, however, that constructed meaning is meaningful only in a particular historical context. As social beings our lives are based on personal and institutional relations, both diachronically and synchronically. It is inaccurate, therefore, to think that certain meanings have certain historical affinities, for example, traditional, colonial, or contemporary (Day 2002, 2). If meaning is contextual, being is relational, thus "meaning assumes form through dialectical interrelationship in which co-implicates mutually constitute each other. The synchronic and diachronic dimensions of relationality reveal the inexhaustibility and perpetual revisability of meaning" (Taylor 1978, 41).

Here, inexhaustibility and revisability become the keys to understanding the construction of meaning. Jarwå dhåsok is a good example. In Becker's (1979) case, the forced etymological interpretation of the name Niwatakawaca by a puppeteer in a certain temporal, cultural, and mythological context emphasizes the identity of a ruthless king. It is probable that the same puppeteer will expand or create a revised jarwå dhåsok of Niwatakawaca in a new context. The variability of context can make jarwå dhåsok exhaustible and revisable. The revised jarwå dhåsok is determined by the perspective and creativity of the puppeteer in his response to a certain sociopolitical condition of the past and its subsequent impacts. The jarwå dhåsok can therefore be discussed from different vantage points. Because of the forced interpretive nature of jarwå dhåsok, the Javanese often refer to it as the result of *diothak-athik gathuk* (finding meaning by tinkering with words playfully), implying a lack of seriousness in its imposed etymological meaning. It may contain a kind of contemporaneous idealism.

The complexity of jarwå dhåsok and its inclusion in mâcâpat per Gus Muwafiq led me to search for the ontological Islamic meaning of mâcâpat. As I mentioned earlier, according to Poerbatjaraka (1952), the Islamic moralistic tale of *Koja Jajahan*, composed circa the seventeenth century, marks the earliest existence of mâcâpat. While subsequent mâcâpat songs were composed later during the Islam-Javanese period, I cannot find any early evidence of the interpretive Islamic meaning of mâcâpat. The earliest reference to such a meaning was made by Hardjowirogo (1952). While Hardjowirogo lists eleven mâcâpat songs and their characters, he does not provide any information about the relationship between mâcâpat and Islam, except the names of individuals who were believed to compose mâcâpat—Islamic saints.

As far as I know, the earliest interpretation of the connection between mâcâpat and Islam appeared in Poedjosoebroto (1978). The book does not provide the author's biography, however a speech on behalf of the director of religious information, Dr. Effendi Zarkasi, states that Poedjosoebroto was the head of PGAN Putri (Pendidikan Guru Agama, or School for Education of Female Religious Teachers). I cannot locate any other information regarding Poedjosoebroto's background, except that at the time this school was under the jurisdiction of the Indonesian Department of Religion, a subdivision of the *Direktorat Jendral Bimbingan Masyarakat Islam* (Directorate General of Islamic Social Guidance).

The book begins with a general introduction to wayang performance, its Indian-based story, and the artistic elements used in wayang (e.g., music, literature, carving, dance, etc.). Essentially, the book contains Poedjosoebroto's fascinating interpretation of the intimate relationship between Islam and wayang. He acknowledges that wayang existed in the pre-Islamic period and discusses how Islamic leaders made adjustments, additions, and alterations to it, appropriating its context, meaning, and musical accompaniment to align with Islamic perspectives. For example, he etymologizes the names of several main characters of wayang puppets deriving from Arabic words (137–80; I will discuss this example later in the chapter). In another example, a highly speculative proposition, Poedjosoebroto (22–32) suggests that Arabic scripts provided the

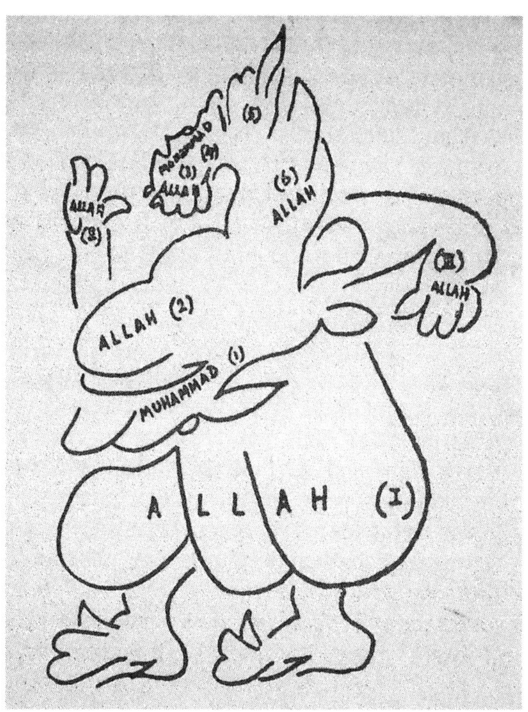

FIGURE 3.1 The Arabic words *Allah* and *Muhammad* in Semar's body.

basis for the carving of some wayang puppets. One example is Semar, a clown servant-cum-god, who always accompanies a knight from the Pandhåwå family. Poedjosoebroto provides a drawing of Semar, consisting of what he sees as the word *Allah* in Arabic script located in Semar's abdomen, chest, hands, head, and face, and the word *Muhammad* in the lower part of the stomach (see figure 3.1).

Returning to the topic of mâcâpat, Poedjosoebroto (194) gives new meaning to the word by slightly altering it to *mancapat*, suggesting a new meaning according to its three syllables: *man* derives from the word *iman*, which means "faith"; *ca* derives from the word *panca*, which means "five"; *pat* derives from the word *pathokan*, which means "pillar". Hence, mancapat refers to the five pillars of the Islamic faith: *shahada* (the confession of faith), *sholat* (daily prayer), *zakat* (giving alms), *puasa* (fasting during the Ramadan month), and *hajj* (pilgrimage to Mecca). This interpretation is highly suggestive because there is no direct relationship between the content of mancapat and the five pillars of Islam. Poedjosoebroto says the names of mâcâpat songs provide guidance or a method to deliver dakwah, which should be carried out patiently and in a good and orderly fashion. Next, Poedjosoebroto etymologizes and gives meaning to each of the names of the mâcâpat songs, as shown in the example:

MIJIL means "borne out": preaching should occur in the right time, place, and circumstances. The song was composed by Sunan Gunung Jati of Cirebon.

PANGKUR derives from the words *deviant* or *rearing*: preaching should not leave behind the Quran and Hadith. The song was composed by Sunan Murya.

KINANTHI derives from the word *accompany*: those who are blind to Allah's guidance should be accompanied and aim for a religious life. It is said that the song was composed by Sunan Giri and Sunan Kalijågå.

DANDANGGULA derives from *dandang* (hope) + *gula* (sugar, sweet), meaning "pleasant and delightful preaching will give hope for happiness." The song was composed by Sunan Kalijågå.

SINOM means "young leaf," such as the young leaf of a tamarind tree or fine hair of a woman's forehead. Happy preaching will lead one to absorb religion as an ornament of life full of hopefulness; a tree or fine hair of a woman's forehead.

ASMARADANA derives from *asmara* + *dana*, which means "love to give" or "glad to give": preaching that results in people who are happy givers, happy giving darma, helping people, without feeling arrogant. The song was composed by Sunan Giri.

MEGATRUH derives from the words *megat* + *ruh*, which means "avoiding bad thinking" or "restraining passion." The song was composed by Sunan Giri.

DURMA derives from the words *dur* + *ma*, which means "retreat from the five Ms" (*maksiat*, immoral behaviors): *madon* (womanizing), *minum* (drinking alcoholic drink), *mada* (consuming drugs), *main* (gambling), and *maling* (stealing). The song was composed by Sunan Bonang, the son of Sunan Ngampel.

MASKUMAMBANG means "floating gold," which means that Allah's teaching is beautiful and good, but heavy. But as long as those who seek for it aim to consecrate Allah, it will become light. The song was composed by Sunan Maja Agung.

PUCUNG means "death" (i.e., wrapped up with white cloth), "peak," "perfect," which means that the Islamic teaching aims for perfection in life in the world and hereafter. (195–200)

Comparing Poedjosoebroto's and Gus Muwafiq's interpretations of the mâcâpat song names, we see a different ordering of the names along with similarities in their meanings (table 3.2).

I do not know whether Gus Muwafiq read Poedjosoebroto's book. What is

TABLE 3.2

POEDJOSOEBROTO	GUS MUWAFIQ
Mijil, borne out	*Maskumambang*, the descent of soul
Pangkur, deviant or rearing	*Mijil*, borne out
Kinanthi, accompany toward religious life	*Kinanthi*, guidance through religion and ethics
Dhandhanggula, bitter and sweet in life	*Sinom*, young in life
Sinom, young leaf or fine hair, ornament of life	*Asmaradana*, falling in love
Asmaradana, love to give	*Gambuh*, male and female in accord (married)
Megatruh, restraining passion	*Dhandhanggula*, bitter taste and sweet Taste
Durma, retreat from the Five Ms	*Durma*, good deed
Maskumambang, Allah's teaching is beautiful	*Pangkur*, leave behind
Pucung, death	*Pucung*, death

clear is that interpreting måcåpat and gamelan as having an intimate relationship with Islam had become, by the mid-twentieth century, a vogue topic among preachers. Indeed, the connection between wayang and Islam similar in content to Poedjoesoebroto's book has appeared in a series of publications up to the present (e.g., Sugito 1984, Suseno 2009, Widadi 2016, Zarkasi 1977).

AFFECT, WAYANG, AND PENGAJIAN (ISLAMIC ORATORY/PEDAGOGICAL EVENT)

It appears that Gus Muwafiq's success as a preacher has largely stemmed from his skill in verbal artifice, the act of making ingenuous tricks, conceits, or puns to persuade others. It is a strategy to bring about effective listening in communicating affect. According to Millie (2017, 26, based on Besnier 1992, 162), "Affect is a result of the listening process that occurs 'in addition to the referential and social communicative functions of language,' and consists of the 'feeling, moods, dispositions, and attitude' that orator and audiences co-create during their interaction."

The affect might be humor, lively verbal delivery in affective structure—such as the imposed interpretation or jarwå dhåsok noted previously—music, or other kinds of proficiency that can restore the audience's fatigue, prevent audience disengagement, or move the audience to tears. In other words, affect is the result of the devices the preacher uses to bring about understanding of the culturally contextualized "intrinsic properties" of his ethical messages. This is in contrast to the *khutbah* preaching at Friday prayer in the mosque, the premise of which is to deliver poetic and performative dimensions of speech as effective properties of rhetoric for successfully delivering ethical subjects.

While I am in general agreement regarding the difference between contextualized and khutbah preaching, my current study of the use of wayang in dakwah shows that the function of affect in contextualized preaching is more than an interlude to remedy the audience's disengagement with the content of the preacher's oratory. In reviewing dakwah by a number of *kyai* (Islamic scholars) in Central Java, I found that wayang and music are not only presented simultaneously but are embedded permanently in the structure of the oratory. Some ulama transform a full wayang performance for preaching, while others incorporate only one or two episodes, which I will be discussing in the following sections. First, I briefly discuss the form of today's wayang performance and its relevance to dakwah.

As in most forms of cultural performance, wayang has developed through several iterations throughout history. As Indonesia was gradually globalized, particularly since the 1980s, wayang transformed in number of significant ways. While I discuss these developments in more detail in chapter 4, here I highlight a few key differences in contemporary performance from the wayang of the past. First, the light source of today's wayang performance is an electric bulb instead of an oil lamp. This change to electric light has brought about number of consequences. Wayang spectators have grown to prefer watching a puppet play not from the shadows of the puppets behind the screen, but from the side of the puppeteer and musicians. The electric light source has thus changed the two-dimensional wayang stage into a three-dimensional stage. In this regard, the electric light does not function to produce shadows, but as a spotlight similar to a Western proscenium stage. Second, the use of a sound amplification system is standard in today's wayang, usually with multiple large speakers and several microphones to amplify the sound of the puppeteer, singers, and many gamelan instruments. Typically, a puppeteer has his own crew to run the sound system.

Finally, the most distinctive innovation in today's wayang performance is the expanded scenes of Limbukan and Gårå-Gårå, the two scenes containing mostly humorous dialogue and musical interludes of lighthearted pieces. Appearing in the second part of the first major division of the play, the main puppet characters appearing in the Limbukan scene are two funny-looking ladies-in-attendance, a fat Limbuk and her skinny mother Cangik. Appearing in the first section of the second major division of wayang performance, the main puppet characters in the Gårå-Gårå are the clown-servant Semar and his three sons, Garèng, Pétruk, and Bagong. Considered as intermezzo, in the past the duration of each of these scenes was around fifteen minutes, and the dialogue included contemporary affairs. In contrast, in today's wayang performance, each of these scenes is expanded to more than two hours. The scene often includes the presence of guest stars, who may be singers of Indonesianized Western popular music, traditional dancers, comedians, or even VIP guests. The scene is full of dialogue between the puppeteer and *pesindhèn* (female singers of the gamelan) and the guest stars. The pesindhèn, wearing attractive attire and makeup, are seated on an elevated stage to the left of the puppeteer, facing the audience. In both Limbukan and Gårå-Gårå, the puppeteer may also act as an emcee, asking singers to sing songs requested by the audience.

It is worth noting that the rise of wayang dakwah occurred in the same timeframe as the development of contemporary wayang. That is, contemporary wayang and wayang dakwah developed at a time when Western capitalism was shaping economic development in Indonesia. The rise of wayang dakwah has been further spurred by shifts in the socioreligious climate in Indonesia, namely the deepening of Islamization, along with the global geopolitical environment post-9/11 (i.e., the September 11 attack, consisting of airline hijackings and suicide attacks against targets in the United States by the Islamic extremist group Al Qaeda).

The history of religio-intellectual contact and transformation between Indonesia and Islam has resulted in diverse interpretations of the religion in Indonesian communities. Indeed, scholars have had difficulty assigning Indonesian Muslims to any precise category, and often fail to account for the diversity of Indonesia's Islamic communities (e.g., Geertz 1960). This complexity is embodied in the performance practices of contemporary artists in Java. One particularly important facet of this complexity is the controversial nature of the performing arts in Islam (Al Faruqi 1985, Neubauer and Doubleday 2001, Shiloah 1995). In the Shari'a-oriented interpretation, music and figural imagery are seen as seductive arts, which compete with the Quran as a source of imaginative and visionary power (Hodgson 1977). In contrast, Sufi orders view music positively, and use it as a conduit to reach union with God (Trimingham 1971). Regardless of their definition, the performing arts in the Arabic world have historically been as vital to culture as the faith itself (Rasmussen 2010), though the controversy persists.

In twentieth-century Indonesia, this debate has been highlighted by Islamic sociopolitical organizations as they entered onto the cultural performance scene. For example, Muhammadiyah and Nahdlatul Ulama—two of the largest Islamic organizations in Indonesia—promoted two opposing views of the performing arts: the arts as an obstacle to Islam, and the arts as an embodiment of Java-Islam syncretism (Thoyibi et al. 2003). This disagreement reflects themes that are rife in Indonesian national politics. During one of Indonesia's worst cases of mass violence in 1965,[11] for example, thousands of people were killed, resulting in the decline of older, less formal institutions, which supported and sponsored cultural performances (Ricklefs 2012). In contrast, Suharto's New Order government lifted previous bans on Western popular culture (a ban that was launched by the previous Old Order government), while also adopting policy to develop and preserve traditional performing arts (Yampolsky 1995). The combination of these two elements—popular culture and traditional performing arts—has since become the premise for contemporary artistic performance.

The events of 9/11 are the other force that has led to the rise of dakwah activity in Indonesia. An increasingly contentious global geopolitical environment has marked life experiences in the post-9/11 world and has brought issues of religion and culture to the forefront of public consciousness. This is especially true for Muslim cultures, which have been repositioned in unprecedented ways. In Indonesia, the aim has been to portray the true and good nature of Islam.

One commonly held (if historically flawed) perception is the view of Islam as "against the performing arts." Indonesia, the largest Muslim country in the world—and recently a site of extreme Islamic resurgence both internally and externally—has many thriving artistic traditions, which call into question from some Islamic factions the role and use of the performing arts in contemporary Muslim cultures. This question has surfaced as a result of recent dialogue between the radical *wahhabi* movement (named after its pioneer, Muhammad Ibn 'Abd al-Wahhab) and the incorporation of Western-influenced, globalized cultural trends. Calling the recent penetration of Islamic radicalism a form of Islamic reformation in Javanese society, Ricklefs (2012, 392) began to see a negative consequence; that is, older art forms such as wayang and gamelan have been culturally denatured. If the art forms have revived, it is only because local authorities support them for the purpose of tourism or for marking unique local identities. Ricklefs goes on to say that even if Islamic reformers do not aim to discredit older art forms, eventually, modernization and the globalization of entertainment will lead to the abandonment of these art forms. Ricklefs's pessimistic opinion about the future of traditional performing arts deserves consideration, though it is too early to declare such a dramatic outcome.

What is clear is that wayang has inspired wide-ranging discourses. This is because wayang is a multimedia performance genre that commands colorful and deep historical, aesthetic, religious, and emotional affiliations (Anderson 1996, Arps 2016, Kayam 2001, Mrazek 2006, Grounendael 1985). The multifaceted meanings of wayang are sustained and enriched by the fact that in our contemporary world, wayang also illuminates (a) the effects of Indonesia's sociopolitical and religious conflicts, (b) Java's cultural encounters with global Western influences, and (c) Java's deepening Islamic conservatism. This assertion highlights the change, continuity, and expansion of the meaning, content, and context of wayang. Overall, wayang is shaped by intercultural and interreligious contact, which can create diverse fusions or hybrid cultural productions, and diverse reactions among scholars and audiences. The inclusion of wayang performance in Islamic dakwah is a case in point.

My interest in closely studying gamelan and wayang from an Islamic perspective emerged in 2010, when a group of ethnomusicologists specializing in Indonesian music asked me to contribute a chapter for a book on music and Islam in Indonesia. Although I had never before written an essay devoted to Islam and the performing arts, I ventured to write a chapter addressing Islam in the context and development of wayang and gamelan, roughly from the sixteenth to the twentieth century. The key point focused on the dynamic encounters between Islam and Javanese performing arts, one of the main themes of this book. I pursued my interest by doing archival and ethnographic research on this topic. Between 2014 and 2018, I carried out research intermittently in Java, investigating wayang kulit and wayang golèk performances, especially in the east, center, and west-north coastal area of the island where Islam began to spread in the sixteenth century. I also extended my research to the central and southwest interior of Java.

DAKWAH, HUMOR, AND POPULAR MUSIC: KI JOKO GORO-GORO[12]

In researching the use of wayang kulit for dakwah, I ended up studying dakwah by Kyai Mastur of Jepara and Kyai Abdurochim of Demak—the latter became the focus of my study. I attended a number of Kyai Abdurochim's dakwah and interviewed him once in his home. Here is an excerpt from my field notes (2017):

> My research assistants and I came to the event quite early. I saw technical persons were busy setting up and testing a very elaborate amplification system with several gigantic loudspeakers, configuring a computer projector, and positioning a pair of large screens. Soon thereafter, a group of musicians arrived, setting up their instruments—a drum set, electric guitar, keyboard, and a few gamelan

> instruments. They were testing the right mode of their mediated sounds. Then, to welcome the audience, the musicians played pieces from a genre of the most popular pop music: an Indonesian-Western-Indian-Middle Eastern musical hybrid called dangdut. This music is known for its very lively dance craze rhythm. The audience kept arriving, now reaching several hundreds. Segregated, men and women sat down on the mats, chatting, but detaching themselves from the rhythmically very animated dangdut. They were waiting for the arrival of Kyai Haji Abdurochim, a very charismatic preacher who is known for his use of wayang puppet play in his pengajian (Islamic oratory/pedagogical event); his use of wayang puppetry has led him to become one of the most popular preachers in Central Java, so much so that he is also intimately known by the name Ki Joko Goro-Goro (Ki is an address to an honorable person, Joko is a common name given to supposedly a vibrant man, and Goro-Goro is one of the humorous scenes in wayang performance).

At this juncture in attending Ki Joko Goro-Goro's pengajian, I was reminded of Pemberton's (1987) article, in which he discussed the performance of refined gamelan pieces at a wedding ceremony. His point was that refined gamelan pieces evoke a sense of detachment, a kind of invisibility assumed by the guests as they are seated, immobile on chairs, loyally following a predictable, step-by-step ritual of events. It struck me at the time that the guests' detached reception to gamelan that Pemberton discussed was no different from the invisible reception of the audience in the pengajian. However, the pengajian audiences were not listening to refined gamelan pieces, but to dangdut, a genre of popular music that has the power to inspire people to dance, or to make their hips move naturally. I asked myself, why did this dangdut fail to induce the audience to move their hips? Why were they responding to dangdut the same way guests respond to refined gamelan pieces at a wedding ceremony? The answer must depend upon the performance context of the music and how it is given meaning by its listeners. In other words, the meaning of music is heavily situated. Like gamelan for a wedding ceremony, dangdut in pengajian is part of a predictable ritual that makes people stay still, waiting for the main event to occur.

Unlike Gus Muwafiq's dakwah, music is an important component of Ki Joko Goro-Goro's pengajian, consisting of a Javanese-Western hybrid ensemble: a basic rock-band ensemble mixed with a few gamelan instruments. Featuring three or more singers, the musicians performed not only dangdut, but also a Middle Eastern style of *sholawatan* (singing to praise the Prophet Muhammad) and lighthearted gamelan pieces. This musical mixing, where musicians switch easily from one genre to another, is a feature of Ki Joko Goro-Goro's preaching.

Sometimes the music functions as an interlude; other times the music and its sung texts closely relate to the content of the oratory. In either case, the music contributes to the playfulness and lively atmosphere, the crux of Ki Joko Goro-Goro's dakwah.

Another feature of Ki Joko Goro-Goro's preaching is the inclusion of wayang scenes that present profuse humorous dialogues, including vulgar and pornographic jokes. In fact, the name Kyai Joko Goro-Goro, by which he is known, was adapted from the name of the scene Gårå-Gårå (also spelled Goro-Goro) in typical wayang performance (referenced earlier). Through the voice of a certain wayang character (Cangik), he explained how he adapted his preaching name:

Cangik (CN): True, isn't it, girl? Today's pengajian contains unusual things.

Limbuk (LB): What else we can do, Ma. Because if it doesn't contain unusual things, it cannot get sold.

CN: That's not true, girl. We forget our own history. What I have learned from reading is that it was *walisångå* who preserved culture through *budi daya*. *Budi* means etiquette; *daya*, finding a way to do it—the ways in which walisångå embrace people to come [to pengajian].

LB: Like that, Ma.

CN: Yes, girl. After I read the history of Sunan Kalijågå using wayang for proselytization, hence I used wayang too, with Semar, Garèng, Pétruk, and Bagong appearing. At that time, this scene was called Goro-Goro. That's why I am known as Kyai Joko Goro-Goro.

LB: What's its meaning?

CN: *Go* means *Golèk* (searching), *Ro*, *roso* (inner feeling). *Semar*, *Ki Samar*, *taspiranti sparimur samirun samir—tancut tali wondå* (prepare well for hard work), *Nålå Garèng* (Nala Gorin), searching; *Pétruk* (fatruk), one should be serious in carrying out *amar ma'ruf nahi mungkar* (carrying out what is right, forbidding what is wrong); the meaning of wayang is *owah-owahané tiyang* (the changing of human behavior). It was Sunan Kalijågå who was doing this teaching.

LB: Like that, Ma.

CN: Yes, that was the order of things. In the past, a proselytization employed the arts. That's why you don't say that art is *kharom* (forbidden by religion).

LB: That is true, Ma. Sometimes that's what people say, those who don't like what we're doing.[13]

The fact that he calls himself by the nickname Goro-Goro, the name of a humorous scene from wayang performance, indicates that his decision to incorporate wayang scenes in his pengajian was inspired by a particular segment of contemporary wayang performance. By the time wayang dakwah emerged, the expanded version of the Gårå-Gårå scene (as well as the Limbukan scene) has become one of the features of the play. The presence of three singers wearing heavy makeup and elaborate Islamic-style attire in Ki Joko Goro-Goro's pengajian also mirror the singers in contemporary wayang performance, though they are smaller in number. The singers also sat on the floor to the right of Ki Joko Goro-Goro, facing the audience, again maintaining the staging of contemporary wayang performance.

The use of an elaborate sound amplification system is standard practice in this kind of preaching. As in contemporary wayang performance, a microphone attached to a specially designed metal plate is hung around the neck of the preacher. Each singer has her own mic, as does each instrument in the ensemble. Typically, the sound system has four or more gigantic speakers, which are placed in the four corners of the audience space. In addition, four monitored speakers are placed in front of the stage, facing the preacher and musicians. It is not uncommon to film the event live, and project the image on a screen placed a distance from the stage for audience members seated further away to watch. The result of these elements is *spektakuler* (from English, spectacular), the adjective commonly used to describe contemporary wayang performance.

As discussed previously, Ki Joko Goro-Goro incorporates only one or two scenes of wayang performance into his preaching. This means that a wayang stage is set up during the oratory just before the wayang scene is about to start. Unlike typical wayang performance, Ki Joko Goro-Goro's wayang stage does not use a screen. It consists of only a piece of banana log, elevated by wood legs at two sides of the log. Wayang puppets are arranged in a screen located at the back of the stage but are used only as decoration for the backdrop. The stage has no wayang box. When Ki Joko Goro-Goro needs wayang puppets, his assistant takes them from the backdrop.

During his oratory, Ki Joko Goro-Goro mostly sits on a decorated chair, only occasionally standing up. When a wayang scene is about to happen, usually toward the end of the preaching, Ki Joko Goro-Goro gives a verbal cue to his assistants to pick up and move the wayang stage—the elevated banana log covered by a cloth, which says: ANGELELURI BUDHAYA JAWI MANGGA SAMI NGAJI NGUGEMI AGAMI MANUT TINDAK LAMPAHIPUN PARA WALI (Preserving Javanese Culture, Let Us Carry out Quranic Study to Embrace Religion, Following the Path of Wali).

The stage is placed in front of the preacher. Since the wayang stage does not use a screen, Ki Joko Goro-Goro's head and shoulders can still be seen by the

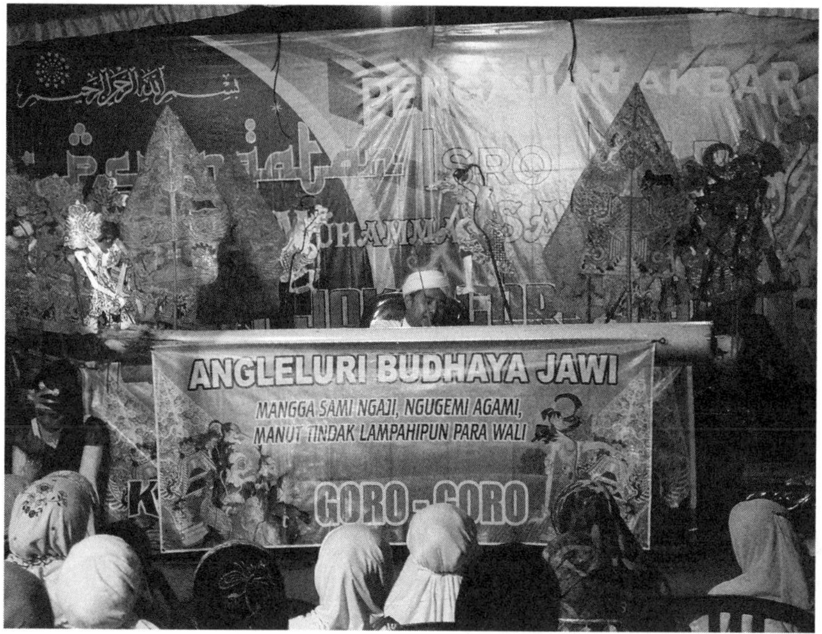

FIGURE 3.2 Ki Joko Goro-Goro's wayang stage. Photographed by Ciptono Hadi.

audience. Since wayang in dakwah is only an interlude (though it is permanently embedded in the structure of the preaching), the wayang stage is simplified. Consequently, the wayang concept is also simplified. In addition to the absence of a screen, there is only one banana log—as opposed to the two used in typical wayang performance (one positioned lower than the other), which create a three-dimensional theatrical space. Having observed Ki Joko Goro-Goro's oratory extensively, both live and on YouTube, it is apparent that his ability to move the puppets is elementary, though he has a sense of musical rhythm and is a good singer. In this sense, the materiality of the wayang becomes part of the artifice strategy—an ingenious trick through which the Hindu stories of wayang are Islamized.

What does this strategy yield for the audience? I begin to unpack this question by quoting narration from Ki Joko Goro-Goro's preaching:

> Janåkå appears with folded hands, praying *tahajjud* and *tajjad. If he appears before midnight, the puppeteer must be crazy.* Janåkå is from the word *janatuka*, [which means] "heaven." Arjunå is *arcunaja. Arcu* means "aspiration," *unaja*, "safe and sound." *Rojana sarjana*, **if you want to enter heaven, you need to see Puntådéwå [the oldest of the Pandhåwå brothers], who will lead you to**

> **righteousness and bring you to Quranic study (pengajian). After the pengajian, let us pray; crazy people are cured, since they carry out the five times of prayers. I-S-L-A-M means Isak, Subuh, Luhur, Asar, Magrib—the five times [of praying]. You will enter heaven. At half past one, you should stay awake.** *Let me emphasize, if you want to enter heaven, you should be awake at night; right gentlemen? [Audience: "Right!"] . . . Pee. You are awake just to pee; if not peeing [for yourself], peeing for [someone else].* **That is not the way to enter heaven. It is difficult to enter heaven, because there are many crazy people, many monsters; you can imagine their faces. They are gigantic spiritual beings. They are giving birth daily. This is the boss of Iblis, the king of satans**—*can you pick up that puppet closer to me? That Cakil is too far away.* **This is the boss. Every day, they are giving birth. They cannot die; they will die at the same time as the end of the world. Thus, today the world is full of spiritual beings. Careful! In the street, pengajian will be disturbed [by them], in the house, disturbed, in the street, disturbed.** *Cakil cannot die. Janaka kills him, but tomorrow there will be another Cakil again. Actually, his death is caused by stress, because one of his teeth is too long, therefore, he cannot spit. I am tired thinking about this [Cakil]. Ah, I am tired, but it is not time to stop yet. My army of Satan, you must disturb all pengajian. Satan, come here, Satan!*[14]

This wayang scene typifies the content of Ki Joko Goro-Goro's dakwah. The narration contains three main elements, indicated by different font styles: (a) the Islamization of Hindu characters (underlined), (b) moral teaching (bolded), and (c) humor (italicized). In the first case, Janåkå (also known as Arjunå)—the middle Pandhåwå brother in the Hindu *Mahabharata* epic—is explicitly Islamized. Janåkå is not doing meditation, but *sholat* (Islamic prayer), and his names (Janåkå and Arjunå) are given an Islamic interpretation. Puntådéwa, the oldest Pandhåwå brother, is treated as if he is an ulama: one should study the Quran with him. In the second case, the audience is reminded how difficult it is to enter heaven, since Iblis and Satan interfere. Lastly, the humor is self-explanatory: referring to peeing with the implication of a sexual act; jokingly asking someone to pick up the Cakil wayang puppet because it is too far for him to reach it; and a silly joke—Cakil's long teeth causing him stress and death.

Four clown-servants are the main characters in the midnight wayang scene whose content is full of humor and interludes of light music from which Ki Joko Goro-Goro adapted his name: Semar, Garèng, Pétruk, and Bagong. Javanese people believe these clowns were created by the Javanese, since they cannot be found in *Ramayana* and *Mahabharata*, the Hindu epics on which wayang stories are based. However, many Islamic proponents and preachers opine that the names of these clowns derive from Arabic words. Indeed, Ki Joko Goro-Goro did Arabicize the names of these clowns. This trend has led me to investigate the source of this interpretation. Poedjosoebroto's *Wayang Lambang Ajaran Islam* (Wayang as a Symbol of Islamic Teaching) (1978), which I mentioned earlier in connection with Gus Muwafiq's preaching, discusses in depth the relationship between wayang and Islam. Sure enough, he puts forward the following interpretation about the Islamic meaning of the names of punakawan: Semar is also called *Ismaya*, which derives from the Arabic *Asma-Ku*, referring to a symbol of worship or *mismar*, which means "nail" or "fix," symbolizing permanency. Garèng or Nala Garèng comes from the Arabic word *Khoiran*, which means "goodness" or "doing good" (Arabic *Amar Ma'ruf*). *Nala* is an Arabic word, which means "to receive." In Javanese, *nala* means "heart." Pétruk is from the Arabic word *Fatruk*, which means "hence leaving behind," meaning leaving behind badness, or in Arabic, *nahi munkar*. *Bagong* or *Bagho* means "conflict between thought and feeling, also between badness and goodness."

In addition to Poedjosoebroto's book, an earlier text by Sastroamidjojo (1964) provides a further interpretation in passages about Islam and wayang. On the names of pånåkawan, Sastroamidjojo quotes Moeso, explaining that the name Semar derives from the Arabic word *Simaroen*, which means "nail"; Nolo Garèng is a corruption of the Arabic word *Nala Korina*, which means "I acquire friends"; and Pétruk derives from *Fatruka*, "those who have left the mundane world." Bagong is not mentioned.

Noticing that Sastroamidjojo quotes Moeso, I traced the primary source. Moeso's interpretation was published in 1925 in the Dutch journal *Djowo*. In addition to the Islamic meanings of three pånåkawan quoted by Sastroamidjojo, Moeso gives Islamic meanings to Togog and Såråitå, two pånåkawan antagonists. *Togog* derives from the Arabic word *Togien*, which means "excessive or bad character," and *Såråitå* from *Sara jat*, which means "born in darkness." Moeso also explains the Islamized symbolic meaning of Gunungan and the scene Gårå-Gårå scene. To date, this is the earliest reference I have been able to find regarding Islamizing the names of pånåkawan. Moeso does not provide any references.

My Meeting with Ki Joko Goro-Goro

Before I had a chance to attend Ki Joko Goro-Goro's preaching, I had observed him only by video. I had long wanted to interview him, though my initials attempts through calls, text messages, and intermediaries were to no avail. Rumor has it that it is difficult for anyone to meet him. Eventually, my research assistant was able to contact his assistant, telling him that a professor from the United States was going to attend his preaching, and that the professor would like to meet him.

At the event, as my assistant and I waited patiently for Ki Joko Goro-Goro to start his oratory, rumor spread through the crowd that the preacher was stuck in traffic somewhere; hence his sermon would be late. After the musicians performed a few pieces, a public announcement came over the loudspeaker: "Attention to Professor Sumarsam, Kyai Joko Goro-Goro would like to meet you, professor." My assistant and I followed one of the event organizers to a house next door to meet Ki Joko Goro-Goro. It was only a brief encounter since he was preparing his preaching and running late because of his delayed arrival. I introduced myself and explained my desire to know more about his dakwah. Ki Joko Goro-Goro explained briefly how it was his calling from God to carry out the dakwah mission. Then, my assistant and I went back to the event, passing through a jam-packed audience. Surprisingly, this brief encounter led Ki Joko Goro-Goro to thank me for attending his preaching at the end of his oratory. The same thing happened when I attended his dakwah a second time. It was a year later, however, and I met him at his home attached to his pesantrèn.

In this second visit, after reminding him that I had previously attended his preaching, he began to tell us about a wayang story that he often incorporates into his program. The story, about Bimå searching for enlightenment, is one of the wayang stories known to contain Islamic teachings. I was familiar with it, as I had discussed it in my prior work (Sumarsam 2011). Notice in the following excerpt how Ki Joko Goro-Goro's version Islamizes the story. He begins by describing the character of Bimå, also known as Werkudårå or Bråtåséna:

> Werkudårå's weapon is his Poncånåkå nail. *Poncå* means five, *nåkå*, sharp. Those who pray five times will have strong faith, which cannot be shaken; sturdy is their faith. To those who are leaving behind the sholat (prayer), they will sit in the heat of hell. . . . Because he is diligent in carrying out sholat, incisive is Werkudårå's prayer; thus, his other name is Bråtåsénå, which derives from [Arabic] *baratasauna*, [which means] those who pray diligently. His countenance is clean and illuminating, so is his heart. . . . With sholat five times, Werkudårå will be able to open the gate of heaven for himself and for anyone who diligently practices sholat. Werkudara brought his parent from the cauldron of Condrådimukå to heaven. Those who practice sholat diligently can take out their parents from the cauldron of Condrådimukå to Surålåyå [the abode of gods].

It is interesting how Ki Joko Goro-Goro mixes and matches this Hindu character with Islam. Here is Ki Joko Goro-Goro's version of the episode of Bimå searching for enlightenment:

Werkudårå met his teacher Durnå. Although he had high *èlmu* [ascetic knowledge], he served Duryudånå [a protagonist of Pandhåwå]. Werkudårå was asked to enter the forest of Pålåsårå to destroy the Reksåmukå mountain. The mountain is like the wealth of the world, which is piled up at any time. There are people who don't give *zakat*, don't want to donate for Quranic study, don't want to move, working only [to accrue wealth]. The mountain was destroyed by Werkudårå. He encountered two twin giants, Rukmåkålå and Rukmåkå. They had large mouths to swallow anything. They said bad things and lies. Their wide eyes were not used for searching goodness. . . . Werkudårå defeated the giants. Then, he plunged into the ocean. . . . There he met Déwå Ruci in the form of a small boy. He asked about the location of the well of *tirtå* [sacred water] . . . Déwa Ruci ordered Werkudårå to enter him through the hole of his ear. Already living with *syariat* [religious law based on Quran and Hadith], Werkudårå entered the ocean of *tariqah* [spiritual path to achieve union with God] in search of a peaceful heart in the form of *haqiqah* [knowledge of ultimate reality], which would enlighten his search [to achieve union with] God. (Author's interview 2019)

In the wayang story, Rukmåkålå and Rukmåkå are the gods Indra and Bayu in disguise, testing the will of Bimå. Werkudårå's familiarity with syariat, then entering the world of tariqah and achieving haqiqah, are the high points of Ki Joko Goro-Goro's Islamizing of the Bimå story.

In the midst of Ki Joko Goro-Goro telling us the story, two guests appeared at the front door: "*kulanuwun* [may I come in]?" Surprised, he let the guests enter and sit down with us, asking them where they were coming from. They replied that they came from Semarang. Then, he continued to tell the story of Déwå Ruci. After completing the story, Ki Joko Goro-Goro asked the guests their purpose in coming to see him. One of them, who looked rather sick, explained that he had come to beg for Ki Joko Goro-Goro's advice. He had a lot of debt, which he could not pay back. He asked Ki Joko Goro-Goro for a "number." While I had no clue what the "number" referred to, Ki Joko Goro-Goro knew it right away. The guest was asking for a lottery number. After a pause, Ki Joko Goro-Goro continued telling the wayang story, but he quickly turned it into moral instruction addressed to the guest who had asked for the number. Among other things, he claimed that he knew the number, but could not reveal it because gambling leads us to hell, and so forth. Then, Ki Joko Goro-Goro asked his maid to bring out a meal, inviting us all to eat. Afterward, he went inside the house and came back with an envelope, which he gave to the guest, explaining to him that he must read the texts in the envelope a thousand times every day. Here we see that it is not uncommon for people to consider a kyai as both Islamic teacher and *dhukun*, a faith healer.

After the guests left, we continued our conversation. I asked him how often he rehearsed with his musicians. Given the kinds of interactions that occur between him and his musicians—which piece and genre of music to play (dangdut, gamelan, sholawatan), which song the singer should sing solo—I thought a rehearsal would be necessary. He answered that they did not rehearse, and only discussed the repertoire on the way to the event. This response was confirmed in my interview with the leader of his music group (August 2019). In that interview, the music director added that much of the learning that occurred among Ki Joko Goro-Goro and his musicians was done through listening to and watching cassettes or videos. In contrast, when I asked Ki Joko Goro-Goro from whom, how, and how long he had learned to perform wayang, his answer was *alahualam*, it was the wish of God. He did not elaborate.

In search of Ki Joko Goro-Goro's biography, I found a 2013 thesis written by Miftachul Ilmi of the Institute Agama Islam Negeri Sunan Ampel Surabaya. The brief biography of Ki Joko Goro-Goro provided in the following paragraphs is drawn from Ilmi's work. When Ilmi wrote his thesis in 2013, Ki Joko Goro-Goro was thirty-eight years old, indicating he was born in 1975. Ki Joko Goro-Goro's father passed away when he was six years old. He grew up under the supervision of his uncle, and studied religion in his uncle's pesantrèn in Sidorejo, a nearby village to where Ki Joko Goro-Goro was born in the village of Wonowoso. Aside from studying religion, one of the Ki Joko Goro-Goro's favorite activities was to watch wayang performances. He had his own collection of wayang puppets, and he liked to wear *blangkon* (a traditional Javanese hat). These are typically uncommon practices among young boys, especially those studying at pesantrèn. Ki Joko Goro-Goro soon became known for his ability to preach and deliver speeches, into which he incorporated wayang stories. To further his skills, he took a course designed for religious propagators (*mubalig*). His then went on to be educated at the Sekolah Tinggi Agama Wali Songo (the Islamic College of Wali Songo) in Semarang. Despite Ki Joko Goro-Goro's reticence to discuss the subject with me, from Ilmi's thesis it is clear that his interest in wayang began during childhood and persisted throughout his education as a preacher—indeed, it was a large part of what led him to fame.

Ilmi further documented Ki Joko Goro-Goro's incorporation and Islamization of wayang in his dakwah. Ilmi argues that Ki Joko Goro-Goro's use of wayang is method of *dakwah Bil-Hikmah*, that is, delivering words of truthfulness, honesty, and sincerity, which is supported by *dalil*, argumentation as mentioned in the

Quran. In this regard, wayang is considered a means to deliver religious messages through entertainment. In Ki Joko Goro-Goro's words:

> This dakwah of cultural art (*seni budaya*) is done as an encirclement (*perangkul*), not hammer (*pemukul*). The *mauidhotul chasanah bil hikmah* through art is beautiful and a blessing. What it means to preach with culture or budaya derives from *budi* and *daya*. Budi means to teach (*ngulangi*), daya to make an effort. This means to embrace people [to strengthen their religious piety] through wayang—wayang means the behavioral changing of people (*wahwahaning tiyang*). (Ilmi 2013, n.p.)

However, Ilmi does not delve into the kinds of humor and/or musical interludes Ki Joko Goro-Goro embeds in his dakwah, despite these being key aspects of his fame. The inclusion of humor, including bawdy and/or pornographic jokes, in a religious event raises questions of its appropriateness. How do we explain this intersection between religion, humor, and popular culture? The answer depends on how we define religion. On the one hand, religion can be defined as a formalized, organized system of beliefs, practices, and rituals designed to facilitate closeness to God; we can call this the traditional, formal, or official theological perspective. On the other hand, religion can be seen as those practices and rituals carried out by religious laity in their everyday lives, consisting of a range of activities, such as gift exchange, cremation, hymn singing, and other lived and practiced religious belief which may have religious significance or contain spiritual potency. People who are attached to the former (e.g., formal theologians) may dismiss or even condemn the use of popular culture or humor in a religious event (Forbes and Mahan 2005, Ray and Dempsey 2010, Rinallo et al. 2013). To them, the latter religious practices, and the combination of sublime experience with things aimed at consumers' secular consumption, is contradictory (Rinallo et al. 2013). Yet, this sacred-secular hybrid presentation is common in many socioreligious events in Indonesia and elsewhere in the world.

Studies of religion show that humor is often present, whether modest or bawdy, through physical or verbal expression. In chapter 1, I discussed a pair of court jesters, canthang balung, who perform all sorts of funny movements during the processional event to celebrate the life of Prophet Muhammad. In another example in Japan, Gerbert (2013) relays a story where the Goddess of Fertility shuts herself in a cave. Other gods try unsuccessfully to lure her to come out. Finally, another goddess of fertility succeeds in getting her to come out by "dancing on an upturned tub, stamping her feet resoundingly, 'pulling out the nipples of her breasts,' and pushing down her skirt to expose her private parts, causing the eight hundred myriad deities to roar with laughter" (55, based on Chamberlain 1981, 64).

Expectations about the need for reverence and what is an appropriate attitude have made people uneasy to talk about the presence of humor in religious practice. This is especially the case regarding humor in holy books. In Islam, humor appears in the Quran and in Hadith, the Arabic texts that delineate the definition of Islam. However, the interpretation of strict Islamic rules has caused humor and other joyful forms of expression (including music) to be viewed as the "unlawful enjoyment of worldly pleasures. Accordingly, even today they suffer from restrictions in traditionalist Muslim societies, while enjoying relative freedom in others" (Marzolph 1991, 178). Mir (1991) lists and describes a number of humorous episodes in the Quran. For example, in S. 27:17–18, Solomon, who understands animal languages, hears an ant instructing its companions at the approach of Solomon's army: "Ants, enter into your holes, lest Solomon and his troops should crush you, without being aware of it." Solomon, according to the passage, "smiled, breaking into laughter." He, too, must have seen the situation in a humorous light. (181–82).

Humor may create or contain paradox, ambiguity, incongruity, and inconsistency. Within these conditions, humor can teach us certain morals or practical wisdom. We can find this seemingly odd juxtaposition in the oratory of both Gus Muwafiq and Ki Joko Goro-Goro. The following examples show this kind of humor in Ki Joko Goro-Goro's oratory as well as illustrating his use of rhyme (in bold).

Bolongan-bolongan iki lho pinjere **doså** . . .	Our bodily cavities are the root of our sins . . .
Itungen lambe siji; irung loro, *telu*; *mripat* mripat loro, **limå** kuping loro = pitu.	Please count: the first is lip; second nose; third [and fourth] two eyes; fifth two ears = seventh.
Sing loro aku roh **nggoné**, ning ra ngerti **jenengé**.	These last two, I know where they are, but I don't know their names.
Iki alat sètan sing paling mandiiii.	These cavities are Satan's most powerful device.
Såyå ombå såyå gedhé nglakoni **doså**.	The wider the cavities the more they deliver sins.
Mula gusti Allah **ndadèknå bolongan sångå**.	Thus, Allah created nine of them.
Sing metu **såkå kånå** ora **ånå** sing énak, elèh Cangkem sing metu **åpå**?	What is coming out from them is nothing good, ah, all are gross bachin kabèh.

Alaaaah, gumoh, watuk, iler, *liak utah-utah*, uahhh ora ana sing énak.
Iki **ngandaknå** nèk jeroan iki bosokan nggo **doså**.
Irung sing metu **åpå**?
Upil, umbel, mimisen kuwi é ra énak kabèh.
Måtå, dolok, lodok emh ya Allah gusti ésuk-ésuk lèk mrèntèk kebaké **kåyå ngånå**
Kuping isiné **åpå**?
Cukil watu iki ora ånå sing ´nak.
Bolongan ngisor sing ngarep uyoh, lanang kadang metu santené.
Sing wédok, saos, kecap.
Sing mburi gedhang **gorèng**.
Wis ora ånå sing énak jan kåyå ngèné bosokan **kabèh**.
Iki lho nèk jenengan ajeng kementhèl, thik gembagus, kemakii åpå?[15]

What's coming out from the mouth?
Walah gumoh, cough, saliva, phlegm, vomit, ah, none is good.
This all shows that what's inside of us is rotten stuff, the place of sins.
What is coming out from the nose?
Snot, mucus, nosebleed, nothing good.
From the eyes, mussy stuff, oh my God, all is coming out everywhere in the morning.
What is inside the ears?
Ear dirt, nothing good.
The lower front cavity, pee, sometimes coconut, sing milk coming out from man.
From woman, ketchup sauce.
From rear cavity, fried bananas.
Ah, nothing good, all are rotten stuff.
That is what will happen if you are arrogant. Think about it.

This humor is clearly vulgar, but the beginning and closing sentences instruct the audience to interpret the "dirty" things that come out of the nine holes in the body as the root of sin. Hence, arrogance should be avoided. As highlighted throughout this discussion, the spectrum of the meanings infused through the use of pop culture and comic expression in ritual is wide ranging, and depends upon individual and collective contexts. As Ray and Dempsey (2010) suggest, pop culture and ludic expression are incorporated in ritual not only for temporary comic relief, but also for the social, religious, and psychological dividends they yield. This idea also applies to the songs and sung texts performed in dakwah for their effects on spiritual potency. As I show in the following sections, the formation and transformation of religiously charged potency is very complex and may involve contradiction and paradox.

"ILIR-ILIR": FROM A SONG OF POSSESSION TO ISLAMIC TEACHING

Lir-ilir lir-ilir, tanduré wis sumilir
Tak ijo royo-royo, tak sengguh pangantèn anyar.
Cah angon cah angon pènèknå blimbing kuwi
Lunyu lunyu pènèknå kanggo mbasuh dodotirå
Dodotirå dodotirå kumitir bedah ing pinggir
Dondomånå jrumatånå kanggo sébå mengko sore
Mumpung padang rembulané
Mumpung jembar kalangané
Sun surakå surak hiyo

The wind is drifting (*lir-ilir*),[16] the planted plan has fully grown.
All is green, as if it is newlyweds.
Hi shepherd, climb that starfruit tree.
Even though it is slippery, you do it.
It will be used for washing *dodot*[17] clothes.
Their dodot clothes, the batik (*kumitir*),[18] are ripped off.
Sew it, fix it, it will be worn for the afternoon's homage,
While the moon shines brightly,
While the space to play is wide,
Let's cheer, yay.

This text is from the children's song "Ilir-Ilir." I offer this translation, though I cannot understand the "true" meaning of the song, as the text is difficult to decipher. It is not uncommon for the Javanese to consider such texts—the text as a whole or phrases within it—as holding symbolic meaning. Like the diverse ways people interpret måcåpat and wayang, "Ilir-Ilir" has been given a variety of meanings.

As with other traditional children's songs, the composer of this song is unknown. In recent decades, as the text came to be interpreted with an Islamic meaning, Javanese Muslims have attributed the song to one of the walisångå, either Sunan Kalijågå, Sunan Giri, or Sunan Ampèl. There several versions of the melody, though most are similar, with one notable exception (as I later discuss): a version by the music group Kyai Kanjeng, which was founded by the prominent Islamic preacher Ainun Abdul Madjid (known as Cak Nun) of Yogyakarta.

I have not found any ethnographic works that trace the meaning of "Ilir-Ilir," though a review of blogs, newspapers, journals, and theses confirms that its text is interpreted widely as intimately connected to Islamic teachings and values. Take, for example, the version of the text that appears in the online journal of Nahdlatul Ulama (Saefullah n.d.), one of the largest Islamic political/social organizations in Indonesia:

Lir-ilir, lir ilir tandure wis sumilir.
Like watering a plant, Islam will become more fertile, since it is promoted by wali and *mubaligh* (Islamic missionary).

Tak ijo royo-royo, tak sengguh kemanten anyar.
Green is a symbol of Islam, like newlyweds, it draws the attention of society.

Cah angon-cah angon, penekno blimbing kuwi.
Shepherds refer to those who hold power, hoping they can shepherd people to embrace Islam. Starfruit has the shape of five angles, symbolizing the five pillars of Islam.

Lunyu-lunyu penekno, kanggo masuh dodotiro.
Though slippery and difficult, climb so that Islam can be found, enabling us to purify *dodot* cloth. Dodot is an attire worn by the royal leaders of the past.

Dodotiro-dodotiro, kumitir bedah ing pinggir.
Your attire and religion have worn down because they are mixed with animism and ritual, which contradict Islamic teaching.

Dondomono jrumantana, kanggo sebo mengko sore.
Broken religion should be fixed with Islam so that you can face God later in the afternoon.

Mumpung jembar kalangane, mumpung padhang rembulane
While you are still alive, you have a chance to repent to God.

Suraka surak horeeee
Be happy, you all are hoping to receive blessings from God.

The author adds the following comments: "Through this song, Sunan Kalijaga invited each Muslim, including royal leaders of the past, to embrace Islam, though in making Islam grow and fertile we encounter many difficulties and challenges. But if we are not giving up, God will endow us happiness" (Saefullah n.d.). Compared to my translation at the beginning of this section, this text is more interpretive than strictly a translation, pointing to the song's idealistic Islamic value in promoting the religion. This is further apparent in the interpretation of "Ilir-Ilir" offered in the newspaper *IslamPos* (Saputra 2016):

Lir-Ilir Lir-Ilir.

The song is started with ilir-ilir, which means "wake up," "live," or "be aware." What is needed is to awake your soul, your conscience, or your thought. There is also an element of wind here, meaning the way to feel alive should involve the moving of air, hence ajakan to dzikir.

Tanduré wus sumilir, Tak ijo royo-royo tak sengguh temantèn anyar.

The dzikir chant causes the tree to become green and beautiful. The tree refers to anything which is beneficial to us. Temanten anyar (newlywed) might mean Javanese kings who started to embrace Islam, who are only at the beginning level of devotion, just like the newlywed.

Cah angon cah angon pènèkno blimbing kuwi.

Why *cah angon* (shepherd boy)? Because it is the shepherd who can guide us to the right path. Why *blimbing* (star fruit)? Because the color of star fruit is green and it has five sides, indicating the five pillars of Islam. Why *pènèkno* (to climb)? This is an instruction from wali to Javanese kings to instruct their subjects to embrace Islam.

Lunyu-lunyu pènèkno kanggo mbasuh dodotiro.

Though with great difficulty, we must carry on washing our clothes, referring to the clothes of *taqwa* (piety).

Dodotira dodotiro kumitir bedah ing pinggir.

The clothes of the piety should be cleaned; the bad ones should be thrown away. Put together beautiful clothes.

Dondomono jlumatono kanggo sébo mengko sore.

This is a message from wali that eventually you'll die and meet the Creator to justify your deeds. Hence, you should perfect your Islamic faith.

Mumpung padang rembulané, mumpung jembar kalanganné.

Wali advises us to perfect our faith when we have the opportunity to do it, as long as we are still alive.

Ya surako surak hijo.

Greet these callings with cheers of gladness. Practice them according to Islamic law as a sign of happiness.

Again, the author does not translate the text, but interprets it to support Islamic teachings and values. This strategy is similar to the practice of jarwå dhåsok, the imposed interpretation of word(s) discussed previously.

It is important to note that originally, "Ilir-Ilir" was an old, lighthearted children's song (I will say more later about the history of this song). Nonetheless, it is interesting that the "true" meaning of the text is difficult to decipher, so it is subject to diverse interpretations. It is as if one is trying to interpret the uninterpretable: why would a song text with hidden/symbolic meaning be sung to a lighthearted melody? Why are Javanese Muslims eager to interpret the song text as having an intimate relation to Islam, as well as to attribute one of the walisångå, either Sunan Ampèl, Sunan Kalijågå, or Sunan Giri, as its composer? Combined with the exploration of the genesis of "Ilir-Ilir," these questions are crucial to our understanding how individuals, a group of people, or society gives meaning to music.

"Music is booth deeply rooted and transient," Slobin (1996, 1) aptly states. As will be apparent later, "Ilir-Ilir" is deeply rooted in a certain original usage and context, but it then "dissolves into space while simultaneously settling into individual and collective memory" (1) to be transformed to a different meaning and context. Looking at the use of "Ilir-Ilir" in the context of Islamic preaching in contemporary Java, I suggest that it is connected to the rise of the Islamic interpretation of traditional songs and song texts in the context of particular sociopolitical circumstances. In this regard, the Islamization of Javanese song and the performing arts in general has happened as a consequence of the rapid development of dakwah activity during President Suharto's New Order government, especially starting in the 1970s.

The term *Orde Baru* (New Order) was created by Suharto's regime. It represents the self-naming of a new regime with a promise for a new way to govern the nation after the fall of the previous Sukarno regime, which the new regime called *Orde Lama* (Old Order). In 1965, one of the most horrible events in Indonesian history happened: the fall of the Old Order government allegedly caused by a thwarted communist coup d'état. It began with the killing of five generals by a group of military officers from the air force, who were later linked to members of the Communist Party by a certain faction of the army led by General Suharto. This series of events led to bloody conflicts throughout Indonesia aimed at exterminating the communists and their allies by killing thousands of members of the party. This led to the rise of the New Order government with Suharto as president.

It is well-known that governments in Southeast Asia have vested interest in the shape and survival of their traditional performing arts (Lindsay 1995). Indonesia is no exception. This applies to both the Old Order and New Order regimes, although Suharto's personal involvement in the arts was not as deep as Sukarno's. The cultural and political context has shaped national government policy and structure. During the New Order period, two modes of sociopolitical development occurred. First, the New Order's government policy encouraged the development of the traditional performing arts. Noticeably, the government paid special attention to preserving, fostering, and developing the performing arts through all sorts of activities, including organizing festivals and competitions.

At the same time, the government was working to maintain good relationships with Islamic organizations. These combined to increase the linkage between the traditional arts and Islam. The Islamic interpretation of the song text of "Ilir-Ilir" and the publication of Poedjosoebroto's (1978) *Wayang Lambang Ajaran Islam* (Wayang as a Symbol of Islamic Teaching) are two of the best examples of the fruits of this development.

President Suharto's autocratic style of governance, combined with widespread corruption and a global economic crisis, led to his resignation and the downfall of the New Order government in 1998, after three decades of his presidency. Subsequent regimes have led Indonesia toward a more democratic style of governance, allowing the voices of the masses to be heard. This period is known as *Reformasi*, during which a significant number of sociopolitical, religious, and cultural organizations developed. These organizations have often critiqued the government and society in general. It was in this context that Islamic dakwah activity experienced rapid growth, hence the birth of the dakwah using gamelan Kyai Kanjeng founded by Emha Ainun Nadjib (Cak Nun). Mixing gamelan, Western, and Middle Eastern instruments, Kyai Kanjeng provides the musical interludes that support Cak Nun's oratory. The ensemble focuses its performance on the Arabic style of sholawatan, a song praising the Prophet Muhammad.

One of the signature sholawatan pieces Cak Nun performs is "Ilir-Ilir," though with a newly composed melody for the original text. Rasmussen (2005) describes the medley in Cak Nun's sholawatan performance, in which "Ilir-Ilir" alternates with the style of "Sholawat Badar," sung to the same melody, with *Mawwal* (a nonmetric modal improvisation of prayer) as an interlude. Here, I quote Rasmussen's explication, including the texts and translations of "Ilir-Ilir," "Mawwal," and "Sholawat Badar." Note that Rasmussen identifies the melody of "Ilir-Ilir" as a Javanese song that everyone knows from their grandmothers; as I will explain, this is not the case.

> An archetypal example of the work of Kiai Kanjeng and Emha Ainun Nadjib is the piece-Ilir-ilir, a gending dolanan, or traditional Javanese song that "everyone knows" from their grandmother. The lyrics in the Javanese language (even more localized than the Indonesian national language) are attributed to Wali Sunan Ampel, one of the original nine prophets (Wali Songo) that brought Islam to Indonesia. The melody, too, is Javanese as opposed to Arab, a sound that is reinforced by the accompanying gamelan instruments. The central section of Ilir-ilir features the Arab sound of global Islam in language, melody, scale, and accompaniment. It is a solo supplication by Emha himself singing in Arabic and in the Arab style of a mawwal, a nonmetric modal improvisa-

tion, accompanied by drone. The mode is maqam Nakriz with its distinctive augmented second between the third and fourth degrees (for example C, D, E-flat, F-sharp, G.) The timbre, ornamentation, and phrasing are also derived from Arab musical practice. Furthermore, his pronunciation is laced with just a touch of tajwid, the system of rules in Quranic recitation that govern pronunciation, accent, duration, and elision of syllables within the sacred text. His solo supplication is followed by the very popular Arabic-language song in praise of the prophet Muhammad entitled Sholawat Badar, but with the same Javanese Ilir-ilir tune. (82)

JAVANESE TEXT FOR *LAGU DOTANAN* (CHILDREN'S SONG) "ILIR-ILIR"

Ilir-ilir tanduré wus sumilir	The crops are blowing in the wind
Tak ijo royo-royo tak sengguh temantèn anyar	So very, very green, like newlyweds to me
Bocah angon pènèkna blimbing kuwi	Herder boy, climb that star fruit tree
Lunyu-lunyu pènèken kanggo masuh dodotira	Quickly climb it, to wash my robe
Dodotira kumitir bedhah ing pmggir	The robe's hem is torn at the edge
Domana jrumatana kanggo séba mengko soré	Ply the needle, sew it up, for the great occasion tonight
Mumpung gedhé rembulané, mumpung jembar katangané	Now, while the moon is full and the yard is wide
Ya suraka surak iyo	Shout "hooray!"

Translation by Marc Perlman

"MAWWAL"

Allahu munaghfirlanaa, Ya Ghaffaar.	God is forgiving, oh forgiver.
Allahu munaflahlana abwaabar-rahmah.	God is beneficent to us. Doors of mercy,
Allahu munaflahlana abwaabalbara-kah	Doors of blessing, doors of strength, power, doors of pardon.
Abwaabalquwwan, abwaabal aafiyah waabwaabalkahiraat.	God is forgiving, oh forgiver
Allhummaghfirlanaa Ya Ghaffar	

Rough translation by John Eisele and Anne Rasmussen

"SHOLAWAT BADAR"

Shalaatullah Salaamulah	Prayers of God, Blessings/the good things of God
'Alaa Thaaha Rasuulilillah	Upon Taha (a Sura of the Quran) the prophet of God
Shataatullah Salaamullah	Prayers of God, Blessings/the good things of God
'AlaaThaaha Rasuulililah	Upon Taha (a Sura of the Quran) the Lover of God
Shalaatullah Salaamulah	We have arrived at the saying of the "bismillah"
'Alaa Yaasin Habiblillah	And the peaceful one/this the prophet of God
Tawassalna bi bismillah	And all the strivers toward God
bil haadi Rasuulillah	With the family badri (name/the moon) oh God
Wa kulli mujaahidin lillah	With the family badri (name/the moon) oh God
Bi ahlilbadri ya Allah	Oh God preserve/make safe the community
llahi sallimil ummah	From revenge
Mlnat afaati wannikmah	And from woe and from obscurity
Wa min hammin wa min ghummah	
Bi ahlil badri yaa Allah	

Rough translation by John Eisele and Anne Rasmussen

It is not far-fetched to suggest that Kyai Kanjeng composed a new melody for "Ilir-Ilir" in order to match the religious style of sholawat in general (see figures 3.4 and 3.5). Cak Nun acknowledged that he changed the original melody of the song, and changed its tuning system from sléndro to pélog, around 1996–1997 (personal communication through Hairus Salim, July 2020). Toto Rahardjo, one of Kyai Kanjeng's musicians, confirmed Cak Nun's acknowledgment, adding that the original melody was totally changed, accompanied by a new musical arrangement.

Notably, the medley of songs on which "Ilir-Ilir" and "Sholawat Badar" center express Cak Nun's idea of "Indonesia's flight from darkness," as he "speaks to the crisis of faith among the Indonesian people." This is confirmed by the title of his VCD that contains "Ilir-Ilir," *Berhijrah dari Kegelapan* (Flight from Darkness, Rasmussen 2005). The inclusion of the Arabic "Mawwal" and "Sholawat Badar" songs is meant to strengthen the Islamic modality of his message.

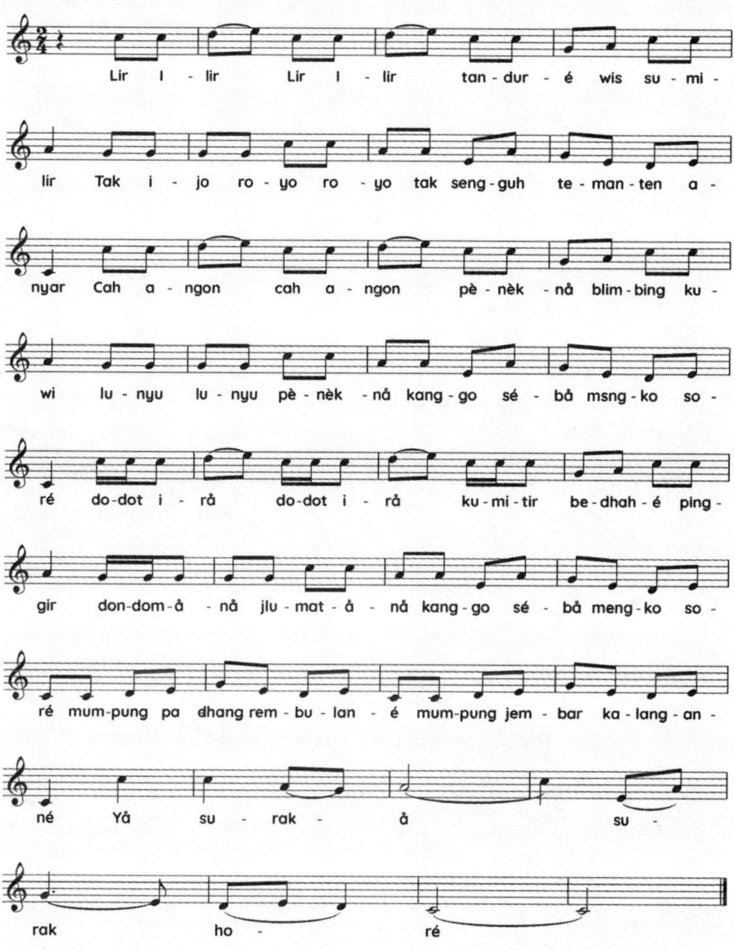

FIGURE 3.3 The song and lyrics of "Ilir-Ilir," *sléndro*. Transcribed by the author.

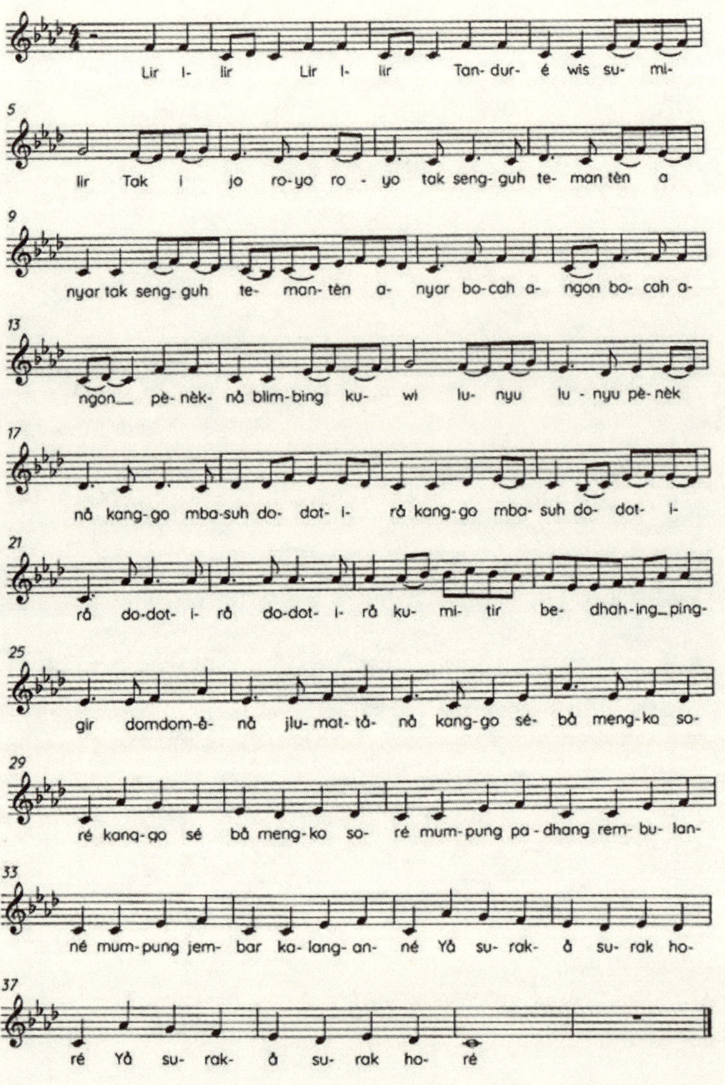

FIGURE 3.4 Kyai Kangjeng's version of "Ilir-Ilir" Sholawatan. Transcribed by the author.

It is important to note here that Cak Nun knows well the original melody of "Ilir-Ilir." In fact, before he and Kyai Kanjeng composed a new melody and arrangement for the song, he sang "Ilir-Ilir" in its original melody in the sléndro tuning system. He sang the song as part of an oratory titled "Renungan Ilir-Ilir." Opening it with a score of questions pertaining to the crisis of the past and what to do in the future, the speech was full of introspection and retrospection about the past and the future Indonesians must contemplate. He offered solutions by asking his listeners to enter the world of "Ilir-Ilir." He then sang the original melody of the song, one or two lines at a time, followed by his interpretation and comment of their meaning. Here is an example of the beginning of the oratory.

> Lir ilir lir ilir tanduré wus sumilir, tak ijo royo-royo tak senggo temantèn anyar.
>
> It is as if only today Kanjeng Sunan Ampèl tells us about ourselves, about everything we have experienced, but we aren't able to understand it. It has been five centuries since he sang the poems, but there is no guarantee we will understand them. In fact, his words tell us about the A B Cs of our life, making us not confused about our history from one day to another. It is about the history of a nation whose peak of destruction lay in its inhabitants, who are not able to acknowledge that the destruction has been indescribable.
>
> "Wake up from your death," says Sunan Ampèl. "Recover from your decades of unconsciousness; wake up from your comfortable, long sleep." This nation is really a piece of heaven. It is as if once the heavens leaked, spraying prosperity and beauty, forming glorious Indonesia. You can plant all kinds of seeds of prosperity on top of its highly fertile soil. It is not possible to find God's living being hungry in the middle of green lands consisting romantically of rows and rows of islands. It is even possible for you to carry out and celebrate a newlywed of development, which you can achieve more than what other nations anywhere can achieve. But we haven't been thanking God for His mercy in giving us a piece of heaven. We have wasted the gift of God through planting injustice and harvesting greed.[19]

Here, Cak Nun contextualized "Ilir-Ilir" within the era of Reformasi, the era full of challenges. What is relevant to our discussion in the following sections is that Cak Nun knows well the origin of the melody of "Ilir-Ilir": he sang each line of that melody (although in a nonmetrical way) before he gave his interpretation of the lines.

From the Royal Interpretation to the Folksong of Possession

In light of the various interpretations of "Ilir-Ilir" and the use of the song as a powerful sociopolitical, religious, and cultural message, a question regarding the original performance context of "Ilir-Ilir" lingers in my mind. We know that "Ilir-Ilir" has been discussed in terms of its intimate relationship with Islamic dakwah, and the text of the song has been subject to diverse interpretations, but its original meaning is tough to pin down. In search of older references to "Ilir-Ilir," I came across the 1913 volume *Serat Raryå Saråyå*, written by a learned member of the royal court of Surakarta, Kangjeng Pangeran Haryå Kusumådiningrat, with additional information about the melody written by Dutch scholar D. Van Hinloopen Labberton. This is the oldest Javanese reference to "Ilir-Ilir" I have found. Written in Javanese script, the section on "Ilir-Ilir" includes the text and its meaning. As you see in table 3.3, the court elite perspective colors the interpretation:

Kusumådiningrat's interpretation is not easy reading; it contains abstract ideas, symbolism, and aspiration, all the while reflecting his elite/royal perspective. Notably, references to Islam are absent from the interpretation, as are links to other older Javanese references. Instead, this interpretation suggests a very different perspective than its Islamic interpretation today.

In subsequent research, I found another reference to "Ilir-Ilir," written by Totilawati in 1974, which shows the song as one in a series accompanying the children's ritual play *Nini Thowong* or *Nini Thowok*. This play involves the use of a female effigy, whose head is a coconut shell mounted on a basket (the body). The following passage offers my translation of Tutilawati's brief essay, which appeared in the monthly Javanese magazine *Jayabaya*:

> Usually, *Nini Thowok* is performed during the full moon, between the tenth and fifteenth [of the Javanese month], after *ngisa* prayer, hence about 9:00 p.m. However, its preparation began in the afternoon. Toward the time of the *magrib* prayer, the teenage girls who would present the play got together, bringing stolen things to make the Nini Thowok effigy: *siwur* or *jébor* (water dipper made of coconut shell), *kukusan* (rice steamer), *gandhik* (mortar for grinding herbs or spices), *ublik* (small oil lamp), etc. Commonly, the leader of the ritual was an old lady, who was appropriately in the position of grandmother. First, the available stuffs were used to construct a human-like figure. The water dipper was smeared with white powder, reddened (as lips), and smeared with eyebrows. Then, the incomplete effigy was brought to a place

TABLE 3.3 *Serat Raryå Saråyå*

Hilir ilir, Tandurè wong semilir Tak ijo royo-royo Dak sengguh temantèn anyar	Being awakened, [those who grow up as] members of the royal blood look as if radiance illuminates from their faces, as if they have received sacred knowledge.
Cah angon pènèken blimbing kuwé Lunyu-lunyu pènèken Dienggo ngumbah dodotira	People who observe the way of life, to achieve the final judgment of life, though hard, its way has been provided, need to perfect and widen the apparatus [of life].
Dodotira kumitir bedhah pinggiré	You should choose dignified clothes, because the golden painted edges of the cloth, called *balenggi*, which should be fixed, can only be worn by the high-ranking members of the royal elite, the *Kaliwon* rank or above.
Domana jlumatana Dinggo séba mengko soré	We should make an effort to unite, carrying out our responsibility in life until we die. This is because *soré* [afternoon] is at the end of the day.
Mumpung Mumpung gedhé rembulané mumpung jembar kalanganné suraka surak ngayo	This all should be done while you're still young; do it with happiness.

Composed by Kangjeng Pangéran Haryå Kusumådiningrat in Surakarta, with added information about the melody of the piece by D. Van Hinloopen Labberton in Batavia. Published by the Widya Pustaka Organization and sold in the Jamurdwipa bookstore in Bogor, 1913.

believed to be haunted, such as an unused well, underneath a large banyan tree, or even the cemetery. There, old people burned incense, and the one who was charged to lead the ritual read a prayer. During the time of Queen Pembayun, the prayer was "Please let me play the Nini Thowok," followed with another prayer: "Please heavenly maiden come down to the earth, entering into this effigy," etc. While the leader read the prayer, the effigy Nini Thowok stayed laying down on a *tampah* (winnow, a wide tray of woven bamboo). Repeatedly, the teenage girls thickened the powder, applied lipstick, and strengthened Nini Thowok's broad band (bound around the stomach), making it very pretty. After completing the prayer, the sleeping Nini Thowok was left there.[20] (Totilawati 1974, as cited in Ras 1979)

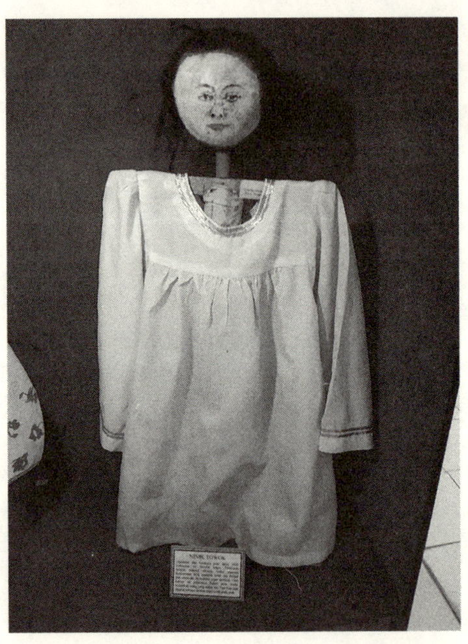

FIGURE 3.5 The effigy of Nini Thowong. Reproduced courtesy of Zaenul Fattah.

Subsequently, the teenagers sang a short song. The leader of the ritual prayed, asking the ancestors to help the village to invite a celestial nymph. Then, a short song was sung to accompany the procession of the effigy. Four teenagers held the effigy. After the completion of the procession, a series of songs were sung to invite *widadari* (celestial nymphs) to join the ritual. "Ilir-Ilir" was sung to call the wind to come. Other songs were sung to invite the nine widadari, to accompany the widadari putting on makeup, and so forth. The teenagers sung a livelier song, joined by the audience, and stood the effigy up. At this time, the audience teased the effigy, making out as if the effigy was alive, and chasing it. (Totilawati 1974, as cited in Ras 1979)

Totilawati does not mention an association between "Ilir-Ilir" and Islam. In fact, in a much older report of the same ritual play, Hurgronye (1906, 206) explains that the Islamic orthodoxy relegated its original superstitious nature to obscurity. Referring to the same play but with a different name, *Brendoeng*, Hazeu (1901) reported that he witnessed it in Semarang for the purpose of calling for rain. Hazeu cited Raffles's book *The History of Java* (1817), stating that the effigy was male and moved by two children to the music of gamelan; Raffles calls it *Brindung*.

Faith and Knowledge in "Ilir-Ilir"

The point I want to make is that the *Nini Thowong/Nini Thowok* play has been in existence for at the least two hundred years; its original meaning is different than what Cak Nun's Kyai Kanjeng intended. This transformation from one meaning to another in the performing arts is not uncommon. Cak Nun has a particular explanation of this transformation according to his theological convictions. As he stated in a recent sermon, there is a clear distinction between *ilmu* (knowledge) and *iman* (faith): "If there is something you can approach, touch, analyze scientifically (*secara ilmu*), there is something else larger, which can be approached not with knowledge, but with faith." In his discussion of Idul Fitri (the celebration after the Ramadan fasting month), he defines *fitri* as a supranatural (*ghoib*) phenomenon. Culturally, in Indonesia, the day of Idul Fitri is the time when family and friends apologize to each other for what they have done wrong. Cak Nun thinks this tradition only scratches the surface of the meaning of fitri. The deeper meaning of fitri is apologizing to God. "If you want to pass the gate of the supranatural world, you don't do it with argumentation and knowledge. [Rather], you should do it by believing in God, acceptance (*ikhlas*) of God. Then you should add a promise that you should always pray (sholat) so that you will be listed in the online God's large computer. Then you should always offer help around, *sodhakoh*."

I suggest that Cak Nun's line of thought can be applied to theological experience in listening to or singing "Ilir-Ilir." On the one hand, "Ilir-Ilir" can be approached through cultural analysis, as what I and others have done. On the other hand, Cak Nun suggests that listening to or performing "Ilir-Ilir" should be considered a spiritual experience allowing devotees to enter the supranatural world. Here, we are encountering a complex discourse about the interaction between faith and knowledge, the subjective and the objective experience. For the former, one can enter a supranatural world during the Fitri or by listening to "Ilir-Ilir." However, as a preacher Cak Nun is compelled to give a reason for subjective experience by contextualizing it (in the case of "Ilir-Ilir") with the crisis the Indonesian must encounter, in the past and at present. I see the dynamic, interactive, and complex dialogue between subjectivity and objectivity in Cak Nun's commentary as following Hegel (1977). Taking subjectivity as the point of principle, Hegel explains that beauty and truth present themselves in feelings and persuasions, in love and intellect—subjectivity and objectivity in dialogue.

> The intellect scrupulously distinguishes the objective from the subjective, and the objective is what is accounted worthless and null. The struggle of subjec-

> tive beauty must be directed precisely to this end: to defend itself properly against the necessity through which the subjective becomes objective. That beauty should become real in objective form, and fall captive to objectivity, that consciousness should seek to be directed at exposition and objectivity themselves, that it should want to shape appearance or, shaped in it, to be at home there—all this should cease; for it would be a dangerous superfluity, and an evil, as the intellect could turn it into a thing (*zu einem Etwas*). Equally, if the beautiful feeling passed over into an intuition that was without grief, it would be superstition. (57)

If Cak Nun had not discussed "Ilir-Ilir" in the context of contemporary Indonesia, the whole exercise would have been no more than superstition.

The important point emerging from this discussion is the complex interaction between objectivity and subjectivity. It would be difficult to pin down which comes first. Cak Nun began by objectifying "Ilir-Ilir" ("let us enter the world of 'Ilir-Ilir,'" he says) in contemplating the present and past issues of Indonesia, and then subjectified it for religious experience by composing a new melody for it in the sholawatan style.

Further Implications and Recapitulation

This discussion of "Ilir-Ilir" has illustrated the dynamic way that meanings of the song are formed and transformed in relation to the context of performance. In a more recent analysis, Chan (2017) adds a further layer of complexity, tracing the possible origin of *Nini Thowong* to the tradition of spirit-basket divination associated with the Chinese goddess Zigu from as early as the fifth century. In this regard, Chen leads us to think not only about the migration of Chinese people to Indonesia, but also about their contribution to Indonesian culture and society, and the issue of Sinophobia. Originating from South China, the Chinese migrants brought their cultural traditions with them and introduced them to Indonesia, and they were subsequently developed and hybridized with Indonesian culture.

Indeed, "Ilir-Ilir" has gone through a long historical development. From a children's song used in a ritual possession, to a call for rain and to ward off evil spirits, it turned into a sholawatan song used to strengthen the Islamic faith of devotees. The process did not stop there. As tourism became an important project of the state at the local and central levels, *Nini Thowong* has been commodified for tourist consumption, for example, by the group Nini Thowong Sando Budoyo in the village of Grudo Parangrejo in Yogyakarta province, which Chen discusses.

These circumstances have inspired contemporary carriers of *Nini Thowong* to innovate the play, making it more attractive to tourists, adding gamelan to accompany the songs, and changing the simple traditional clothing of the effigy to more attractive modern dress. This is not the place to elaborate on the Chinese and tourism connections of "Ilir-Ilir" and the *Nini Thowong* ritual play. The key point is the continual revision of meaning in music and the performing arts through different historical eras and socioreligious contexts.

Indeed, this is the key point of this entire chapter. It is about change and the variability of context throughout history, which has led to the revision and multiplication of meanings. Music and the performing arts can have multiple meanings because they have been constructed on the basis of interplay between simultaneous voices and cultural texts, each of which has a different perspective. When all meanings are combined, they bring about harmonized and/or contested simultaneity, generating multiple meaning possibilities to be received by multiple audiences in multiple ways. "Ilir-Ilir" has gone through multiple transformations, from a song in the context of ritual play, through which the song texts are given multiple meanings. Ki Joko Goro-Goro's preaching consists of multiple elements to be presented in multidimensional performance. Catering to the millennial generation, Gus Muwafiq constructs his preaching by combining old and new elements with a sense of modernity. By investigating Cak Nun, Ki Joko Goro-Goro, and Gus Muwafiq's preaching intertextually and ontologically, the heterogenous significances and meanings of performing art are revealed. This transformational process and its results are open-ended, as I illustrate in chapter 4.

THE HISTORY AND RELIGIOSITY OF GAMELAN SEKATÈN

The discussion of "Ilir-Ilir" reminds us that tradition is constantly revisable, and the past will never be completely erased. This is an approach Becker (1993) illustrates by using the term *palimpsest* to discuss the archaeological meaning of Javanese gamelan, as I mentioned in chapter 1. It also implies that meaning is constructed based on context, but lives are based on personal and institutional relations. If meaning is contextual, being is relational, thus "meaning assumes form through dialectical interrelationship" (Taylor 1978, 49). It follows that the synchronic and diachronic dimensions of relationality reveal the inexhaustibility and perpetual revisability of tradition.

With this premise in mind, I will discuss a specially designed gamelan that consists of distinct instrumentation: gamelan Sekatèn or Sekati. Performed once a year to celebrate the birth of Prophet Muhammad, gamelan Sekatèn can be found in the courts of Yogyakarta (Yogya), Surakarta (Solo), and Cirebon. I illustrate how gamelan Sekatèn in different localities signifies certain identities and characteristics that are inherently local. Its meaning and development are also shaped by local history.

In my previous work, I have written about gamelan Sekatèn at the Kasunanan court of Surakarta (Sumarsam 1981, 54–73). I am also the narrator of and a consultant on a documentary film on gamelan Sekatèn, "Gift of Wali: The Gamelan Sekaten."[21] The documentary was recorded in 1997 when I was given permission to play gamelan Sekatèn at the Kasunanan court, playing the *demung* (a metallophone-type instrument) of this sacred ensemble.

My interest in revisiting my study of gamelan Sekatèn stems from an event that occurred in 2021. It was a monthly program called "Nusantara Arts Gamelan Masters Guest Lecture Series." I was invited as one of the guest masters to present my thoughts about gamelan history. In my presentation, I discussed gamelan Sekatèn as one of the oldest ensembles. At the end of the lecture, Marc Perlman, whose early major study focused on Javanese gamelan, commented that he doubted the old age and uniqueness of gamelan Sekatèn. He suggested the possibility that gamelan Sekatèn is a regular gamelan but made in a larger size. This is because the *bonang* of gamelan Sekatèn is a two-row bonang as in any regular gamelan, although it is played differently. Perlman made a good point in doubting the age of the Yogyanese and Solonese gamelan Sekatèn, since there are other ancient and special gamelan in these courts that have bonang with only one row of gongs. Perlman's observation spurred me to research deeper into the history and characteristics of three gamelan Sekatèn in the courts of Surakarta, Yogyakarta, and Cirebon. Additionally, I briefly discuss gamelan Sekati in the village of Temaga in Bali.

Perlman's comment reminded me about gamelan Sekatèn in Cirebon, which is quite different than gamelan Sekatèn in Solo and Yogya. The gamelan Sekatèn in Cirebon is a small ensemble with smaller-sized instruments; the gamelan Sekatèn in Surakarta and Yogyakarta is a large ensemble with larger-sized instruments. More importantly, the bonang in Cirebon is a one-row bonang, not a two-row bonang as in Surakarta and Yogyakarta.

Questions emerged about the meaning and historical connections between the gamelan Sekatèns in Cirebon and those in Yogyakarta and Surakarta. Believed to have been created during the early period of Islamized Java by Sunan Kalijågå, gamelan Sekatèn is performed once a year in a religious festival called Mawlid Nabi or Garebeg Mulud (because it was held in the Javanese month of Mulud). The event commemorates the birth of the Prophet Muhammad.

In the court capitals of Surakarta and Yogyakarta, a pair of Sekatèn gamelan has been and is still played in front of the mosque. A common popular interpretation about gamelan Sekatèn in Surakarta and Yogyakarta is that due to the exceptionally large size of its instruments, musicians should strike them with extra energy to produce a loud sound that can be heard from afar. Hence, gamelan Sekatèn would attract people to listen and therefore be proselytized.

The Cirebonese also believed that their gamelan Sekatèn was created by Sunan Kalijågå. It is also performed once a year during the Garebeg Mulud festival. However, the gamelan Sekatèn in Cirebon is performed in an open palace pavilion without walls, not in front of the mosque. The number and size of the instruments in the ensemble are smaller in comparison to gamelan Sekatèn in Surakarta and Yogyakarta. Hence, the gamelan Sekatèn in Cirebon cannot produce loud sounds. These two facts have led me to question the role of gamelan Sekatèn in Cirebon.

Along with Cirebon, there are several other small Javanese court gamelan believed to be archaic ensembles that have a one-row bonang—gamelan Monggang, Kodhokngorèk, and Cåråbalèn. If we consider one-row bonang older than two-row bonang and small ensembles older than large ensembles, the archaic nature of gamelan Sekatèn in Solo and Yogya comes into question. Furthermore, why are Solonese and Yogyanese gamelan Sekatèn similar (large ensembles and large instruments), when Cirebonese gamelan Sekatèn is distinctively different? Unfortunately, conventional historical evidence is lacking on the genesis of these gamelan Sekatèn. Therefore, the findings presented here are based on myths and contemporary historical perspectives.

The main point about the three gamelan Sekatèn is that they have existed and performed in the context of the same event, each with a distinctive musical style, uniqueness, and, in the case of Solo and Yogya, similarity. I therefore wondered whether these differences and similarities were shaped by the identities and character of the communities in which they were created. By way of an answer, I will first explain the identity and character of the Solonese and Yogyanese court communities, which developed as the result of certain historical events in the eighteenth century. The events consisted of a series of intrigues in Central Java among Javanese princes in their struggle for power. This occurred at a time when the Europeans, especially the Dutch, entered the scene of Javanese history as traders, monopolizing trade and beginning to intimidate and interfere in the political life of Javanese royal families for their own benefit.

> [The intrigues began] with the sacking of Paku Buwana II's court of Kartasura by Chinese and Javanese rebels in 1742. Subsequently, the Dutch defeated the rebels and reinstalled Paku Buwana on the throne. (At this point, because of

> the destruction of his court in Kartasura, Paku Buwana moved his palace to Surakarta.) But a number of princes, especially the nephew of the king (Mas Said) and the king's half-brother (Pangeran Singasari), who had opposed the king and helped the Chinese insurrection, continued their insurgency. The intrigue worsened when the king's own brother Mangkubumi defected to the rebels. Thus, two sides were established in the eighteenth-century Javanese war of succession. The rebels, led by Mas Said and Mangkubumi, contended with the men led by Paku Buwana II, who was assisted by the Dutch. After the death of Paku Buwana II in 1749, the war continued into the reign of Paku Buwana III (r. 1749–1788). The young king governed the court so poorly that many of his officials, including the crown prince, defected to the rebels.
>
> Having experienced almost continuous war since the Chinese rebellion in 1743, in 1752 all parties began to take another course of action: the way of negotiations. First, Mas Said began to negotiate with the Dutch. Then Mas Said and Mangkubumi broke their alliance, and Mangkubumi began separate negotiations with the Dutch. These negotiations resulted in a division of territorial control between Paku Buwana and Mangkubumi, and in Mangkubumi's agreement to help the Dutch to defeat Mas Said. In 1755, a treaty was signed at Giyanti. The Mataram kingdom was then permanently divided between two major courts, the Susuhunan (Kasunanan) of Surakarta and the Kasultanan of Yogyakarta. Mangkubumi became the first sultan of Yogyakarta, taking the name Hamengku Buwana I. (Sumarsam 1995, 48–49)

Because of the partition, each court felt it necessary to establish its own identity and character in many aspects of life, including customs, rituals, attire, literature, and the performing arts. How these differences developed is challenging to trace because of the lack of historical evidence. However, Carey (1986, 19) has found evidence from oral tradition:

> When the victorious Mangkubumi met Sunan Pakubuwana III (r. 1749–88) at the village of Jatisari, mid-way between Giyanti and Surakarta, on 15 February 1755, he was asked by the Surakarta ruler to make a choice between "tradition" and "modernity" with regard to his new court at Yogyakarta. The actual Javanese terms used, according to this oral tradition, were *wadhah* "container" and *wiji* "seed/essence"—the first referring to the outward forms of the Javanese tradition and the second to its intrinsic essence, an essence which could be refracted through an ever-changing outward appearance. The purpose of this selection was to ensure that in the ensuing period, when the Mataram kingdom was divided, the two halves would evolve in a clearly distinct cultural pattern

from each other, thus underlining the irrevocable nature of the political and territorial division agreed two days earlier at Giyanti.

Faced with this choice, the oral tradition asserts, Mangkubumi opted for the former (i.e., the wadhah or container), thus implicitly leaving his Surakarta rival with the possibility of developing a more "modern" court style.

Such is the background of the courts' fabricated identity and character in establishing their differences from each other. Because of Mangkubumi's rebellion and his leadership and strength in his struggle for power, and owing to his success in establishing the second major court of Mataram, the Kasultanan of Yogyakarta, he earned his fame as a heroic figure in fighting his opponents; hence the heroic character of the Kasultanan court of Yogyakarta reverberated as an identity trait of the community.

How has the difference between Yogyanese and Solonese court identity and character been practiced in the life of the members of its community? Lindsay (1980, 90) has answered this question in terms of how each court has defined itself from one another in a stylistically opposite way: "To wear the batik *parang* pattern Yogyakarta style was not to wear it with the diagonals running up to the right, as in Surakarta, but the other way around. To play *imbal* (interlocking) patterns on the *demung* in Yogyakarta was not to stress the on-beat, but the off-beat."

Lindsay acknowledges that it is difficult to make a connection between political events and artistic activity (93), a challenge I illustrate in the analysis of gamelan Sekatèn that follows. I propose that music as a "pattern of sound produced by human interaction" (Blacking 1976, 26) embodies an imagined identity and character of the community in which the music is produced. This allegorical reading through music should be approached from the perspective of human imagination in musical reception. That is, when people watch a performance or listen to music, they will be able to perceive it as a form of synthesis of many aspects coming out of that imagination, rather than as what they visually see or hear alone. "In the imagination these different aspects coincide with each other, whereas in real life it is necessary to alternate between different viewpoints" (Cook 1990, 88). To this end, I next describe the manner in which Yogyanese and Solonese gamelan Sekatèn produce their loud sounds, which allegorically informs us about the identity and character of the community.

Producing loud sounds on large gamelan Sekatèn results from the way musicians strike their instruments. In playing a metallophone-type instrument (demung, *saron*, and *peking*), a musician lifts the mallets above their head, then strikes the instrument with extra energy. The timing of this physical act of playing the gamelan instrument is different for Yogyanese musicians than for musicians in Solo. Solonese musicians create loud sounds according to the usual norm of playing the composition. That is, they play loudly and at a fast speed (*sesegan*) when the music reaches the end of the composition, a kind of climax of the presentation. In contrast, Yogyanese musicians do this loud playing from the beginning to the end of the piece. The melodic leader of the ensemble, the bonang player, plays the introduction of the piece. In gamelan Sekatèn, this introduction is called *racikan*, consisting of long, unmetrical melodies. On every important structural point of the melodies of the introduction, the other instruments would punctuate in unison with the end tone of that structural point.

Producing with consistency a loud gamelan sound from the beginning to the end of the piece is uniquely the Yogyanese treatment of playing gamelan Sekatèn. This practice "violates" the general rule of playing; that is, musicians play loudly when the tempo of a piece is fast, and play softly when the tempo is slow. Thus, the juxtaposition between a piece performed in slow speed and loud-sounding production is unique to Yogyakarta gamelan Sekatèn. This means that Yogyanese musicians must exert extra energy to produce loud sounds from their instruments for a considerable amount of time; so much so that it is necessary for two musicians to stand by to play one instrument, while facing each other. They switch playing the instrument when one musician cues the other to take it over to sustain producing loud sounds.

Another noted difference in the melodic treatment between Yogyanese and Solonese musicians is the stylistic playing of bonang. In a technique of playing called *pipilan*, the Solonese musician plays more elaborately than the Yogyanese bonang player does—the latter would play in a more straightforward style (see the comparison in table 3.4).

Historical Construction of the Identity and Character of Gamelan Sekatèn

Considering the differences between gamelan Sekatèn in Cirebon and Bali and gamelan Sekatèn in Yogyakarta and Surakarta—ensemble size and volume—in our analysis of the relationship between music and community identity and character, and their historical connections with Solonese and Yogyanese gamelan Sekatèn yields complex, challenging, and fascinating discussion and analysis.

As noted earlier, according to tradition, gamelan Sekatèn in Java were created by Sunan Kalijågå, although historical evidence to support this belief is lacking. Nonetheless, Javanese people from different strata of society—laymen, bureaucrats, Islamic ulama and preachers—deeply believe that Sunan Kalijågå is the creator of gamelan Sekatèn, so much so that if someone objects to this belief,

TABLE 3.4 Comparison between the melodic styles of bonang Sekatèn of Surakarta and Yogyakarta

Bonang Sekatèn of the Surakarta style. Gendhing "Rambu" (excerpt)

Balungan	. . . 5 . . . 6 . . . 5 . . . 6	. . . 5 . . . 6 . . . 5 . . . 3
Bonang	. 5 3 . . 5 3 . 6 5 3 . 3 5 3 .	6 5 3 . 5 5 3 . 6 5 2 . 2 5 2 .
Balungan	. . . 5 . . . 6 . . . 5 . . . 6	. . . 5 . 2 . . . 1 . . . 3 . 2
Bonang	. 5 3 . . 5 3 . 6 5 3 . . 5 3 $\overline{.6}$	$\overline{.6}$3 6 . 5 . 3 . 2 3 1 . 3 1 3 .

Bonang Sekatèn of the Yogyakarta style. Gendhing "Rambu" (excerpt)

Balungan	. . . 5 . . . 6 5	. . . 6 . . . 3 . . . 5 . . . .
Bonang	5 6 5 . 5 6 5 . . 6 6 6 5 5 . .	6 3 6 . 6 3 6 . . 5 5 . . 5 . 5
Balungan	. . . 6 . . . 5 . . . 3	. . . 1 . . . 2 . . . 3 . . . 2
Bonang	6 5 6 . 6 5 6 . . 3 3 . . 3 . .	1 2 1 . 1 2 1 . 3 2 3 . 3 2 3 .

Transcribed by the author.

heated debate ensues. This underscores the importance of tradition (often in the form of myth) as a source of people's beliefs. Next, I illustrate this myth-history relationship pertaining to gamelan Sekatèn by reviewing *Babad Sekatèn* (*The Chronicle of Sekatèn*) composed by Siswaharsaya (1934) in relation to gamelan Sekatèn in Cirebon.

Regarding the origin of gamelan Sekatèn, *Babad Sekatèn* tells us about the downfall of the kingdom of Måjåpahit, the last Hindu-Buddhist empire (thirteenth to fifteenth century), whose king (Brawijaya) transferred his power to his son, Raden Patah, who was a Muslim. At that time, most of the population still embraced Hindu-Buddhism, whose ritual included providing offerings to deities. One time, King Raden Patah met with the Islamic saint (wali) Sunan Kalijågå, who proposed to find the most effective way, on a mass scale and peacefully, to change people's religion from Hindu-Buddhism to Islam. One of the ways to do this was to use wayang performance as a tool to teach Islam to the people. Sunan Kalijågå also proposed another ideal way to Islamize the people:

This text from *Babad Sekatèn* illustrates the court events and rituals presumably happening in the kingdom of Demak during the early Islamization of Java. More importantly, the author of the babad confirms a common and deeply held

TABLE 3.5

Pupuh I: Dhandhanggulå

<table>
<tr><td>21. Pamikaté mrih janmå kèh prapti
Ing paséban masjid kering kanan
Sinungan gamelan gedhé
Tinabuh siyang dalu
Praptèng bedhug ing tengah ratri
Imbal gantyå giliran
Saben-saben pupuh
Yèn mirang gongså tinatab
Pårå janmå yekti busekan marani
Mring ungyaning gamelan</td><td>To make many people attend, in
the left- and right-side hall of the mosque
should be placed a large gamelan
to be played in the day and evening
until the hour of midnight,
taking turns in playing them. Each time
a piece is performed,
if people hear gamelan,
for sure many people will rush to come
to where gamelan is located.</td></tr>
<tr><td>24. Ing plataran masjid dèn rakiti
Ambeng-ambeng ingkang warnå pepak
Winangun kadyå sesajèn
Kang ngémbå caranipun
Janmå Budå lamun sesaji
Ngajèni pårå déwå
Sesembahanipun
Ing ngriku prå janmå kathah
Kinèn ngepang ambengan kang wus sinaji
Miwah sinungan artå</td><td>In the courtyard of the mosque, install
all sorts of complete ritual foods,
which should be made like an offering,
imitating the ways
when Buddhist people presented offerings,
paying homage to deities,
their worshippers.
Many people
were asked to sit in a circle around the
ritual foods.
Money was also provided.</td></tr>
<tr><td>25. Pangepungé ambengan sesaji
Dèn dongani mawi båså Arab
Déné surasèng dongané
Nenuwun ing Hyang Agung
Mugå-mugaå sakyèhing janmi
Samyåa pinaringånå
Iman mring Hyang Agung
Angrasuk agåmå Islam
Nut sréngaté panutan kita Jeng Nabi
Muhammad Rasullullah</td><td>The encircling of ritual foods
is accompanied by prayer in Arabic.
The meaning of the prayer is
a request to the exalted one,
hoping all people
were given
faith by the Exalted one
to embrace Islam,
following the prescription of the Prophet
Muhammad, the messenger of Allah.</td></tr>
<tr><td>27. Dé wanciné kang sidekah nenggih
Tinangguhnå ring ri adi Islam
Yèku mengeti wiyosé
Jeng Nabi muhammadun
Salalahu ngalail ngalam
Yèku tanggal ping rolas
Mulud wulanipun
Ing malemé ariåyå
Prå ngulåmå myang prå wali samya
dhikir
Sembahyang harjamaah</td><td>The ritual is held
in the day of the Islamic holiday,
to commemorate the birth of
the Prophet Muhammad,
may Allah's peace and blessings be
upon him,
which is on the twelfth
of the month of Mulud.
In the evening before the celebration,
Ulama and saints perform dhikir litany
and Friday's prayer.</td></tr>
<tr><td>30. Prå prajurit sajroning nigari
Nyutrå miwah tamtåmå kalawan
Numbakanyar sakabèhé
Kinèn samektèng kéwuh
Bedhil tumbak warastranèki
Miwah tabuhanirå
Gong bèri myang tambur
Puksur teteg lan kemanak
Iku kabèh pedah kinaryå ngurmati ing
ari adi Islam</td><td>The military of the kingdom,
Nyutra, tamtama, and
numbakanyar, all
were ordered to stand by with
their guns, lances, arrows,
and their musical instruments:
large gong, drums,
puksur, teteg, and kemanak,
all were played to celebrate the
Islamic holiday.</td></tr>
</table>

31. Kapindhoné supadyå prå janmi Samyå kènyut kasengsem tyasirå Mring adèn-adèn kang tinon Déné ari punikå Sang aprabu miyos tinangkil Munggwing ing Sitibentar Ingayap prå arum manggung myang cèthi biyådhå samyå ngampil upacaraning narpati banyak dhalang kacu mas	The second aim is to make people attractive in their hearts to the presence of the aden-aden offering. Today The king enters the palace chamber in Sitibentar hall, accompanied by those beauties, ladies-in-attendance holding the king's ceremonial swan, golden handkerchiefs,
32. Sawunggaling myang dwipanggå rukmi Sarwå retnå kang ardåwalikå Lar badhak kanan kéringé Tabuh saddhå sang prabu Nulyå tedhak saking Sitinggil ginarebeg prå biyådhå Praptèng alun-alun Kinurmatan kålåntåkå Miwah bedhil ngurmati mawanti-wanti Gongså munyeng monggangan	chicken and elephant figurines made of gold. Swan figurines also gold. Mountain-shaped peacock feathers were placed on the left and right side. At noon the king exits from Sitinggil chamber, accompanied by ladies-in-attendance. When arriving at the courtyard the sound of cannons heralds him and rifle guns sound many times to pay homage to him. The gamelan Monggang is sounded.

Pupuh II: Sinom

1. Sang Srinåtå dupi myarså Mring sabdaning Sunan Kali Dhahat ascaryèng wardåyå Nulyå matur mring prå wali Mangkånå sabdå aji Ambå kalangkung panuju Mring karsanyå Jeng Sunan Malah ambå amewahi Tetuguran winiwitan sadèrèngnyå	When the king hears Sunan Kalijågå's pronouncement, he is very happy. Then he speaks to the wali. Here is what the king said: I very much agree with your wishes, wali. I even add with awakening as the beginning of the event.
2. Ing antårå saptå dinå Tempuking kang ari adi Pra bupatyå moncå pråjå Kang samya tur bulu bekti Sawusé samyå prapti Masanggrahan néng lun-alun Ngiras ngleremaken anggå Rèh saking lumaku tebih Sapandhèrèké nèng pasébannyå priyanggå	For about seven days when the holiday comes bupati from outlying area come to pay homage to the king. When they come they should rest in the courtyard to cool off their bodies since they have walked from far away. They stay in each compound with their entourage.
3. Miwah kalangkung prayogå Ri praptanirå prå dipati Kang pradonggå wiwit munyå Saking bangsal Sripanganti Binektå maring masjid Samargå-margå tinabuh Supadyå prå janmå Samyå kèlu anut wingking Marang masjid kasengsem dening gamelan	It is even better if when they arrive gamelan should begin to be sounded in the Srimanganti hall. Then the gamelan should be brought to the mosque, playing it on its way to the mosque so that people are interested, following it from behind, so that they are coming to the mosque because of their interest in listening to gamelan.

Siswaharsaya 1934, in Atmosiswartoputra 2021, 52–56.

belief that gamelan was performed in the mosque to make people interested to come and listen to the gamelan, providing the opportunity to be Islamized—the idea proposed by Sunan Kalijågå. However, babad is a literary work. It does not represent factual events. Rather, the content of babad is based on the imagination of its author, on the author's interpretation (in this case poetically presented) of real events of the past but infused by what the author has experienced in his life. I suggest that Siswaharsaya's *Babad Sekatèn* follows this pattern. The origin of gamelan Sekatèn was described by Siswaharsaya based on what he saw and experienced as part of his life in 1930s Sekatèn festivals in Yogyakarta or Surakarta, and the belief of the people in the community. He imagined that the story he told in *Babad Sekatèn* was also happening in the kingdom of Demak in the sixteenth century. It is in this context that we should understand the difference between the content of literary work and historical documents.

Like Soedjatmoko's views on the usefulness of myth in reconstructing history, Kuntowijoyo (2004, 1) sees the content of history and literary works as complementing each other: "Structurally, in history there is evidence, information, and fact, useful to explain about reality. In the structure of literary work there is structurization, possibility, expression, and imagination, useful to evaluate reality. In the meantime, the substance of history is the objectification of life because it must be aware of changes. Literary work is the subjectification of life, and its reference is eternity."

This seems to be a nonissue when we look only at Yogyanese and Solonese gamelan Sekatèn. But when we take into consideration gamelan Sekatèn in Cirebon, we encounter certain issues. Knowing that Cirebonese gamelan Sekatèn is distinctively different than Solonese and Yogyanese gamelan Sekatèn, can we still apply the concept that music is an allegorical reading of the community that produced it? This is a challenging question to answer because our evidence is limited to traditional historiography. But it must be done since both Javanese and Cirebonese people have the same belief that their gamelan Sekatèn were created by Sunan Kalijågå during the Islamic kingdom of Demak. In other words, we need to explain the differences and similarities while taking into account the varying performance contexts.

As I mentioned earlier, Cirebonese gamelan Sekatèn is different: it has a smaller ensemble with smaller instruments, it has one-row bonang, physically it looks archaic, it produces a softer sound, and it is performed in the hall located in the court compound. All things considered, I lean toward the view that Cirebonese gamelan Sekatèn is older than Solonese and Yogyanese gamelan Sekatèn, as I explain in the following discussion.

In *Music in Java*, Jaap Kunst (1973) says that Islam adopted gamelan Sekatèn from the formerly indispensable music of all Hindu ceremonies. But he does not explain the nature and practice of pre-Islamic gamelan Sekatèn. In *Hindu Javanese Musical Instruments* (1968), Kunst mentions *sakati* (a variant name of gamelan Sekati) two times: *sakati* from sung poetry (*kidung*) *Undhakan Pangrus* (116) and *gong sakati* from kidung *Arjuna Pralabda* (80, 103). The reference to gong sakati is brief: "lawan gong sakati ambarung" (and gong sakati is performing together). Noticeably, the kidung from which the word *sakati* comes was composed in Bali. Since in Bali the word *gong* means "ensemble," it is not far-fetched to speculate that gong sakati means gamelan Sakati.

I later found an audio recording of gamelan Sekati on the website of Danker Schaareman, a well-known researcher of Balinese music. It is a gamelan Sekati from the village of Temaga, Bali, recorded by Theo Meyer in the 1960s. No photo or any information accompanies the audio recording. Schaareman said that people believed deeply in the sacredness of this gamelan, so much so that taking photos of the instruments was not allowed. Listening to the recording led me to conclude that it is a small ensemble with one instrument leading the melody, which reminds me of the small Cirebon gamelan Sekatèn.

Unfortunately, I cannot find any conventional historical evidence of the timeframe for the creation of this Balinese gamelan Sekati. I can only hypothesize that it was brought to Bali when Java was Islamized. I searched further to find corroborating evidence to the thesis that Balinese gamelan Sekati existed during the pre-Islamic period. My research on Sanskrit-based Old Javanese kakawin sung poetry did not yield anything on gamelan Sekati. Almost giving up my search, eventually I found the term *sekati* in reference to music mentioned in *Sejarah Melayu* (Malay Annals). It is said that when the king of Malaka Mansur Sah visited Måjåpahit, all kinds of music and musical instruments were played to herald his presence. One of these was the sekati. The *Malay Annals* were composed and rewritten several times from the fifteenth to the seventeenth century. So, at least based on mythological account, the existence of gamelan Sekati in pre-Islamic Java, perhaps during the time of the great empire Måjåpahit, cannot be ruled out.

Assuming this is true, I thought more about the similarities between Cirebon and Balinese gamelan Sekati in size and instrumentation, and I compared the pieces performed by them. A rather stunning revelation emerged—the musical idiom and performance style of these two gamelan Sekati are similar. In fact, the contour of the melodies as they are shaped by the tone at the end of each phrase is also similar.

Does this prove that Balinese and Cirebon gamelan Sekati are older than gamelan Sekatèn in Yogya and Solo? Yes and no. No, because we do not have enough conventional historical evidence to prove the contention. Yes, by inference, if we consider how maritime trade made it possible for a cosmopolitan interweaving of cultures to occur, as Vickers (1993) has shown us. In the case of Java's north coast and Bali, maritime trade led to the formation of Pasisir community complexes, which facilitated intellectual exchanges and movements of people, literature, and performing arts in the area; hence the possibility of gamelan Sekatèn moving from Måjåpahit to Demak, Cirebon, Blambangan, and Bali.

Gamelan Sekatèn of Cirebon, Yogyakarta, and Surakarta in Historical Perspective

According to Cirebonese tradition, Cirebonese gamelan Sekatèn came from the kingdom of Demak, and only one gamelan existed during the period of Demak. It is not clear in which period of Demak gamelan Sekatèn was sent to Cirebon. Following Atmosiswartoputra's (2021) analysis, there are a few possibilities. The first is that after the death of the second king of Demak, Raden Trenggånå, the gamelan was brought to the court of Pakungwati in Cirebon by his wife Ratu Ayu (she was the daughter of the power holder of the court, Sunan Gunung Jati). Another possibility is that the name of Trenggånå's wife was Ratu Ayu Mas Nyåwå, who brought gamelan Sekatèn to Cirebon as *tondhå asih*, the sign of love. The third possibility is that the wife of Sunan Gunung Jati, the sister of Raden Trenggånå, brought the gamelan Sekatèn to Cirebon. Atmosiswartoputra concludes that the last possibility is closest to the truth.

If we follow a Cirebonese perspective, Yogyanese and Solonese gamelan Sekatèn did not come from Demak since the only gamelan Sekatèn, the small-sized ensemble and instruments producing a soft sound, was brought to Cirebon. It is said that afterward there was no gamelan Sekatèn in Demak. We know that in the late sixteenth century the political and cultural center moved to Mataram, on the inland of Central Java. We do not have any clues about the existence and development of performing arts in the early period of Mataram. According to contemporary perspectives, performing arts that have been inherited by the modern courts of Yogyakarta and Surakarta attribute their creation to Sultan Agung, the infamous ruler of Mataram (reigned 1613–1645), including gamelan Sekatèn as we know them today.

To conclude, this discussion illustrates the dynamics of how we can maneuver between historical evidence and mythological (literary or oral) information, belief and fact. At times, myth and history not only interact but collide, as I have shown in the case of the genesis of gamelan Sekatèn. The history-myth collision may trigger debate and discussion among members of society because it may undermine people's beliefs. We learn from this discussion the possibility that among the three gamelan Sekatèn in Java, the Cirebonese gamelan Sekatèn is the oldest and was the first to appear in Demak. Although evidence is very thin, it is possible that Cirebonese gamelan Sekatèn, and Balinese gong Sekati of Temaga, existed during the pre-Islamic period. This leads me to conclude that Solonese and Yogyanese gamelan Sekatèn are likely younger than Cirebonese gamelan Sekatèn. The former was created not in Demak during the heyday of the Demak kingdom, as many people believe, but during the era of Sultan Agung.

What does this tell us about "the in-between" in life? First, we encounter the in-between in discussing past historical events since we must deal with the dynamic interaction, collision, and collaboration between history and myth. We must deal with dialectical dualism between what people believe and what historical facts tell us. I can see heterogeneous perspectives—congruent and incongruent, agreeable and contradictory to one another—when we try to link present and past events. In the final chapter, I turn to more recent discourse and developments through an analysis of wayang from the nineteenth to the twenty-first century.

FOUR

Discourses on Wayang from the Nineteenth Century to the Present

There are two main transitional periods in Java's history in which the development of Javanese cultural tradition has impacted wayang shadow puppet performance: (1) the transition from the Hindu-Javanese to the Islam-Javanese world beginning around the fifteenth century, and (2) from the Hindu-Islam-Javanese world to the period of Western-influenced, global cultural trends in our contemporary world. Each of the transitions has brought about the development of hybrid cultural expression. During the first period, the Hindu and Islamic elements were all syncretized and absorbed into the complex indigenous matrix of Javanese culture. During the latter period, the already fabricated hybrid culture became imbued with Western culture, and recently with the deepening of Islamization, which has added to the complex contextualization of Javanese performing arts in general.

In any event, Hindu and Islam have become the foundation of the development of Javanese hybrid culture. Speaking of the early history of Southeast Asia, historian Olivier Wolters even prefers to use the term *Hinduization* rather than *Indianization* of Southeast Asia, emphasizing religion as a conduit for cultural transformation. In line with the fundamental tenets of religion, it is not far-fetched to suggest that *convivencia*—the concept of peaceful coexistence of multiple faiths and traditions[1]—had been on the minds of those who were responsible for making sociopolitical and cultural transformation occur.

The question is, how far can convivencia be achieved? This is a relevant question, but it will be difficult to draw a general picture of the success or failure of socioreligious and cultural traditions of Hindu-Javanese, then Hindu-Javanese-Islamic harmonized interfaith relations. This is because each period has its own dynamic concepts and shapes of identity, otherness, and culture (Akasoy 2010,

497), albeit closely or distantly related. The following discussion aims to address this dynamic from the viewpoint of contemporary discourses but without disregarding past perspectives. Particularly, the localized incorporation of Western-influenced, global cultural trends has brought issues of religion and culture to the forefront of public consciousness in discourses about rearticulating Indonesia's spiritual, regional, and national identity.

To illustrate the dynamic of contemporary discourse on Islam within wayang, I'll begin with some relevant events. On June 18, 1994, as an epilogue of a wayang performance by dhalang Purbo Asmoro at the hall of the MPR/DPR (People's Consultative Assembly/People's Representative Council), the representative of the wayang organization Pepadi Jakarta asked the late Abdurrahman Wahid (Gus Dur, who in 1999 became the president of Indonesia) to give a speech about wayang.[2]

Listening to this speech, I was expecting to hear Gus Dur talk about wayang in its relationship to Islam. This is because he was a prominent leader of the Islamic community, the son and grandson of prominent Islamic scholars (the founder of Nahdlatul Ulama and the well-known Tebuireng pesantrèn in Jombang), and he had an impeccable Islamic education, including his study in Al Azhar University in Cairo and the University of Baghdad. However, Gus Dur failed to satisfy my expectations. He did not speak about wayang and Islam; instead, he talked about the relationship between wayang and Indonesian nationalism, democracy, and politics. He prefaced his talk by acknowledging that he was not a professional wayang goer since most of the time his pesantrèn elders would not allow him to watch wayang performance, not because they were anti-wayang but because they wanted him to focus on studying religion. The local sugar factory sponsored an annual wayang performance, and village chiefs in the vicinity also often sponsored wayang because of their economic success. Thus, the young Gus Dur watched wayang performance as *kenakalan* (mischievous, being naughty), because of a conflict of interest with his pesantrèn elders.

During the question-and-answer session, Dr. Abdullah—a retired admiral of the navy, Universitas Indonesia professor, and expert on Javanese culture and philosophy—was the first to comment on Gus Dur's speech. He prefaced his comment by saying that he appreciated Gus Dur's perspective on wayang. Then, he spoke at length about wayang as a tool for religious propagation. Referencing *The Helligen van Java* by the Dutch scholar Rinkes, he explained the role of Sunan Kalijågå as dhalang, performing wayang for proselytization. Rinkes's reference is *Babad Cirebon*, the source examined in chapter 3.

As mentioned previously, Javanese people profoundly believe in the important role of Sunan Kalijågå in promoting Islam through wayang performance. Abdullah's comment on Gus Dur's speech confirmed this belief. However, the sources he invoked, including *Babad Cirebon* itself, fall short in explaining how Sunan Kalijågå conducted this proselytizing activity. *Babad Cirebon* only explains that the audience of Sunan Kalijågå's wayang performance was required to recite Kalimah Shahadat as a payment to watch the performance (Rinkes 1996, 135–36). In so doing, the audience was automatically converted to Islam. In other words, while showing how wayang performance functioned as a religious initiation rite, there is no explanation of how wayang storytelling was used to promote Islam. The only mention of the direct link between wayang and Islamic propagation mentioned in the babad pertains to the story of Déwå Ruci. The babad mentions that after becoming familiar with Kalijågå's teaching, the king of Demak drafted a text of a wayang story modeled after a wayang play about Bimå's unification with the deity (134).

Abdullah offered fascinating comments on this Déwå Ruci story. His interpretation of the passage from *Babad Cirebon* was that it was Sunan Kalijågå who composed the story of Déwå Ruci. He explained that there is a connection between the meaning of the wayang performance of the story of Déwå Ruci and Quranic chapters (*surah*) *al-baqarah* and *al-madinah*. He went on to say that the Javanese believe in *alam ghaib* (unseen world), and one can enter it. Then he asked himself, is there a similar story in the Quran? His answer was positive: the *alam ghaib* can be found in Quranic verse 16, *surat aidin*, which says that in carrying out the teaching of *tarekat* (the path of Islamic mysticism), the Sufi practitioners can go together with *jin* (supernatural creature). Jin cannot be found in *syariah*, but tarekat recognizes it. In following tarekat, the practitioners can receive water. Referring to the work of the liberal Indonesian Muslim scholar Nurcholis Madjid, Abdullah said that this water is called *maahayadi*, water of life. This is in congruence with the story of Déwå Ruci, in which Bimå is searching for the sacred water of life.

Two points are important here: (1) The fact that Abdullah can make a connection between wayang (especially the story of Déwå Ruci) and Quran is fascinating. There are a few instances in which Javanese intellectuals are doing the same, at many different levels. One of the most complete works that illustrates this is Poedjosoebroto's book *Wayang Lambang Ajaran Islam* (Wayang as a Symbol of Islamic Teaching) which I discussed at length in chapter 2. (2) Abdullah claimed that the story Déwå Ruci was composed by Sunan Kalijågå, confirming and enhancing Javanese belief about the role of Sunan Kalijågå in spreading Islam through wayang. However, his assertion is contested by historical evidence. That is, the story of Déwå Ruci is based on a Hindu-Javanese story, *Nawaruci*. In other words, it is a story composed before the arrival of Islam. I have no reason to believe that Abdullah was unaware of this fact. This is because a dissertation written by Prijohutomo, published in 1934, is about *Nawaruci.* The complete text of *Nawaruci* and its Dutch translation are included in the dissertation, followed by the text of *Déwå Ruci* composed by a well-known eighteenth-century *pujonggå* (poet/man of letters) of the court of Surakarta Yåsådipurå I. However, for whatever reason, Abdullah skips this historical fact, preferring to explain that Sunan Kalijågå was the creator of the story of Déwå Ruci.

Comparing the texts of *Nawaruci*, composed during the Hindu-Javanese period, and Yåsådipurå's *Déwå Ruci*, composed during the Islam-Javanese period, is beyond the scope of this chapter. In this regard, I refer readers to Arps's (2016) study of this topic. Examining the religious dimension of this textual transformation, he concludes that Yåsådipurå appropriated *Nawaruci* with "a miscellany of ideas and images from various [Islamic] sources. They [the two texts] do have Sufism in common, particularly devotional practice and mystical doctrine and exercise in tarekat contexts." This is another illustration of how the interaction and collision of history and myth continue to be a principal theme in our discourse about wayang.

LIGHT AND POWER: WAYANG AS A SHADOW PLAY

As I mentioned in the first chapter, based on passages from old Javanese literary works, we learn that wayang existed in Java around the ninth century, although we don't know its specific form. Then, we know from a number of *kakawin* literary works from the eleventh century that it was a shadow puppet play. And it has been suggested that aside from the fact that wayang stories were based on the Indian epics *Mahabharata* and *Ramayana*, the aesthetics and structure of Indian theatrical performance might have influenced wayang performance. To what degree this is the case cannot be ascertained.

Claire Holt (1967), following the works of Rassers (1959, 95–215), Hazeu (1897, 3), and Kats (1923, 41), believed that as it developed wayang took a form that became distinctly Javanese in three respects.

> [It] has evolved from ancient indigenous initiation rites; the fact that all parts of wayang's technical equipment are designated by indigenous and not by Indian terms; and the presence of the strikingly original figure of the servant clowns who have a very prominent role in wayang play but no counterparts in the Indian epics. These clowns are thought to be purely Indonesian mythological divine beings (seemingly demoted to the status of servants but actually powerful) who preceded the Indian epic heroes on the shadow screen. (131)

The form of the ancient indigenous initiation rites is a matter of conjecture. Regarding comical figures in wayang, Holt is quick to remind us that they "do appear on the ancient Indian stage as the *vidushaka*, 'an ugly and ridiculous Brahman'" (131). She suggests it was this vidushaka that was depicted in the Javanese reliefs and literature (115), but she does not make any direct connection with wayang. Nonetheless, the jester *vidhusaka* in ancient Sanskrit Indian stage and in its contemporary form is a central figure whose actions often dismiss the plot altogether. For example, according to Gamliel (2014), in Koodiyattam theater in Kerala, the vidushaka is in favor of telling stories from "folktales, local versions of popular Hindu epics and, above all, descriptions of scenes from daily life in Kerala. It may be marriage, food, prayers, love affairs, social behavior and even contemporary political issues . . . [The portrayal is] satirical and highly amusing, which makes it popular among spectators usually less concerned with the more serious and dignified aspects of a Koodiyattam performance" (3).[3] It seems that these vidushaka acts are not unlike *pånåkawan* jesters in Javanese wayang.

Other specifically Javanese aspects of wayang are the all-night duration of the performance, a single puppeteer fully in charge of performing the play, the extreme stylization of the puppets, the gamelan accompaniment (either small or large ensemble), and the structure of the plot. For deeper discussions of the background of wayang, see the work of Holt (1965), Brandon (1970), Brakel (1981), and Sumarsam (1988, 2003). Here, I will focus on another essential Javanese dimension of wayang: the symbolic and metaphorical meaning of the performance. Several scholars have written on this topic, including Mangkunegårå VII (1957 [1933]), Keeler (1987), and Becker (1979). Using Alton Becker's "Text-Building, Epistemology, and Aesthetic in Javanese Shadow Theatre" as a starting point, I will proceed with my own interpretation.

A linguistics professor/philologist specializing in Old Javanese and the language of wayang, Becker proposes that any wayang story includes four major epistemologies: (1) that of the demons—the direct sensual epistemology of raw nature; (2) that of the ancestor heroes—the stratified, feudal epistemology of traditional Java; (3) that of the ancient gods—a distant cosmological epistemology of pure power; and (4) that of the clowns—a modern, pragmatic epistemology of personal survival. All these epistemologies coexist in a single wayang. That is, nature time, ancestor time, god time, and the present time are all equally relevant in an event, though the scope of each event is different. The linearity of Western drama, which presents unambiguous temporal-causal sequences, cannot be applied to wayang performance, whose plot structure is based on multiple timeframes and multiple epistemologies. "In wayang, we [Westerners] might say that Gatsby, Godzilla, Agamemnon, John Wayne, and Charlie Chaplain . . . do appear in the same plot, and that is what causes the excitement; that clash of conceptual universes is what impels the action" (224). In other words, epistemological coincidence in wayang is the underlying structure of the play from which the real subtlety of the performance arises.

However, Becker carried out his study in the 1970s. Since then, wayang has evolved. In fact, current wayang performances are radically different than wayang plays three decades ago. I will focus on one aspect of this evolution, the formation of contemporary wayang as a result of the changing light source used for wayang performance.

It is not incorrect to describe wayang performance as two-dimensional, with flat puppets performing against a flat, two-dimensional screen. However, if we consider other aspects of the play—narration, puppet movements, a pair of banana logs in low and high positions, and the social hierarchy of wayang characters—the audience can imagine that the wayang performance happens three-dimensionally. As can be seen in figure 4.1, a scene viewed from the shadow or puppet side, Ben Arps aptly explains that the puppets' on-screen position gives us a clue to help us imagine the scene as it is happening in three-dimensional space.

In a wayang performance, two levels of banana logs are set at the bottom of the screen. When a puppet is planted on the lower banana log, its body from the waist down cannot be seen from the puppet side, indicating that from the shadow side the puppet is seen as if the figure is sitting down cross-legged.

Imagining the three-dimensionality of wayang performance can especially be achieved from the shadow side of the stage behind the screen, and the use of *blèncong* (an oil lamp) produced a certain aesthetic trajectory, which I will discuss later. Thus, the light source in wayang performance is important not only in technical terms but also in its symbolic meaning. A lively debate about this aspect of wayang appeared in nineteenth-century Javanese literary work.

The debate is about which of the four main elements of a wayang play—puppeteer, puppets, blèncong oil lamp, and *kelir* (the screen)—is the oldest, from which other elements come into existence. One participant indicates that the screen must have been the first, since before the puppeteer and puppets are at hand, and before the lamp is lit, the screen exists already. Another participant asserts that the puppeteer is the oldest; the screen and puppets all are his, and the lamp is lit and hung by him. The third participant suggests that the puppets must be the oldest, since in planning the performance, the puppet is first to exist, not the puppeteer, screen, or blèncong. The main figure in the literature dismisses all three replies. He argues,

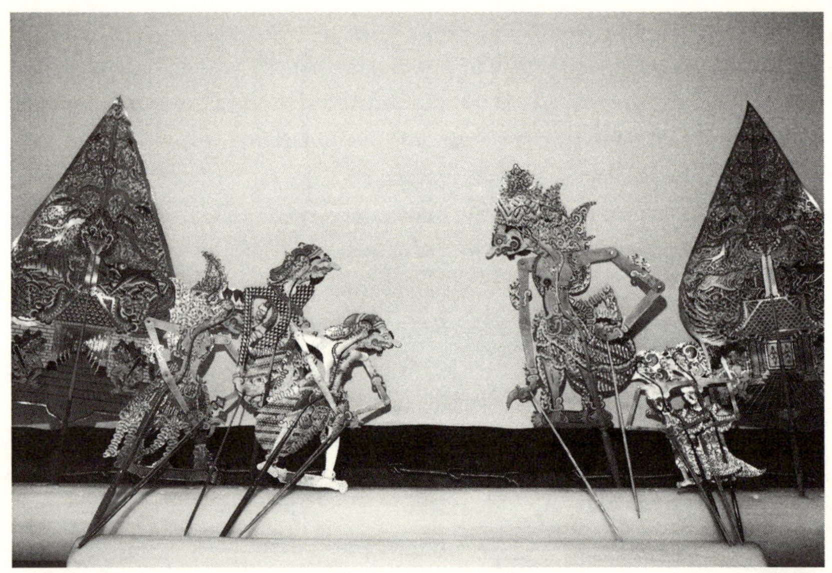

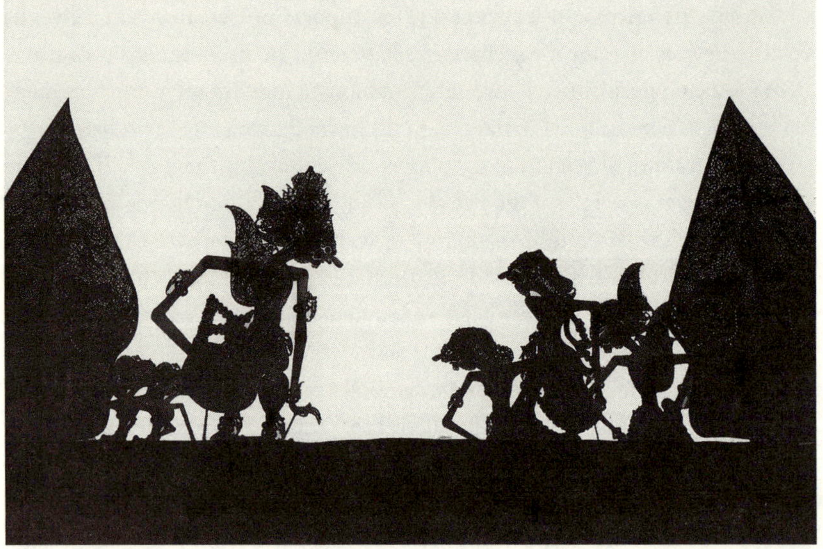

FIGURE 4.1 Imagining three-dimensional space based on Bernard Arps's sketch (2016). From behind the screen, the puppet is seen as either sitting down cross-legged or standing up, depending on the position of the puppet. Photographed by Feri Arifianto.

For even though the screen's set up,
Wayang-puppets and gamelan prepared,
Musicians seated with
The puppeteer, if all's still dark,
The dhalang's at a loss,
To pick unable, or reject,
Or give the proper speech to any of the puppets.

The audience cannot recognize
Each wayang-puppet for itself,
And everything's mysterious,
Obscure and hidden from the eye.
It's when the blèncong comes
To life, and flares up brilliantly,
That from the bottom to
The top the screen is visible
With the Kurawa [enemy cousins] and Pandhåwå [hero brothers]
left and right.

The puppeteer beneath the lamp
Can now select, can now reject
Each wayang-puppet in its turn
By weighing it reflectively.
And, then he sets one forth
Whose form is called "the one-who-yearns."
What makes this possible
I think, therefore, the lamp is older than the rest.[4]
(Translation by Anderson 1981, 135–36)

Hence, light is the older than the other elements, which also implies that light symbolizes Power, a concept presented as one of the main themes of the wayang story about Déwå Ruci. The main story is the journey of the second Pandhåwå brother, Bimå, to search for enlightenment or mystical union with God. He must go through all sorts of obstacles, and at the end he meets his own spiritual personification, a small-sized figure named Déwå Ruci, who instructs Bimå to enter his body cavity. There the first thing he sees is a radiant light, and then Bimå encounters bright, multicolored lights as expansive as the ocean. It has been suggested that the pervasive mention of lights as Power is inspired by an Islamic mystical teaching called Nur Muhammad (the light that is Prophet

Muhammad), a doctrine of stages of emanation, which culminate in the perfect man, *insan kamil* (Arps 2007).

The traditional oil lamp used as the light source in wayang performance does not produce a steady illumination but rather a flickering reddish/yellowish light. The older generation of wayang connoisseurs hold the opinion that the oil lamp produces a certain effect: the flickering light makes the shadows of the puppets on the screen appear as if they are "breathing." Moreover, the older generation also believes that by watching wayang in shadow, the performance sends them to an imaginary world.

The traditional concept of wayang shadow play changed significantly when blèncong oil lamps were replaced with electric bulbs. Gradually, the concept of wayang as shadow play changed from an imagined three-dimensional pictorial performance (especially if viewed from the shadow side behind the screen) to a full view of the three-dimensional wayang stage when viewed only from the puppet side, in front of the screen. Rather than producing shadows, electric lightbulbs function more like spotlights in a proscenium theater. The strong, sharp light of the bulb (halogen is preferred) provides a bright, steady light that allows viewers to see the puppets and their movements clearly. Electric lights also produce sharp shadows, both behind and in front of the screen. Shadows of puppets appear in front of the screen when the puppeteer holds the figures at a distance from the screen and closer to the light source. Juxtaposing wayang puppets and their shadows in front of the screen makes for a thrilling visual presentation. This compelling display has made it more interesting to watch wayang from the puppet side.

This concept of the three-dimensional wayang stage has also encouraged many puppeteers to create more elaborate and sophisticated techniques of puppet movements. Given the larger space now available when the light source is moved higher up, a contemporary puppeteer can manipulate puppets in new and remarkable ways. For example, performing a somersault has now become a standard movement for any puppet of strong character. Some puppeteers can make giant puppets do double or even triple somersaults. Concomitantly, as wayang increasingly became a three-dimensional performance, many dhalangs added colored bulbs, smoke machines, and other special effects to the performance.

Subsequently, additional nontraditional elements and practices have been incorporated into wayang, which have made three-dimensional performances more prevalent. They are (1) the incorporation of Western musical instruments and a Western style of Indonesian/Javanese pop music; (2) the presence of six or more female singers with alluring makeup and sensuous attire (positioned on a raised stage to the right of the puppeteer and facing the audience); and (3) the presence of guest artists such as singers of Indonesianized-Western popular music, stand-up comedians, and VIP guests. It has also become standard practice in today's wayang for the puppeteer to dialogue with the singers and guest artists on topics that have nothing to do with the story being enacted in the play. The overarching point is that the electric bulb as the light source of wayang performance has inspired and triggered these developments.

If light symbolizes power, then when the electric light bulb replaces the blèncong oil lamp, does the light still symbolize Javanese Power? This is a relevant question because Javanese believe that lights are not only a symbol of power, but power itself. According to Moertono (1972, 56), the light that is traditionally and symbolically conceptualized as power is manifested in bright luminescence, a "star," and a dazzling blue, green, or white ball of light streaking through the sky. One of the most fascinating stories about this light symbolizing power tells of a power transfer from King Amangkurat III to his successor, Pangeran Puger. "The story is told that the [dead] king's manhood stood erect and on the top of it was a radiant light (tjahja), only the size of a grain of pepper. But nobody observed it. Only Pangeran Puger saw it. Pangeran Puger quickly sipped up the [drop of] light. As soon as the light had been sipped, the manhood ceased to stand erect. It was Allah's will that Pangeran Puger should succeed to the throne" (56).

If light is the source of power, these stories imply that Javanese Power is concrete, not an abstraction of certain patterns of human interaction, such as the word that authority or legitimacy expresses. Instead, in the words of Anderson (1972, 7), for the Javanese, "power exists independent of its possible uses. It is not a theoretical postulate but an existential reality, an intangible, mysterious and divine energy which animates the universe. It is manifested in every aspect of the natural world, in stones, trees, clouds, and fire."

But light from electric bulbs is the result of technological advancement, and does not come from the natural world. And the use of electric bulbs as the light source in wayang performance is a result of Java-Western sociopolitical/economic encounter. It is not too far-fetched here to say, therefore, that today's wayang has developed as the result of the strength of Western cultural influences on Javanese culture. The implication is that electric light has an impact on the role of the puppeteer in three areas: it changes his relationship to and interaction with his sponsor, his audience, and his puppets; there is more pervasive interaction with his guest artists; and it creates a change in the structuring of time. In this regard, the boundary between the world of wayang and the world surrounding it becomes ambiguous.

It is true that these three impacts happen for the most part in two particular scenes of wayang performance, the Limbukan and Gårå-Gårå, both containing mostly slapstick/humorous dialogs and musical interludes of lighthearted pieces. But the expanded version of these scenes, from a half hour or less to two to four hours, cause the puppeteer to reconfigure the structure of the story, to use shorter or condensed musical accompaniment, to shorten narrations, etc. Significantly, the fact that the puppeteer must share his performance with other performers and guest stars, including VIP guests who might be high-ranking government officials or leaders of a political party, his power is compromised.

Certainly, this did not happen when the dhalang was fully in charge of the performance. In a conversation about a dhalang's status once the performance has begun, Ward Keeler, who studied wayang in Central Java in the 1970s, reported:

> No one has the authority to interrupt his performance at any time. Even a king, I was often told, must defer to the dhalang during the performance: it is the dhalang who is in charge (*kuwasa*) until the performance ends. To tell the dhalang to stop lays a person—whether one of the sponsors, an important political figure, or a policeman—open to misfortune, a divine punishment for this usurpation of the dhalang's authority . . . By the same token, it is the dhalang who must take responsibility (*tanggung jawab*) for the proceedings. If spectators get into a fight, if thieves take advantage of the hubbub to burglarize a neighbor's house, if any type of misfortune occurs, it will be seen as a failure of the dhalang's potency to maintain the security of the ritual scene and surrounding area. So closely is the dhalang's influence tied to events that take place in the hamlet during his performance that if a baby is born nearby, the dhalang is said to have received a boon of mystical energy (*wahyu*). The newborn is taken to the dhalang, who cradles the baby in his arms and gives it a name. The child is then called the dhalang's *anak sampiran* (*anak*, "child"; *sampir*, "to carry something slung over one's shoulder"), establishing a bond that should be maintained throughout their respective lifetimes. If, on the other hand, anyone in the hamlet dies, the dhalang will be thought to exert an inauspicious aura." (Keeler 1987, 169)

This leads us back to the question of the impact of electric light on the meaning of wayang performance. I would say that it is a metaphor for and realization of the continuing dynamic effects of Javanese-Western encounters on Indonesian sociopolitical and cultural development. Since electric lights originated from the advance of human technology, their impact on wayang can be explained in light of that development.

How do we explain this development? Some dhalangs I have spoken to replied to this question by following a trope stated by a popular, innovative dhalang, Ki

Nartosabdho: *Nuting jaman kelakone* (innovation happens) as society changes from one era to another. The scholar and cultural commentator Umar Kayam (2001) viewed contemporary wayang performance critically, contextualizing it within the sociopolitical and cultural conditions of Suharto's New Order government in the following ways.

Throughout its history, the New Order government gradually produced great changes in the lives of Indonesians, particularly the Javanese. Foreign loans, foreign investments, the exploitation of natural resources, and the ideology of development have made it possible for the government to form a highly capitalistic structure of economic life. Almost every institution and space in the economic and marketing fields has experienced the high-level distribution and exchange of money. However, this tendency was not automatically accompanied by the process of political liberalization and the birth of an autonomous middle class. In the political arena of the New Order, the state formed a centralized and feudalistic structure. Power was centralized in the hand of President Suharto alone, which then flowed down with diminishing strength through related families, the bureaucratic network, and their cronies.

Kayam goes on to say that a hybrid capitalist and feudalistic orientation implemented by the Suharto regime did enhance the country's economic prowess; yet it primarily favored those elite groups within the government and nongovernmental institutions. Consequently, this socio-economic landscape prompted individuals belonging to those selected elite groups to embrace wayang as their favorite performing art.

This is because wayang has long been known as *adiluhung* (superb beauty) art, representing the peak of the feudal civilization of the past. Members belonging to the elite social groups I mentioned previously became so influential that a new ceremonial event was created: before a wayang performance begins, to honor his role, the sponsor of the performance hands over the puppets (usually the main characters in the story to be presented) to the puppeteer. But more importantly, the sponsors of wayang performance in this period were able to influence wayang artists to create lively performances that would satisfy the sponsor's taste or his understanding of the taste of the audience. In addition, it is not uncommon for the puppeteer during one of the humorous scenes (Limbukan or Gårå-Gårå) to acknowledge the generosity of the sponsor and the presence of VIP guests, even inviting them to be guest stars and sing or give a speech.

In my previous study, I traced the early development of contemporary wayang. I concluded that it had a close affinity with the campaign activity of the ruling political party, Golongan Karya (Golkar).

The committee responsible for this *wayang kolosal* project was called Pantap, an acronym of Panitya Tetap Apresiasi dan Pengembangan Seni Pewayangan Jawa Tengah (the Permanent Committee for the Appreciation and Development of Central Javanese Wayang). Kuwato wrote a dissertation on wayang Pantap, and the following section is drawn from his work.

According to Sudjadi, the head of Ganasidi, the aim of Pantap was to attract the interest of Indonesian youth to wayang in the face of the dominance of Western popular culture. This was to be achieved by promoting younger dhalangs and improving their skills, and by making wayang performances more attractive to youth. Performing wayang with two or more dhalangs made it possible for them to learn from each other and to develop complementary skills. Pantap wayang performances were held once a month in the courtyard of the office of the central Javanese government (Setwilda Propinsi Jawa Tingkat I Jawa Tengah): each performance was broadcast by government-sponsored television and radio. In this way the Pantap committee hoped that the assigned dhalang would become well-known and be hired to perform more often.

To make the performance more attractive, the Pantap wayang appended new elements to the traditional wayang format, including the appearance of stand-up comedians and guest stars, a new stage setup with two or three screens, and the addition of another stage with its own lighting for the comedians and guest stars (including rock or dangdut singers). The wayang was performed on an elevated wooden stage, 20 meters wide by 10 meters deep; a yellow carpet covered the stage floor. One thousand folding chairs were placed to the front, left, and right of the stage, and a camera for the live television broadcast was front and center. A small (12 by 3.5 meters) stage was set up and connected to the main stage, to be used by comedians, *pesindhèn* singers, guest singers and dancers, and any other attractions incorporated in the Limbukan and Gårå-Gårå scenes. In front of this small stage, inside the terrace, fifty chairs and several tables were placed on a yellow carpet to accommodate government officials. (Sumarsam 2003, 72–73)

COLONIAL AND POLITICAL TRAJECTORY

The previous section discusses how tradition undergoes innovation (see Hobsbawm and Ranger 1983), or put another way, continuity and change in tradition (Holt 1967). The performing arts, or literature for that matter, are subject to evolution or renewal in response to historical and social change. The specificity or details of what has triggered change and renewal is a subject of lively discussion and debate. Richard Schechner addressed this question in his thought-provoking article, "Wayang Kulit in the Colonial Margin" (1990). He postulated that in the mid-nineteenth century the Dutch imposed certain values on Javanese court artists, which brought about "normative expectations" for the style of wayang performance. In the 1920s, this "normative" style was propagated by dhalangs from the schools of puppetry in Yogyakarta and Surakarta. Subsequently, it has been used by twentieth-century Western scholars as the basis of their studies. In this sense, the normative expectation of wayang became not only the experience of the Javanese under (Dutch) colonialism, but also the experience of Westerners interested in wayang (27). Schechner charged that colonialism had shaped a "normative expectation" of wayang performance, which recent scholars have helped to perpetuate through their writing, their sponsorship of performances, and their failure to study other types of nonnormative wayang performance. Indeed, this is a serious charge. Part of the context of Schechner's critical analysis was the works of Alton Becker. Becker and his wife's project of sponsoring wayang performance at the University of Michigan in 1988, with the dhalang Midiyanto, was often targeted in Schechner's analysis.

Keeler (2003) responded at length to Schechner's polemical jibe, charging that he exaggerated his claims about the nineteenth-century development of so-called "normative" wayang in the absence of compelling evidence. Keeler is also of the opinion that Schechner was misled by the role of dhalang. Whereas the dhalang appears to be a fully autonomous author, who is creating, controlling, and rendering his own text, those appearances may lead Westerners to think that the dhalang is a performance artist *avant la letter*. But in practice, Keeler explains, the dhalang does not systematically organize scenes or dialogues in order to construct political arguments; rather, he peppers his performance with only occasional political remarks. Along this line, Keeler also reminds us of the social position of the dhalang as client to his sponsor. That is, he must be wary that advancing political criticism could jeopardize his commercial viability, or even endanger himself through harassment, or risk being arrested if his sponsor is the state.

In her book *Shadows of Empire: Colonial Discourse and Javanese Tales* (1996), Laurie Sears also enters the debate. Sears proposes that the process of negotiation between colonial power and indigenous traditions was manifested allegorically in wayang stories, starting in the eighteenth to early nineteenth century. This, she asserts, "was part of the machinery of colonial rule" (299). One of the examples Sears puts forward is the work of the learned courtier and puppeteer K. P. H. Kusumådilågå's *Serat Sastråmirudå* (1933 [1879]). Sears explains that Kusumådilågå received his knowledge of wayang from the younger brother of Paku Buwånå IV (reigned 1830–1858), K. G. Boeminåtå, who was an expert on wayang, gamelan, and dance. Kusumådilågå's knowledge of wayang was published in the Solonese newspaper *Bramartani* in 1877 and 1878 by a certain man from Mangkunegaran. Eventually, the article was published as *Serat Sastråmirudå* (The Book of Sastråmirudå) in 1930; reputedly, it became a standard of wayang performance for any dhalang to follow.

Sears argues that Java's colonial intellectual atmosphere with its premise of maintaining "authentic" Java-Hindu presentation of wayang tales influenced the production of *Serat Sastråmirudå*. She contends that the question/answer format of the book and the rules prescribing wayang performances followed the methods of the production of knowledge commonly used by Dutch scholars. Even the story used to represent the book, the story of Pålåsårå, has been published, annotated, and freely translated in Javanese script by the Dutch scholars Roorda, Poensen, and te Machelen. In a nutshell, *Serat Sastråmirudå* was the precursor of the court style of wayang performance in setting out the rules for correct performance, marking a sharp distinction from the village wayang style. Sears concludes that the court style of wayang performance was created in the 1920s with the establishment of the court wayang school, which "can be interpreted as *a creative Javanese adaptation to Dutch scholarly attitudes and the aesthetic preference of Dutch educated Javanese*" (150, my emphasis).

Sears's and Schechner's studies are important because they fruitfully juxtapose history and cultural criticism. But, as the prominent scholar of Indonesian history Ricklefs (1999, 550) puts it regarding Sears's study, "Her evidence in the period she covers, the eighteenth to early twentieth century, is thin, and lacking in extensive research on unpublished Javanese manuscript." However, she does not let the absence of evidence silence her. Despite the criticism, I find Sears's arguments relevant to my present study. She proposes that wayang performance should be thought of as allegories of its time, context, and place, and as a metalanguage for political and cultural commentary (Sears 1996, 11). Sears goes on to say:

> Because the stories can be used to comment on the vicissitudes of daily life, and thus commentary changes with each telling, it becomes increasingly difficult to fix the "meaning" of any story. Each story has the potential to be renewed in each telling, and each new telling leaves its traces on the story told. The persistent ability of stories both to change and change past and present marks the constitution and celebration of these stories as allegories. (11)

In the following sections, I will discuss particular wayang events and a wayang story by applying Sears's point, examining the process of formation and transformation of a particular wayang story from one performance to another.

ALLEGORY, MEANING, AND TRANSFORMATION

The first example is a wayang story that seemingly represents an allegorical reading of society, but essentially was intricately used as a tool to gain political power. As mentioned in the previous chapter, it is not uncommon for the Javanese to use certain wayang characters in political discourse, for example, to portray political figures or colonialists during the early period of Indonesian independence.

During the New Order government, this portrayal of political figures by wayang characters came to the attention of the public at large when President Suharto implied that he identified himself as Semar, one of the most beloved clowns but also a wise and powerful figure. In so doing, the president pronounced himself as having humble origins, but now become a powerful figure and protector of the people (Pausacker 2004, 233–34). Suharto asked Pepadi, the national organization of dhalangs, to gather twenty dhalangs to meet him. He asked them to promote through their performances the importance of understanding Pancasila—five principles of Indonesian state political philosophy—and its significance in the life of the people. Pepadi came up with a story to convey the President's theme: an important figure with a humble background explaining Pancasila. Pepadi assigned five dhalangs (Anom Suroto, Timbul Hadiprayitno, Sugito Purbotjarito, Panut Darmoko, and Subono) and three Pepadi officials with extensive knowledge of wayang (Solichin, Roesman Hadikoesoemo, and Ekotjipto) to compose the story, "Semar Mbabar Jati Diri" (Semar reveals his identity), with the subtitle "Ismojo Mbangun Jiwo" (Ismojo constructs the soul) and "Sastro Hanggojati" (The literature of the true self). Subono (personal communication, 2022), the youngest dhalang and the descendant of dhalangs, who was trained at the Institute of the Arts in Surakarta, claimed that he wrote a rough draft of the script, which he completed in consultation with the other dhalangs and officials. Subsequently, Pepadi published the story as a monograph in 1995. As a show of reverence to the president, many dhalangs, senior and junior, performed the story, albeit in different versions.

The story was set during the period after the end of the *Mahabharata* epic, centering around King Parikesit (the great grandson of the middle Pandhåwå brother, Prince Arjunå), who ruled a kingdom inherited from his Pandhåwå ancestors. The king felt his reign had shortcomings, because he was unable to bring prosperity to his people. His grandfather advised him to emulate the Pandhåwå by running the kingdom on the basis of the five principles of Pancasila.[5] His grandfather also reminded the king that it would be appropriate for him to ask for advice from Semar. Full of hope, the king departed to search for Semar.

In his absence, the kingdom was attacked by antagonists, but to no avail. In the last scene of the story, Parikesit and his priest Curigånåtå meet Semar. Semar explained the official national motto of Indonesia, a concept mentioned in a Javanese-Hindu literary work, *Sutasoma*: *Bhineka Tunggal Ika Tan Hana Dharma Mangrwa* (they are indeed different but of the same kind since there is no duality in truth). The original meaning referred to the idea that there should be no difference between Buddhism and Sivaism. The Indonesian nationalists adapted it to mean that while the Indonesian people are diverse, they are united; hence the motto "Unity in Diversity." Semar also explains Pancasila, the five foundational philosophical ideas of the Republic of Indonesia: (1) belief in one God; (2) just and civilized humanity; (3) democracy based on unanimous deliberations of representatives; and (5) social justice for all.

Finally, at the heart of the matter Semar reveals his identity: his existence and the conditions of man and his creativity, which are embedded in the six sections of the twenty alphabets.

Hå, hånå urip, there is a life before the creation of human beings.
Na, genå or nglegenå, a human life inside the womb is still neutral.
Caråkå, aside from receiving five senses (*poncå indriyå*) a human being with good character is also equipped with the ability to create (*ciptå*), to feel (*råså*), and to carry out its desire (*karså*).
Dhåtåsawålå, which means uncontested life essence.
Pådhåjåyånyå, good forces and bad forces are equal. A human being is judged on his or her good or bad behavior only at the end of their life.
Mågåbathångå, the soul detaches from the body. A good soul resides in heaven, a bad soul in hell.

The twenty Javanese alphabets, usually divided into four sections, have been interpreted in different ways. The most popular interpretation describes a conflict between two servants of Ajisåkå of Majesthi, Dorå and Sembådå. One time Ajisåkå asked Dora to accompany him to kill a giant king, Dewåtåcengkar, whose habit was to eat humans. Before departing, Ajisåkå asked Sembådå to guard his weapon, saying that Sembådå should give the weapon back only to him. After successfully destroying Dewåtåcengkar, Ajisåkå asked Dorå to return to Majesthi to pick up his weapon. However, Sembådå refused to give the weapon to Dorå, in keeping with his master's directive. The two fight and both die because they are equally powerful in battle.

The interpretation of the meaning of Javanese alphabets in Pepadi's story of "Semar Mbabar Jati Diri" differs than that of the traditional interpretation. It holds that one should understand the concept of a Javanese philosophy known as *sangkan paraning dumadi* (the origin and destination of creation) and moral advice that human beings should have excellent character and practice the act of devotion to God to receive God's blessing. Clearly, Pepadi also responded literally to the president's request to create a wayang story that would explain through performance the foundational philosophy of the state, the Pancasila, and pronounce the good virtue of humanity through interpreting the meaning of Javanese alphabets.

All in all, the story "Semar Mbabar Jati Diri" came about because the president requested a group of dhalangs to create a story, rather than it being a story created by dhalangs to reflect sociopolitical/historical circumstances. In other words, the portrayal of the president as godly-wise Semar is not a manifestation of sociocultural allegory but is rather based on Suharto's desire to be like Semar. In that sense, the portrayal of the president as Semar parallels his autocratic regime, which was known for suppressing critical voices directed against them.

Despite Suharto's suppression of dissent, some indirect criticism has come from different corners of society, including from musicians. One of the best examples is a song called "Pétruk Dadi Ratu" (Pétruk becomes king). The song was popularized by the late Mus Mulyadi, a well-known singer of a genre of Javanese popular music called *Campursari*. Here is part of the lyrics.

MAJALAH TEMPO 2004

Pétruk dadi ratu,
Nyonggå pincuk udut srutu.
Ratu Surålåyå
Patihe Narådå.
Yen lungguh
Sikil jigang munggah mejå,
Cengèngas cengèngès.
Tambur kon nabuh déwa,
jrèng jrèng jrèng jréng.

Pétruk becomes king,
holding up a container [for food],
smoking a cigar
[as if he is] the king of heaven.
Narådå is his minister.
Pétruk sat down,
his leg on the top of the table.
He is laughing without reason.
Pétruk asks gods to play drums
[onomatopoeic sound of drums].

Pétruk dadi ratu,
Nyonggåa pincuk udut crutu
Déwa déwå bingung,
Pétruk ngaji mumpung.

Pétruk becomes king,
holding up a container (for food), smoking a cigar.
Gods are confused.
Pétruk takes opportunity [for his own benefit]

Dipolné dipolné	without any limit,
Nggoné dadi jalwå tukung.	as if he is a large chicken,
Mbendinå mangan	eating every day,
Nganti wetengé mlembung.	so much so that his stomach is swollen.
jrèng jrèng jrèng jréng . . .	[onomatopoeic sound of drums]
Pétruk dadi ratu.	Pétruk becomes king,
Nyonggå pincuk udut crutu.	holding up a container (for food), smoking a cigar.
Dadi ra karuan	Everything becomes a mess.
Ilange tatanan,	The loss of order.
Ukumé kuwåså	But punishment is in the hand of God.
Wekasan si Bagong tekå.	Finally, Bagong arrives,
Si Pétruk digèrèt	dragging around Pétruk.
Bali dadi menungså.	He resumes his usual being
jrèng jrèng jrèng jréng.	[onomatopoeic sound of drums].

People listening to the song might associate it with a wayang story because its content is similar to a story about the clown Pétruk becoming a king who haphazardly uses his power to govern his kingdom (I will return to this story later). In fact, the composer of the song, Andjar Any, intended it as a critique of the authoritarian President Suharto. This fact was revealed after Suharto died, when Anjar Any was interviewed by a journalist for *Tempo* magazine. He said that in order to criticize the president and avoid trouble, he had to choose the language carefully.

After the downfall of Suharto's regime, during the era of reformation, much of the general public perceived Indonesia's presidents as inept, and this was reflected in how they were portrayed in wayang. President Habibie was likened to Garèng and Gus Dur was likened to Bagong (Pausacker 2004, 235), both clown-servants known for being slow and stupid. Pausacker goes on to say that the stories of Garèng, Bagong, and Pétruk holding power temporarily was a trend during the era of Reformation. The story "Pétruk Becomes King" was one of the most well-known stories at the time but for another reason: it depicted the importance of the voice of the commoners.

Carangan

It is common to categorize wayang stories into two general groups: standard (*pokok* or *asli*) and branch (*carangan*). In 1986, a group of Indonesian and American scholars launched research on this topic, resulting in a three-volume work. They reviewed nearly twenty books by Indonesian and European scholars and conducted interviews with thirty dhalangs for the purpose of defining carangan. They offered remarkably varying conclusions, ranging from finding carangan stories to be autonomous (deviating from standard, pokok or asli stories), to seeing carangan as any stories not found standard books of wayang, to claiming that all wayang stories are carangan.

I suggest that the rich variety of meanings attributed to these stories can be explained by our understanding of the word *carangan*. Derived from the root word *carang* (branches of a tree), *carangan* denotes the multiplication of a branch as a tree grows. This metaphorical allusion to plants is commonly used to show the process of augmentation or variation in gamelan, as apparent in the terms *cèngkok*, *kembangan* (floral decoration), and *wiletan* (entwining). In particular, the term *cèngkok*, which is associated with the word *cangkok*, denotes the processes of transplanting, grafting, pruning, and nurturing (Day 1981, 76). It makes sense, therefore, that finding the precise definition of *carangan* is difficult. A carangan story does not derive from any standard story. It does not involve planting the seed, so to speak, but they grow from the branch itself. As a carangan story might grow out from one branch to another, subtle or drastic change might happen to the story. That happens with the Pétruk-as-king story, which has gone through both subtle and drastic changes of meaning.

As noted previously, Pétruk is one of the clown servants (*pånåkawan*) of the middle Pandhåwå brother. The other pånåkawan are Pétruk's younger brothers Garèng and Bagong, and their father, Semar. In contrast to other puppets, the pånåkawan puppets are distinctive for their funny shapes and physical deformities. Semar is known for being immensely fat, with a heavy breast and behind, his uncontrollable farting, and seepage always coming from his eyes. Garèng is a dwarf with disjointed and crooked arms and has yawning sores on his feet, so he always walks with a limp. Pétruk is of scrawny build, is tall, and has a long nose. Bagong, like Semar, has a fat belly and behind and a flat nose. The story has garnered all sorts of interpretive meanings, usually about a commoner taking power. The anthology of Pétruk-as-king stories, in performance and written documents, is critical to this study.

Gus Dur as Semar, Jokowi as Pétruk

As I mentioned earlier, I was surprised to learn that in his speech on wayang Gus Dur did not make any connections between wayang and Islam. Instead, he focused on the relationship between wayang and Indonesian nationalism, democracy, and politics. This does not mean that his knowledge of wayang was minimal. He often watched wayang and hired prominent dhalangs to perform (Al Qurtuby 2022). That is why his family and colleagues hired the well-known dhalang Ki Enthus Susmono to perform in a thousand-days-after-his death commemoration. Many of his colleagues and admirers testified that he was a big fan of wayang. Indeed, his younger daughter even said that wayang was one of his favorite traditional performing arts (NU Online 2012).

The most important way to understand Gus Dur's relationship to wayang is as an allegory of the Indonesian politics of his era. This concerns the portrayal of Gus Dur as Semar, one of the most beloved characters in wayang. What is distinctive about Semar is that he is a clown-servant of paradoxical character and iconography. "He is ornamented like a woman, his clothes are those of man, yet his face is that of neither man nor woman. He is the repository of the highest wisdom, yet this flashes from in-between his gentle jokes, his clowning, and even his persistent uncontrollable farting" (Anderson 1996, 6). Mulyono (in Laksono 1978, 25) elaborated.

> What manner of creation is this, who stands leaning on his belly? or is it, who sits rocking on his buttocks?
>
> The mid-day sun is sallow beside the radiance of his face.
> How can such brilliance emanate from one as pallorous as a corpse?
>
> No parent, no children has he. His smile misted in tears.
> Bleak perils of humanity, softened in the gentle rain of his compassion.
>
> Goodness itself, this god made man, who
> Dominates the *satria* with servitude.
>
> Kings grovel before him; gods honour him;
> Even the Most-High does his bidding.
>
> Invincible through non-deeds, omnipotence in inertia.
> Here lies the source of his *sakti* (divine might).

Dawn at dusk, sunset at daybreak.
The perfect being: Ismaya.

How can the portrayal of Gus Dur as Semar be allegorically interpreted in the context of the sociopolitical conditions of the time? To answer this question, we need to recount a series of tragic events that began in 1965. I previously described these events in chapter three to contextualize the song "Ilir-Ilir" by Cak Nun and his Kyai Kanjeng Ensemble. The alleged coup d'etat attempt by the Communist Party (Partai Komunis Indonesia, PKI), followed by the kidnapping and killing of six army generals by air force officers, also allegedly linked to the Communist Party and the left-wing president, Sukarno, triggered a staggeringly ugly and horrific response. Thousands of members of PKI and its allies were killed by forces under the command of General Suharto, and Sukarno's government was overthrown, with Suharto's New Order government taking power. After more than three decades of authoritarian governance and economic decline, public pressure to restore democracy and eradicate corruption led to Suharto's resignation in 1998.

Subsequent regimes, led by Presidents Habibie, Megawati, and Yudhoyono, have led Indonesia toward a more democratic style of governance, allowing the voices of the masses to be heard. This period is known as *Reformasi* (Reformation), which saw a flourishing of sociopolitical, religious, and cultural organizations. However, the next three presidents were unable to implement further political reforms (Jones 2012, 162). Essentially, the supposed Reformation period was an unending transitional period. I suggest that the wayang scene Gårå-Gårå (the world in turmoil) represents this transitional period.

However, this scene should not be interpreted literally. Rather, the wayang depiction of the world in turmoil uses humor and musical interludes to represent the period of transition toward finding solutions. Hence, the presence of clown-servants—Semar and his sons—is compulsory in this scene. As noted, Semar is a clown-cum-god character. As such, he epitomizes a perfect democratic ideal, namely that those of the highest status are in perfect unity with those of the lowest status: *manunggaling kawulå lan gusti* (a perfect union between the commoner and the Lord) is a philosophical expression that captures well the meaning of this concept.

This brings me back to Gus Dur's relationship with wayang. People's portrayal of Gus Dur as Semar aligns with the presence of Semar in Gårå-Gårå, representing allegorically an important figure in the world of unending transition. In fact, people consider Gus Dur's physical form to be like that of Semar (short, rather plump body), which made the comparative identification almost automatic, easily leading to an allegorically deeper reading of Gus Dur as symbolizing a union between commoners and Lord, from which his power emanated during the continuing transitional period of reforming the nation. Gus Dur, like Semar, is known for his witty humor as well as being a repository of wisdom.

In a similar vein, the story about Pétruk becoming a king is fascinating for the rich interpretations of its meaning. My research suggests that it is one of the best examples of a complex transformation of a story as its context and meaning change from one period of history to another. Existing for more than two centuries, the Pétruk-as-king story not only signifies the importance of the voice of commoners but, in its early form, it was also associated with a colonial campaign to disdain Javanese rulers for their inability to govern. In our contemporary era, the present-day President Joko Widodo is portrayed as Pétruk.

The Pétruk-as-king story became a lively topic of discussion in political discourse after the period of Reformasi following the resignation of President Suharto, especially through mass media. In 2014, during the presidential campaign, people came up with a satire that portrayed candidate Joko Widodo (Jokowi) as Pétruk becoming a king, in both good and unflattering ways—good because of his humble background as a commoner; unflattering by predicting he would be unable to govern. The same portrayal of President Jokowi as Pétruk returned during the second term of his presidency, in an even more pointed way because he was portrayed by Fadli Zon, who previously had been an important figure in an opposing party (Garindra); at this time, Zon was second in command of the house of representatives. Jokowi seemed to ignore the negative side of his portrayal of Pétruk becoming a king. Instead, he confirmed the positive side of the portrayal by buying a large painting, an image of a large gathering of people witnessing a procession, congratulating Pétruk wearing a crown walking with Garèng behind him, followed by Semar driving a chariot.

The use of the Pétruk-as-King story in political satire persisted during Jokowi's presidency. Jokowi's 2021 visit to Yogyakarta to encourage people to get the Covid-19 vaccine is a case in point. The event was organized by a group of Yogyakarta performing artists under the leadership of a prominent poet and performing artist named Butet Kusudiarjå. I imagine the performers must have been excited to hear that President Joko Widodo would be accompanying their Covid-19 vaccinations. Several of them wore costumes for wayang wong performance.

Seven dancers wearing Pétruk-like masks greeted the president, leading him into the hall; the Pétruk masks were to remind everyone of the comparison of Jokowi to Pétruk becoming a king. Opinions about this comparison were divided. One camp believed Jokowi-as-Pétruk represented the importance of common-

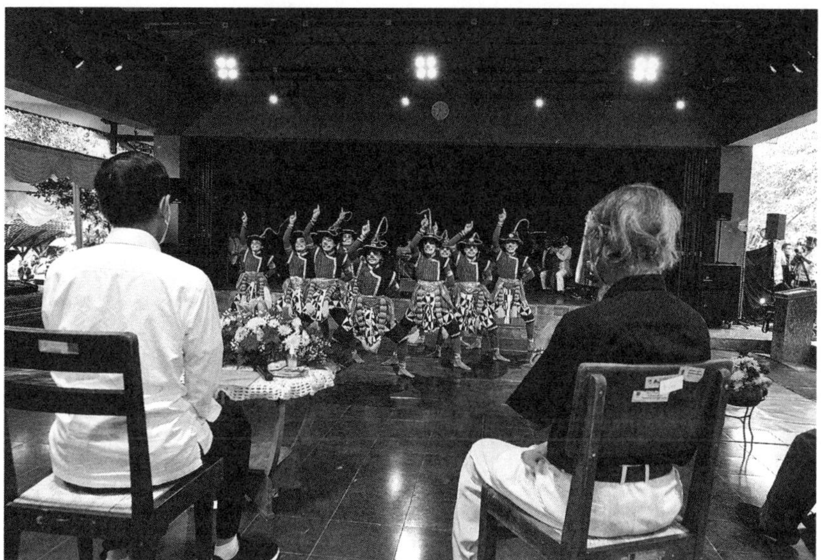

FIGURE 4.2 Dancers wearing masks of Pétruk (or Pinokio?) to greet and perform for President Joko Widodo during his to visit to Yogyakarta encouraging people to get Covid-19 vaccinations. Reproduced courtesy of Agus Suparto, a photographer of the office of the Indonesian President Joko Widodo.

ers' voices in a democratic society. The other camp interpreted the Pétruk mask dancers not as Pétruk, but as Pinocchio—when Pinocchio lies, his nose grows longer, thus suggesting that Jokowi's presidency is characterized by lies. How did Jokowi respond? He told Butet, the head organizer of the event, "lucu mas" (that's funny, brother).

The lively public discussion of the portrayal of Jokowi as Pétruk becoming king shows that wayang is not only rich with imagery, but also with metaphor and political commentary. The Pétruk-as-king story is a very old, very funny, and very popular story. How can a clown-servant become a king? Is it a satire of a grassroots voice in a democratic society, as many have interpreted it? Since the story has existed since the nineteenth century, might colonialism have been involved in its formation? In the following sections I attempt to unpack the formation and transformation of the story throughout history. My assumption is that different meanings of the story are determined by place, time, and circumstances. In other words, the meaning of the story is shaped by its performance context.

Certainly, this assumption is nothing new. As Laurie Sears rightly states, wayang performances should be thought of as allegories of their time, context, and place, and as a metalanguage for politics and commentary (Sears 1996, 11). "Because the stories can be used to comment on the vicissitudes of daily life, and thus commentary changes with each telling, it becomes increasingly difficult to fix the 'meaning' of any story" (11). Sears's point is about the formation and transformation of a wayang story from one performance to another, but in my opinion the plot and meaning of such a story might change according to the sociopolitical and cultural circumstances of a certain historical period. Whereas the Pétruk story has existed in three periods of history, its plot, meaning, and even the name of Pétruk as a king and the name of his kingdom have kept expanding and changing, bringing about rich interpretations of its meaning.

How does the storyline go in wayang performance? When was the story composed? I will answer these questions, tracing the Pétruk story from written documents from the early twentieth century and the nineteenth-century manuscript from the Kasultanan court of Yogyakarta. But first I will briefly mention the position of the Pétruk-as-king story in relation to other stories.

To begin, here is a synopsis of the story based on what is commonly presented in twentieth- and twenty-first-century wayang performances and some published monographs.

> The story begins with princess Mustakawèni, disguised as the prince Gathutkaca, stealing a powerful pusåkå Kalimåsådå from Yudhistirå, the king of Ngamartå. In her journey with the pusåkå, the princess meets one of the sons of Arjunå, the prince Priyambådå, who is accompanied by his clown-servants Semar, Garèng, Pétruk, and Bagong. Through a very intense fight, Priyambådå seizes the pusåkå from Mustakawèni's hands. To make sure the pusåkå will not be taken away again by Mustakawèni, Priyambådå asks Pétruk to keep it.
>
> Pétruk knows that Kalimåsådå is a very powerful pusåkå. A desire comes to his mind to try out the efficacy of the pusåkå. Leaving Priyambådå behind, Pétruk departs to the kingdom of Sonyåwibåwå with the aim of subjugating the kingdom. Pétruk's wish is blessed by the gods Guru and Narådå (they are in disguise as the minister of the king Bèlgeduwèlbèh), who are concerned with the safety of pusåkå Kalimåsådå. Successful in making the king of Sonyåwibåwå surrender, Pétruk declares himself the new king with the name Bèlgeduwélbèh or Thongthongsot. He changes the name of the kingdom from Sonyåwibåwå to Lojitengårå. There he becomes powerful and subjugates many kingdoms. King Bèlgeduwèlbèh also orders his army to attack the kingdom of Ngastinå, and jails its king, Duryudånå, his entourage, and all his brothers.
>
> In the meantime, the king of Ngamartå Yudhistirå and the king of Dwåråwati Kresnå hear about the rising powerful King Bèlgeduwèlbèh. They order their forces to destroy the kingdom of Lojitengårå, but none of them can win the battle. Kresnå, who knows who King Bèlgeduwèlbèh is, asks Semar (Pétruk's

father) and Garèng (Pétruk's older brother) to fight the fake king. They are successful in forcing King Thongthongsot to take off his kingly attire, and he becomes Pétruk again. The ministers also reveal their identities as Guru and Narådå. The two gods explain that what Pétruk has done is under their watch, and they give a present to Pétruk for his success in keeping Kalimåsådå safe. The end.

Decolonizing and Nationalizing the Story

Notice from the synopsis of the Pétruk-as-king that Bèlgeduwèlbèh is one of Pétruk's names. What's in this name, which is unusual, strange, and un-Javanese-sounding? The most common interpretation is that it must be a form of mockery—the name of a Dutchman. When I posted the question of the origin of the name Bèlgeduwèlbèh on the gamelan listserv decades ago, the late Professor Ernst Heins replied that the name came from the Dutch words *wel edel bey*: the salutation "yours truly" for ending a letter. Responding to my recollection of Heins's reply to my inquiry, Matthew Cohen (2021, personal email) interprets the name Bèlgeduwèlbèh as coming from the phrase *veel geduvel bij*, or "a lot of hassle."[6]

Regarding the name of Pétruk's kingdom, Loji Tengårå, both sound like Javanese words, but the word *loji* derives from the Dutch word *loge* (lodge). *Tengårå* means "signal." The other name of Pétruk-as-king is Thongthongsot; *thong* is an onomatope for signaling alarm or a signal from the head of a village to call his subordinates to meet him (the device is called *kenthongan*, a large wood tube with an opening in one side). *Sot* means "curse," such as *disotaké*, to put a curse on someone. Does Thongthongsot mean "calling someone to be cursed"? That would be a bit of a far-fetched interpretation. However, along with the meanings of the names Bèlgeduwèlbèh and Loji Tengårå, such an interpretation is in line with the idea that the story of Pétruk becoming king is Javanese satire directed at the Dutch colonialists for their unlimited control.

The question is, why was Pétruk dressed as a Dutch commander (figure 4.3)? Instead of searching for historical reasons for the Dutchification of Pétruk, contemporary interpreters of this story prefer to give it a universal meaning. That is, in a democratic society, commoners must have their voices heard. Further investigation of nineteenth- and twentieth-century sources—monographs, newsletters, and manuscripts—about the Pétruk-as-king story will help answer this question.

My archival research led me to identify a script of the story written by a certain Hardjosoemarto in 1950. I haven't yet found the original script, but I found its Indonesian translation published by Balai Pustaka (a state agency) in 1962 and

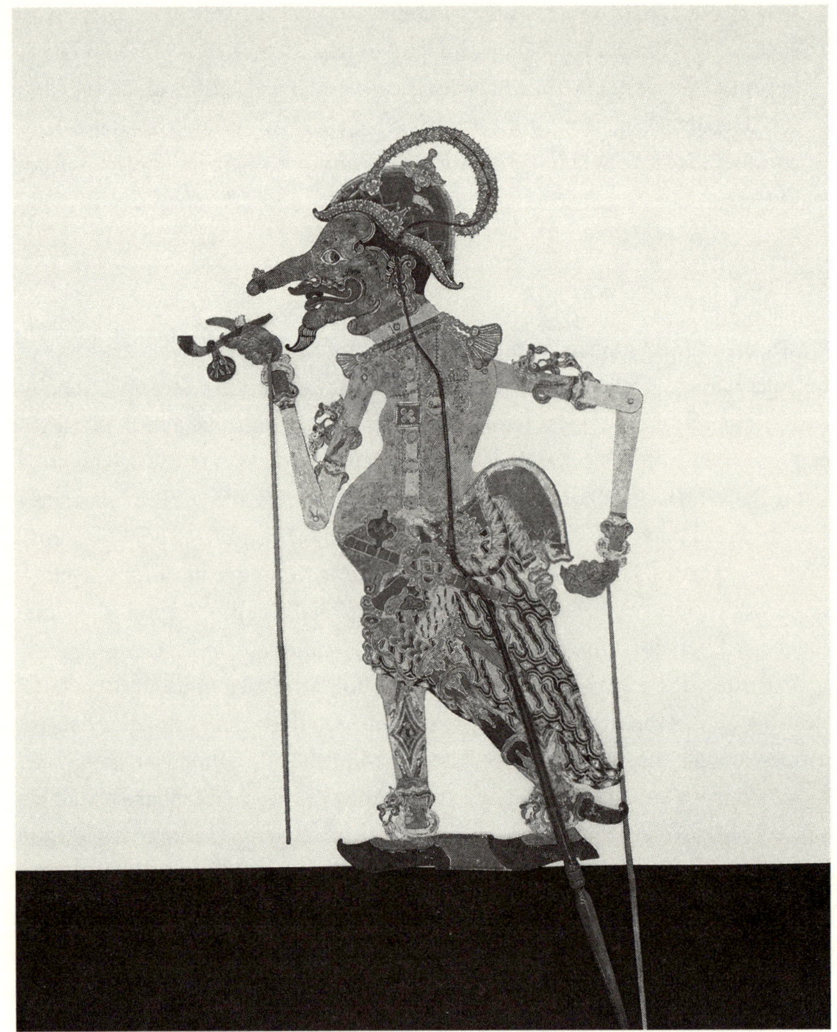

FIGURE 4.3 The Dutchification of Pétruk in the Pétruk-as-king story with the name Bèlgeduwèlbèh. Reproduced courtesy of Yale University Art Gallery.

reprinted in 1963, entitled "Petroek Djadi Radja." Basically, the story is not much different than the story I summarized earlier, but it is written in the form of a Western-style script. That is, the script was meant to be performed as *sandiwara*, "drama" or "play" in the Indonesian language, so that it could be known and possibly performed by non-Javanese people from other Indonesian regions. It does make a sense that through a state-sponsored publication, a wayang story was introduced to the Indonesian general public so people would become familiar with each other's cultural performances as part of government campaigns to promote awareness of national diversity. From a different perspective, the fact that it was wayang story—wayang was and is one of the most celebrated Indonesian performing arts—through which understanding Indonesia's cultural diversity was launched, suggests that the idea was to define national culture as the peak (*puncak-puncal kebudayaan*) of Indonesian regional culture, as mentioned in the 1945 Indonesian Constitution of the State (*Undang-Undang Dasar '45*).

I also found a monograph entitled *Pétroek Dados Ratu. Tjarangan Bebanjolan* (*Pétruk Becomes a King: A Branch of a Humorous Story*), followed by the Dutch translation *De Nar Als Vorst, Javaansche Klucht* (*The Servant as Prince, Javanese Absurdity*). Published in 1911, the essay was a composed by Maijer Ranneft, the assistant resident in charge of the director of domestic affairs. The first part of the essay contains Ranneft's introduction to wayang and the translation of a detailed script of the Pétruk-as-king story. The second part is a script of the same story written in Javanese scripts by Raden Mas Mangkoe Hamidjaja of Magelang. Further research led me to discover that the essay is a reprint of an article by the same author (1906, 111, 113–77) that appeared in *Bijdragen tot de*

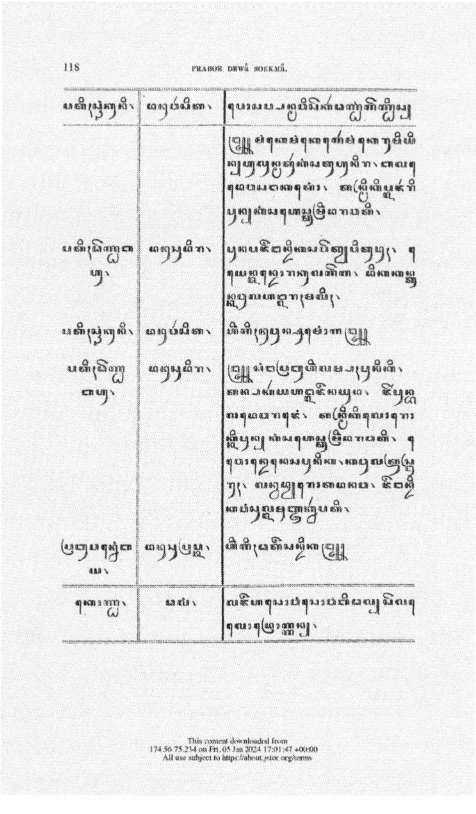

FIGURE 4.4 Excerpt of the Javanese scripts for the story "Praboe Dewa Soekma" by Raden Mas Mangkoe Hamidjaja of Magelang. From Ranneft 1906, 118.

Taal-, Land- en Volkenkunde van Nederlansch-Indie (*Journal of the Humanities and Social Sciences of the Netherlands East Indies*).

It is worth noting the involvement of the Dutch in producing the script and commentary and pondering the reasons why. The title of Ranneft's article is "Praboe Dewa Soekma, of Petroek als vorst (uit de wayang orang)" ("Praboe Déwå Sukmå, or Pétroek as a Prince [from the wayang wong performance]"). The first part contains background about wayang, and the second part, the detailed script of the story, includes the dialogue among the characters and the dhalang's narrations. The basic storyline is somewhat like the story in previous publications, but the detailed plot is expanded, and the names of some characters are different. What immediately caught my attention was the name of the King Pétruk and his kingdom. His name is not Bèlgeduwèlbèh or Thongthongsot, as is common in today's story, but His Majesty Déwå Sukmå (Deity of Soul). His kingdom is called Nusakambangan.

Ranneft's translation of the script was based on the performance of wayang wong dance drama taking place in and sponsored by the Javanese regent of Magelang. According to the regent, the performance was based on a manuscript owned by the sultan of Yogyakarta. In my research, I was made aware of the existence of the Pétruk story in this manuscript before I came upon Ranneft's article. Written in the early to mid-nineteenth century, the title of the manuscript is *Serat Kandha Pétruk Dados Ratu*. The Pétruk story is preceded by three sections of the story of Jaya Semadi, which was presented in a three-day performance. The fourth section of the manuscript, "Pétruk Dados Ratu," is a later addition that was performed on the fourth day of the event. The 104-page manuscript is dated September 13, 1872. Written in Javanese scripts, it contains longer, more detailed, and different variations of the story. I'll highlight a few narratives that are drastically different than the narratives from the early twentieth century and the ones we know today.

The two most striking differences are the names of Pétruk-as-king and the names of his kingdom. His name is His Majesty Déwå Sukmå (the name that appears in Ranneft's text). His second name (perhaps a nickname?) is Singsèh Cithothok. He has a wife and four concubines and four close disciples. The name of his kingdom is Nusakambangan, and he has a *wihara* (Buddhist temple) in Bangkalan, Madura. I must acknowledge that I don't have enough references to interpret the distinctiveness of this Pétruk story.

Another striking difference about this manuscript is the reason why Pétruk must leave the princely Madukårå residency. Here, he leaves because his master Arjunå once was angry at him and grasped his *kucir* (a hair style for children), pulling out one of his hairs. Pétruk was offended and very upset. Therefore, he left, accompanied by three of his close disciples. Arriving in the middle of a forest, Pétruk meditates (*hamemati rågå*). Gods give their blessing, asking Pétruk to conquer the kingdom of Nusakambangan and declare himself its king.

How should we interpret the meaning of this story as it is told in the court manuscript? According to Soedarsono (1984, 234), the Pétruk-as-king story represents Hamengku Buwånå V's criticism of the Dutch governor general, Commissary General Leonard Pierre Joseph Burggraaf Du Bus de Gigsignies. He explains that the governor general had no Javanese blood, but he acted as if he was a Javanese king. The accuracy of this interpretation should be questioned, however. After a great revolt against colonialism from 1825 to 1830 (known as the Java War), a more effective regime was established in which the Dutch consolidated their total control of Java and its courts. This new situation is reflected in the opening of the court wayang wong play, which began with a recitation of Hamengku Buwånå's gratitude for the support and love of His Lordly Father the Dutch Resident, His Lordly Grandfather the Governor General, and His Lordly Grandmother the Queen of the Netherlands. In this context, it is unrealistic to suggest that Hamengku Buwånå V was brave enough to criticize Dutch authority.

Unfortunately, there is no contemporaneous evidence to help us reconstruct the meaning of the Pétruk-as-king story as presented in the court manuscript. But a recent essay by Sri Margana (2019), "Religion, Communism, and Ratu Adil: Colonialism and Propaganda Literature in 1920s Yogyakarta," sheds some light. He proposes that after the implementation of the Cultivation System, which forced Indonesians to produce agricultural goods for export to benefit the Dutch colonial government, the Dutch consolidated their control of Java through various forms of propaganda, including films, pamphlets, posters, and books. In Yogyakarta, the Dutch Resident Dingemanns published four Javanese stories, in the Javanese language. One of them is entitled *Caritanipun Simin diukum pangadilan amarga dadi Ratu Adil palsu* (The story of Simin, punished by the court for falsely claiming to be the Just King). Sri Margana argues that the story presents a colonial perspective of the Ratu Adil movements. "Simin, a commoner, portrays himself as a king, reflecting elements of the wayang (shadow puppet) story 'Pétruk dadi Ratu' that had been popular since the nineteenth century." Dingemanns presents Simin as a fake king who abuses his position and gives himself a pompous and even bawdy title. "This fourth story may be understood as colonial mockery of commoners' subversive activities, portraying them as lacking political savvy" (247).

There is no evidence that the Simin story was inspired by the Pétruk-as-king story. However, there seems to be a pattern that shows a connection between the two. Earlier, I asked why the Dutch became deeply involved in writing about the story and translating it into Dutch. I suggest that such activity related to Dingemanns's propaganda campaign. The point being made is that only the Dutch can rule Java, not the Javanese, as represented by Simin. I must admit that this is highly speculative opinion, but it is true that in general the Dutch showed a deep interest in Javanese performing arts in the court of Yogyakarta. The author of *Babad Ngayogyakarta* says of the Europeans, "*sami suka ningali*" (all were enjoying watching the performance) (Lindsay 1991, 100). Lindsay wonders whether they were truly enjoying it or if the author was simply following a conventional narrative. In any event, it seems clear that colonial contexts prompted the development of the court wayang wong. Soedarsono even points out that the use of a script read by *pamaos kandha* (a narrator) indicates the influence of Western culture on the court wayang wong.

PRESERVATION AND DEVELOPMENT

As I noted earlier, Gus Dur was known for being a big fan of wayang. Because wayang has become a widely celebrated Indonesian cultural production, the state often holds wayang performances and/or festivals at the national or regional level. It is not uncommon for political organizations to sponsor wayang performances as part of their campaigns. The most notable example was the government political party, Golkar. As discussed earlier, Golkar sponsored spectacular wayang performances, using longer screens and multiple puppeteers.

There are also two national organizations, the National Secretariat of Indonesian Wayang (Sekretariat Nasional Wayang Indonesia, Senawangi) and the Indonesian Association of Puppetry (Persatuan Pedalangan Indonesia, Pepadi), whose founders and administrators are active or retired high-ranking government officials. The regional branches of these nonprofit organizations often sponsor wayang performances, festivals, and seminars.

As the government and government officials have more conspicuously become patrons of wayang, a series of formalized ceremonies signifying an attribution to those holding power were created to present before the beginning of a performance. Commonly, this bureaucratic ritual consists of an opening remark by a master of ceremonies about the order of the event, singing the national anthem, a prayer led by a religious figure, a speech by someone on behalf of the sponsor, sometimes a speech by a VIP guest (usually a high-ranking government official), and the sponsor handing over wayang puppets to the dhalang. This preperformance ceremonial event has become a standard way to open a wayang performance, not only for government-sponsored wayang but also for privately sponsored wayang performances (without singing the national anthem) to celebrate rites of passage.

At wayang performances sponsored by the government or its allies, it is not uncommon for a government official to deliver an introductory speech. Certainly, the kind of speech is determined by his or her familiarity with and knowledge of wayang. Some high-ranking officials have deep knowledge of wayang that they learned in the environment where they grew up, and giving such an introductory speech is not a challenge for them. Gus Dur, for example, had no problem delivering speeches for such events because of his familiarity with wayang tradition. The point is that this phenomenon shows the increasing shift of wayang patronage from sponsors holding wayang for private events to government or government-related sponsors. In this context one can predict the familiarity of certain government officials with wayang. I will relate a story about my encounter with such an official—not through a personal meeting but through reading his writing.

As part of the 2018 International Gamelan Festival, which was held in Surakarta, I was invited to write a book in Indonesian on gamelan. Since I didn't have enough time to write a brand-new book, I offered to publish a selection of my articles in English translated into Indonesian, thematically arranged. In the conclusion of the book, I included a section deriving from the new research I had carried out since 2007 under the auspicious of grants from the National Endowment for the Humanities and the American Council of Learned Societies.

Aware that the event was by design an international festival, the organizing committee also felt it was necessary to publish a book in English. They invited me to reprint three of my previous articles on wayang. Entitled *Contextualizing Wayang and Gamelan to History, Islam, and Nation State*, the book focused on the relationship between Javanese performing arts and Islam. When the publisher asked me to approve the draft of the book, I was surprised to learn that the foreword was attributed to the current minister of education and culture, Muhadjir Effendy. I have no proof that he actually wrote the foreword. My publisher told me that even if an assistant wrote it, the minister must have been the one who came up with the ideas. I was pleasantly surprised to find the foreword insightful and thoughtfully written, and concluded that the minister must know something about wayang and Islam.

The minister explains in his foreword (Sumarsam 2018, v) that, according to Javanese tradition, Javanese Islamic saints (*wali*) played an important role in the propagation of Islam through gamelan and wayang. However, he quickly qualifies that so far there is no strong evidence to support the claim. Moreover, the relationship between Islam and performing arts appears to be somewhat distant. Certain Islamic factions even view gamelan and wayang with a degree of taboo. In turn, the minister questions: How can the teaching of Islam be conveyed through wayang and gamelan? In response, he explains that the three essays within this thin book written by Sumarsam do not directly address this inquiry. Instead, the essays in the book offer historical and contemporary perspectives to show the connection between Islam, wayang, and gamelan.

The minister makes an important point, which makes me ask, who is Muhadjir Effendy? From reading this brief foreword, it seems clear that he must be knowledgeable about Islam and wayang, since he properly contextualizes my book. Even more surprising is the fact that Minister Muhadjir Effendy was and is one of the leaders of Muhammadiyah, an Islamic organization that tends to emphasize modernization, and that sometimes questions the role of the performing arts in society. I also discovered that the minister's father was a dhalang, and that the minister himself has learned to perform wayang.

My point about the involvement of high-ranking government officials in the performing arts is to show an intimate link between cultural performances and social and national identity. That is, the role of patronage of the arts contributes to shaping the form of wayang performance. Before Indonesia became an independent country, Javanese aristocracy (the king and his family) were important patrons of the performing arts; hence the establishment of courtly identity, character, and performance style. After independence, the status of the court changed from being power holders in society to being followers of the government of the Republic of Indonesia. As more and more prominent government officials became keen patrons of wayang, the courtly identity of the performing arts shifted to become the national identity of Indonesia. The courts still maintain their cultural traditions and are lauded by the government as a symbol of national pride and cultural heritage. It is in this context that the involvement of government officials in performing arts activity, at a national or regional level, takes place. Their involvement has brought complexity to traditional structures and changed the significance of wayang patronage.

Gus Dur's and Bung Moko's Critical Views

The role of government as an important patron of cultural performances is sometimes a subject of debate in Indonesia. For example, in an essay, Gus Dur (2001, 3–4) questioned the government's interference in the development of art. He argued that the state must have nothing to do with culture. He defines culture as the result of social interaction between members of the community, individually and collectively; it is a live process, not a treasure that can be inherited. To him, art is not only aesthetic expression, but it can also cleanse the conscience of society, acting as a catharsis of sociopolitics, and as a vehicle of cultural change. That is why Gus Dur was skeptical about the Department of Education and Culture launching Cultural Congress (Kongres Kebudayaan), the state-sponsored forum that since the early twentieth century has been a routine platform for guiding the development of culture. Gus Dur is of the opinion that culture ought not to become a minister's political gimmick, something resulting from the bureaucratization process (4).

Another towering Indonesian scholar who had the same perspective as Gus Dur was the late Soedjatmoko (also known intimately as Bung Moko). In mid-1979 he was invited to lecture before artists, instructors, and lecturers at the Jakarta Institute of Education and Culture (Lembaga Pendidikan dan Kebudayaan Jakarta, LPKJ) at the Taman Izmail Marzuki Arts Center. The main topic of his lecture was the life of the traditional arts in the era of modernization. He argued that Indonesia was in the middle of transitioning from a traditional to a modern society. In this context, it made sense that people would be ambivalent about positioning the traditional arts in Indonesia. Bung Moko explained that Indonesia was lagging behind in economic development in this period and that poverty was widespread. Therefore, his idea was for Indonesians to create a new but simple civilization.

Bung Moko noted that there was a gap between urbanization and traditional village life. The former involves an expanded lifestyle that includes and was influenced by Western materialistic culture; this lifestyle is not congruent with the traditional village lifestyle. Traditional arts cannot accommodate the modern lifestyle of urban people. On the other hand, while urban people are heavily influenced by Western culture, they cannot totally ignore traditional culture. He asserted that because of the narrowing of external cultural space (*menciutnya ruang luar*) caused by modernization, people should pursue the development of their own internal space (*memperkembangkan ruang dalam*) so they can appreciate aesthetic expression, uplifting humor, and searching for the meaning of life through spirituality. According to him, artists through their creations have an important role to play in this internal search for the meaning of life.

After his closing remarks, Bung Moko invited the audience to ask questions. Unfortunately, the audio of the first question cannot be heard clearly. But I can deduce from his answer that the question was about the role of government in providing resources to artists to produce their works. Listening to Bung Moko's answer, from his use of strong words and his gradually rising his voice, it is clear he was angry. "I am sorry, the question may be wrong . . . totally wrong;

please, don't be angry. The problem is whatever the government can do, the present or future government, it would have a small impact." He emphasized that Indonesians should reform their country with the understanding that it has a dense population and limited material resources. In this regard, artists have an important role in providing the development of internal space he referred to earlier. There should be no crisscrossing between the creativity of artists and public institutions. None of this, he emphasizes, can be dealt with by government policy. If government has a place, it is only marginal.

> [It is] artists with their freedom who can much more determine the life of the arts in the future and the ability to provide a place and to enjoy the beauty in their daily life. Thus, I think in the framework I have explained earlier, do not ask the government what they can do. They cannot do anything in encountering the breadth and the primary issues . . . We should search for ways to [guide] the hearts of Indonesian society, Indonesian nation. [In this regard] the artist is the key. The question is, can they open the key to the creativity of most Indonesians? The main issue is the dynamic of society, the dynamic among the artists, how far they can orient themselves to the market for elites and extended to tourists, or how far they feel that they are the manifestation, the mouthpiece of the anxiety of culture in their socio-environment.[7]

Bung Moko's stance regarding the minimal role government should play in the development of the arts parallels Gus Dur's critical view of the bureaucratization of culture and performance as exemplified by the government-sponsored Cultural Congress. Nonetheless, such critical views from towering nationalist figures had no impact on the policy of the Indonesian government. The Kongres Kebudayaan, which started late in the colonial era, has become an important gathering for Indonesian intellectuals. The last congress was held in 2018, with the theme "Having Identity in Culture" (*Berkepribadian Dalam Kebudayaan*), which can be interpreted as searching for a distinctive national identity within or according to Indonesian culture.

Indeed, the Cultural Congress was born in 1918 as part of the search for national identity in the spirit of national awakening. As explained by the historian Har Tilaar (in Supardi 2017, x), "During the first Congress in 1918, Indonesian society was under the control of colonialism. Indonesian culture was seen as inferior, and anything coming from the West was the best thing. The 1918 Cultural Congress began to make [Indonesians] aware of the pride and confidence toward their own culture; thus, the nation and people of Indonesia had given birth to the National Awakening in 1908, the Youth Oat (*Sumpah Pemuda*) in 1918 and the revolutionary independence in 1945." The encounter with Western culture and its negative and positive influences have inspired Indonesians searching for national identity. This is a consistent theme of subsequent congresses. The debate about accommodating or rejecting Western culture has been and remains the main thread of the conversation about the search for national identity.

Cultural Policy

It is in the context of this debate that the Indonesian government became deeply involved in the development of culture and cultural expression. That is, the concept and execution of cultural policy is seen as a way of building national identity. From the period of Indonesia's national awakening to the present, institutions affiliated with the development of government and, after independence, the government itself, felt compelled to direct the development of Indonesian culture. In the words of Article 32 of the Constitution, "The Government shall develop the National Culture of Indonesia," which is defined as "the culture that emerges as a product of the minds of all the Indonesian peoples. Earlier and indigenous cultures as represented by the local cultures all over Indonesia are a definite part of national culture. Cultural endeavors shall be aimed at developing civilization, culture and (national) unity, without denying novel elements from foreign cultures which may develop or enrich national culture as such and improve the human dignity of the Indonesian nation."[8]

Right after the declaration of independence in 1945, the Ministry of Education and Culture was created to carry out that constitutional charge. Its Cultural Department consisted of three divisions, Archeology, Art, and Languages. Today, the art division is called Cultural General (Jendral Kebudayaan), and it is under the Ministry of Education, Culture, Research, and Technology (Kementerian Pendidikan, Kebudayaan, Riset, dan Teknologi). Through its national and regional agencies, it provides funding for schools of performing arts, theatrical and musical groups, and artistic projects by certain individuals or cultural groups. The division also provides funding for arts festivals, arts competitions, and the like. All in all, the government became an important patron of the arts. This was definitively solidified in 2017 when the government enacted the Law about the Development of Culture (Undang-Undang No. 5 Tahun 2007 Tentang Pemajuan Kebudayaan). The law lists ten cultural objects—oral traditions, manuscripts, customs, rites, traditional knowledge, traditional technology, arts, languages, folk games, and traditional sports—that should be preserved, documented, sustained, and developed with the help of government funding.

It is clear from this list that the state pays close attention to Indonesia's traditional ways of life, not only as historical heritage to be recorded but also as cultural practices that people should follow and refer to in positioning their cultural identity and carrying out their daily lives. In performing arts, the law encourages contemporary artists to actively perform traditional repertoire for the sake of conservation and preservation, and to use them for reference in creating new works. The question is, since the government and its officials are the sole sponsor of artistic projects, to what degree does the sponsor influence the content of artists' works?

This question reminds us of contemporary wayang performance in which, as I mentioned earlier, an artist must acknowledge the presence of his sponsor or his well-known patrons literally or figuratively, for example by asking the sponsor to ceremonially hand over a puppet to the dhalang, and by the dhalang inviting the sponsor or government officials to deliver a speech or be a guest star. These kinds of practices did not exist in traditional wayang performance.

Another example is when the sponsor asks a dhalang to incorporate certain messages into his performance, especially during the humorous Gårå-Gårå and Limbukan scenes. A lecturer at the Institute of the Arts in Surakarta, Bambang Suwarno (2006, 4–5), reported the ways in which a well-known dhalang, Ki Nartosabdho, responded to the diminishing popularity of wayang performance during the Orde Baru era by featuring the humorous Gårå-Gårå scene, and incorporating into it many light songs of his own composition to create an intimate atmosphere with his audience. In addition, he presented important figures, such as Kresnå, Bålådéwå, Werkudårå, and Arjunå as if they were just regular human beings rather than serious figures discussing serious matters. Anom Suroto, as a supporter of the New Order government, communicated government policies to his audience by incorporating them in any scenes he thought fit. As ways to make the younger generation interested in wayang, and potentially more receptive to the government's messages, the late Manteb Soedarsono made the puppets' movements remarkably acrobatic and employed colorful lighting and sound effects.

The preceding discussion is about framing wayang performance as it happens in-between the world of opposite-complementary dualism. On the one hand, the dhalang follows certain traditional rules, practices, and stories, but on the other hand he must incorporate nontraditional ideas or adjust the content of the story according to circumstances of the time and place of his performance. I have discussed this topic at length in terms of wayang story functioning as allegory to sociopolitical reality. In Javanese discourse on wayang this is called *sanggit*, the manifestation of creativity in the moment of performance.

On a conceptual level, this reminds us of Gus Dur's and Bung Moko's comments about assuming the state will have a marginal role in the development of culture and cultural performance. Lindsay (1995) has studied the importance in

Southeast Asia of the state as patron of the arts, underscoring the basic accepted premise of the educative value of regional cultural heritage as a civilizing agent of human behavior, hence taking it for granted as a source of pride and sense of identity without being problematic (659). Building national identity is the key purpose of the state's cultural policy, but the diversity of cultural expression in Indonesia's archipelago has made national identity difficult to define. It is in this context that Bung Moko's assertion that the state should not do much to support cultural diversity and Gus Dur's critical view of the Cultural Congress become relevant. The health of the performing arts as impacted by being in-between two ideas—that culture develops as the manifestation of society responding to social, political, and cultural change, and that the government has a duty to guide the development of culture—will most likely be an open-ended topic for future discussion.

Wayang and UNESCO

All in all, the government has been and still is committed to overseeing the development and promotion of Indonesian culture. To promote Indonesian culture abroad, the state sponsored groups of performing artists on what are known as *misi kesenian* (cultural mission). "Soft cultural diplomacy" is the term commonly applied to this type of endeavor. The first such cultural mission was in 1954; under the first president of Indonesia, Sukarno, the state sent an Indonesian performing group to China. Since then, there have been a score of cultural missions to many countries, including the large "Indonesia Floating Fair" in 1961, in which a ship carried performers and exhibitions to Hawaii, Japan, Hong Kong, the Philippines, and Singapore.[9] Other missions included the World's Exposition at the 1964 New York World's Fair, the 1970 Expo in Osaka, Japan (for which I was selected as one of the musicians performing Javanese and Balinese music), and the 1984 Vancouver World's Fair.

Another opportunity for the government to carry out cultural diplomacy through the arts is UNESCO's World Heritage program. In 2003, Indonesian wayang was one of the Southeast Asian performing arts to make the list of "Masterpieces of the Oral and Intangible Cultural Heritage of Humanity." Subsequently, *keris*, *batik*, Panji stories, and recently gamelan have been listed. I will not examine the process of Indonesia making the list (see Foley 2014, Boonstra 2014, and Smith and Okagawa 2009). In what follows, I discuss the relevance of the World Heritage program to the recent development of wayang.

There are six criteria of cultural expressions and spaces a country must meet to be accepted into UNESCO's World Heritage program:

1. Demonstrate their outstanding value as masterpieces of the human creative genius.
2. Give wide evidence of their roots in the cultural tradition or cultural history of the community concerned.
3. Be a means of affirming the cultural identity of the cultural communities concerned.
4. Provide proof of excellence in the application of the skill and technical qualities displayed.
5. Affirm their value as a unique testimony of living cultural traditions.
6. Be at risk of degradation or of disappearing.

Among these criteria, cultural identity, a unique testimony of living cultural tradition, and a risk of degradation or of disappearing are relevant to our discussion of the development of today's wayang performance. As discussed previously, modern Western culture and technology have been incorporated into contemporary wayang, resulting in performances featuring a long humorous scene with the presentation of Indonesian popular music, the presence of guest stars, and a new type of light for the performance (from an oil lamp blèncong to electric bulb. Do these developments lead to "affirming the cultural identity" and "a unique testimony of living cultural tradition," as UNESCO has in mind? Indeed, UNESCO (2008) is concerned about the integrity of wayang, as can be seen in an essay on its website five years after it declared wayang a World Cultural Heritage. "Implementation of the National Action Plan for the Safeguarding of the Wayang Puppet Theatre of Indonesia" says that in contemporary Indonesia, "wayang is pressed to serve popular tastes that sometimes do not appreciate its traditional refined way of weaving humor into serious social and political issues, and it is believed that this special role may have contributed to wayang's survival over the centuries" (1). The concern is strengthened by the following quotation, taken from another UNESCO essay: "The Wayang Puppet Theatre still enjoys great popularity. However, to compete successfully with modern forms of pastimes such as video, television or karaoke, performers tend to accentuate comic scenes at the expense of the story line and to replace musical accompaniment with pop tunes, leading to the loss of some characteristic features."[10]

Regardless, UNESCO did support the implementation of the national plan for safeguarding wayang. The plan has been carried out with a budget of US $149,986 (funding source from Japan Funds-in-Trust), aiming to make more effective transmission of wayang knowledge and the skills to perform from master artists to young artists, to revitalize the activity of wayang community studio (*sanggar*) and wayang practitioners, and to make audio-visual educational kits and guidebooks about various forms of wayang to enhance the general public's appreciation (UNESCO 2013).[11] In this way, two of the six criteria required for receiving designation are strengthened: (1) providing proof of excellence in the application of the skill and technical qualities displayed, and (2) avoiding the risk of degradation or disappearance. However, these plans do not address UNESCO's concerns about the development of wayang performance that presents excessive scenes of humor and popular music.

This leads us to think about the meaning of cultural heritage as UNESCO defined it. Conceived and debated during the 1970s, the concept initially applied to monuments and objects of valuable inheritance but was then expanded to include "tradition or living expressions inherited from our ancestors and passed on to our descendants, such as oral traditions, performing arts, social practices, rituals, festive events, knowledge and practices concerning nature and the universe, or the knowledge and skills to produce traditional crafts.[12] UNESCO's convention explains each of them in detail, emphasizing the importance of safeguarding the wealth of knowledge and skills to produce them so they can be passed on to the subsequent generation.

UNESCO's concern that today's traditional performing arts are under threat because of the popularity of Western popular culture in non-Western countries is highly relevant to our discussion of wayang and gamelan. In many cases traditional music has become standardized, bringing about the abandonment of traditional practices. For example, the UNESCO convention says of the explosion in popularity of Western popular music, "Though it performs an important role in cultural exchange and encourages creativity that enriches the international art scene, the phenomenon can also cause problems. Many diverse forms of music may be homogenized with the goal of delivering a consistent product. In these situations, there is little place for certain musical practices that are vital to the process of performance and tradition in certain communities."[13]

However, by the time the convention was established in 2003, Western popular culture had already penetrated Indonesian culture. Western musical instruments and Indonesianized or hybridized Western popular had been incorporated into wayang performance in a number of scenes. It is also an open question whether at the time traditional performing arts were at risk of degradation or of disappearing (criteria 6). It is possible that such a statement, which was also mentioned in the application the Indonesian committee submitted to UNESCO, is more rhetoric than reality. A study of wayang in the late 1990s by Umar Kayam (2021) demonstrated the exuberant persistence of wayang tradition—albeit with aspects of Western popular culture and technology incorporated into it—as indicated by the large number of dhalang and wayang groups in the Yogyakarta special province, Central Java, and East Java. This was still true when the study was published in 2001.

Since cultural transformation is inextricably linked to the influence of foreign cultures, the question becomes in what way the concept of heritage is associated with cultural identity. Smith and Akagawa (2009) think that the link between heritage and cultural identity is difficult to understand, but they rightly suggest that "a key consequence of heritage is that it creates and recreates a sense of inclusion and exclusion. At global, national and local levels, heritage, however defined, is used to define a sense of place. Current and dominant definitions about 'tangible' and 'world heritage' establish an international hierarchy of cultural relevance, status and sense of place. Ultimately, whatever the ICHC [Intangible Cultural Heritage Convention] does or does not achieve, the development of international debate about intangible heritage—and thus the nature of heritage more generally—has the potential to rework not only definitions of heritage but global and local senses of place" (7). In this regard, the development of wayang in the context of UNESCO's Intangible Cultural Heritage project has created a paradox. On the one hand, its idea is to preserve the knowledge and skills of traditional performing arts, while on the other hand, Western technology and cultures have penetrated into wayang tradition for a long time.

Readers should be familiar now with the idea that the wayang-UNESCO encounter represents a dynamic dualistic interaction, i.e., the theme of the present study. It shows the complexity of Javanese society searching for a balanced coexistence in the context of the global public sphere through the program of Cultural Heritage for Humanity. Wayang practitioners whose performing art is on UNESCO's list of Intangible Cultural Heritage were very proud having such an honor bestowed on their tradition. Many dhalangs announced it proudly in the Limbukan and Gårå-Gårå scenes. But does this recognition change their performance practice? I don't think so. For the state, which feels responsible for supervising the preservation and development of performing arts, the Intangible Cultural Heritage for Humanity designation has encouraged it to better promote Indonesia, aiming toward social, political, and economic success. Whether wayang is an endangered practice or not is not their priority.

The idea of acknowledging commonality in worldwide cultural production is indeed a monumental project, considering the heterogeneity of the history and development of each society of the world in terms of the dynamic of the transformational process of culture by reflecting and contemporizing the past. UNESCO's concern about wayang is a small example of a complex issue the organization encounters. In her essay "World Heritage and Cultural Economics," Kirshenblat-Gimblet (2006) is pessimistic about the result of such a meta project:

“the masterpieces on UNESCO’s intangible heritage list could never do the work that world heritage is intended to do, namely, to model a particular vision of humanity in terms of a global cultural commons” (196).

This discussion of wayang revolves around the topic of cultural production when society is searching for a balanced coexistence between Java and the West through creative exploration—notwithstanding the result. This evolution is happening as Javanese society lives in the in-between world, still in a period of cultural transition when the Javanese have to take a stance about their deepening encounter with Western cultural influences.

CONCLUSION

In 1965, Claire Holt, in her monumental work *Art in Indonesia: Continuities and Change*, noted that Java has long been the center of attention of scholars studying Indonesia. This is because through much of its history, Java has been "the principal locus both of power and of converging insular and international commerce," and has "provided the bulk of historical records" (3).

Holt made that statement almost six decades ago. Is Java still the focus of study? Perhaps. I would say a certain methodology has led to Java remaining one of the subjects garnering the most scholarly attention. That methodology takes into consideration extensive historical sources and contemporary cultural theory and criticism by delving deeper into examining Javanese literature of the past, linking it with Javanese traditions in the present, and reviewing discourses about Java by past and present scholars. This process is common to any study, but it seems that the richness of historical sources and the view of culture as an unending transformational process have maintained the interest of Javanists. Often, the research consists of intensively reading old manuscripts, translating them into English, and analyzing them diachronically or synchronically, or in their cultural contexts (e.g., Florida 1995, Robson 1995, Soebardi 1975). Another trend is to analyze links between past and present traditions by quoting texts extensively from old manuscripts (e.g., Acri 2015, Day 2020, Meyer 2021, Pemberton 1994, Vickers 2020, Zoetmulder 1974).

The present study follows this methodology. In doing so, I highlight the interactions of various religio-sociocultural relationships, and discuss resulting heterogeneous perspectives, inconsistencies, eclecticisms, and even paradoxes within Javanese society throughout inter-historical and intercultural moments. Following the premise that the performing arts are an expression of the total social and cultural life of people (Turner 1990), I suggest that the social drama of wide-ranging religio-sociocultural expressions are performatively realized in the performing arts.

This conclusion reflects the case studies presented throughout the book, which touch on a range of themes such as transhistorical complexity and ambiguity, incongruity, politicization, allegory, and patronage and the advancement of culture. As a coda, I return to the overarching theme of the book—the world of dualism, the in-between, and liminality—by way of a metaphorical reading of a contemporary picture and verses of music drawn from the nineteenth-century *Serat Tjenṭini*.

As a point of departure, I ask: what strategies and methods should one employ in understanding the performing arts in the context of the historical development of Java's complex and diverse society? As I have suggested throughout this book, I propose the notion of the dialectical multiplicity of dualisms. I define "dualism" not as "the idea or belief that everything has two opposite parts or principles" per Britannica,[1] but as a push-pull, dynamic interaction between opposites from which the dynamic complementarity of balance and opposition occurs (Becker 1979). These dualisms include stasis/motion, sacred/secular, day/night, lord/servant, good/evil, male/female, left/right, traditional/contemporary, history/myth, ethnicity/nationality, and many more.

I included "the in-between" in the title of the book because I was inspired by my initial discussion of the interaction between history and mythology. Thinking further, I began to see wider implications of the "in-between" concept in processes of sociocultural change and continuity, creating a process Turner (1979, 1982, 1990) calls "rite-of-passage." Such a process creates a "liminal phase" that happens at the time of cultural flux or on the threshold of change. What happens in the liminal phase, the in-between, or a time between times can be characterized by ambiguity, indefiniteness, and blurred conventions within which exploration, creativity, innovation, and change can occur.

TRANSHISTORICAL COMPLEXITY AND AMBIGUITY

Understanding the world "in-between" or in a "liminal phase" has led me to better see processes of cultural formation and transformation as creative explorations in search of new methods and methodologies, expanding new meaning, and negotiating or rejecting older forms during times of cultural flux. The process becomes even more complex when we consider the liminal phase over a long span of history. In chapter 1, I examined contemporary events, tracing them back many centuries to understand the impact of Indian culture on the development of Javanese performing arts. One of my examples traces the link between the twentieth-century court jesters *canthang balung* and *vidu* priests-cum-performers mentioned in the ninth-century kekawin *Ramayana*, which relates to the idea of finding archaeological meaning through the concept of palimpsest (the present cannot completely erase the past) proposed by Becker (1993) and earlier by G. P. H. Hadiwidjojo (1953).

Other examples include Gus Muwafiq's proselytizing regarding the transformation of the twelfth-century Hindu Tantric pancamakara ritual practice into the sixteenth-century Islamic slametan ritual meal, and the story of the transformation of the weapon Kalimahoshada mentioned in the twelfth-century kekawin *Bharatayudha* to pusåkå Kalimåsådå in its association with the sacred Islamic confession Kalimah Sahadat. It is always a challenge to trace transformational processes that occurred many centuries ago. The point is, the world "in-between" or the "liminal phase" at a time of cultural flux allows creativity and exploration to occur, yet ambiguity or ambivalence accompany the creative and exploratory process.

In dealing with such a long time span in studying cultural transformation, I began to see patterns of congruity and incongruity in cultural practices and discourses as a consequence of intercultural and interreligious encounters in the process of formulating new forms of a more transient culture. In contemporary Java, terminology such as "local genius" or "local wisdom" (*kearifan lokal*) are used to describe the ability of people to localize foreign cultural elements in the formation of local cultural identity. Sometimes, such an identity is considered highly unique and becomes locally valued expressive culture. Other times, because of the cultural and religious diversity of Indonesia, such forms garner scrutiny or criticism.

For example, localizing Quranic reading by using a gamelan tuning system could be considered the product of a local genius. But when Yaser Muhammad Arafat presented a televised Quranic recitation in the *pélog* gamelan tuning system at the formal occasion of the 2015 *Isra Mi'raj* (the Journey and Ascension of the Prophet Muhammad) in the presidential palace, certain conservative Muslims were highly critical of such a Javanized Quranic reading because of its deviation from the original practice. Arafat, who is a lecturer at the Indonesian Islamic University (UIN) Sunan Kalijågå, had to defend himself.[2] He proved historically that the tradition of Quranic reading in the Javanese style was an old practice. When the Arabic style of Quranic reading became known throughout the region in the 1960s and especially the 1970s, this older practice became marginalized. The point is that within Islam, we find dualistic views, including both defenders of legalistic forms of Islam and those who profess Java-Islam syncretic mysticism.

It is well-known that the discussion of the role of the performing arts in Muslim society around the world is fraught with ambiguity and lively debate. The performing arts may be positioned in terms of *haram-halal* polarity or as "in-between." The localization or syncretization of Islam has intensified the debate about whether, for example, Islamic music from the homeland of Islam can be mixed with local music. I mentioned this issue in my previous study (Sumarsam 2011, 54) by referencing the eighteenth-century *Serat Cabolèk*, an experiment of wayang performance accompanied not by gamelan, but by *terbangan* (an Islamic ensemble consisting mainly of frame drums), which triggered lively debate about its appropriateness. One interlocutor laughed at this Islam-Javanese cultural hybridity, while another gave an example of certain well-known *santri* (devoted Muslims) who practiced it with finesse.[3]

In contemporary Java, such contestation can trigger national debate, resulting in highly charged emotional responses. This happened recently when a certain popular preacher made a critical statement about wayang during a televised sermon, saying that wayang performance is forbidden (*haram*) in Islam. Responses from some dhalangs and wayang organizations were swift, nasty, and unprecedented. A few dhalangs created a puppet portraying the preacher and ripped apart and burned it in a scene of their performances. One wayang organization threatened a lawsuit against the preacher. The national dhalang organization tried to cool down the situation right after these responses happened. The controversy receded when the preacher apologized publicly for what he had said.

As I mentioned earlier (following Turner), the liminal phase provides a stage for uniquely structured events to detach from mundane life, and to present ambiguous ideas and emerging symbolic forms, such as those performed by maskers and clowns. I discussed masked dances with the Panji story originating from East Java. When this story was introduced to the courts of Surakarta and Yogyakarta, it developed into one of the most grand and sophisticated performances. This can be thought of as a symbolic legitimation of power, which Moertono (1968) calls the cult of glory in the legitimation of kingship. Tracing the genealogical tree of real or mythological figures was one way to enhance the greatness of the king and his kingdom. During the period of the fourteenth-century Måjåpahit Empire, the Panji story was an important reference to mutual social interaction between Java and wherever the story landed (Vickers 2020, 282). Since the kings of Mataram (now the courts of Surakarta and Yogyakarta) believed they were descendants of the Måjåpahit dynasty, fostering and classicizing the Panji story in their theatrical performances was a form of tribute or paying homage to their forebears, while also providing a means to enhance their power.

INCONGRUITY

Clowns are always an integral part of the story of Panji and many others, including the Damarwulan story and stories based on *Mahabharata* and *Ramayana*. Clowns in Javanese stories not only perform "a set routine characterized by broad, graphic humor, absurd situation, and vigorous physical action," as defined by *Britannica*,[4] they also express levity whose source of amusement may include abusing and poking fun at the most exalted of patrons. This personality is closer to the role of a jester in other parts of the world. That is, a jester is considered to have special power that can be absorbed by his patrons to enhance their power.[5] Here is a partial definition from *Britannica* about the fool or jester: "Often deformed, dwarfed, or crippled, fools may have been kept for luck as well as for amusement, in the belief that deformity can avert the evil eye and that abusive raillery can transfer ill luck from the abused to the abuser. Fool figures played a part in the religious rituals of India and pre-Christian Europe, and, in some societies, such as that of Ireland in the seventh century BC, they were regarded as being inspired with poetic and prophetic powers."[6]

Javanese clowns, like Semar in wayang stories based on *Mahabharata* and *Ramayana*, and Bancak and Doyok or Sabdåpalon and Nåyågénggong in the Panji story, are given the name *pånåkawan*; *pånå* means wise, *kawan* means close friend. Particularly regarding Sabdåpalon and Nåyågénggong, people believe that these jesters were the best friends (*abdi kinasih*) of the Hindu-Buddhist king Brawijaya of the Måjåpahit Empire, meaning that the king might ask them for advice. The story has it that when the king of Måjåpahit was defeated by the Islamic king of Demak, he decided to convert himself and the whole Måjåpahit population to Islam. The two jesters disagreed and left the kingdom, disappearing. Some people in contemporary Java believe and predict that these jesters will appear again at some point in the future.

Such is the power of the jesters to inspire people to prophetic phenomena; that is, by positioning the jester in the in-between world, as a manifestation of incongruity and a blurring of hierarchy and distinction. In chapter 4 I discussed Semar as an example of this incongruity in the extreme—Semar as a clown-cum-god personification. It is true that in contemporary thought, Semar is a jester who holds this position. But in an older wayang tradition, still represented symbolically in East Javanese wayang performances today, the clown Bagong is believed to be Semar's image—Semar and Bagong as internal-external entity. In the performance, Semar and Bagong are placed inside a figure of a mountain (*gunungan*) in the middle of the screen. The clown pair is used ceremonially for the opening and closing of any performance, regardless of the story being presented.

More to the point of the interactive dualism concept is the relationship between Semar and Togog. Both jesters are the manifestation of gods. Semar is assigned to accompany the good character or knight (*satriyå*), while Togog accompanies evil giants (*rakseså*). On the surface, it looks as if this represents foremost good versus evil. However, in any story, both jesters advise good behavior—realizing the concept of complementarity in the dualism of the opposite.

Incongruity is also typical of the humor presented by Ki Joko Goro-Goro, a preacher whose sermons are full of humor. In chapter 3 I discussed some of his humorous preaching. Here I cannot resist reiterating what I described there, which illustrates the incongruity between the human bodily reality and the human bodily life function. The five bodily openings sustain life. However, Ki Joko Goro-Goro describes them as the centers of sin, producing unclean stuff. He begins by listing the bodily openings: mouth, nose, eyes, ears; then of the last two, he says, "I know where they are in our body, but I don't know their names." He describes these five bodily openings as "Satan's tools": "Nothing good comes out from any of them . . . What is coming from the mouth? Ah, there are slobber, cough, saliva, mucus, vomit—none of them is delicious. This means that what's residing inside of you consists of rotten material that produces sin." He continues talking about unclean stuff coming from the nose, eyes, ears, and the two unnamed bodily openings—the front private part and the back private part. The moral advice is that we should be humble, not arrogant people, as there are sins inside us. This is an example of levity, which is condemned by conventional forms of proselytization, but is common in preaching at community events, which contain a mixture of seriousness and humor. Here, the humor aims not only to attract the congregation to listen to the presentation, but also to bestow moral and spiritual values.

POLITICIZATION

Seriousness and levity are also employed by other preachers, for example Gus Muwafiq and Cak Nun. There is no predictable balance between the two elements. For many preachers, in the present study exemplified by Ki Joko Goro-Goro and Cak Nun, music is also an integral part of the preaching. Even if the music consists of lighthearted songs, the lyrics may contain religious and moral teachings. In some cases, music may serve as a conduit for, give meaning to, or be associated with politics and history. Cak Nun is a champion of this. In recomposing and recontextualizing the song "Ilir-Ilir," Cak Nun made a critical link to the suppression of critical voices by Suharto's New Order government by preaching what ought to be the "right" governing behavior according to his interpretation of the lyrics of the song. Here, the topic of knowledge and spirituality becomes an interesting philosophical discussion. Cak Nun believes that you can approach some questions scientifically, but that some larger issues must be approached not with knowledge, but with faith.

From a musical perspective, the song "Ilir-Ilir" has a long history and unique context. It is mentioned in references from the nineteenth century as one of the songs performed to invite celestial nymphs to enter a human effigy in the Nini Thowok children's play so that the effigy can move by itself. To conform with Islamic proselytization, the Kyai Kanjeng ensemble changed the melody of "Ilir-Ilir" to a *sholawatan* style, with Arabic lyrics sung intermittently with the Javanese lyrics. This is an example of music that is not only transient, but also changes significantly according to the context in which it is given meaning—the world in-between provides a cultural space for exploration and creativity.

Whether such creativity results in a form of exaggeration or is closer to historical evidence is an open question, that is, an ambiguous phenomenon in a liminal phase. Yet, it is a strategy preachers use to make their oratory more attractive. For example, it is almost routine for Gus Muwafiq to exaggerate the superiority of gamelan. He says that no other music surpasses the complexity of gamelan because its instruments are made of bronze—a highly complex material. Certainly, Gus Muwafiq exaggerates in this statement to attract the attention of his audience—they should be proud to have the most complex music in the world.

ALLEGORY

Cultural performance representing socioreligious allegory is one of the main themes of this book. Allegory is defined as "a symbolic fictional narrative that conveys meaning not explicitly set forth in the narrative."[7] In this study, the scope of allegorical reading is quite broad, encompassing a range of cultures in their interhistorical contexts. In this regard, I presented Sears's and Schechner's work as frames of reference for my examination of the story of Pétruk becoming king. I suggested that allegorical interpretations of wayang stories can be very fluid and sometimes contradictory to one another, depending on how the story has been conceived, performed, and reenacted from one period of history to another, or from one performance context to another. The Pétruk story can convey different meanings, such as the importance of the voice of the commoner or the exploitation of colonialized people. I further suggested that in the nineteenth to early twentieth centuries, the story was an allegory for the colonial government's portrayal of the stupidity of the Javanese. The point is, allegorical readings can be difficult to decode, depending on what we know about the performance context and the period of history, and how much evidence can be found in reading between the lines.

Interpreting the meaning of allegory is challenging because of the highly indirect process of constructing it. This is similar to the process of a dhalang incorporating indirect descriptions or criticism of certain persons or events into their performance. In the discourse of wayang, according to Bambang Suwarno (2006), a senior, now retired dhalang and lecturer at the Indonesian Institute of the Arts in Surakarta, there are two ways a dhalang does this: *medhang miring* (to hit with a sword slantingly) and *nyampar pikolèh* (slapping but reaching the target). The former is an indirect description or criticism, the latter uses another event to portray a particular event or criticism. Such variation makes interpreting allegorical meanings a challenging task.

When the construction of allegory is not indirect, can it still be called allegory? The portrayal of certain important individual figures in society is one of the best examples of a direct process of constructing allegory. According to *Britannica*, "symbolic allegory" occurs when a character "is not merely a transparent vehicle for an idea, but rather has a recognizable identity or narrative autonomy apart from the message it conveys."[8]

An example of this symbolic allegory is the portrayal of the current president of Indonesia, Joko Widodo (intimately known as Jokowi) as the clown Pétruk in the story of Pétruk becoming king. This happened during the period of his campaign and after he became president. The process of constructing allegory is more clearly defined in this case, as it was based on the popularity of a towering figure and political rival. Supporters of the president were proud of this depiction, since Pétruk is a commoner with a humble background—Jokowi began his career as a furniture salesman—and they interpreted the comparison as indicating the importance of grassroots voices. Others, however, held a critical view of the president, viewing the comparison as suggesting he was a stupid clown who did not have the ability to govern.

The portrayal of the second president of Indonesia, Suharto, as Semar is another example of symbolic allegory, though the portrayal was very much the result of his own action: he asked dhalangs to portray him as Semar, a jester-cum-god manifestation. The portrayal of President Wahid as Semar is closer to the definition of personification allegory, that is, an embodiment of human nature and an abstract concept,[9] since his portrayal represents the world in transition in the Gårå-Gårå (world in turmoil) scene of wayang performance.

PATRONAGE AND THE ADVANCE OF NATIONAL CULTURE

The portrayal of high-ranking government officials as wayang characters indicates the importance of wayang as a mirror of society, while highlighting the intimate relationship between wayang and government officials (albeit the Javanese) as its patrons. One of the reasons for the popularity of wayang is its wide-ranging patronage, encompassing different classes of society, from commoners to the royal family and the State and its officials. However, systems of patronage have changed over the centuries.

We learn from history that after the Islamization of Java, in the nineteenth century society was divided into two broad camps: people who were devoted Javanese Muslims called themselves *putihan* (the white ones), while those who considered themselves nominal Muslims were called *abangan* (the red ones; Ricklefs 2012, 17). This division was not rigid; the groups often overlapped. The *abangan* were the main patrons of wayang and gamelan, while the *putihan* were patrons of Islamic performing arts originating from the homeland of Islam. Because the *abangan* dominated the population, it is no surprise that wayang and gamelan became widespread.

The patronage of wayang and gamelan decreased rather drastically after the horrible national tragedy in 1965, when allegations that communists calling themselves the September 30th Movement killed six army generals with support from left-leaning President Sukarno was the pretext for a coup by General Suharto, who overthrew Sukarno, the country's first president, and took power. Thousands of members of the Indonesian Communist Party and its allies from all levels of society, including farmers, youth, artists, and high-ranking officials, were killed. The mass murder was carried out primarily by militant Islamic forces under the direction of Suharto. Calling his regime the New Order (*Orde Baru*), Suharto ruled Indonesia from 1966 until his resignation in 1998.

Mystery and controversy persist regarding who masterminded the September 30th Movement and for what purpose, as well as about Suharto's role and motivation in destroying the Communist Party and its members. What is relevant to our discussion here two particular consequences of these events: the deepening of the Islamization of Indonesia and the decrease in patronage of traditional performing arts. The increasing infiltration of Western popular culture and modern economic instability have further contributed to the decline of patronage of traditional performing arts.

In the late 1960s to early 1970s, the State required that each performing group be registered identification cards were issued to indicate that performers were not ex-members of the Communist Party (Suanda 1981, 38). Only artists who held the cards could perform. The timing of performances had to be adjusted (i.e., when a performance would start or end), so they would not coincide with the five-times-a-day schedule of Islamic prayer (39); this signaled the direction Indonesia was moving toward the deepening hold of Islam, and further diminished sponsorship of the traditional performing arts.

In the early 1970s the situation gradually returned to normal, except for a few restrictions. Subsequently, the State realized the importance of building a national cultural identity (*jati diri*). In the 1980s, the Orde Baru government launched a campaign to preserve, foster, and advance traditional performing arts. Through its national and local offices of culture, the government organized all sorts of activities, including performing arts festivals and competitions. However, the deepening of Islamization continued to complicate and spur debate about the character of Indonesian traditional performing arts.

One result of the New Order government's interest in wayang and gamelan was the creation of spectacular wayang performances sponsored by the government's political party Golongan Karya (Golkar). I have discussed this topic in previous work (2013) and again in the present study (chapter 4). I also discussed the important role of the State in preserving, fostering, and developing indigenous Indonesian culture as a conduit for national character building, in part by encouraging students at all levels to study and practice traditional arts. Alongside this, the State also maintains the importance of organizing the Cultural Congress (*Kongres Kebudayaan*), usually biannually, as a means of directing the development of national culture. As the culmination of these efforts, in 2017 the State enacted a law on the Advancement of Culture (Undang-Undang Republik Indonesia Nomor 5 Tahun 2017, the Law of the Republic of Indonesia Number 5 of 2017).[10]

This law has wide-ranging content. Its aim is to advance the future civilization of Indonesia, whose diverse regional cultures are considered assets and key to a national cultural identity. It states that the advancement of the culture requires "Protection, Development, Utilization and Capacity Building/Empowerment . . . to achieve a politically sovereign, economically independent, and cultured Indonesian society" (Undang-Undang Republik Indonesia Nomor 5 Tahun 2017, 2). The law takes a comprehensive approach, encompassing not only cultural identity, but also cultural diversity, political sovereignty, and economic independence (the importance of the practices of "creative industry"), highlighting the complexity of the Indonesian State wherein one domain of statecraft interweaves or interacts with another. This complexity of cultural development reminds us of Soedjatmoko's criticism that it is unwise for the government to address the challenge by supporting artists in their artistic expression. It also calls to mind

Gus Dur's dislike of the bureaucratization of culture through the institution of the Cultural Congress. Both critics believe in the power of artists to express social drama autonomously.

In part because of the Covid-19 pandemic, implementation of the Law on the Advancement of Culture has been delayed and partial. One development has been the documentation of the culture and performance of various ethnic groups, to be presented on a television program called *Indonesiana.* Criticisms have begun to appear in webinars, newspapers, and journals about the State exercising control to direct the participants toward certain artistic forms. It is too early to comment on the implementation and criticism of this new law, but questions persist about how state control of the "Advancement of National Cultures" will play out, particularly the impact when cultural development results from top-down policy rather than bottom-up creativity.

The commonly expressed reason why the State cares deeply about cultural development is concern about the impact of Western culture on the traditional cultural identity of Indonesia. However, the law does not address this aspect of cultural development, and it even explicitly defines Indonesian national culture as the result of "the overall processes and results of inter-cultural interaction living and developing in Indonesia . . . which is marked by the existence of inter-cultural interaction among local cultures or with other cultures from outside Indonesia in the dynamic processes of global change." The text qualifies, however, that "It is in this context [i.e., interaction with foreign cultures] that the Indonesian nation encounters various problems, challenges, and opportunities in advancing the National Culture of Indonesia" (Undang-Undang Republik Indonesia Nomor 5 Tahun 2017). But this worry only applies to the future advancement of cultures, and does not consider retroactively the impact of Western culture on traditional culture in the performing arts. The incorporation of Western culture and technology in contemporary wayang performance and its bureaucratization (see chapter 4) are not addressed or questioned in the law beyond the one acknowledgment that external influence occurs.

CODA

By way of conclusion, I ask readers to consider figure 5.1. The picture appears on the November/December month of a 1978 Javanese calendar (Becker 1987, viii). It consists of four parts. The circle in the middle contains an inscribed verse in Javanese script, the picture of the instrument kendhang, saron, and kenong. The part on the top contains an inscribed verse, a picture of two cakras on the left and right sides, and a crown on the bottom. Attached to the bottom part of

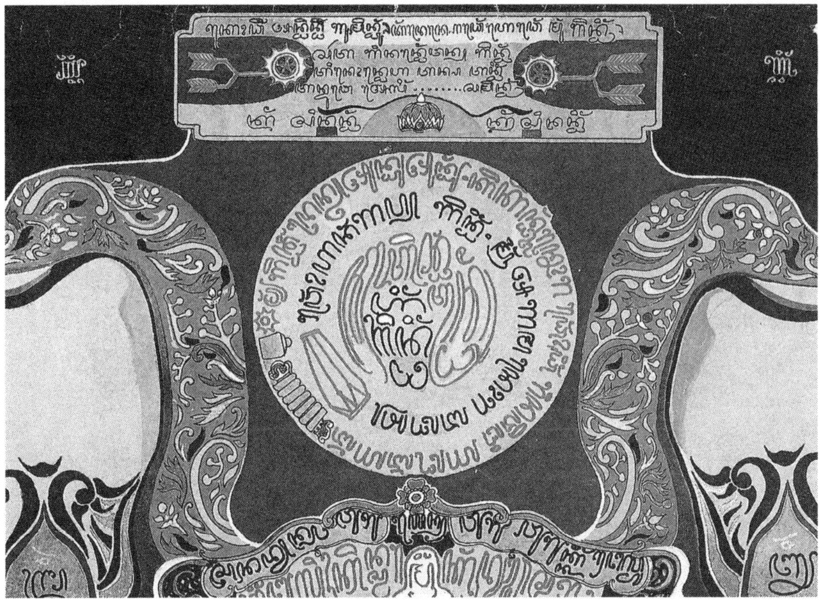

FIGURE 5.1 A picture on the 1978 Javanese calendar with verses from *Serat Tjenṭini* appearing in the top, middle, and bottom parts of the picture.

the image on the outer left and right sides are the pictures of two serpents with a flora/fauna design. Another inscribed verse, though incomplete, appears on the bottom part of the picture.

Alton Becker (1987, ix–xx) used the picture and verses for an opening remark in the second volume of *Karawitan: Source Readings in Javanese Gamelan and Vocal Music*, a four-volume set on gamelan and vocal music containing a series of translations of works by Javanese authors. Becker used the image to explain the challenging process of translating the verses as they are shaped and framed by the picture. I approach this image as an iconographic form, that is, its use by an artist or artists to convey a particular meaning. My assumption is that the picture and the verses can be thought of as a metaphoric reading of the inherent dualism and the world in-between in Javanese society. There is the top-bottom dualism, the two-cakras dualism inside the top part of the picture, and the serpent-like wings dualism. The circle in the middle is a gravitational center.

In what way does one part of the picture relate to the others? To answer this question, we need to understand the meaning of the verses inside the picture. Two verses on the top and middle parts of the picture are written in a genre of *mâcâpat* (sung poetry). Three sentences appear in the bottom part of the picture that are taken from other verses.

TABLE 5.1 Verses to figure 5.1

Verse in the top box

Kodheng andhendheng gumendhung	Losing mind, stubborn, arrogant,
Kang dèn èdheng hamung gendhing	[musician] is boasting only gendhing,
Sartå ginandhèngan gendhang	linking it to gendhang [drum].
Tinondhéå tanpå tandhing	Compared [to anything], none surpassed [the musicians' stand].
Tan duwé éling samendhang	[They] don't have any idea, even a little
Kang sinandhang kang sinandhing	self-understanding or anything else.

Verse in the middle circle

Mung gendhing dèn undhung-undhung	Gendhing is the only boastful item,
Kekandhangan nora dhong dhing	without understanding anything else.
Rinå wengi andhang-adhang	Day and night awaiting
Wong ananggap	people who would hire them.
Mring agåmå nora dhangan	On religion, they understand none,
Katendhang tundhung ing gendhing	since gendhing defeated them all.

Incomplete verse in the bottom box

Sanadyan wuru yèn	Although drunk, if
Wuru-wuruking ngèlmu	drunkenness is for searching sacred knowledge . . .
Ingulihken swårå mring kang duwé swårå	Let the sounds be returned to the owner of the sounds.

The verses were quoted from the *Serat Tjenṭini*, a literary work composed in the late eighteenth to early nineteenth century, known for its encyclopedic content. Based on the version of *Serat Tjenṭini* published by Bataviaach Genootschap van Kunsten en Wetenschappen (1915, vols. 7–8, 203) the box at the top contains verse 43 from canto 277e; in the middle part is verse 44 from canto 277e, both in måcåpat sung poetry *Kinanthi*. Both verses describe the musician's passionate involvement in music as antithetical to the proper mindfulness of and devotion to God. The third section of framed writing at the bottom paraphrases text derived from the two lines of verse 21 and the last line of verse 31.

Together with other verses in mâcâpat *Pucung* (see table 5.2), they describe the sacred knowledge embedded in rasa of the gendhing (verses 1, 2, and 10) and a mystical interpretation of the musician's "drunken" infatuation with music, placing greater emphasis on the meaning of the totality of the playing of the composition (*gendhing*) by the full ensemble of musicians (verses 21 and 31). However, according to the text, even the total sound of the complete musical ensemble would not bring about a transcendental experience (*rasa*) if its sacred knowledge (*èlmu*) could not be internalized. This is because èlmu is embedded in rasa inside the gendhing.

Becker (1987) gives us a hint about the meaning behind the picture and verses: the picture shows "the way cultural coherence works: a few deep metaphors bind various things together, make them resonate and mutually reinforce each other, and make the world seem orderly, reasonable, and harmonious" (ix). In my view, Becker's reading of *Serat Tjenṭini* can be expanded to include the perspective that the world is full of dynamic interactions and interrelationships of different

TABLE 5.2 Canto 277e, verses 1, 2, 10, *Pucung*

Sacred knowledge embedded in rasa of the gendhing

1. Kang poenikå dhi ragil Koelawiryèku Mungguh gagendhingan Mrih sampurnaning awaril Kedah dunungaken ing ilmu rasanyå	1. Therefore, my brother Kulåwiryå, Concerning the playing of gendhing, to truly understand its meaning, it must be explained through the sacred knowledge of its rasa.
2. Ungelipun gamelan srancak puniku Pan unining gongså Tan dadyå wredining ilmu Mung gendhingé dhi ragil kang dadyå råså	2. The sound of a set of gamelan is merely the sound of a metal instrument, not revealing the meaning of ilmu [sacred knowledge]. Only the gendhing my brother can become rasa.
10. Dhé punikå dhaupé marang ing èlmu Unining gamelan Sami lan unining lambé Gendhingé punika jatining niat	10. Concerning the marriage between gamelan and sacred knowledge, the sound of gamelan is the same as the sound of our lips. Gendhing is the true niat [striving after the sublime].

TABLE 5.3 Canto 277e, verse 21

A mystical interpretation of the musician's "drunken" infatuation with music

21. Gih punikå wong niågå bongså wuru Senadyan wuruå Yèn wuru wuruking èlmi Wuru cengeng èkramé mikrad munajad	21. Such is the musician's drunkenness. Although drunk, if drunkenness is for searching sacred knowledge, the drunken ones will receive blessing from God.

TABLE 5.4 Canto 277e, verse 31, *Pucung*

The importance of the sound of a full ensemble as divine

31. Kang kadyèku dhi ragil pamuntunipun Swaraning gamelan Gendhing gendhèng swaranèki Ingulihken swårå mring kang duwé swårå	31. That is the answer, brother. The sound of gamelan is the sound of instrumental and vocal music. Let the sound return to the owner of the sound.

elements and aspects of life, normative or not. This implies that the picture with the verses and other related verses beyond those appearing in the picture reflect poetically the characterization and presentation of Javanese life (Day 2021). They are a metaphor for society living in the in-between world, in the liminal phase, in the dualistic interactions from which innovation and the exploration of new ideas stem. Two main points stand out about the description of gamelan: (a) the picture and verses portray dynamic dualistic interactions and competing opinions, and (b) the conclusion about the importance of hearing the complete ensemble as a conduit for understanding sacred knowledge, in which rasa can be found inside gendhing, is notable.

Regarding the second point, when *Serat Tjenṭini* mentions gamelan and religion, its author is very open minded, describing on the one hand the negative attitude of musicians toward religion, and on the other hand the deep religious significance of achieving rasa within gendhing. In the late eighteenth and early nineteenth centuries, the period when *Serat Tjenṭini* was composed, debate about the role of religion in society appeared very often in literature. As I mentioned in chapter 4, a lively discussion about the light source of wayang performance as the oldest and most powerful element appears in the nineteenth-century *Serat Gatholoco*. A metaphoric reading of wayang in *Serat Tjenṭini* also highlights the ambiguity of its explication.

It is not uncommon to find in the discourse about wayang that, symbolically, the dhalang represents God, and his creations are a set of shadows cast on a screen. The verses in question (see table 5.5) tell us that the dhalang and wayang are integral parts of the allusion to the concept of the universe; so are other wayang paraphernalia. This means that the relationships between the Absolute and the Contingent, God and human, are indeed very complicated.

TABLE 5.5 Canto 279e, verses 2–5, *Megatruh*

The ambiguity of the metaphoric reading of the relationship between wayang and dhalang

2. Kaé Kidang Wiråcåpå lon amuwus Dhi ragil Kulåwiryèku Mungguh purnaning pandulu Susurupaning ringgit Kakékat´ringgit tinonton	2. Brother Wiråcapå says slowly: "My younger brother Kulåwiryå, regarding the true perspective of the knowledge of *wayang*, it is hidden from the spectators.
3. Janmåtåmå karyå lèjeming pandulu Sasmitaning Hyang sejati Dhalang lan wayang dinunung Panganggoné Hyang mawarni Karyå upamèng pandulon	3. From those who strive for the in nermost truth, God is the only one to beckon. Dhalang and wayang are considered two of God's apparel, metaphorically speaking.
4. Kelir jagad gumelar wayang pinanggung Asnapun makluking Widi Gedebog bantålå wegung Balèncong pandaming urip gamelan gendhinging lakon	4. The screen is the unfolding world where puppets are staged, [they are] God's' various creations. The banana log is the great earth. The blèncong lamp is the light of life. Gamelan is the song of the story line.
5. Titahing Hyang tanpå wilis ing tumuwuh Kabèhé dadya ling-aling Kang tan olih ing pituduh Tan mulat ing Hyang sejati Kandheg warnå rupèng kono	5. God's creation is growing countlessly. All becomes concealment, without guidance. Without observing the true God, it stops as metaphor only.

TABLE 5.6 Canto 279e, verses 22–23, *Megatruh*

The allegory of dhalang as God	
22. Hyang måhå gung punikå dhalang linuhung Pangkat lahiring jasmani Myang istidlal kang maujud Dadining ringgit nèng kelir Dhalang kang murbèng lelakon	22. The Exalted One is an honorable dhalang, creating the birth of the physical body, and the referential realization of whatever happens with the puppet on the screen. The dhalang determines the story.
23. Inggih dhalang sejati punikå ratu Kang murbå solahing urip kang sinèrèn mring Hyang Agung nampèni ajading takdir tabiat bawaning kang wong	23. The true dhalang is the king [who is] in charge of life behavior. Blessed by the Great One, receiving freedom of destiny, the character and behavior of man.

Some of the subsequent verses (see table 5.6) clearly show the allegory of dhalang as God. As Zoetmulder (1971, 89) suggests, the true meaning of dhalang and wayang can be "discovered only when one sees them as external to the various ways in which God acts and works in the world." This relationship indicates the heterogeneity of life in-between, full of complexity, ambiguity, eclecticism, and even paradoxes.

Returning to the first point, the description of gamelan emphasizes the plurality of sounds, and acknowledges that each instrument has its own timbre and character, which facilitate a sublime experience. In its compositional design, each instrument or group of instruments is assigned to a particular function in the ensemble. But in trying to categorize these functions, exceptions always emerge. This is because categorization is a shorthand or reductive explication of the multidimensionality of musical practice. It is common to use binary terms to categorize the function of gamelan instruments: *pamurba/pamangku* (those which are supervised/those which are supported) instruments playing melody (*pamurba lagu* and *pamangku lagu*) and those instruments performing rhythm (*pamurba irama* and *pamangku irama*).[11] Notwithstanding that these characterizations are widely taught and well-known, they cannot explain the full gamut of performance practice of each instrument or group of instruments. This is because different types of compositional processes and different genres of gamelan pieces involve a variety of performance techniques on many instruments.

A distinctive characteristic of knowledge production in *Serat Tjenṭini* is notable here, a tradition called *santri lelånå* (wandering student of Islam): santri litterateurs wandered from one place to another in search of teachers of mystical lore, esoteric knowledge (*èlmu*), and other knowledge of various fields. The richness of *Serat Tjenṭini* is possible because of its diverse interlocutors. As Anderson (1991) explains:

> [They included] the architects who envisioned, planned, and supervised the construction of Java's myriad mosques, palaces, and fortifications; the puppet masters (*dhalang*) who over generations built the varied traditions of the shadow play; the expert musicians who created the panoply of Javanese musical genres; the adepts of the many branches of Islamic learning; not to speak of dancers, actors, sculptors, smiths, painters, curers, astrologers, magicians, folk botanists, martial-arts teachers, burglars, and so on . . . Some were drawn into the service of royal courts and provincial lords . . . Others preferred the freedom of the road—joining Pigeaud's memorable swarm of *zwervers en trekkers*—peddling their specialties on the broader social market (for example, actors and teachers of martial arts). Still others, such as kyai and *guru ngelmu* (teachers of mystical lore), would settle in rural retreats, drawing to themselves acolytes and clients by word of respectful or astonished mouth. (275–76)

It makes sense that the content of *Serat Tjenṭini* encompasses all elements and aspects of Javanese lives because of the diverse fields and diverse professionals performing and presenting their crafts, from which the knowledge is produced. For this reason, *Serat Tjenṭini* has earned its reputation as a comprehensive encyclopedia of Javanese life in eighteenth- and nineteenth-century Java. But *Serat Tjenṭini* is more than an encyclopedia, it is also a narrative of the characterization and representation of everyday lives (Day 2021). All things considered, I suggest that the verses in *Serat Tjenṭini* represent a deep metaphor for people's lives in society, a complex society in the context of unending cultural and religious transformations.

Inspired by the tradition of student wanderers as the producers of knowledge in *Serat Tjenṭini*, I close this conclusion with a personal anecdote. Before entering the United States, my journey with gamelan was quite extensive. I performed in different cities in Java, as well as for seven months at the Expo '70 in Osaka, Japan, had brief visits to perform in Manila (Philippines) and teach at the Indonesian Embassy in Canberra, Australia, and finally settled at Wesleyan University in 1972, where I have remained. While at Wesleyan, I have travelled to many universities in the United States, Australia, Asia, and Europe, teaching summer school, running workshops, serving as an invited guest musician or dhalang, and delivering papers at conferences.

In the 1980s, my American colleagues gave me an opportunity to write an essay on my teaching experience at Wesleyan. The title of the essay was "Opportunity and Interaction: The Gamelan from Java to Wesleyan" (Sumarsam 2004). As the editors of the book in which it was published suggested, my essay included a reflection on my experience. By then, I was also interested in history. The result was an essay consisting of a collage of personal accounts and historical reports on the presence of gamelan at Wesleyan and beyond.

The experience I acquired from wandering around the world with gamelan is partly responsible for my ability to produce knowledge through this work. This brings me back to *Serat Tjenṭini*. That is, the knowledge production of *Serat Tjenṭini* was the result of Islamic students' wandering in search of teachers, esoteric knowledge, and all sorts of mundane knowledge. I am not claiming that my production of knowledge is in any way comparable to the production of knowledge in *Serat Tjenṭini*, but in the same spirit, I consider myself a wanderer. I will continue to wander with gamelan, searching, producing, and sharing more knowledge.

Nyuwun pangèstu pårå kadang / Wish me luck
Maturnuwun / Thank you

GLOSSARY

adiluhung: an adjective, which means great beauty, "classical," refined, respectable, beautifully embodied in, pertaining to literary works and performing arts.

alamkara: literary embellishment, a practice by Balinese puppeteers of ornamenting their performance. Originally an Indian term: ornamentation or embellishment in composing or performing poetical texts or musical or theatrical performances.

alus: the concept of Javanese refinement contained and revealed in the inner and external realm of human experience.

babad: traditional Javanese historiography; legend or myth that might be considered a semi-historical event of a certain locality.

Bhairawa: a Hindu tantric deity, the terrible fearsome manifestation of Shiva.

biduan: from *bidu*, a singer at a shamanistic séance in Malay, related to Javanese *vidu* (*widu*), an ancient performer of various genres of performing art.

blangkon: traditional Javanese hat made of batik cloth.

cakra (also spelled *chakra*): the visualization of center energy, the main scriptural teaching of Buddhist or Shivaistic Tantra.

candi (*candhi*): temples believed to be the sanctuary of gods and places of worship.

canthang balung (also called *lurah bhadut*): court jesters whose jobs include singing *senggak/alok* (vocal interjections) in the gamelan accompaniment for the *serimpi* court dance, dancing in processions of Islamic religious festivals, and supervising the *talèdhèk* dancers/singers.

dakwah: preaching to strength or deepen Muslims' faith; religious propagation.

dangdut: a genre of popular music that has the power to inspire people to dance, or to make their hips move naturally.

dewa-raja: god-king; a belief system in Southeast Asia that grew out of a mixture between Hindu and indigenous traditions to consider a king as a divine universal ruler.

dhalang: a puppeteer in Javanese and Balinese puppet plays, whether a shadow play using two-dimensional puppets to project shadows behind the screen, or a play using three-dimensional wooden puppets without a screen.

dhanyang: the spirits of local ancestors believed to be the guardians of a village.

dhukun: faith healer, ritual specialist.

dzikir (*dhikir*): Islamic prayer for achieving religious ecstasy by reciting continuous repetition of a formula, usually comprising different names of God.

gamelan: A music ensemble consisting predominantly of gong- and metallophone-type instruments, but also including string instruments, xylophone, drum, flute, and vocalists; cultivated and developed mostly in Indonesian islands, particularly Java and Bali.

gambuh: the name of *måcåpat* sung poetry; older form of Balinese *wayang* presenting Panji story; Balinese dance drama presenting the Panji story.

Gårå-Gårå (*Gara-Gara*; *Goro-Goro*): the beginning scene of the second part of *wayang kulit* performance, featuring clowns with their humorous dialogues.

gendèr: a metallophone with ten to fourteen bronze or iron keys suspended by cords in a wooden frame over tube resonators, played with two disc-type mallets.

gendhing: a generic term for any gamelan composition; a generic term for a gamelan composition with a relatively long *gongan* rhythmic structure.

iråmå (*irama*): tempo; the expanding and contracting of *gongan* rhythmic structure accompanied by changes of the density levels of the instruments in the ensemble.

jarwå dhåsok (*jarwo dhosok*): meaning based on etymologically forced or imposed interpretation.

kakawin (*kekawin*): Old Javanese poetic genre adapted from Indian sung-poetry *kavya*.

kamanak (*kemanak*): a pair of bronze instruments that have the shape of hollow banana.

Kasultanan: the official name of the sultanate court of Yogyakarta.

Kasunanan: the official name of the court of Surakarta.

kavya: Sanskrit court poetry of India.

kawi: poet; Sanskrit-based Old Javanese language.

kethoprak: a genre of folk-dance drama.

kidung: a poetic genre from the Middle Javanese period.

kraton (*keraton*): court.

Kyai Kanjeng: an ensemble created by the prominent preacher Cak Nun and his musicians, consisting of a mixture of Western musical instruments and gamelan instruments tuned to the Western diatonic tuning system.

Langendriyan: Javanese dance opera with the dialogue in the form of sung-poetry and sung by the dancers and accompanied by gamelan.

Limbukan: a humorous scene in the first division of *wayang kulit* performance, consisting of dialogue between two lady clowns, skinny Cangik and fat Limbuk (the name of the scene derives from this character).

lontar: dried palm leaves on which manuscripts of all sorts are written.

mabasan: see *macarita*.

macarita: recitation; a tradition of the public reading of literary works; in Bali, *mabasan*.

Mahabharata: an Indian epic introduced and rewritten by Javanese poets during the Hindu-Javanese period, with the theme of the conflict between the Kurawa and Pandhåwå brothers.

Mangkunegaran: the minor court of Surakarta.

mantra: a prayer or hymn of power potency that opens a *wayang* performance.

mimbar: elevated seat of honor in the mosque from which a preacher delivers sermons.

musryik: idolatry.

Nini Thowong (*Thowok*): a ritual play using a female effigy, which spirits enter through the singing of a series of songs.

Pakualaman: the minor court of Yogyakarta.

pånåkawan (*punåkawan*): jester or clown, the companions of the knight in the *wayang* story.

Panji: indigenous Javanese stories associated with the period from the eleventh to the thirteenth centuries, the time of the Kediri and Singosari kingships.

pancamakara: a ritual of Hindu Tantrism involving the Five Ms: *mada* (drinking liquor), *maithusa* (sexual intercourse), *mudra* (meditation), *matsya* (eating fish), and *mamsa* (eating meat).

pathet: modal classification of *gendhing* (gamelan composition). There are three *pathet* in each of the tuning systems.

pengajian: the study of Quran, liberally applied; Islamic oratory/pedagogical event.

pesantrèn: Islamic boarding schools.

pesindhèn: female singers of the gamelan.

pujangga (*pujonggå*): royal court poets and chroniclers.

pusaka (*pusåkå*): a magically charged relic of inheritance.

pustaka (*puståkå*): letter; library.

raket: old term for *wayang topèng* (masked dance drama).

Ramayana: an Indian story whose theme is the adventure of Rama and his wife Sinta.

rasa: inner feeling.

rasa sejati: true rasa.

salunding: an ancient instrument: xylophone with bamboo or metal keys.

senggakan: a stylized vocal interjection within the gamelan accompaniment for the *serimpi* dance form or certain *gendhing*.

serimpi: a highly refined Javanese court dance genre from the Kasunanan court of Surakarta.

sholawatan: singing to praise the Prophet Muhammad.

slametan: a ritual and communal feast.

Sufi: the Islamic brotherhood whose members practice mysticism.

talèdhèk: dancer-singers, in the past also known as prostitutes.

Tantrism: a Hindu sect whose ritual practice includes transgression of social norms (see *pancamakara*).

tembang: a form of Javanese sung poetry.

ulama: Islamic scholars.

walisångå: the nine Islamic apostles believed to be responsible for introducing and spreading Islam in Java and beyond.

wayang golèk: a puppet play using three-dimensional wooden puppets presenting Islamic *Ménak*, *Mahabharata*, or *Ramayana* stories.

wayang klithik: a puppet play using two-dimensional wooden puppets presenting the Damar Wulan story, portraying a semihistory of the fourteenth-century Måjåpahit era.

wayang krucil: a puppet play using two-dimensional wooden puppets presenting the Panji story (see *Panji*).

wayang kulit: a shadow puppet play using two-dimensional, flat leather puppets. Considered the oldest wayang performance, the wayang kulit presents stories based on the Hindu *Mahabharata* and *Ramayana* stories. It is also referred to as *wayang purwå*.

wayang topèng: masked dance-drama presenting indigenous Javanese stories based on the Panji stories (see *Panji*). In the past, it also told stories based on the *Mahabharata* epic and the *Ramayana* stories.

wayang wong: a Javanese dance drama with characters and stories drawn from the wayang shadow puppet performance.

widu (*vidu*): an ancient performer-singer of all kinds of performing arts, who also is believed to endow power.

widu mawayang: widu performing *wayang*.

wondå (*wanda*): the various temperaments of a puppet character in *wayang*.

NOTES

Introduction

1. *Sareng sakenyarirå Sanghyang Predangga Pati,*
gumantyå mring Sanghyang Ratri,
kapanjutan imå-imå,
gamburå lawan ancål(å).
Imå-imå mégå, gamburå segårå, ancålå puncaking gunung.

Sanghyang Anon [Manon] methik pupusing gebang siwalan tunggal,
nedak kinèn dhå-pådhå,
tinètèsan asta gangga ganggané wirantanu.
Astå namaning tangan, [gong] gangga banyu, wira tulis, tanu mangsi.

The quotation is taken from a documentary video of wayang golèk performance in Tegal, which I sponsored and organized, assisted by my research assistant Ciptono Hadi.

2. Here, I use the term *recitation* to mean a formal reading, usually from memory, in which the recited words serve as verbal magic, mantra, or invocation to attain power and blessing from the gods, in this instance for the success and safety of Warnoto's performance.

3. See Kees W. Bolle, Jonathan Z. Smith, Richard G. A. Buxton, et al. s.v. "myth," *Encyclopaedia Britannica Online*, last updated November 13, 2023, https://www.britannica.com/topic/myth/Myth-and-history.

4. *yekā n śīrṇa dinuk ring astra wara pustakamaya lumarap*
mabhrāpan maṇi hemadaṇḍa tumanem nḍaḍa sang ahulun
tan pendah kadi wangkawanginum I rah nṛpati mamulakan
ndah śaktinya tinut ri jīwa nira ing amarapada.

5. See Ali Mustofa Official, "Nonton Bareng (LAKON SAKRAL) Drs. Ki Sigit Manggolo Saputro Lakon Kalimosodo Kajarwo," YouTube, June 6, 2021, video, 5:51:29, https://www.youtube.com/watch?v=lRFSLLJV3Mg. The scenes of the meeting between walisångå and Yudhistirå, the explanation of Sunan Kalijågå about pusåkå Kalimåsådå, and Yudhistirå moksa can be found toward the end of the video (4:43:00–5:31:00). The performance was presented on March 19, 2011, commemorating the second anniversary of Ganggeng Samudra (a court-associated Islamic organization to safeguard morality) in Sleman, Yogyakarta. In his opening remark, the dhalang acknowledged the presence of G. B. P. H. Yudaningrat, the brother of King Hamengku Buwånå X. According to dhalang Ki Gondo Suharno (personal communica-

tion with author, 2018), the idea of composing the story of Kalimosodo Kajarwo came from him. Ki Gondo Suharno was the dhalang who performed wayang kulit at Yale University and wayang golèk at Wesleyan University for the visit of Sultan Hamengku Buwånå X to Wesleyan University in 2018.

6. *Dadi dadalang kekembung* [tetembung]
anama Ki Seda Brangti
apahe [upahe] *yen ababarang*
ika kalimah kakalih
singa gelem nguchapake
ya dadi tanggane nyuling.

Regarding the word *kekembung*, I have consulted Doddie Yulianto, who is an expert on Cirebonese wayang and culture. He said that the word *kekembung* should be *tetembung*, which means "given the name of." And *apahe* should be *upahe*.

7. See the next section for the name Sèh Malåyå in the context of the story Nabi Kilir.

8. *Sang Ratu Wahdat lingira*
Pasemone nafi isbat iku yayi
Wayang tengen lan kiwa.

Kang kiwa puniku maring nafi
Kang tengen puniku maring isbat
Pandhåwå maring nafine
Isbat Karowa iku
Isbat iku pon asal nafi
Nafi pon asal isbat
Musbat kang den rebut
Kresna kang dadi pahesan
Kresna kaca pahesaning ringgit kalih
Kalah menang ing kaca.

Mulane ku arebat nagari
Iya musbat iku kang den rebat
Mulane perang dadine
Nagara kang den rebut
Korawendra rebut nagari
Lan jenenging Pandhåwå
Iku semunipun
Mulane wong asawala
Nafi isbat kang den rebut iku yayi
Ing mangke tekeng kina.

9. I would like to thank Tony Day for his suggestion to see the complexity of the discourse about Sunan Kalijågå's immersion in the world of wayang as a tool for proselytization by looking at essays on this topic by other scholars, especially Meyer and Quinn.

10. *Seh Mlaya umatur aris*
kalangkung nuwun patikbra

Kalijaga tur sĕmbahe
nanging hamba matur tuwan
anuwun babar pisan
sajatine suksma luhur
kang wasta iman hidayat

11. Sumarsam (2003), 73.

ONE *Indian Origin and Inspirations*

1. Sarkar (1959, 98) notes that the significance of this word (*tangkin hyang*) is not known; it could pertain to the names of persons, plays, or stories.

2. 9. *Makaphalā svasthā sang hyang dharma muang prajah kabaih kahlamnya hinyūnnakan ton-tonan mamidu sang tangkil hyang sinalu macaritta rāmāyaṇa mamisang tangkil hyang si nalu macarita bhimma kumāra mangigal kica.*
 10. *ka si jaluk macarita rāmāyana mamirus mabañyol si mungmuk si galigi mawayang buatthyang macarita bhimma ya kumāra.* (Sarkar 1959, 90)

3. Wirâthâparwâ is the fourth book of the *Mahabharata* epic. It tells stories of the sojourn of the Pandhâwâ brothers in exile at the court of the king of Wirâtâ after they lost a game of dice with their cousins, the Kurâwâ brothers, as a result of a power struggle and long conflict over inheriting land from their ancestors. To hide their identities, the five Pandhâwâ brothers disguise themselves under assumed names and employments. The oldest brother Yudhistirâ assumes the identity of a brahmin with name Kangkâ; the second brother, Bimâ, becomes a cook and wrestler with the name Balâwâ; the middle brother, Arjunâ, becomes a eunuch and music and dance teacher with the name Wrehatnâlâ; Nakulâ becomes a charioteer with the name Grantikâ; Sadewâ becomes a cowherd with the name Tantipâlâ; and the wife of Yudhistirâ, Drupadi, becomes a lady-in-waiting of the queen of Wirâtâ with the name Salindri. Eventually, the Pandhâwâ brothers succeed, completing their thirteen-year exile, and were given land to build their own kingdom, called Amartâ.

4. The discussion of the Indian-influenced Old Javanese scripts and literacy is drawn from Hunter (1966) and Supomo (1993).

5. Desiring the annihilation of all hostile powers, the hero devoted himself to the performance of his sacrifice on the battlefield. Gradually he used as flower offerings the head ornaments from the hair of his fallen enemies; as grains, the forehead ornaments of deceased kings; and the burning palaces of his adversaries as his sacrificial firepit, into which he constantly sacrificed the decapitated heads of his foes while fighting valiantly in their chariots. (Supomo 1993,164)

6. See also Supomo (1996, 27).

7. Acri also mentions the studies by Sedyawati (1982); Royo-Iyer (1991, 1998, 2003) on pictorial evidence of dance performances depicted on the wall of *Candi Prambanan*; Soedarsono's studies on the origin of wayang, wayang wong dance drama, and wayang topèng dance drama in the ancient Central and Eastern Javanese kingdom (ninth to fifteenth centuries); Emigh (1984, 1996); and Coldiron (2005a, 2005b, 2007). According to Acri (2014), the first two scholars "did not go beyond the identification of the formal features displayed by the dancing characters and their links to *karana*-poses as codified in the Sanskrit *Natyasastra*"; and the last two "did not provide concrete text-historical evidence linking with specific groups and traditions . . . [and]

limited themselves to posit a common, and rather generic, 'Tantric root' for South Asian (i.e., Orissan) and Javano-Balinese masks and masked performers."

8. For a lengthy summary of Arjunawiwaha, see Zoetmulder (1974, 235–37). Here is a brief summary of the story. A demon king Niwåtåkawåcå threatens to attack the heavens. Knowing that the demon king cannot be killed by gods, the god Indrå seeks assistance from the second Pandhåwå brother, Arjunå, who at the time is in penance on the Indrakilå mountain. Before doing so, Indrå sends beautiful celestial nymphs to test Arjunå's meditation by seducing him, but they are unable to awaken him. Hence Indrå visits Arjunå, and a conversation ensues about power and pleasure. Knowing the success of Arjunå's penance, the demon king Niwåtåkawåcå sends Mamangmurkå to destroy the forest where Arjunå is meditating. In the form of a wild boar, Mamangmurkå attacks him. At that time, the god Guru, disguised as a hunter, arrives. Both the god Guru and Arjunå dispatch their arrows, killing the boar. A dispute arises, developing into a fight about who killed the boar. Eventually, the hunter transforms back to the god Guru, presenting Arjunå with an arrow called Pasupati. The story has it that Niwåtåkawåcå can be killed through his particular vulnerable spot. A celestial nymph, Supråbå, with whom the demon king is falling in love, is able to make the king reveal his vulnerable spot: on the tip of his tongue. Hearing this, while in a combat with the demon king, Arjunå shoots his arrow, hitting the king's tongue and killing him.

9. *koṅ taṇḍaṅ koṅ kaniṣṭākuṭa makuvu-kuvuṅ koṅ kaśmala kuvoṅ*
tan pomah tā katṛṣṇā laku vidu mavayaṅ kom guṇya saguṇa

10. *sahana niṅ abanyol denyāṅguyvākəna puraci*
aṅigəl-igəl agəṅgṅan koṇṭol paḍa mətətəṅ
vəlu sakəbəh agasyak ndan moghāvədi vəkasan
kaguyu-guyu kagman yan prāptaṅ vəlu sabaṭaṅ (5)

pirus amirusi menmen denyāmet pacəh acəməh
rabi nika bisa pantəs denyābhāvaka maṅəyəh
laki nika mulat aṅdrəṅ kahyūn-hyūn aṅuṅas-uṅas
kadi vəḍus anut a jyan yan təṅhā təka muriṅis (6)

ikaṅ ama caṅah olih guyv aprih paḍa sinurak
tkap ika nini-niny elik masvāmi vərə-vərəh
paḍa bisaṅ avayaṅ vvaṅ denyāṅguyvakən atarik
pacəh ika kaki-kaky akrak ginyat mulih akusa (7) (Acri 2014, 8–9)

11. *meh rahināsĕmu bang hyang aruna kadi netra ning ogha rapuh*
sabda ni kokila ring kanigara sakĕtĕr ni kidung ning akūng
lwir wuwus ing winipañca papĕtak ing ayam wana ring pakagan
mrāk anguhuh bhramarāngrabhas kusuma ring parahasyan arūm

TWO *Center-Periphery, Court-Rural Dynamics*

1. Consulting Riana's (2009) translation of *Negarakertagama*, Vickers corrected Robson's translation of verse 5. Riana's translation is as follows: "Firstly, Sri Kerta Wardhana requests that the King played drum (*mamanjaki*), there in the middle of the stage which was hastily

decorated. The King's Queen wore beautiful headdresses and sang a song. Her singing style was interesting, causing big laughs." In other words, to Vickers and Riana, *sori* means "queen," *rahajeng* means "beautiful," *mamanjaki* means "drum," and *tekes* means "headdresses."

2. 4. *hāryya raṇāḍikāra lali yan hatur i narapati*
hāryya mahāḍikāra ta dulur nika paṛṇ amuwus,
ān/ para handyan āpti mihate siran arakhĕrakhĕt.
a juga liṅnira t-hĕr umāntuk/ hadadadakan

5. *çrī kṛtawarddaneçwara mamanjaki sira rumuhun,*
ṅkāna rika witāna ri tṅah rinacana dinadak
çorinireki gitada lawan/ tkĕsira rahajöŋ,
sotan ulah karāmyan ikanaŋ guyu juga winanun

6. *ndāluwaran sireki dataŋ narapatin aṅadĕg.*
gitaniranyat aṅdani girahyasĕn iṅ umulat.
çorinireki suçrama nirukti lituhayu wagĕd
gita nikāṅhiribhirib aweh ṛsĕpaniṅ umulat

7. *çri naranātha tan sipi wagusnira tlas arasuk*
asta tkesnirekin upabhāryya rahayu sawala
tusniṅ amatya waṅça wicaksaṇa tĕtĕs iṅ ulah
Etu nika pabañwal anibākĕn ucapan aṅne

8. *naŋ nawanātya kapwa tinapaknira tinĕwĕkakĕn.*
asya makādi tan pat ikan guyu paṛṅ aslur
mwaŋ karunāmanun tanis aweh skĕl upuhara luh.
etu nikaŋ tumon/ pada kamanun aṅĕnaṅĕn (Pigeaud 1960, 70)

3. 59b. *pun Caraŋ-Lĕŋkara pukulun anapĕṭĕta gumuyu rahaden Siŋhamatra tumuli*
samâdandan kaŋ aŋrakĕt iriki ndan rahaden mantri lagy akon aŋaturana iŋ raden
Wirastrasari kĕḍinira aŋunḍaŋ tĕka mĕnḍĕk anembah iŋ sira rahadyan //

60a. *ndan liŋe pukulun lĕmah tatampakanira milw aniŋalana rakĕt*
lalaŋkaran liŋira raden mantri /

60b. *nĕngeh ta gambuh anyar paŋrakĕtira apañji Wireswara punaŋ linihuŋ mĕnĕŋ raden*
Warastrasari

4. His essay, on the circulation of the Panji story throughout Southeast Asia, proceeds by reconstructing early forms of performance, and especially through understanding of gambuh dance drama by examining many early manuscripts from the regions.

5. 8. *Karem olah kaprawiran*
Myang saliring rèh pangrèh ing dumadi
Nanging samudayanipun
Lelangen pakumpulan
Siniwi mring kadéyan myang punggåwå gung
Sang Panji waskithèng gitå
Mardawaning olah rawit

9. *mila sru oneng ing nålå*
Labet marcåpådå dèrèng amanggih
Pradonggå renggan kalangwun
Kang kadyå Lokånåntå
Éling-éling yèn titisé sanghyang Wisnu
Sanalikå wus kadriyå
Dènyå karyå gitå rangin

10. *Sang Panji sigrå matah*
Kadang catur myang kadéyan kang warni
Kålåwijå ugi catur
Pinurih lelawanå
Dènyå karyå gamelan Asmåråbangun
Tandyå tumandang pinarak
Prak parapé nambut kardi

11. *Angastå uthuk namanyå*
Kanan kéring kinaryå molak malik
Sinom prådå pasang jungut
Sadhiyå ngarsèng råkå
Ngastå sapit angentas badhé puniku
Kabektå mring lelandhesan
Séla hitem kang piranti

12. *Dé kang badhé malu gongså*
Radèn Wirun angastå palu alit
Andågå madyaning palu
Palu ageng dyan Kalang
Dhoyok, Bancak, Sebul, Palèt samyå nglamus
Lamus warni sakawan
Ageng dhårå dhiré alit.

6. 5. *Tetanggapan mengko bengi*
åpå wayang åpå gambyong
åpå bebagoran telu iku
endi kang prayogi
salah siji sedhéngah
Ki Wiråbråjå turirå

6. *Inggih sumonggå (n)Jeng Kyai*
kerså kang pundi siniyos
kang råkå linigirå mungguh aku
bagor baé becik
lakonné Narawangsa
yèn ora Jayakusuma

7. *Dhå-pådhå wong kéné iki*
dhemenané kang tinonton
amung totopèngan kèh wong (n)dulu

tinimbang lan ringgit
tlèdhèk karucil purwå
topèng gedhéning tontonan

7. 9. *Sang kusumå dèn lêlipur*
yå tå lêjaring kang galih
warnanen dalu semånå
Radèn Inowanèngpati
arså klangenan ringgitan
Rahadèn Kudå sasimping

10. *Kinèn angringgit sang bagus*
gedhog seksånå wus nyimping
kelir balèncong pinasang
dhasaré anyar kang ringgit
mubyar kang sungging predåpå
sembådå wangunnyå luwih

11. *Ki Sogèng lawan Ki Cekruk*
kang sami ngladosi simping
gamelan sampun tinåtå
kang sami nabuh ing gendhing
sagunging pårå kadéyan
myang prå wedånå pangarsi

12. *Kang ngrebab Dyan Wukir santun*
angendhang Radèn Permadi
Dyan Jåyåmirutå bonang
panrus Dyan Andågå nenggih
anabuh barung ing bonang
kang egong Dyan Jayèngpati

13. *Keng nyaron gambang calempung*
lukat ngethuk ngenongi
ajangkep pårå wedånå
Radèn Wasi Jayèngrêsmi
tansah nèng wurining dhalang
Rahadèn Panji sesimping

14. *Radèn Panji Marabangun*
ningali nèng lebet kelir
lan garwå asesaréan
Kusumå Retnå Jinali
miwah sagunging pårå dyah
samyåtap caket kang kelir . . .

17. *Kang mulat jejel supenuh*
samyå kayungyun ing ati
dhedhalang wasis ukårå
keng panjak apekik-pekik

lakoning rigit winedhar
mungel walgitå maarti

18. *Panji Anom kalanipun*
ngawulå mring Prånåragi
risang panji kasatriyan
ambedhah negårå Bali
nyabrang ing segara rupak
menang dènirå ajurit

8. Sinom

17. *Pårå nåtå susuruhan kang linanggar*
Ingamuk saking wuri
Kang dadyå pangarså
Senåpati pamungkas
Sira Aryaa Banaspati
Kanthi punggåwå
Astå kang surå sekti

18. *Wadyåbålå kawan lekså pipilihan*
Kawan èwu turanggi
Nulyå tinengeran
Kinèn nempuh ing yudå
Gong kendhang salompèt muni
Surak gumerah
Kadyå nengker wiyati

19. *Wadyåbålå ing wuri dhedheng anyirap*
Papanjeran rinakit
Myang sagung wahånå
Råtå liman turonggå
Kebekan muareng Jambi
Yåtå Pangarså
kagådå nempuh wani

20. *Pårå dhaèng kawan èwu sikep pedhang*
Wahånå kudhå sami
Mangsah anarajang
Surung sereng amagas
Wadyå ingkang pacak baris
Gègèr jangginggat
Dèn amuk saking wuri . . .

22. *Mantri Jurumalang asru atatanyå*
Mungsuh såkå ing ngendi
Tambung laku cidrå
Ngamuk såkå ing wuntat
Ora nganggo tåtå titi
Lir bajak alas
Déné dhapur prajurit.

(Panji Dadap II 1980 [mid-nineteenth century], 170–71)

9. For the program of the festival, see https://festivalpanji.id/home/.

10. This section is adapted from the paper "From Texts to Invocation: *Wayang* Puppet Play from the North Coast of Java," which I presented at Cornell University in March 2019. The essay is published in *Sounding Out the State of Indonesian Music*, edited by Andrew McGraw and Christopher J. Miller (Ithaca, NY: Cornell University Press, 2022), 157–73. A similar version of the paper with a different introduction appears in *Performing Arts and the Royal Court of Southeast Asia*, vol. 2 (Leiden: Koninklijke Brill, 2024), 227–44.

11. For discussions of contemporary wayang kulit performance, see Kayam (2005), Mrázek (1999, 2000), and Sumarsam (2013). One notable difference between wayang performance in the past and today (starting around the 1980s) is the presence of extended scenes referred to as *Limbukan* and *Gårå-Gårå*, which contain lighthearted musical interludes and humorous dialogue between clown-servant puppets and the *pesindhèn* (singers), guest artists, and VIP audience members. Typically, the dialogue has no relationship to the story of the play.

12. The names of the pieces are "Lompong Keli," "Ayak-Ayakan Sanga," and "Kratagan 'zek."

13. In wayang kulit, the dhalang's narration is called *janturan*. In the wayang golek of Tegal it is called *ngabor*, which is similar to Javanese wayang kulit, where a piece called *Kabor* is often performed as the first scene representing the kingdom of Hastina.

14. *Sareng sakenyarirå Sanghyang Predonggå Pati. Gumantyå mring Sanghyang Ratri. Kapanjutan imå-imå gamburå lawan ancål(å). Imå-imå megå, gamburå segårå, ancålå puncaking gunung.*

Sanghyang Anon [Manon] methik pupusing gebang siwalan tunggal. Nedak kinen dhå-pådhå, tinètèsan asta gangga gangganè wirantanu. Asta namaning tangan, [gong] gangga banyu, wira tulis, tanu mangsi.

Samyå rebutan papan mboten wènten ingkang saged nututi antawisipun. Sawenèh wonten ingkang nuwakaken papan, sawenèh wonten ingkang nuwakaken tulis. Awit praptané balé dumadi inggih minati[?] anyar pinanggih al warak al wahi, dumugunipun akhiré jaman.

Kamongkå sadèrèngipun papan gumelar, tulis sampun gumantung. Sadèrèngipun tulis gumantung, papan kang sampun gumelar. Saicaling papan tulis, pårå pujonggå sami manunggal ngre . . . gengaken, sami ngunggung aksårå.

Tibaning mangsi anèng papan nimbulaken leksårå sawidak kalih cacahé. Leksårå suwi-dak-kalih kapundhut tigang-dåså kabucal mengalèr dhawahipun wonten tanah Bandi? Israel inggih wonten tanah Arab inggih tanah Mesir[?]

Leksårå punika [terik] tesih gundhul dèrèng dipun paringi sandhangan mbénjang lamun sinandhangan saged ngawontenaken kitab Jabur, Injil kelawan Torek lan al-Quran.

THREE *Linking the Present to the Past through Preaching, Ritual, and Levity*

1. As I mentioned in the introduction and in chapter 1, the pancamakara Tantric ritual practice consisted of consuming five essential elements: *madya* (wine), *matsya* (fish), *mamsa* (meat), *mudra* (parched grain or drug), and *maihuna* (sexual intercourse). I also discuss the pros and cons of this ritual.

2. *Tumpeng ingkung* refers to a set of sacrificial food, consisting chiefly of two main dishes: *tumpeng*, a cone of rice (*tumpeng*) surrounded by other dishes, and a cooked whole chicken (*ingkung*).

3. Agus Prasetyo, "Gus Muwafiq Risalah Kitab Jamus Kalimosodo Sunan Bonang," YouTube, January 8, 2019, video, 57:14, retrieved July 2, 2023, https://www.youtube.com/watch?v=ohyufiflRao. Javanese Text:

karena ternyata di Tuban dan sekitarnya, termasuk di pedalaman Jawa Tengah, ini ada satu aliran yang sangat ekstrim. Aliran yang sangat ekstrim itu dikenal dengan istilah aliran Bhairawa Tantra. Aliran Bhairawa Tantra itu suatu aliran yang samasekali tidak representasi Hindu, juga tidak representasi Budha. Dia muncul di tengah-tengah tradisi Hindu dan tradisi Buda. Tradisi Hindu itu mengajarkan dharma dan menahan hawa nafsu. Jadi orang yang paling baik itu matinya muksa dalam agama Hindu. Lha muksa itu satu harus ngalami yang namanya Upanisad. Upanisad itu menghilangkan jatidiri. Jadi sampai orang tidak ada yang kenal. Setelah itu baru melakukan kabumian. Kabumian adalah laku hidup seperti bumi. Bumi itu semakin diuyuhi semakin subur, semakin dicangkul semakin subur, jadi manusia semakin dihinakan semakin mwnunjukan kualitas kemanfaatannya.

Habis itu baru ngalami yang namanya Upawasa. Upawasa itu duduk terdiam begini, lantas nanti tidak makan tidak minum dan tidak menyentuh isteri. Nanti tubuhnya otomatis pelan-pelan jadi kecil-kecil-kecil-kecil terus lap ilang, muksa. Nah di beberapa tempat di tanah Jawa ternyata itu tidak efektif karena banyak yang gagal. Melakukan upawasa, tubuhnya sudah mengecil-mengecil-mengecil imannya nggak tebel ada yang ingat isterinya, ada yang ingat kambingnya. Itu berhenti dia. Tubuhnya besar lagi nggak bisa, hilang lagi ndak bisa, yang kemudian jadi jengglot utawa Betara Karang. Maka bagi teman-teman yang ketemu Jengglot jangan mau ya dibohongi harganya mahal. Itu produk gagal, itu produk gagal muksa.

Nah ini kemudian orang punya aliran baru yang ternyata berbalik dari aliran itu, yaitu aliran ngumbar hawa nafsu, dikenal dengan istilah pancamakara atau malima. Jadi upacaranya ini laki perempuan uda kabeh, telanjang semua, ngedhep arak, menghadap tumpeng ingkung menungsa, untuk apa—mengumbar hawa nafsunya. Sahwat di bawah perut ini dilakukan melakukan diumbar dengan hubungan seks bebas, akal biar nggak banyak terlalu banyak pikiran dikasih minum arak, supaya nanti perutnya ini ndaak krucak-krucuk, lha ini dikasih makan tumpeng ngono lo. Nah, saat mereka yang dibutuhkan bukan muksa tapi cukup dia ngraga sukma. Nah ngraga sukma dilakukan supaya pas sukmanya ini keluar, tubuhnya nggak bergerak, kasih makan daging manusia . . . Nah, ini menghasilkan ilmu baru di tanah Jawa yang luar biasa ekstrim.

4. *Ya wis aku jangan dibunuh. Saya nggak saya ikut kamu. Aku melu aku melu kowe ora pa pa nanging aku aja dipateni. Ya wis ndak apa apa kamu ndak saya bunuh, tapi kamu harus merubah perilakumu. Iya. Ya wis muter-mutermu tetep ndak apa apa. Maka muternya tetep dibiarkan saja ndak apa apa, tapi aja wuda, lanang wedok aja uda, jangan melakukan hubungan sing bebas. Arak ini ndak boleh luakmalkom . . . boringsun kan diganti, ganti wedang putih atau kopi atau teh. Nah tumpeng ini halal, maka ndak ada masalah, ndak apa apa. Nah ingkung pitik, ingkung menungsa, ini diganti sama ingkung pitik, ini sama Sunan Bonang. Nah mantra ngraga sukmanya diganti kalimat thaokid Lhailahlhailolah. Maka kalau sekarang kita ketinggalan ada tumpengan yang merajalela se sampek ke Malaysia bahwa juga ada tumpeng, itu sebetulnya adalah Sunan Bonang yang melestarikan.*

5. In 2019 Gus Muwafiq was in the hot seat because a portion of his preaching was interpreted by other preachers as being empty of imagination. The controversy was about his description of how, being taken care by his grandparents early in his life, the Prophet Muhammad was often *rèmbèsen* (having an unclean nose or eyes). This statement triggered outrage from other

preachers and from conservative Muslims in general, so much so that Gus Muwafiq had to apologize by making a statement online.

6. 50. . . . *Anggelasah asungsun timbun marindhih*
lir babaganing pisang.

51. *Wor winor lan jalu miwah èstri*
sadhéngahnèå kang katindhihan
kang kawudan becik baé
tan ånå ukumipun
wus tatané wong dul birai
singå menang sualnyå
sålå-silahipun
santri kang kasor èlmunyå
asrah jiwå rågå myang bojonèki
katur sumonggèng kersä.

7. I would like to thank Acri, whose essay (2019) led me to revisit and expand my discussion of this topic. In fact, in a footnote, he mentions my work, observing that my analysis, along with Cohen's (2011), "have tended to focus mainly, or uniquely on the Sufi elements," which is true. The discussion I put forward here is drawn from Acri's essay, the main aim of which is to expand and fine-tune Zoetmulder's (1994) discussion of the same topic.

8. *Datan samar satibané pati*
kang sampurnå kang sinelir ikå,
tan ånå kèksi wujudé,
kang sampurnå puniku,
pan wus kartå negårå singgih,
tegesé kang sampurnå
anirnakken riku,
alam pipitu wus sirnå,
pan wus bersih sirnané alam puniki,
tunggalé ambiråwå

Ratuning alam pan wus kahesti,
abiråwå wastané punikå,
alam nenem iku liré,
sirnå wétan puniku,
lawan kulon kidul lor iki,
ing luhur lawan ngandhap,
miwah kayu watu,
tuwin bumi langit ikå,
ngawang nguwung kumandhang ing angin warih,
samodrå lan dahånå

9. *Contoh kalau kita ini bangsa besar. Orang Arab punya alat musik bernama terbang, terbuat dari kayu dan kulit. Orang Eropa punya gitar dari kayu dan tali. Kayu tinggal tebang, kulit tinggal potong. Mudah. Tapi orang Indonesia punya alat musik bernama gamelan yang berbuat dari*

logam. Hanya bangsa yang menguasai ilmu pertambangan dan metalurgi yang maju mampu membuat alat musik dari logam. Makanya jangan malu menjadi bangsa ini. (Retrieved July 3, 2023, https://www.youtube.com/watch?v=CkiNzcBedWw.)

10. *Mulå kitå sedåyå diwulangi tembang kehidupan, ingkang kawitan dikenal kanthi jeneng Masku? Maskumambang. Nåpå tembang Maskumambang? Kumambangé nyåwå medun ngalam, niku ana do? Donyå . . . Sabab Maskumambang niku mudhuné nyåwå, manggon jero rågå sangang wulan manungså ngalami tembang Mi? Mijil . . . Lha nèk wis bar mijil dadi bocah, tembangé Kinan . . . thi. Lha cilik-cilik niki Kinanthi kudu disangoni kanthi agåmå kanthi aklak . . . bar Kinanthi kesusul tembang Si? Sinom, bakal dadi cah enom wis mulai da? Dablek, ra kenèk dituturi. Åpå manèh kok bar Sinom tembangé Asmårå, dånå. Nèk wis mulai ketaman asmårå, jatuh cinta, taek kucing råså co, coklat. Mula nèk seméné-méné niku kulå serahké kyai Komari, mboh dadi åpå pokoké kowe kudu diuleg ngaji . . . Begitu tembang Asmårådånå léwat, nyusul tembang Gambuh, bakal jumbuh cah lanang cah wédok mulai mbangun rumah tangga rabi. Lha nèk wis gambuh tembangé Dhandhanggu gulå. Kepethuk dandang pahit kepethuk gulå legi . . . lha niki pahit uripé olèh dandang merasakan manis getir pahitnya kehidupan. Nèk wis bar Dandanggulå tembangé Dur Durmå. Menungså kudu wis mulai darmå bak . . . bakti . . . kesusul tembang Pang, Pangkur. Ngerti ngerti wis wayahé mungkur såkå ndonyå . . . wis ndang tilik mesjid . . . Nèk ora ndang mungkur mlebu mesjid penjenengan kesusul tembang Megatruh, bakal dicopot rågå sak sukmané. Terakhir tembangé Pucung. Anak menungså mung dipocong . . . Dileboké lawang ciut mulå wong tuwèk jenengé buyut. Siap-siap mlebu lawang ciut.* (Retrieved July 2, 2023, https://www.youtube.com/watch?v=hg-iePw3Ueo.)

11. Allegedly, in the beginning, the violence was caused by the communists' coup d'état, beginning with the kidnaping and killing of six army generals. Allegedly, the coup was aborted by a military faction under the leadership of General Suharto. But these most horrible historical events in Indonesia remain shrouded with uncertainty as to who actually masterminded them, for what purpose, in what way the plot was connected to President Sukarno and his ideology. What is certain is that, led by Suharto, the army launched a ferocious anticommunist campaign, killing many thousands of its members and its allies, and Suharto proclaimed himself president, subsequently ruling the nation repressively for the next three decades, until his resignation in 1998.

12. I adapted this section, with new material added, from a paper I presented at the second symposium of the 2012 ICTM Study Group on Performing Arts in Southeast Asia, "A Preliminary Report on Javanese Wayang and Islamic Dakwah." The paper was published in the PASEA Proceeding *(Re)Producing Southeast Asian Performing Arts and Southeast Asian Bodies, Music, Dance, and Other Movement Arts* (Sumarsam 2013, 200–203).

13. Cangik (CN): *Pengajian kok modèl-modèl saiki yå nduk.*

Limbuk (LB): *Ha yå piyé to yung nèk ora ngéné yå ra pati laris.*

CN: *Ora kok ngono dhuk, awaké dhéwé ki rak kèlingan jaman semono sejarah sing tak wåcå lumantar walisångå angluri budhåyå, é budi lan dhåyå, budi i tåtå kråmå dåyå i usahaning walisångå kanggo ngrangkul manungså bèn dhå gelem tekå kok ndhuk.*

LB: *Ngono yung?*

CN: *He'eh. Lha bareng aku mau bareng jaman semono ndhuk, aku sejarah tak wåcå dakwah kanjeng sunan Kalijågå nggo wayang, aku nggåwå wayang. Semar Garèng Pétruk Bagong sing jenengé jaman semono ki Goro-Goro, aku terkenal kiyai Joko Goro-Goro.*

LB: *Lha artine åpå?*

CN: *Nggo golèk, rå råsâ. Semar ki samar taspiranti samirun samir cancut tali wondå, Nålå Garèng golèk kaapikan, Pétruk fatruk tepigalon såpå sirå mambangå perkårå sing ålå amar ma'ruf nahi mungkar, a wayang iku owah-owahané tiyang. Sunan Kalijågå sing nglakoknå.*

LB: *Ngono yung?*

CN: *He'em. Dadi ånå rèntètanné jaman semono dhakwah kuwi kanggo seni budhåyå, mulå aja sithik-sithik diarani kharom.*

LB: *Lha iyå yung kadang-kadang ngono ki yå ånå wong sing ora seneng.* (Retrieved July 2, 2023, https://www.youtube.com/watch?v=Mc5kZV89R9A.)

14. *Mulå Janåkå metu sedhakep sholat tahajjud sholat tajjad pas setengah siji Janåkå tangi. Mulå Janåkå metu kudu klewat jam rolas, nèk Janåkå metu kok durung jam rolas ki dhalangé édan kang. Mulå Janåkå såkå tembung Janatuka swargamu Arjuna Arcunaja. Arcu pengarep-arep unaja kaslametan. Rojana sarjana ayo nèk kepingin swargå kowé kudu gelem Puntådéwa ngejak keapikan gelem pengajian. Lebar pengajian ayo dhå nglakoni sembahyang wong édan waras nglakoni limang wektu Islam, I-S-L-A-M, Isak Subuh Luhur Asar Magrib limang wektu. Lebar bakal klebu swargå jam setengah siji dhå tangiå, ayo nèk kepingin swargå nèk bengi tangi, yå Pak yå—nguyoh. Kowé tangi mung nguyoh. Nèk ra nguyoh, nguyohi; ngéné kok kepingin swargå. Angèl mlebu swargå mergå nåpå, nèng kono pirang-pirang wong édan, nèng kono pirang-pirang butå; kåyå mengkono kaé rupané, gedhé-gedhé kabèh sétan-sétan. Iki bèn dinå manak bosé, yå iki sing cedak Kang, Cakil kaé nèng kono kadohan. Iki bosé sing jenengé iblis rajané sétan yå iki, iki ben dina manak ra iså mati matiné kukut bareng jagad. Mulå iki dinå wis kebak sétan. Ati-ati waspådå, pengajian, digodhå; nèng prapatan, digodhå; nèng ngomah, digodhå; nèng dalan, digodhå. Iki ora iså mati sing jenengé butå Cakil. Genjot Janåkå modar sésuk ånå wayang Cakil metu menèh. Gårå, Gårå. Iki matiné stres mergå kedawan untu ora iså idu Cakil iki. Pegel aku ngrasaké. Heh lha wis kesel kon ra lèrèn-lèrèn. Wadyå balaning-sun, kabèh wadyå bålå sétan-sétan—nggih—kabèh kaé wong sing dhå pengajian digodhå. Sétan metuå sétan!* (Retrieved July 2, 2023, https://www.youtube.com/watch?v=cnGNV2d9-nI&list=PL4F7086F062DE87A9&index=14.)

15. *Bolongan-bolongan iki lho punjeré doså. Kupiiingki masak Allah nggo ngrungoknå, mlebu kuping tengen tutupånå kuping . . . [penonton] kiwå. Itungen lambé siji, irung loro telu, mripat loro limå, kuping loro pitu. Sing loro aku roh nggoné ning ra ngerti jenengé. Péngin ruh jenengan ngadekå tak dudohi. Iiiki alat sétan sing paling mandiiii. Såyå ombå saya gedé nglakoni doså, mulå gusti Alloh ndadèknå bolongan sångå sing metu tekå kånå ora ånå sing énak, olèh bacin kabèh. Nggih nåpå mboten? Cangkem sing metu åpå? Alah Alaaah, gumoh, watuk, iler, riak, utah-utahuan, ora ånå sing énak. Nggih mboten? Iki ngandhakå nèk jeroan iki bosokan nggo nglakoni doså. Irung sing metu åpå? Upil, umbeeel, mimiseeen, kuwi ora énak kabèh. Måtå, dolok, lodhok emh ya Allah gustiiii ésuk-ésuk lèk mrèntèk kebaké kåyå ngånå. Kuping isiné åpå? Cukil watu bosok, iki ora ånå sing énak. Nggih mboten? Bolongan ngisor sing ngareeep, uyoh, sing lanang kadang metu santenné. Sing wédok, saos, kécap. Sing mburi gedhang gorèng. Wis ora ånå sing énak ta jajal. Kåyå ngéné bosokan kabèh. Iki kulå jenengan ajeng kemlèlthèl, ajeng gemagus, kemaki ki apa?!* (Retrieved July 2, 2023, https://www.youtube.com/watch?v=mtaAVSlD8Z4.)

16. "Lir Ilir" is an abbreviation of "Ilir-Ilir" (the title of the song). Literally, it means a wide bamboo fan. In the context of the song, I interpret it as the fan at work, i.e., the wind is drifting as the result of the moving fan.

17. *Dodot* is a long and wide batik garment (*jarit*) to be worn in a particular way by the court subordinates when they appear before the king or higher-ranking members of the royal family.

18. *Kumitir* has a number of meanings. Here I am relying on Gerick and Roorda (1901): one of its meanings is "a kind of tie-dyed silk fabric," i.e., a batik made of silk. It is possible that kumitir refers the edges of a *dodot*, which is made of silk.

19. *Bisakah luka yang teramat dalam ini nantinya akan sembuh. Bisakah kekecewan dan keputusasaan yang mengiris-iris hati berpuluh-puluh juta saudara kita ini pada akhirnya nanti akan kikis. Adakah kemungkinan kita merangkak naik ke bumi dari jurang yang teramat curam dan dalam. Akankah api akan berkobar-kobar lagi apakah asap akan membumbung tinggi dan memenuhi angkasa tanah air. Akankah kita akan bertabrakan lagi jarah menjarah dengan pengorbanan yang tak terkirakan. Adakah kita tahu apa yang sebenarnya sedang kita jalani. Bersediakah sebenarnya kita untuk tau persis apa yang sesungguhnya kita cari. Cakrawala manakah yang menjadi tujuan sebenarnya langkah-langkah kita. Pernahkah kita bertanya bagaimana melangkah yang benar. Pernahkah kita mencoba menyesali hal-hal yang barangkali perlu kita sesali dari prilaku-prilaku kita yang kemarin. Bisakah kita menumbuhkan kerendah hatian dibalik kebanggaan-kebanggaan. Masih tersediakah ruang di dalam dada kita dan akal kepala kita untuk sesekali berkata pada diri kita sendiri bahwa yang bersalah bukan hanya mereka, bahwa yang melakukan dosa bukan ia tetapi juga kita. Masih tersediakah peluang didalam kerendahan hati kita untuk mencari apapun saja yang kira-kira kita perlukan meskipun barang kali menyakitkan diri kita sendiri. Mencari hal-hal yang benar-benar kita butuhkan supaya sakit . . . sakit . . . sakit kita ini benar benar sembuh total. Sekurang-kurang dengan perasaan santai kepada diri kita sendiri untuk menyadari dengan sportif bahwa yang mesti disembuhkan nomor satu bukanlah yang berada diluar tubuh kita tetapi didalam diri kita. Yang perlu utama kita lakukan adalah penyembuhan diri. Yang kita yakini bahwa harus betul-betul disembuhkan justru adalah segala sesuatu yang berlaku didalam hati dan akal pikiran kita. Saya ingin mengajak engkau semua memasuki dunia Ilir-ilir. . . . Kanjeng Sunan Ampel seakan-akan baru hari ini bertutur kepada kita. Tentang kita, tentang segala sesuatu yang kita mengalaminya sendiri namun tidak kunjung sanggup kita mengerti. Sejak lima abad silam syair itu Ia telah lantunkan dan tak ada jaminan bahwa sekarang kita sudah paham. Padahal kata-kata beliau mengeja kehidupan kita ini sendiri. Alfa . . . beta . . . alif . . . ba . . .' ta'. . . . Kebingungan sejarah kita dari hari-kehari. Sejarah tentang sebuah negeri yang puncak kerusakannya terletak pada ketidak sanggupan para penghuninya untuk mengakui betapa kerusakan itu sudah sedemikian tidak terperi. "Menggeliatlah dari matimu!!!" Tutur sang Sunan . . . Siumanlah dari pingsan berpuluh-puluh tahun. Bangkitlah dari nyenyak tidurpanjangmu. Sungguh negri ini adalah penggalan Surga!! Surga seakan-akan pernah bocor dan mencipratkan kekayaan dan keindahannya, dan cipratan keindahannya itu bernama Indonesia Raya. Kau bisa tanam benih kesejahteraan apa saja diatas kesuburan tanahnya yang tidak terkirakan. Tidak mungkin kau temukan makhluk Tuhanmu kelaparan ditengah hijau bumi kepulauan yang bergandeng-gandeng mesra ini. Bahkan bisa engkau selenggarakan pengantin-pengantin pembangunan lebih dari yang bisa dicapai oleh negeri-negeri lain yang manapun. Tapi kita memang telah tidak mensyukuri rahmat sepenggal surga ini, kita telah memboroskan anugerah tuhan ini dengan bercocok tanam ketidakadilan dan panen-panen kerakusan.* (Retrieved July 4, 2023, https://www.youtube.com/watch?v=K3HhMevwxlw.)

20. *Nini Thowok adaté dianakaké ing wayah padang bulan, antarané tanggal 10 nganti 15, bubar ngisa, dadi kira-kira jam sanga sepuluh bengi. Sok ngonoa persiapan dianakaké wiwit soré. Ngarepaké magrib prawan prawan sing arep nganakaké dolanan iki wis pada nglumpuk, nggawa barang-barang colongan awujud piranti kanggo gawé si Nini: siwur (jébor), kukusan,*

gandhik, ublik, Isp. Sing mimpin upacara adaté wong wadon sing wis umur, wis pantes diundang "embah." Dhisik dhéwé piranti-piranti sing wis ana mau diwangun kaya wongwongan. Batok siwuré diwedhaki, digincu lan diwènèhi alis barang. Yèn uwis, si Nini sing durung dadi mau diarak nyang papan sing dianggep angker, sok sumur mati, sok ngisor wit ringin sing gedhé, malah sok nèng pundhèn barang. Wong-wong tuwa mbakar menyan, banjur sing kapatah dadi pemimpin upacara maca rapal. Dhèk jamané Sri Kanjeng Ratu Pambayun rakitané rapal mau muni: "Kepareng ingsun lelangen Nini Thowok," banjur disambung mantra-mantra liya: "Widadari, widadari, Nini Thowok udhunna nyang bumi, lan lebokna ing golèkan iki . . ." Sajroné pemimpin upacara ndonga, Nini Thowok isih tetep nglumpruk ing tampah. Bola-bali prawan-prawan sing ana kono ngandeli pupuré, ngandeli gincuné, ngencengaké setagèné Nini Towok, nganti ayu banget. Yèn dongané wis rampung, Nini sing isih ngantuk ditinggal ing kono.

21. Resonance Media produced the disc in July 1997. The "Gift of the Wali" can be accessed through YouTube: https://www.youtube.com/watch?v=ERGIaGQsROw.

FOUR *Discourses on Wayang from the Nineteenth Century to the Present*

1. The term is used to describe the relatively peaceful coexistence of Christians, Muslims, and Jews in Spain from 756 to 1032 during the Caliphate of Cordoba.

2. The speech can be accessed at https://www.youtube.com/watch?v=elT-BOG_-Co.

3. See also Kurien 2013.

4. *Sanadyan kelir pinasang, gamelan wus miranti, dhalang niyågå linggih, yèn maksih peteng nggènipun, sayekti durung biså, dhalangé anampik milih, njritakaké sawiji-wijining wayang.*

Kang nonton tan ånå wikan, marang warnanirå ringgit, margané isih petengan, ora kenå den tingali, yèn balèncong wus urip, kantar-kantar katon murub, keliré kawistårå, ing ngandhap miwah ing nginggil, kanan kéring Pandhåwå miwah Kuråwå.

Ki dhalang nèng ngisor damar, biså nampik lawan milih, nimbang ghedé cilikirå, tumrap marang siji-siji, wataké kabèh ringgit, pinates pangucapipun, awit pituduhirå, balèncong ingkang madhangi, pramilané balèncong kang luwih tuwå.

5. The Five Principles are the belief in one God, just and civilized humanity, Indonesian unity, democracy under the wise guidance of representative consultations, and social justice for all the peoples of Indonesia.

6. Cohen explains further, "I see that the 'Wel Edel Bey' is reported here and there in various sources but it doesn't make sense to me as a Dutch expression (though it might be archaic). I also don't understand how the geduvel might become edel. Veel geduvel bij is much closer and 'Belgeduwelbeh' is more or less how a Javanese person without much Dutch would pronounce this phrase." In any event, it is clear that the attire, hat, sword, and some other accessories indicate the Dutchification of Pétruk.

7. *Maaf ya saudara, pertanyaan itu saya kira keliru . . . sama sekali keliru. Kena apa? Jangan marah ya . . . Soalnya, apapun yang bisa dilakuken oleh pemerintah, apakah pemerintah kini ataupun pemerintah berikutnya, itu akan sangat kecil gunanya. Saya coba menggambarkan luasnya permasalahan ini. Kita hanya bisa memperbarui diri kita, dan kebudayan kita, Kita baru bisa belajar hidup di dalam masyarakat yang padat penduduk, dalam situasi materiil yang agak terbatas, kalau setiap manusia Indonesia bisa menjadi seniman. Jikalau seni memegang peranan di dalam kehidupan masing-masing orang Indonesia, dalam hubungan yang kita gambarkan tadi, mengembangken ruang dalam, ini tantangan yang . . . dan apa . . . masalah*

ini oleh negara-negara yang industrinya maju, juga tidak bisa dijawab, tidak bisa dijawab. Di sana kita melihat perpisahan antara seniman profesionil yang seolah-olah mengorbanken atau menyerahken kehidupannya kepada pelayanan keindahan. Dan seorang publik yang apa yang tidak kreatif, yang cuma melihat yang mengapresiasi, untung kalau mengapresiasi dan sebagainya. Kalau saya tadi bicara bahwa tentang keperluan kita yang membina suati sivilisasi yang baru, itu yang saya maksud, diantaranya. Yaitu bahwa garis pemisah antara seniman kreatif dan publiknya silang. Kalau tidak, tidak bisa kita berhasil dalam.apa. usaha pembaharuan yang kita maksudkan. Menghadapi masalah itu, peranan yang dilakuken, bisa dilakuken, atau . . . oleh pemerintah dengan suatu policy, itu marginal saja, itu di.apa.kulitnya saja. Merusak apa kebudayaan tradisionil dia ndak bisa, merperkembangkan dia ndak mampu, ndak mampu, ndak kekurangan duwit kekurangan tenaga dan sebagainya. Saudara-saudara, yaitu golongan seniman yang bebas, dia jauh lebih menentuken hari depan kehidupan kesenian kita. Dan kemampuan bangsa kita untuk memberi tempat dan menikmati keindahan dalam kehidupan kita sehari-hari daripada pemerintah apapun. Jadi saya kira apa, dalam rangka yang saya coba menggambarkan, janganlah kita bertanya lagi pemerintah bisa bikin apa. They cannot do anything, menghadapi luasnya dan pokoknya permasalahan, apakah dia mempunyai atau menyediaken seratus milyar atau duaratus milyar, what difference does it make? No difference. Kita harus mencari jalan kepada hati masyarakat Indonesia, bangsa Indonesia. Dan seniman adalah pemegang kuncinya. Dan pertanyaannya bisakah dia membuka kunci daripada kreativitas mayoritas bangsa. Itu letak persoalannya. Ya jadi, ya saya bisa terangkan, kalau saudara baca GPHNB apa. Itu kan cuman ucapan. Yang yang yang menjadi pokok adalah dinamika di dalam masyarakat, dinamik para seniman, sampai di mana mereka berorientasi kepada pasaran elite gedongan dan kelanjutannya ke turis-turis, atau sampai di mana mereka merasaken bahwa mereka adalah penjelma, penyambung lidah daripada kegelisahan-kegelisahan kebudayaan di dalam lingkungan masyarakatnya. Itu persoalannya. Ya untuk mencari nafkah kita kejat turis boleh, no problem, asal kita jangan lupa bahwa nasib kita dalam ukuran sejarah terhadap diri kita akan kesana. Tidak pada golongan turis, tidak pada golongan asing. Terjawab. (Retrieved July 5, 2023, https://www.youtube.com/watch?v=8SWopGkzYBs.)

8. *kebudayaan yang timbul sebagai buah usaha budinya rakyat Indonesia seluruhnya. Kebudayaan lama dan asli yang terdapat sebagai puncak-puncak kebudayaan di daerah daerah di seluruh Indonesia, terhitung sebagai kebudayaan bangsa. Usaha kebudayaan harus menuju ke arah kemajuan adab, budaya, persatuan, dengan tidak menolak bahan-bahan baru dari kebudayaan asing yang dapat memperkembangkan atau memperkaya kebudayaan bangsa sendiri, serta mempertinggi derajat kemanusiaan bangsa Indonesia.*

9. For an excellent article on these Indonesian cultural missions from the 1950s to 1960s, see Lindsay 2012.

10. UNESCO, "Wayang Puppet Theatre," n.d., retrieved August 10, 2021, https://ich.unesco.org/en/RL/wayang-puppet-theatre-00063.

11. UNESCO, "Periodic reporting on the Convention for the Safeguarding of the Intangible Cultural Heritage," 2013–2014, retrieved August 10, 2021, https://ich.unesco.org/en/state/indonesia-ID?info=periodic-reporting#pr-2014-2014.

12. UNESCO, "What is Intangible Cultural Heritage?" n.d., retrieved August 19, 2021, https://ich.unesco.org/en/what-is-intangible-heritage-00003.

13. UNESCO, "Performing arts (such as traditional music, dance and theatre)" n.d., retrieved August 19, 2021, https://ich.unesco.org/en/performing-arts-00054.

Conclusion

1. *Britannica Dictionary Online*, s.v. "dualism," retrieved July 20, 2022, https://britannica.com/dictionary/dualism.

2. UIN Sunan Kalijaga, "Meet and Greet | Rektor UIN Sunan Kalijaga bersama Yaseer Arafat Dosen Ushuluddin UIN Suka," YouTube, July 1, 2021, video, 30:30, retrieved July 10, 2022, https://www.youtube.com/watch?v=W-OSujdfAJk.

3. "Please do not / hold a performance, my Lord, / in which the relatives of the Prophet of God take part / for this [means] rejecting their example. Indeed, formerly my father, / your servant, was forbidden / to give a tambourine performance with menak repertoire, / this is not permitted in Madura. / Stories about Muhamad and Mursada, Sapingi and Asmarasupi, [may not be included] in the repertory. / [As for] the Madurese tambourine performance, my Lord, / [the story] is only read from a book, / this is not forbidden" (Soebardi 1975, 88–89). The passages that follow suggest that performing wayang stories about the relatives of the Prophet Muhammad is forbidden. But reconciliation prevails: such practice is permissible if the story is read rather than staged. As the last part says, "[As for] the Madurese tambourine performance, my Lord, / [the story] is only read from a book, / this is not forbidden."

4. The Editors of the Encyclopaedia Britannica, s.v. "clown," *Encyclopaedia Britannica Online*, last updated September 12, 2023, retrieved July 20, 2022, https://www.britannica.com/art/clown.

5. The Editors of the Encyclopaedia Britannica, s.v. "fool," *Encyclopaedia Britannica Online*, last updated July 28, 2023, retrieved July 20, 2022, https://www.britannica.com/art/fool-comic-entertainer.

6. Editors of the Encyclopaedia Britannica, s.v. "fool."

7. The Editors of the Encyclopaedia Britannica, s.v. "allegory," *Encyclopaedia Britannica Online*, last updated March 15, 2023, retrieved July 22, 2022, https://www.britannica.com/art/allegory-art-and-literature.

8. Editors of the Encyclopaedia Britannica, s.v. "allegory."

9. The Editors of the Encyclopaedia Britannica, s.v. "personification," *Encyclopaedia Britannica Online*, last updated April 17, 2016, retrieved July 30, 2022, https://www.britannica.com/art/personification.

10. The law can be accessed at http://pemajuankebudayaan.id/wp-content/uploads/2019/06/UU-Nomor-5-Tahun-2017-tentang-Pemajuan-Kebudayaan.pdf.

11. A melodic instrument in charge of supervising (*pamurbå lagu*) is a stringed *rebab* that is bowed; those which are supporting (*pamangku lagu*) are of the *saron* family, *bonang*, *gendèr*, *gambang*, *suling*, and *celempung*. A rhythmic instrument in charge of supervising (*pamurbå iråmå*) is the *kendhang*; the supporting instruments (*pamangku iråmå*) are *gong*, *kenong*, *kempul*, and *kethuk-kempyang*.

BIBLIOGRAPHY

Acri, Andrea. 2010. "On Birds, Ascetics, and Kings in Central Java: 'Ramayana' Kakawin, 24.95–126 and 26." *Bijdragen tot de Taal-, Land- en Volkenkunde* 166, no. 4: 475–506.

———. 2014. "Birds, Bards, Buffoons and Brahman: (Re-)Tracing the Indic Roots of Some Ancient and Modern Performing Characters from Java and Bali." *Archipel* 88: 13–70.

———. 2015. "More on Birds, Ascetics and Kings in Central Java *Kakawin Rāmāyaṇa*, 24.111–115 and 25.19–22." In *From Laṅkā Eastwards: The Rāmāyana in the Literature and Visual Arts of Indonesia*, edited by Andrea Acri, et al., 53–91. Leiden: KITLV iPress.

Adi, Ganug Nugroho. 2018. "Preserving the Rare Art Form of 'Topeng Dalang' from Klaten." *Jakarta Post*, March 19, 2018. http://www.thejakartapost.com/life/2018/03/18/preserving-the-rare-art-form-of-topeng-dalang-from-klaten.html.

Adib, Faishol. 2014. "Mitos Sunan Kalijaga" [The myth of Kalijaga]. *Kompasiana*, June 3. Revised June 23, 2015.

Aichele, W. 1969. "Vergessene Metaphern als Kriteruen der Datierung des altjavanischen Rāmāyana." *Oriens Extremus* 16: 127–66.

Ainur, Muhammad. 2019. *Gus Muwafiq: Menggenggam Dalil, Merawat Tradisi, Menjaga Kebangsaan Indonesia* [Gus Muwafiq: Embracing Islamic law, taking care of tradition, guarding the Indonesian nation]. Jakarta: Laksana.

Akkach, Samer. 1997. "The World of Imagination in Ibn 'Arabi's Ontology." *British Journal of Middle Eastern Studies* 24, no. 1: 97–113.

al Faruqi, Lois Ibsen. 1985. "Music, Musicians, and Muslim Law." *Asian Music* 17: 3–36.

Anderson, Benedict. 1972. "The Idea of Power in Javanese Culture." In *Culture and Politics in Indonesia*, edited by Claire Holt, Benedict Anderson, and James Siegel, 1–39. Ithaca, NY: Cornell University Press.

———. 1974. "The Last Picture Show: Wayang Beber." In *Conference on Modern Indonesian Literature*, edited by Jean Taylor, et al., 33–81. Madison, WI: Center for Southeast Asian Studies.

———. 1996. *Mythology and the Tolerance of the Javanese*. Ithaca, NY: Southeast Asia Program, Cornell University.

Antoun, Richard. 1989. "The Role of the Preacher, the Content of the Sermon: The Case of Luqman." In *Muslim Preacher in the Modern World: A Jordanian Case Study in Comparative Perspective*, edited by Richard Antoun, 67–105. Princeton, NJ: Princeton University Press.

Arps, Bernard. 2011. *Dewa Ruci and the Light that is Muhammad: The Islamization of a Buddhist Text in the Yasadipuran Version of the Book of Dewa Ruci*. Jakarta: Perpustakaan Nasional Republik Indonesia.

———. 2016. "Flat Puppets on an Empty Screen, Stories in the Round: Imagining Space in *Wayang Kulit* and the Worlds Beyond" *Wacana* 17, no. 3: 438–72.

———. 2016. *Tall Tree, Nest of the Wind: The Javanese Shadow-play* Dewa Ruci *Performed by Ki Anom Soeroto: A Study in Performance Philology*. Singapore: NUS Press.

Becker, Alton. 1979. "Text Building, Epistemology, and Aesthetics in Javanese Shadow Theater." In *The Imagination of Reality: Essays in Southeast Coherence Systems*, edited by Alton Becker and Aram A. Yengoyan, 211–43. Norwood, NJ: Ablex.

Becker, Judith. 1988. "Earth, Fire, Sakti and the Javanese Gamelan." *Ethnomusicology* 32, no. 3: 385–91.

———. 1993. *Gamelan Stories: Tantrism, Islam, and Aesthetic in Central Java*. Arizona State University: Program for Southeast Asian Studies.

Berg, C. C. 1954. "Bijdragen tot de Kennis der Panji-verhalen." *Bijdragen tot de Taal-, Land- en Volkenkunde* 110, no. 3: 189–216.

Boonstra, Sadiah. 2014. "Changing Wayang Scenes: Heritage Formation and Wayang Performance Practice in Colonial and Postcolonial Indonesia." PhD diss., Vrije Universiteit Amsterdam.

Brandts Buys, J. S. 1933. "Uit de pers. De tjaṇṭang baloeng's.—Javaansche en Balische kleppers.—Beḍåjå ketawang.—Édan-édanan." *Djåwå* 13: 258–62.

Cahyono, Dwi. 2014. "Akar historis topeng dalang Malang" [Historical roots of Malang's masked dance-drama]. In *Topeng Panji: Mengajak kepada Yang Tersembunyi* [Masked Panji: Invitation to the hidden], edited by Ardus M. Sawega, 128–39. Solo: Balai Soedjatmoko, Semarak Candrakirana Foundation, Pemkab Malang.

Campbell, Joseph. 2004. *Pathways to Bliss: Mythology and Personal Transformation*. Edited and with forwarded by David Kudler. Novato, CA. New World Library.

Carey, Peter. 1997. "Civilization on Loan: The Making of an Upstart Polity: Mataram and its Successors, 1600–1830." *Modern Asian Studies* 31, no. 3: 711–34.

Chan, Margaret. 2017. "The Sinophone Roots of Javanese Nini Towong." *Asian Ethnology*, 76, no. 1: 95–115.

Christianto, Wisma Nugraha. 2003. "Peran dan Fungsi Tokoh Semar-Bagong dalam Pergelaran Wayang Kulit Gaya Jawa Timuran" [The role and function of the characters Semar and Bagong in the shadow puppet play of East Javanese style]. *Humaniora* 3: 285–301.

Clayton, Martin. 1998. "Review of Richard Widdess' *The Ragas of Early Indian Music: Modes, Melodies and Musical Notation from the Gupta Period to c. 1250*." *Bulletin of the School of Oriental and African Studies* 61, no. 1: 164–65.

Cohen, Matthew. 2012. "*Suluk Wujil* and Javanese Performance Theory." *Performing Islam* 1, no. 1: 13–34.

Creese, Helen. 2004. *Women of the Kakawin World: Marriage and Sexuality in the Indic Courts of Java and Bali*. Armonk: M. E. Sharpe.

Damais, L. C. 1970. *Repertoire onomastique de l'pigraphie javanaise (jusqua pu Sindok Sri Isanawikrama Dharmottungadewa)*. Paris: EFEO.

Day, Tony. 2002. *Fluid Iron: State Formation in Southeast Asia*. Honolulu: University of Hawai'i Press.

———. 2023. "Stepping on a Wulu: Minor Characters and Narrative Possibilities in the Sĕrat Cĕnthini." In *Storied Island: New Explorations of Javanese Literature*, edited by Ronit Ricci, 33–65. Leiden: Brill de Certeau, Michel. 1988. *The Writing of History*, translated by Tom Conley. New York: Columbia University Press.

Drewes, G. W. J. 1925. *Dreis javaansche goeroes's: Hun leven, onderricht en messiasprediking*. Leiden: Vros.

Duijker, Marijke. 2010. "The Worship of Bhima: The Representations of Bhima on Java during the Majapahit Period." PhD diss., Leiden University.

Emerson, R. W. 1948. *Nature*. New York: Liberal Arts Press.

Florida, Nancy K. 1995. *Writing the Past, Inscribing the Future: History as Prophecy in Colonial Java*. Durham, NC: Duke University Press.

———. 2019. "Shaṭṭariyya Sufi Scents in the Literary World of the Surakarta Palace in Nineteenth-Century Java." In *Buddhist and Islamic Orders in Southern Asia*, edited by Michael Feener and Anne Blackburn, 153–84. Honolulu: University of Hawai'i Press.

Foley, Kathy. 2002. "First Things: Opening Passages in Southeast Asian Puppet Theater." In *Puppet Theater in Contemporary Indonesia: New Approaches to Performance Events*, edited by Jan Mrázek, 84–91. Ann Arbor, MI: Center for South and Southeast Asian Studies.

———. 2014. "No More Masterpieces: Tangible Impacts and Intangible Cultural Heritage in Bordered Worlds." *Asian Theatre Journal* 31, no. 2: 369–98.

Forbes, Bruce David, and Jeffrey H. Mahan. 2005. *Religion and Popular Culture in America*. Berkeley: University of California Press.

Fox, James. 1997. "Sunan Kalijaga and the Rise of Mataram: A Reading of the Babad Tanah Jawi as a Genealogical Narrative." In *Islam: Essays on Scripture, Thought and Society: A Festschrift in Honour of Professor Anthony Johns*, edited by P. Riddell and A. Street, 187–218. Leiden: Brill.

Geertz, Clifford. 1960. *The Religion of Java*. New York: Free Press.

———. 1973. *The Interpretation of Cultures*. New York: Basic Books.

Gerbert, Elaine. 2013. "Laughing Priest in the Atsuta Shrine Festival." In *Humour and Religion: Challenges and Ambiguities*, edited by Hans Geybels and Walter Van Herck, 54–65. London: Bloomsbury.

Gomperts, Amrit. 2002. "Indian Music, the Epics and Bards in Ancient Java." In *Studien zur Musikarchaologie III: Archaologie für Klangerzeugung und Tonordnung; Musikarchaologie in der Agais und Anatolien*, edited by E. Hickmann, A. D. Kilmer, and R. Eichmann, 573–96. Rahden: Verlag Marie Leidorf GmbH.

Gunawan, Aditya. 2017. "Manuscript Production and Akṣara Mysticism in the Bhīma Svarga." Working Paper no. 26. Singapore: Nalanda-Sriwijaya Centre.

Gungwu, Wang. 1982 [1979]. "Introduction: The Study of the Southeast Asian Past." In *Perceptions of the Past in Southeast Asia*, edited by Anthony Reid and David Marr, 1–8. Singapore: Heinemann Educational Books.

Hadiwidjojo. 1953. "Sesorahipun Pangarsa Paheman Radyapustaka 'G. P. H. Hadiwidjojo' wonten ing Walidyasana" [A speech by the head of Radyapustaka Museum 'G. P. H. Hadiwidjojo' in the Walidyasana Hall]. Typed manuscript. In the author's possession.

Hall, D. G. E. 1981. *A History of South-East Asia*, 4th ed. New York: St. Martin's Press.

Hand, Rachel Elizabeth. 2016. "Knowledge Transmission and the Family in Traditional Javanese Performing Arts." PhD diss., National University of Singapore.

Hardjowirogo. 1980 [1952]. *Serat Pathokaning Nyekar* [The book of the rules for singing]. Jakarta: Balai Pustaka.

Haryono, Timbul. 2006. "Sejarah Seni Pertunjukan dalam Perspektif Arkeologi" [History of performing art in the perspective of archaeology]. Paper presented at the Balai Kajian Sejarah dan Nilai Tradisional Yogyakarta.

———. 2014. "The Kris: Components, Pamor, and Functions." In *Mosaic of Cultural Heritage Yogyakarta*, edited by Inajati Indrisijanti Romli and Anggraeni. Yogyakarta: Bali Pelestarian Cagar Budaya Yogyakarta.

Heehs, Peter. 1994. "Myth, History, and Theory." *History and Theory* 33, no. 1: 1–19.

Hegel, G. W. F. 1977. *Faith and Knowledge*. Translated by Walter Cerf and H. S. Harris. Albany: State University of New York Press.

Hinzler, Heidi. 1981. *Bima Swarga in Balinese Wayang*. The Hague: Nijhoff.

Hobart, Angela. 1987. *Dancing Shadows of Bali: Theatre and Myth*. London: Routledge and Kegan Paul.

Hodgson, Marshall. 1977. *The Expansion of Islam in the Middle Periods*. Vol. 2 of *The Venture of Islam*. Chicago: University of Chicago Press.

Holt, Clare. 1968. *Art in Indonesia: Continuities and Change*. Ithaca, NY: Cornell University Press.

Hooykaas, C. 1973. *Kama and Kala: Materials for the Study of Shadow Theatre in Bali*. Amsterdam: North-Holland.

Hunter, Thomas M. 1996. "Ancient Beginnings: The Spread of Indic Scripts." In *Illuminations: The Writing Traditions of Indonesia*, edited by Ann Kumar and John H. McGlynn, 3–12. New York: Weatherhill.

———. 2007. "The Body of the King: Reappraising Singhasari Period Syncretism." *Journal of Southeast Asian Studies* 38, no. 1: 27–53.

Hurgronye, Snouck C. 1906 [1893–94]. *The Achehnese*, translated by A. W. S. O'Sullivan. Leiden: Brill.

Ilmi, Miftachul. 2013. *Dakwah Melalui Kesenian Wayang Kulit (Studi Metode Kyai Abdurrohim Ki Joko Goro Goro Di Desa Wonowoso Kecamatan Karang Tengah Kabupaten Demak)* [Dakwah through the art of wayang kulit (the study of the method of Kyai Abdurrohim Ki Joko Goro-Goro in the village of Wonowoso the district of Karang Tengah in the province of Demak)]. Thesis, Institut Agama Islam Negeri Sunan Ampel Surabaya.

Jenkins, Ron. 1994. *Subversive Laughter: The Liberating Power of Comedy*. New York: Free Press.

Jones, Ted. 2012. "Indonesian Cultural Policy in the Reform Era." *Indonesia*, no. 93, 147–76.

Kamajaya. 1980–91. *Serat Centhini (Suluk Tambangraras)*. Yogyakarta: Yayasan Centhini.

Kayam, Umar. 2001. *Kelir Tanpa Batas*, Yogyakarta: Gama Media for Pusat Studi Kebudayaan UGM.

Kirshenblat-Gimblet, Barbara. 2006. "World Heritage and Cultural Economies." In *Museum Frictions: Public Cultures/Global Transformations*. Durham, NC: Duke University Press.

Kumar, Ann. 2020. "Panji in Javanese Court Literature and Beyond." *Wacana* 21, no. 1: 135–55.

Kunst, Jaap. 1968. *Hindu-Javanese Musical Instruments*. The Hague: Martinus Nijhoff.

———. 1973 [1949]. *Music in Java: Its History, Its Theory and Its Techniques*. 2 vols. The Hague: Martinus Nijhoff.

Kurien, Mani Elizabeth. 2013. "Kutiyattam: Intangible Heritage and Transnationalism." PhD diss., University of California Riverside.

Kusumådilagå, Kangjeng Pangeran Harya. 1913. *Serat Rarya Saraya* [The book of learning]. Bogor: Widya Pustaka.

———. 1933 [1879]. *Serat Sastråmirudå* [The book of Sastramiruda]. Solo: De Bliksem.

Laksono, Paschalis Maria. 1986. *Tradition in Javanese Social Structure*. Yogyakarta: Gajah Mada University Press.

Leiden University. 2017. "Panji Tales Awarded the Status of World Heritage by UNESCO." https://www.universiteitleiden.nl/en/news/2017/10/panji-tales-awarded-the-status-of-world-heritage-by-unesco.

Lindsay, Jennifer. 1991. *Klasik, Kitsch, Lontemporer: Sebuah Studi Tentang Seni Pertunjukan Jawa* [The study of a Javanese performing art]. Yogyakarta: Gadjah Mada University Press.

———. 1995. "Cultural Policy and the Performing Arts in Southeast Asia." *Bijdragen tot de Taal-, Land- en Volkenkunde, Performing Arts in Southeast Asia* 151, no. 4: 656–71.

Mair, Victor. 1988. *Painting and Performances: Chinese Picture Recitation and Its Indian Genesis*. Honolulu: University of Hawai'i Press.

Majalah Tempo. 2004. "Andjar Any, 68 tahun" [Andjar Any, sixty-eight years old]: 2–3.

Makin, Al. 2016. *Keragaman dan Perbedaan: Budaya dan Agama dalam Lintas Sejarah Manusia* [Diversity and difference: Culture and religion in the crossing of history of mankind]. Yogyakarta: Suka Press.

Margana, Sri. 2007. "Java's Last Frontier: The Struggle for Hegemony of Blambangan, c. 1763–1813." PhD diss., Universiteit Leiden.

———. 2019. "Religion, Communism, and Ratu Adil: Colonialism and Propaganda Literature in 1920s Yogyakarta." *Wacana* 20, no. 2: 233–49.

Marzolph, Ulrich. 1991. "The Muslim Sense of Humour." In *Humour and Religion: Challenges and Ambiguities*, edited by Hans Geybels and Walter Van Herck, 169–87. London: Bloomsbury.

Meuleman, Johan. 2011. "*Dakwah*, Competition for Authority, and Development." *Bijdragen tot de Taal-, Land- en Volkenkunde* 167, nos. 2–3: 236–69.

Meyer, Verena. 2021. "A Wali's Quest for Guidance: The Islamic Genealogies of the Seh Mlaya." *Wacana* 22, no. 3: 675–92.

Millie, Julian. 2017. *Hearing Allah's Call: Preaching and Performance in Indonesian Islam*. Ithaca, NY: Cornell University Press.

Mir, Mustansir. 1991. "Humour in the Qur'an." *Muslim World* 81: 179–93.

Moen, J. L. 1924. "Het Buddhisme op Java en Sumatra in Zijn Laatste Boei Periode" [The Buddhism of Java and Sumatra in its late Buoy Period]. *Tijdschrift van de Bataviaasch Genootschap van Kunsten en Wetenschappen* 64: 521–79.

Moertono, Soemarsaid. 1968. *State and Statecraft in Old Java*. Ithaca, NY: Cornell Modern Indonesia Project.

Moeso. 1925. "Grepen uit de wajang i.v.m. de Islam" [The subject of wayang in connection with Islam]. *Djawa* 2.

Mrázek, Jan. 1999. "Javanese *Wayang Kulit* in the Times of Comedy: Clown Scenes, Innovation, and the Performance's Being in the Present World, Part One." *Indonesia* 68: 38–128.

———. 2000. "Javanese *Wayang Kulit* in the Times of Comedy: Clown Scenes, Innovation, and the Performance's Being in the Present World, Part Two." *Indonesia* 69: 107–72.

———. 2005. *Phenomenology of a Puppet Theatre: Contemplations on the Art of Javanese Wayang Kulit*. Leiden: Konijklyk Instituut Voor Tal Land.

Muwafiq, Gus. 2019. *Nusantara Tidak Akan Bubar* [Indonesian archipelago will not break up]. Tangerang Selatan: Iiman.

Naerssen, F. H. 1937. "Twee joperen oorkonden van Balitung in het Koloniaal Instituut te Amsterdam." *Bijdragen tot de Tall-, Land- en Volkenkunde* 95: 441–61.

Neubauer, Eckhard. 2001. "Islamic Religious Music." In *The New Grove Dictionary of Music and Musicians*, revised by Veronica Doubleday. Oxford: Oxford University Press; online ed., published January 20, 2001. https://doi.org/10.1093/gmo/9781561592630.article.52787.

Olson, Carl. 2015. "Tantric Sex." In *The International Encyclopaedia of Human Sexuality*, edited by Patricia Whelehan and Anne Bolin. Hoboken, NJ: Wiley-Blackwell; online ed., published April 20, 2015. https://doi.org/10.1002/9781118896877.wbiehs503.

Padoux, André. 2002. "What Do We Mean by Tantrism?" In *Root of Tantra*, edited by K. Harper and R. L. Brown, 16–36. Albany: State University of New York Press.

Paku Buwana IV. 1980 [1780–1820]. *Panji Dadap* 2. Jakarta: Departemen P dan K.

Pausacker, Helen. 2004. "Presidents as Punakawan: Portrayal of National Leaders as Clown-Servants in Central Javanese Wayang." *Journal of Southeast Asian Studies* 35, no. 2: 213–33.

Pelras, Christian. 1996. *The Bugis*. Oxford and Cambridge, MA.: Blackwell.

Pemberton, John. 1987. "Musical Politics in Central Java (or, How Not to Listen to Javanese Gamelan)." *Indonesia* 1444: 17–30.

Phalgunadi, Gusti Putu. 1992. *Indonesian Mahābhārata Virāṭaparva*. New Delhi: International Academy of Indian Culture and Aditya Prakashan.

Pigeaud, Theodore. 1960. Vol. 1 of *Java in the Fourteenth Century: A Study of Cultural History*. The Hague: Martinus Nijhoff.

———. 1962. Vol. 4 of *Java in the Fourteenth Century: A Study of Cultural History*. The Hague: Martinus Nijhoff.

———. 1967. Vol. 1 of *Literature of Java*. The Hague: Martinus Nijhoff.

Poedjosoebroto, R. 1978. *Wayang: Lambang Ajaran Islam* [Wayang: Symbols of Islamic teaching]. Jakarta: P. T. Pradnya Paramita.

Poerbatjaraka, R. Ng. 1940. *Panji-verhalen Onderling Vergeleken*. Bandung: Nix.

———. 1952. *Kapustakan Djawi* [Javanese literature]. Djakarta: Penerbit Djabatan.

———. 1968. *Tjerita Pandji dalam perbandingan* [Panji stories in comparison]. Jakarta: Gunung Agung.

———. 1987. "Raden Inu Main Gamelan: Bahan Untuk Menerangkan Kata Pathet" [Radèn Inu plays gamelan: Source for explaining the word "pathet"]. *Bahasa dan Budaja* 5, no. 4: 3–25.

Poerwadarminta, W. J. S. 1939. *Baoesastra Djawa* [Javanese dictionary]. Batavia: J. B. Wolters.

Puaksom, Davisakd. 2007. "The Pursuit of Java: Thai Panji Stories, Melayu Lingua Franca and the Question of Translation." PhD diss., National University of Singapore.

Quinn, George. 2018. "The Tenth Saint and his Antecedents: Continuity in Javanese Narrative Trope." In *Transformation of Religions as Reflected in Javanese Texts*, edited by Yumi Sugahara and Willem van der Molen, 142–59. Tokyo: Research Institute for Languages and Cultures of Asia and Africa, Tokyo University of Foreign Studies.

———. 2019. *Bandit Saints of Java: How Java's Eccentric Saints are Challenging Fundamentalist Islam in Modern Indonesia*. Leicestershire: Monsoon Books.

Raffles, Stanford Thomas. 1982 [1817]. *The History of Java*, 2 vols. Kuala Lumpur: Oxford University Press.

Ranneft, W. Meijer. 1906. "Praboe Dewå Soekmå of Petroek als Vorst. (Uit de Wajang orang)." *Bijdragen tot de Tall-, Land- en Volkenkunde van Nederlansch-Indie* 59, no. 1: 113–77.

Ras, J. J. 1973. "The Panji Romance and W. H. Rassers' Analysis of Its Theme." *Bijdragen tot de Tall-, Land- en Volkenkunde* 129, no. 4: 411–56.

———. 1985. "Kata pengantar" [Preface]. In Vol. 1 of *Serat Kandhaning Ringgit Purwa*, transliterated by R. S. Subalidinata, 6–9. Jakarta: Djambatan and KITLV-Jakarta.

Rasmussen, Anne. 2005. "The Arab Musical Aesthetic in Indonesian Islam." *The World of Music* 47, no. 1: 65–89.

———. 2010. *Women, the Recited Qur'an, and Islamic Music in Indonesia*. Berkeley: University of California Press.

Ray, Selva J., and Corinne Dempsey. 2010. "Ritual Levity in South Asian Traditions." In *Sacred Play: Ritual Levity and Humor in South Asian Religions*, edited by Selva J. Ray and Corinne Dempsey, 1–20. Albany: State University New York Press.

Revire, Nicolas. 2017. "From Gandhara to Java? A Comparative Study of *Bhadrasana* Buddhas and their Related *Bhodhisattva* Attendants in South and Southeast Asia." In *India and Southeast Asia: Cultural Discourses*, edited by Anna Dallapiccola, Anila Verghese, and Mody Mawaz, 280–304. Mumbai: Pramit Prints.

Ricklefs, M. C. 2012. *Islamisation and Its Opponents in Java, c. 1930 to the Present*. Honolulu: University of Hawai'i Press.

Rinallo, Diego, et al. 2013. *Consumption and Spirituality*. New York and London: Routledge.

Rinkes, D. A. 1996. *Nine Saints of Java*. Kuala Lumpur: Malaysian Sociological Research Institute.

Robson, Stuart. 1971. *Wangbang Wideya*. The Hague: Martinus Nijhoff.

———. 1980. "The Ramayana in Early Java." *Southeast Asian Review* 5: 5–17.

———. 1983. "Kakawin Reconsidered: Toward a Theory of Old Javanese Poetics." *Bijdragen tot de Taal-, Land- en Volkenkunde* 139, nos. 2/3: 291–319.

———. 1995. *Deśawarna (Nāgarakṛtāgama) by Mpu Prapañca*. Leiden: Koninklijk Instituut voor Taal-, Land- en Volkenkunde.

———. 1996. "Panji and Inao: Questions of Cultural and Textual History." *Journal of the Siam Society* 84, no. 2: 39–53.

Rowell, Lewis. 1992. *Music and Musical Thought in Early India*. Chicago: University of Chicago Press.

Saefullah, Saad. n.d. "Ilir-Ilir, Ternyata Ini Maknanya" [Ilir-Ilir, this is its obvious meaning]. *ISLAMPOS*. https://www.islampos.com/ilir-ilir-ternyata-ini-maknanya-34471/.

Saleh, Rattiya. 1988. *Panji Thai dalam Perbandingan dengan Cerita-cerita Panji Melayu* [Thai Panji in comparison with Malay Panji stories]. Kuala Lumpur: Dewan Bahasa dan Pustaka.

Saputra, Inggar. 2016. "Model Dakwah Kebudayaan Sunan Kalijaga dalam Syiar Nusantara" [The model of cultural propagation of Sunan Kalijaga in the transmitting Nusantara]. *NU Online*. Senin, May 2, 2016. https://nu.or.id/amp/opini/model-dakwah-kebudayaan-sunan-kalijaga-dalam-syiar-islam-nusantara-Xt3JS.

Sarkar, Himansu Bhusan. 1972 [1959]. Vol. 2 of *Corpus Inscriptionum Javanicarum* [Corpus of the inscriptions of Java]. Calcutta: Firma K. L. Mukhopadhyay.

Sastroamidjojo, Seno. 1964. *Renungan tentang Pertundjukan Wajang kulit* [A reflection of wayang leather puppet play]. Djakarta: Kinta.

Sawega, Ardus, ed. 2014. *Topeng Panji: Mengajak kepada Yang Tersembunyi* [Masked Panji: Invitation to the hidden]. Solo: Balai Soedjatmoko, Semarak Candrakirana Foundation, Pemkab Malang.

Sayid, R. M. 1980. *Sejarah Wayang Beber* [A history of Wayang Beber]. Solo: Reksa Pustaka Mangkunegaran.

Sears, Laurie. 1994. "Rethinking Indian Influence in Javanese Shadow Theater Traditions." *Comparative Drama* 28, no. 1: 90–114.

Sedyawati. 1993. "The Dramatic Principle of Javanese Narrative Temple Reliefs." In *Performance in Java and Bali: Studies of Narrative, Theatre, Music, and Dance*, edited by Ben Arps, 174–85.

London: School of Oriental and African Studies, University of London.

Shiloah, Amnon. 1995. *Music in the World of Islam: A Socio-Cultural Study*. Detroit: Wayne State University Press.

Shiraishi, Takashi. 1990. *An Age in Motion: Popular Radicalism in Java, 1912–1926*. Ithaca, NY: Cornell University Press.

Slobin, Mark. 1996. "Introduction." In *Retuning Culture: Musical Changes in Central and Eastern Europe*, edited by Mark Slobin, 1–13. Durham, NC: Duke University Press.

Soebardi. 1969. *The Book of Cabolek: Critical Edition with Introduction, Translation, and Notes*. The Hague: Martinus Nijhoff.

Soedarsono. 1984. *Wayang Wong: The State Ritual Dance Drama in The Court of Yogyakarta*. Yogyakarta: Dadjah Mada University Press.

Soedjatmoko. 1965. "Introduction." In *Introduction to Indonesian Historiography*, edited by Soedjatmoko, Mohammad Ali, G. J. Resink, and G. McT. Kahin, xi–xxvi. Ithaca, NY, and London: Cornell University Press.

Soewandi, R. M. 1938. *Djedjèrèngan bab: Beksa Tajoeb, Bondhan, Tuwin Wirèng* [The description of tayuban, bondhan, and wiring dance]. Yogyakarta, typed manuscript. In the author's possession.

Stott, Philip, Miranda Bruce-Mitford, J. Dumarçay, Frederick Mathewson Denny, Jan Fontein, and R. Soekmono, et al. 2003. "Indonesia, Republic of [formerly Dutch East Indies]." In *Grove Art Online*. Oxford: Oxford University Press; online ed., published 2003. https://doi.org/10.1093/gao/9781884446054.article.T041100.

Stutterheim, W. F. 1956 [1935]. "A Thousand Years Old Profession in the Princely Courts of Java." In *Studies in Indonesian Archaeology*, edited by W. F. Stutterheim, 91–103. The Hague: Martinus Nijhoff.

Sugito, Bambang. 1986. *Dakwah Islam Melalui Wayang Kulit* [Islamic propagation through the shadow puppet play]. Solo: Aneka.

Sulistyawati, tr. 1985 [1832]. *Kawruh Topeng* [The knowledge of masks]. Surakarta: Sono Poestoko Kraton Soerakarta.

Sumarsam. 1984. "Gamelan Music and the Javanese Wayang Kulit." In *Aesthetic Tradition and Cultural Transition in Java and Bali*, edited by Stephanie Morgan and Laurie Jo Sears, 105–16. Madison, WI: Center for Southeast Asian Studies, University of Wisconsin.

———. 1995. *Gamelan: Cultural Interaction and Musical Development in Central Java*. Chicago: University of Chicago Press.

———. 2003. "Opportunity and Interaction: The Gamelan from Java to Wesleyan." In *Performing Ethnomusicology: Teaching and Representation in World Music Ensembles*, edited by Ted Solis, 69–92. Berkeley: University of California Press.

———. 2011. "Past and Present Issues of Islam within the Central Javanese Gamelan and *Wayang Kulit*." In *Divine Inspiration: Music and Islam in Indonesia*, edited by David D. Harnish and Anne Rasmussen, 45–79. Oxford: Oxford University Press.

———. 2013. *Javanese Gamelan and the West*. Rochester, NY: University of Rochester Press.

———. 2014. *Contextualizing Wayang and Gamelan to History, Islam, and Nation State*. Yogyakarta: Gading Publishing.

———. 2014. "Javanese Music Historiography: The Lost Gamelan of Gresik." In *Producing Indonesia: The State of the Field of Indonesian Studies*, edited by Eric Tagliacozzo, 327–46. Ithaca, NY: Southeast Asia Program Publications, Cornell University.

———. 2022. "From Texts to Invocation: Wayang Puppet Play from the North Coast of Java." In *Sounding Out the State of Indonesian Music*, edited by Andrew McGraw and Christopher J. Miller, 101–11. Ithaca, NY: Southeast Asia Program Publications, Cornell University.

Sunyoto, Agus. 2004. *Sunan Ampel Raja Surabaya: Membaca Kembali Dinamika Perjuangan Dakwah Islam di Jawa Abad XIV–XV M* [Sunan Ampel the king of Surabaya: Rereading the dynamic struggle of Islamic dakwah in Java in the fourteenth to fifteenth century]. Surabaya: LPBA-MASA Press.

Supomo, S., ed. and trans. 1993. *Bhāratayuddha: An Old Javanese Poem and Its Indian Sources.* New Delhi: International Academy of Indian Culture and Aditya Prakashan.

———. 1996. "The Sovereignty of Beauty: Classical Javanese Writings." In *Illuminations: The Writing Traditions of Indonesia*, edited by Ann Kumar and John H. McGlynn, 13–32. New York: Weatherhill.

———. 1997. "From Sakti to Sahada: The Quest for New Meanings in a Changing World Order." In *Islam: Essays on Scripture, Thought and Society*, edited by Peter G. Riddell and Tony Street, 219–36. Leiden: Brill.

Suseno, Budi Dharmawan. 2009. *Wayang Kebatinan Islam* [Wayang as an Islamic spiritualism]. Kasihan, Bantul: Kreasi Wacana.

Suwarno, Bambang. 2006. "Situasi Wayang Kulit Purwa Sekarang" [The condition of today's shadow puppet play]. *Lakon* 3, no. 1: 1–11.

Tan, Ta Sen. 2018. *Cheng Ho: Penyebaran Islam dari China ke Nusantara* [The propagation of Islam from China to Nusantara]. Jakarta: Kompas.

Taylor, Mark C. 1978. "Toward an Ontology of Relativism." *Journal of American Academy of Religion* 16, no. 1: 41–61.

Thoyibi, M., et al. 2003. "Sebuah Proses Panjang" [A long process]. In *Sinergi Agama and Budaya Lokal: Dialektika Muhammadiyah dan Seni Lokal*, edited by M. Thoyibi, Yayah Kisbiyah, and Abdullah Aly, 205–46. Surakarta: Muhammadiyah University.

Tondhakusuma, Raden Mas Harya. 1870. *Serat Kyahi Gulang Rarya* [The book of Kyahi Gulang Rarya]. Manuscript MN 80/3/SMP 618. The Reksa Pustaka library of the Mangkunegaran Palace, Surakarta.

Totilawati. 1974. "Nini Towok." In *Javanese Literature since Independence: An Anthology*, edited by J. J. Ras, 380–84. Leiden: Brill.

Trimingham, J. Spencer. 1971. *The Sufi Orders in Islam.* London: Oxford University Press.

Turner, W. Victor. 1979. "Betwixt and Between: The Liminal Period in Rites de Passage." In *Reader in Comparative Religion: An Anthropological Approach*, edited by William Armand Lessa and Evon Z. Vogt, 4th ed., 234–42. New York: Harper and Row.

———. 1982. *From Ritual to Theater: The Human Seriousness of Play.* New York: PAJ Publications.

———. 1990. "Are There Universals of Performance in Myth, Ritual, and Drama?" In *By Means of Performance: Intercultural Studies of Theatre and Ritual*, edited by Richard Schechner and Willa Appel, 8–18. Cambridge: Cambridge University Press.

van Groenendael, Victoria M. Clara. 1985. *The Dalang behind the Wayang: The Role of the Surakarta and Yogyakarta Dalang in Indonesian-Javanese Society.* Dordrecht: Foris.

Vickers, Adrian. 1993. "From Bali to Lampung on the Pasisir," *Archipel* 45: 55–76.

———. 2005. *Journeys of Desire: A Study of the Balinese Text Malat.* Leiden: KITLV Press.

———. 2020. "Reconstructing the History of Panji Performances in Southeast Asia." *Wacana*

21, no. 2: 268–84.

Wagner, Fritz. 1988. *Art of Indonesia*. Singapore: Graham Brash.

Wain, Alexander. 2007. "The Two Kronik Tionghua of Semarang and Cirebon: A Note on Provenance and Reliability." *Journal of Southeast Asian Studies* 48, no. 2: 179–95.

White, David Gordon. 2003. *Kiss of the Yoginī: "Tantric Sex" in Its South Asian Contexts*. Chicago: University of Chicago Press.

Widadi, Subur. 2016. *Membaca Wayang dengan Kaca Mata Islam* [Reading wayang with Islamic perspectives]. Makamhaji, Sukoharjo: C. V. Farishma Indonesia.

Widdess. Richard. 1993. "Slendro and Pelog in India?" In *Performance in Java and Bali: Studies on Narrative, Theatre, Music, and Dance*, edited by Bernard Arps, 186–96. London: School of Oriental and African Studies, University of London.

Wiratama, Rudy. *Pakem Pedhalangan Wayang Gedhog Gaya Yogyakarta* [The texts of the synopsis of wayang gedhog stories of Yogyakarta style]. Sleman, Yogyakarta: MirraBuana Media.

Wirjosuparto, Sutjipto. 1968. *Kakawin Bharata-Yuddha*. Djakarta: Bhratara.

Wolters, O. W. 1999 [1982]. *History, Culture, and Region in Southeast Asian Perspectives*, rev. ed. Ithaca, NY: Southeast Asia Program Publications, Cornell University.

Yampolsky, Philip. 1995. "Forces of Change in the Regional Performing Arts of Indonesia." *Bijdragen* 151, no. 4: 700–25.

Zarkasi, Effendi. 1977. *Unsur Islam dalam Pewayangan* [Islamic elements in wayang]. Bandung: Alma'arif.

Zoetmulder, P. J. 1974. *Kalangwan: A Survey of Old Javanese Literature*. The Hague: Martinus Nijhoff.

———. 1982. *Old Javanese-English Dictionary*. The Hague: Martinus Nijhoff.

———. 1994. *Pantheism and Monism in Javanese Suluk Literature: Islamic and Indian Mysticism in an Indonesian Setting*. Leiden: KITLV Press. First published in Dutch in 1935.

Zurbuchen, Mary Sabine. 1987. *The Language of Balinese Shadow Theater*. Princeton, NJ: Princeton University Press.

INDEX

Page numbers in *italic* refer to tables and figures.

MUSIC / CULTURE

A series from Wesleyan University Press
Edited by Deborah Wong, Sherrie Tucker, and Jeremy Wallach

The Music/Culture series has consistently reshaped and redirected music scholarship. Founded in 1993 by George Lipsitz, Susan McClary, and Robert Walser, the series features outstanding critical work on music. Unconstrained by disciplinary divides, the series addresses music and power through a range of times, places, and approaches. Music/Culture strives to integrate a variety of approaches to the study of music, linking analysis of musical significance to larger issues of power—what is permitted and forbidden, who is included and excluded, who speaks and who gets silenced. From ethnographic classics to cutting-edge studies, Music/Culture zeroes in on how musicians articulate social needs, conflicts, coalitions, and hope. Books in the series investigate the cultural work of music in urgent and sometimes experimental ways, from the radical fringe to the quotidian. Music/Culture asks deep and broad questions about music through the framework of the most restless and rigorous critical theory.

MUSIC/CULTURE FALL 2024

Benjamin Barson
Brassroots Democracy: Maroon Ecologies and the Jazz Commons

Donna Lee Kwon
Stepping in the Madang: Sustaining Expressive Ecologies of Korean Drumming and Dance

Sumarsam
The In-Between in Javanese Performing Arts: History and Myth, Interculturalism and Interreligiosity

A COMPLETE LIST OF SERIES TITLES CAN BE FOUND AT
https://www.weslpress.org/search-results/?series=music-culture

ABOUT THE AUTHOR

Sumarsam received his PhD from Cornell University. He has devoted his life to playing and studying Javanese gamelan and wayang puppet play. His books include *Gamelan: Cultural Interaction and Musical Development in Central Java* (1995) and *Javanese Gamelan and the West* (2013). He is currently Winslow-Kaplan Professor of Music at Wesleyan University. He has been the recipient of the National Endowment for the Humanities and the American Council of Learned Societies fellowship (2016–2017), the Indonesian Bintang Satyalencana Cultural Award (2017), and the Yale Institute of Sacred Music fellowship (2019–2020). He was named an honorary member of the Society for Ethnomusicology in 2018.